Find Info Like a Pro

Volume 1

Mining the Internet's Publicly Available Resources for Investigative Research

Carole A. Levitt and Mark E. Rosch

(Previous edition entitled *The Lawyer's Guide to Fact Finding on the Internet* by Carole A. Levitt and Mark E. Rosch)

CD-ROM included

LawPractice Management Section

MARKETING • MANAGEMENT • TECHNOLOGY • FINANCE

Commitment to Quality: The Law Practice Management Section is committed to quality in our publications. Our authors are experienced practitioners in their fields. Prior to publication, the contents of all our books are rigorously reviewed by experts to ensure the highest quality product and presentation. Because we are committed to serving our readers' needs, we welcome your feedback on how we can improve future editions of this book.

Screen shots reprinted with permission from their respective owners. All rights reserved.

Cover design by Andrew Alcala.

Nothing contained in this book is to be considered as the rendering of legal advice for specific cases, and readers are responsible for obtaining such advice from their own legal counsel. This book and any forms and agreements herein are intended for educational and informational purposes only.

The products and services mentioned in this publication are under or may be under trademark or service mark protection. Product and service names and terms are used throughout only in an editorial fashion, to the benefit of the product manufacturer or service provider, with no intention of infringement. Use of a product or service name or term in this publication should not be regarded as affecting the validity of any trademark or service mark.

The Law Practice Management Section, American Bar Association, offers an educational program for lawyers in practice. Books and other materials are published in furtherance of that program. Authors and editors of publications may express their own legal interpretations and opinions, which are not necessarily those of either the American Bar Association or the Law Practice Management Section unless adopted pursuant to the bylaws of the Association. The opinions expressed do not reflect in any way a position of the Section or the American Bar Association.

Printed in the United States of America.

12 11 10   5 4 3 2

Library of Congress Cataloging-in-Publication Data

Levitt, Carole A.
    Find info like a pro : mining the Internet's publicly available resources for investigative research / by Carole A. Levitt and Mark E. Rosch.
        p. cm. — (Find info like a pro : mining the Internet's publicly available resources for investigative research ; v. 1)
    Includes index.
    ISBN 978-1-60442-890-2
    1. Legal research—United States—Computer network resources. 2. Legal research—Computer network resources. 3. Internet research. I. Rosch, Mark E. II. Title. III. Title: Mining the Internet's publicly available resources for investigative research.
    KF242.A1L4785 2010
    340.072′073—dc22

                                                        2010005637

Discounts are available for books ordered in bulk. Special consideration is given to state bars, CLE programs, and other bar-related organizations. Inquire at Book Publishing, American Bar Association, 321 N. Clark Street, Chicago, Illinois 60654.

Contents at a Glance
Volume 1

Contents

For Searching Public Records Online, see *Find Info Like a Pro,*
Volume 2: Mining the Internet's Public Records for Investigative
Research

Contents at a Glance
Volume 2

About the Authors

 Carole Levitt is a nationally recognized author and speaker on Internet research. She has over twenty years of experience in the legal field as a law librarian, legal research and writing professor, California attorney, and Internet trainer. She is a skilled online searcher, focusing on legal, public record, investigative, and business research. She is also coauthor of *The Cybersleuth's Guide to the Internet* (IFL Press 2009).

As President and founder of Internet For Lawyers (**www.netforlawyers .com**), she provides customized Internet research training to legal professionals (with continuing legal education credit). Ms. Levitt has presented at the ABA TechShow; LegalWorks; LegalTech; the annual meetings of the American Bar Association (ABA), the National Association of Bar Executives, the Association of Continuing Legal Education, and the California State Bar Association; the worldwide Gibson, Dunn & Crutcher corporate attorney retreat; law firms, bar associations; and library associations throughout the country. Ms. Levitt serves on the Executive Council of the ABA's Law Practice Management (LPM) Section, as well as serving as the acquisitions chair for the section's publishing board. Previously, she was chair of the California State Bar's Law Practice Management & Technology Section and served on the Executive Board of the Los Angeles County Bar Law Practice Management Section, among various other professional association activities.

She was a regular contributor to the *Los Angeles Lawyer* magazine's "Computer Counselor" column for eight years and has also written for numerous magazines, newsletters, and Web sites such as *California Lawyer, Trial, The Internet Lawyer, Computer and Internet Lawyer, Research Advisor, Nashville Lawyer, FindLaw, CEB Case N Point*, and *LLRX*.

Ms. Levitt received her Juris Doctorate from the John Marshall Law School, where she graduated with distinction and was a member of the school's law review. She earned her BA in Political Science and her MLS at the University of Illinois. Ms. Levitt can be contacted at **clevitt@netfor lawyers.com**.

Mark E. Rosch

 As Vice President of Internet For Lawyers (IFL), Rosch is the developer and manager of the Internet For Lawyers Web site. He writes and speaks about how to use the Internet for research and on technology implementation for the legal community. He is also coauthor of *The Cybersleuth's Guide to the Internet* (IFL Press 2009).

Mr. Rosch has also written about the application of computer technology in the law office for *California Lawyer, Law Technology News, Law Office Computing, Los Angeles Lawyer, Los Angeles Daily* and other publications. Additionally, he has presented at the annual meetings of the ABA, the National Association of Bar Executives, the Association of Continuing Legal Education, the California State Bar, and in-house at various firms.

Mr. Rosch is a member of the ABA and served as a Vice Chair of its LPM Section education board. He is also a member of the Association of Continuing Legal Education (ACLEA), having served as chair of ACLEA's entrepreneur's section and its marketing section. He has also served on the Academy of Television Arts & Sciences' Public Relations Steering Committee, and the Television Publicity Executives Committee.

During his nearly twenty years of marketing experience, Mr. Rosch has developed and supervised the publicity, promotions, and marketing campaigns for numerous and varied clients, from legal portals to new media developers. He has also provided Web management consulting to the State Bar of California Law Practice Management & Technology Section's Web site and various law firms and solo practitioners.

He graduated from Tulane University, in New Orleans, with a BA in Sociology. Mr. Rosch can be reached at **mrosch@netforlawyers.com**.

Acknowledgments

Mark and I would like to thank and commend the ABA LPM Publications staff (Tim Johnson, Kimia Shelby, Denise Constantine, and Trish Cleary) for all their hard work in producing this book. They were very patient with all our changes (only some of which can be blamed on the ever changing nature of the Internet). We also appreciate your encouragement and belief in this book.

We'd like to thank our parents, but we can't . . . because they don't use the Internet and don't even own computers. But seriously, we do thank them for believing in us when we first launched Internet For Lawyers over ten years ago and for teaching us that we can do anything (almost) that we put our minds to.

Preface

In 1999, we combined Carole's dual background as a lawyer and law librarian with Mark's background in marketing and his penchant for technology to create Internet For Lawyers and teach lawyers how to use the Web effectively and efficiently. To create our first seminars and training materials, we reviewed a lot of Internet research books to find the most useful sites for lawyers that were available for free on the Internet. In all of the books we used, we never found an Internet research book that was everything we thought such a book should be.

When the ABA asked us to write a new edition of Joshua Blackman's *The Internet Fact Finder for Lawyers*, which was re-titled *The Lawyer's Guide to Fact Finding on the Internet*, Second Edition, our goal was to write a book that would save researchers time and money and help them avoid frustration. We looked at it as our chance to write the book we had been searching for, but never found—and our chance to correct all the pet peeves we found in other books. We wanted to share what we learned about the best of the hundreds of Web sites we've used while conducting real-world research or while testing for evaluation purposes.

With our second revision, the Third Edition of the book grew to more than 800 pages with new Web sites and updates to sites we had discussed previously. Going forward, we knew that creating a series of more narrowly-focused books would make this information easier for our readers to find and use.

Not Just for Lawyers

Even though this book is published by the largest association of lawyers in the world, it's *not* just for lawyers. This book is for anyone who needs to conduct investigative or background research (without spending a dime, in most cases) and can answer "yes" to at least one of the following questions:

- Are you a business owner trying to verify the Social Security number of a potential new hire?
- Do you need to find a missing deadbeat client to collect on a debt?
- Do you need help putting together a list of potential customers?
- Are you trying to find someone's address or phone number, even a cell number?
- Would you like to know how to access expensive databases for free—databases that include millions of newspaper and magazine articles, biographical profiles, company profiles, and more?
- Do you want to learn the ins and outs of social networking sites so you can uncover information about people or find a missing person?

Finally, we hope that the research strategies discussed in this book will teach you how to find information about yourself currently on the Internet and how to get some of it taken down (or at least how to keep your information off the Internet going forward).

What's New in this Book?

As we embarked in this new direction, we decided to focus first on the category of resources we get asked about most frequently—investigative research. We began with a thorough review of the last edition to identify the topics we wanted to cover in this new book and to completely deconstruct the arrangement of that material into smaller, more manageable chapters. Then, as we have in the past, we began testing and reevaluating each site discussed in those relevant chapters. We updated our discussion about each site by pointing out any new (or deleted) features and new URLs (if they changed). We also refreshed almost every single screen shot.

We then added new information, including detailed discussions of new Web sites, a new chapter on social media sites (like MySpace, Facebook, and LinkedIn) and microblogging services (like Twitter), and information affecting Internet research such as: (1) Internet privacy issues; (2) security breaches of commercial databases; and (3) how to get information from Internet sites admitted into evidence; and much more. After all that, we decided the investigative research book was still too long, so we broke the book into two books. The first book (this book), focuses on "publicly available information" found free (or for low cost) on the Internet, while the second book will focus on public records found free (or for low cost) on the Internet.

We're always pleased to learn from our readers how these books met our goal—to help them save time and money with their Internet research and to avoid frustration.

Our goal with this new edition remains the same.

This Book Differs From Other Internet Books— It Will Empower You!

The following was a rundown of the pet peeves we had with other Internet research books, and an explanation of how we hoped our books overcome those shortcomings in order to empower you to become a more efficient and effective researcher.

But, Is It Free?

The authors of the other Internet research books rarely warned us if the Web site they were describing was a pay site. There's nothing more bothersome than going to a site expecting to find information for free, and instead being greeted by a registration and payment screen asking for your credit card. On the other hand, these other authors usually also failed to bother to clue us in when a site was free.

We know, as it is with most anything, that price is a major consideration when deciding between alternative research resources—and we all agree that free is better (all other things being equal). Our first goal, then, was to label the Web sites we included in the book to show whether they are free (or free but requiring registration) or require payment. Some sites have different levels of access. For example, a Web site might offer some limited information for free and then charge for more extensive information (such as those sites that are free to search but require a paid subscription to view the full text of search results). Some sites are completely free, while others, though costing no money, require registration to access all or part of the sites.

However a Web site is arranged, it's good to know before you get there. We label the sites with the icons shown below to indicate what kind of access is offered. If we use more than one icon, it means the site offers varying levels of access.

 Pay   Free   Registration Required

We also tell you when free is not better—that is, when you're not going to find it for free or when free won't be the most efficient route. In such instances, we recommend a pay site. We want to save you time and money by clueing you in—in advance.

So, What's the Purpose of This Site and What Content Does It Offer?

Some of the authors of other books we reviewed simply pointed to a laundry list of Web sites but failed to describe their content or failed to indicate the purpose of the site. Our second goal was to provide an overview of each site's content and to suggest in what situations the Web site should be used. When applicable, we also suggest alternative sites. We want to save you the frustration of visiting Web sites that don't have the content you need or don't allow you to search in the manner you want. For example, if you need to know the owner of a certain piece of real estate in Los Angeles, we recommend a pay site to find that information, and explain that while the Los Angeles County assessor's office offers a free, searchable Web site, it doesn't allow you to search by owner's name, only by the property address. Even then, the free site does not provide the owner's name—only the assessed value.

What's with This Alphabetical List of Titles?

Some Internet research books we looked at listed Web sites in alphabetical order by the name of the site. A research book is not useful if it's simply an alphabetical list. Even one of the authors of this book, who is a librarian by training and who lives and dies by alphabetical order, doesn't find it useful when organizing a research book— in fact, she abhors it. And this is from someone who organizes her spice rack (and even the credit cards in her wallet) alphabetically.

We want to save you time and money by thinking the way you do. So, our third goal was to organize by subject. Researchers don't think in alphabetical title order, they think in subject order. To make this book more useful, we have chosen to organize it in subject order.

But, Which Sites Are We Recommending, and Where Should You Start?

Even those few authors who did organize their books by subject couldn't stay completely away from alphabetical order. They always seemed to revert to an alphabetical list of Web sites within each subject when it would have been more meaningful to organize in a way that showed the reader in which order they should use the sites, starting with the most useful. The reader seeks and depends on the judgment of the author, who is the expert searcher. The author is there to guide searchers down the superhighway—to draw the road map, showing the searcher which sites to stop and visit in order to gather the most useful information.

Our fourth goal was to list the Web sites in a meaningful order within each topic. Thus, our list of sites begins with what we judge to be the best starting-point sites. We want to save you time and money by listing sites in a way that quickly displays our judgment of each site—by showing you which ones to begin with, and then which sites to visit next. We only show you the best sites.

Are There Any Tips or Tricks to Using This Site?

Most other Internet research books failed to provide practical tips and tricks about the Web sites listed in the book. Our book is designed to save searchers from the wrong turns, dead-ends, and even wrong destinations that we encountered along the way while evaluating the sites. To do this, we include tips about the best aspect of each site (content and functionality) and a how-to for those sites that have great content but are not intuitive to use. For example, some Web sites bury the search function, or their most useful information. Some sites use cryptic labels for parts of the site, such as **More** or **Download**. We tell you what you'll find if you click on the **More** or **Downloads** link and very often, that's where the most useful information is found!

Conventions Used in This Book

You might have noticed the boldfaced terms **More** and **Download** in the previous paragraph. Throughout the book we will use boldfaced type to indicate exact text that appears in links (URLs), buttons, drop-down menus, Web site names, etc. of the sites we discuss. Additionally, we will use *italics* to indicate exact text, search terms/keywords used in sample searches we conducted to evaluate the sites we discuss.

Our goal is to uncover that information and those features for you—to translate those sites for you. We want to save you time and money by detailing the information we learned by visiting and testing out the hundreds of sites included in this book.

Show Me the Site

Finally, most authors failed to display the Web sites that they described. The Internet is a graphic-intensive medium, chock-full of icons and links—not just text. When getting driving directions, most people find it useful to look at a map while the instructions are being given. It's the same with the Internet. So, rather than just describe Web sites, we also provide screen shots of the more important sites, or the ones that have some hidden trick.

This book is written in a style that mixes narrative with a standardized template presentation. First, we give you an introduction to the topic in a narrative fashion, and then we highlight the best sites in a template format so you can quickly learn about each individual Web site. The template, as shown below, displays the site name, whether it's free or not, its URL, its purpose, its content, our view of the site, and our tip or tips for using the site.

Internet For Lawyers

Articles, tips, and links: Online CLE: **$**

http://www.netforlawyers.com

Purpose:	To provide information to the legal professional about how to use the Internet for legal, business, and investigative research.
Content:	The site offers articles about Internet research and also has online CLE courses to help you hone your Internet research skills by having you test out the sites discussed in the CLE articles in order to answer the quiz questions. Some of the articles explain how to find free case law on the Internet, how to find information about companies, and how to find free public records.
Our View:	It's our site, so we're probably a bit biased, but here goes! You'll like the clickable links included in the articles—it makes it easy for you to visit the sites for your own research. The online CLE quizzes are probably the least expensive you'll find on the Internet at $15 per credit hour.

Figure I-1. netforlawyers.com is the Web site of the authors. It provides articles and tips about conducting Internet legal research and also promotes their live seminars, many of which are based on the content of this book.

Tip: Use the red tabs at the top to navigate the site, or use the search box in the upper right-hand corner to search with keywords. The **LIVE MCLE** tab informs you about in-house courses and the **CALENDAR** tab tells you in which city (from Alaska to Atlanta) you can attend an Internet For Lawyers bar-association-sponsored seminar.

How to Use the CD

To make it easier to locate and access the sites you want to use in the book, we have included a CD-ROM that features links to all of the sites discussed in the book. The sites are all arranged by name and by topic so you can easily navigate to them without typing URLs into your browser! All of the links are included as a PDF file and requires the free Adobe Acrobat Reader to view.

Also provided is the helpful Checklist for Finding and Verifying Experts featured in the book, as well as a Source Credibility Checklist, a handy Methodology Checklist, and more. These are included as Microsoft Word files so that you can copy them to your hard drive, print them out, and make notations for your own Web searches.

Keeping Up to Date

We have been teaching legal professionals where to find the information they need on the Internet at seminars since 1999. So nobody knows more than we do that useful new sites appear on the Internet daily. That's why we are working to keep you up-to-date on these developments by including a free companion blog to inform you of the newest sites and any useful new developments at old favorites. You can find the blog online at **http://www.netforlawyers.com/blog**.

Introduction

How Lawyers Can Become Internet Detectives

In legal practice, research involves *much* more than the case law, statutes, and regulations explained in law school. For example, lawyers need to find current addresses to serve parties or to contact potential heirs. Other lawyers need to "dig up dirt" about the opposition or need to unearth background information about potential clients/hires. The Internet is extremely well-suited to investigative detective tasks. To become an Internet detective, lawyers need to learn how to find both public records and "publicly available information" on the Internet. This book focuses only on "publicly available information," while the companion book, Find Info Like a Pro, Volume 2: Mining the Internet's Public Records for Investigative Research, will focus on public records.

Most lawyers are familiar with the concept of public records, which we define as records stored at government agencies, available for public inspection—whether in person or over the Internet for free or in a pay database. The concept of publicly available information, however, might not be as familiar to lawyers.

Publicly available information, as defined by The Federal Trade Commission, Bureau of Consumer Protection's Division of Financial Practices is:

- Any information that a financial institution has a *reasonable basis to believe* is lawfully made available to the general public from:
  - Federal, state, or local government records;
  - Widely distributed media; or
  - Disclosures to the general public required by federal, state, or local law.

The Federal Trade Commission offers these as examples of publicly available information:

- Fact that an individual is a mortgage customer of a particular financial institution where that fact is recorded in public real estate records
- Telephone number listed in the phone book
- Information lawfully available to the general public on a Web site (including a Web site that requires a password or fee for access)

On the other hand, our definition of publicly available information does NOT include "federal, state, or local government records" or "Disclosures to the general public required by federal, state, or local law." Instead, we define publicly available information as any information found on the Internet (via a Web site, blog, social networking profile, etc.) that is NOT a public record.

Some examples of publicly available information (for purposes of this book), would be:

- Biographical information
- Articles from newspapers and magazines
- Address, fax, or phone numbers (home or work)
- E-mail addresses

While most of this book focuses on free information found on the Internet, we also include pay databases that compile information from a variety of sources (such as publicly available information, public records, proprietary information, and nonpublic/nonfinancial information).

If you're not yet convinced that you should bother with the Internet, or if you're uncertain whether anything of practical value is available on the Internet, read the war stories scattered throughout the book from practicing lawyers describing how they've used the Internet to find background and investigative information to solve problems, settle cases, and win at trial. In most of the war stories, we note the lawyer's name. But if a matter is still ongoing, to protect the confidentiality of the parties (and in one case an innocent dog) we need to shield the lawyer's name.

And, if you're still not convinced that you should bother with the Internet, we'll discuss some cases where even judges are using the Internet to help them make decisions while other judges (sometimes implicitly and other times explicitly) imposed a "duty to Google" upon lawyers.

Do Lawyers Have a Duty to Google?

Duty to Google

In 1999, a district court cautioned against relying on data from the Internet as "voodoo information." *St. Clair v. Johnny's Oyster & Shrimp,* 76 F. Supp. 2d 773, 775 (S.D. TX. 1999). Today, fortunately, judges are telling attorneys that they have a "duty to Google" as part of their due diligence procedure. Not only are judges admitting information from the Internet into evidence, sometimes they're the ones conducting the Internet research to help make judicial decisions.

For example, in a recent Indiana decision, the court was incredulous that the plaintiff failed to "Google" the missing defendant (Joe Groce) as part of his due diligence process. The court stated, "We do note that there is no evidence in this case of a public records or Internet search for Groce . . . to find him. In fact, we [the judge] discovered, upon entering 'Joe Groce Indiana' into the Google™ search engine, an address for Groce that differed from either address used in this case, as well as an apparent obituary for Groce's mother that listed numerous surviving relatives who might have known his whereabouts." The court upheld the defendant's claim of insufficient service of process and affirmed the dismissal of the case. *Munster v. Groce,* 829 N.E.2d 52 (Ind. App. 2005) *available at* **http://caselaw.lp .findlaw.com/data2/indianastatecases/app/06080501mpb.pdf**.

In a similar case, the court noted that the investigative technique of merely calling directory assistance to find a missing defendant has gone "the way of the horse and buggy and the eight track stereo" now that we have access to the Internet. *Dubois v. Butler,* 901 So. 2d 1029 (FL App 2005) *available at* **http://www.4dca.org/May2005/05-25-05/4D04-3559.pdf**.

In a recent Louisiana case, a trial court judge nullified a tax sale after the judge conducted an Internet search and determined that the tax-delinquent owner was "reasonably identifiable" and would have been locatable if the government had run a simple "Internet search" to locate the named mortgagee. The government claimed to have conducted a public records search and a Lexis-Nexis search. The appellate judge upheld the trial court's nullification of the government tax sale. Part of the basis of the appeal was whether it was appropriate for the trial court judge to have conducted an Internet search. The appeals court stated, "Nevertheless, we find any error the trial court may have committed by conducting the Internet search is harmless, because the trial court's ultimate conclusion that the tax sale violated Dr. Weatherly's due process rights is legally correct." *Weatherly v. Optimum Asset Management,* 928 So.2d 118 (La. App.

2005), *available at* **http://www.la-fcca.org/Opinions/PUB2005/2005-12/2004CA2734Dec2005.Pub.10.pdf**.

Duty to Google Questioned

The court, in a recent Pennsylvania case, took the opposite view of the above cited cases and ruled that a Google search, which a county performed to locate someone who owed back taxes on a property, was insufficient. The court held that instead of a Google search, the county should have used the telephone book! The court noted that if Northampton, Pennsylvania's tax collectors had looked up the missing defendant's telephone number in the telephone book, they might have been able to reach him (the telephone number in the telephone book was correct while the telephone number found using Google had been disconnected). The court, taking a very literal approach, concluded that the county's service by publication was insufficient because, by law, it was required to search the countywide telephone book to find an address to mail notice of a tax sale to a delinquent owner. *Fernandez v. Tax Claim Bureau of Northampton County,* No. 1600 C.D. 2006 (Pa. Commw. 5/30/07), *available at* **http://www.pacourts.us/OpPosting/Cwealth/out/1600CD06_5-31-07 .pdf**.

If the law specifically requires a certain manner of research, follow that literally, even if it means a "horse and buggy" search of the telephone book instead of an online Google search.

While it is common to "Google" someone to find a phone number or address, there are also many other phone directories free online to search, such as WhitePages.com (**http://www.whitepages.com**) or Anywho (**http://www.anywho.com**). If the free resources yield no results, try one of the pay investigative databases (discussed later in this book). In either case, always cross-check your search results by trying several ways to find a person. For example, verify results by checking more than one Web site or database.

Standard of Care

Diane Karpman, a California ethics expert, asks the question, "Will the use of technology change the standard of care?" In a scenario where the average lawyer uses online resources to find the most current information, while another lawyer fails to, then "the failure to do so is below average and therefore below the ordinary standard in the community. Falling below the average, typical, ordinary standard in the community opens the door to charges of professional negligence. In this case liability would not be for failing to use technology, but for failing to find the information that other lawyers could find and use for their clients' benefit." ("Keep Up or Face Peril," 20 GPSOLO, Number 4 [June 2003]) *available at* **http://www.abanet.org/genpractice/magazine/june2003/keepup.html**.)

CHAPTER**ONE**

Finding and Backgrounding People

Finding versus Backgrounding

This book is about finding people and obtaining background information about them. Lawyers frequently have to find people, from a missing heir to an expert witness. Finding involves, primarily, locating someone's contact information. This could range from a home, e-mail, or work address, to a home or work telephone number (landline or cellular) or, to even a facsimile number. Other times, lawyers need to "background" a person. Backgrounding can be defined simply as finding information about a person's background. It's a term commonly used by private investigators. There are two major ways to find and background people: by searching through public records and by sifting through bits and pieces of "publicly available" information.

Public Records versus Publicly Available Information

While public records are filed with government agencies, publicly available information is not. Publicly available information is that information that you voluntarily provide to a private entity or publish in a public place (such as the Internet). For example, you provide your phone number and address to a private entity—the telephone company. You publish information on the Internet—from postings to an online community, to the content on your own Web site, to the information you provide to Classmates.com. That information is now publicly available and may be found by anyone surfing the Internet. It may also be sold to marketing companies or public record database companies. In a recent study, 70 percent of the respondents gave personal information to a commercial Web site to get a product or service (but only 29 percent did so to a government Web site). The fact is that information about each of us is scattered among countless computer files held by the government, by private entities, and now by the public entity known as the Internet.

This book focuses on locating and using the publicly available information on the Internet to find and background people. We'll discuss both traditional resources found on the Internet—such as phone directories, and nontraditional resources—ones that you'll need to "think outside the box" to find, such as online communities (Google Groups, Facebook, MySpace, etc.). Some of this publicly available information contained within nontraditional resources would never be found on a pay database, yet could provide you with the "smoking gun." However, pay databases also have a place in the search for missing people and backgrounding people, and will be discussed later in this book. These databases combine public records, publicly available information, and other information sources such as credit headers (See page 216).

Try the Internet First

There's nothing as convenient or as cheap as using the Internet to search for people via publicly available information. This is not to say that the Internet provides access to all information about a person. For example, there is no comprehensive site on the Internet to search for all e-mail addresses for free. If you need to search for something like that, you'd need to use a pay database in addition to free resources, and even then, you might not find what you're looking for. However, the convenience of the Internet's perpetual availability from almost any computer (or handheld device) with an Internet connection, and the negligible cost of using the Internet, makes it a logical first choice for finding and backgrounding people, even if you end up accessing a fee-based database later.

Privacy Issues on the Internet

Computers are incredibly useful tools if you're looking for someone or backgrounding them, and slightly scary if you're concerned about personal privacy (especially your own). After we've already disclosed personal data, it is difficult to recall it. Some sites do offer you the chance to remove your data, however. For instance, if you find your contact information available on Google's PhoneBook database, you can have it removed by filling out a form at **http://www.google.com/intl/en/help/pbremoval.html**. Some other Web sites used to offer this option, but no longer do, such as Switchboard.com. In order to protect our personal privacy, the most useful thing we can do is to be aware of the power of digital communications, and be cautious about what personal data we release. But if you're looking for someone, maybe because they owe you money, or because an estate you're administering owes them money, or just simply to invite them to a reunion, computers make the process easy, and even fun.

Offline Searching

Keep in mind that although the free Internet and pay databases can be useful sources for public record and publicly available information research, a comprehensive search may also involve physically traveling to court houses, government agencies, and other archives (public and private) to review paper records. It's estimated that only twenty percent of public records are online.

Backgrounding People

Although we noted that the term backgrounding is one used by private investigators, which conjures up images of cloak and dagger surveillance, it actually refers to investigating a person via research instead of by surveillance. Backgrounding can be as straightforward as finding someone's biography in a *Who's Who* type of directory or finding their telephone listing in a free online telephone directory or as offbeat as finding out something mentioned about them in a posting in an online community or in an eBay feedback profile. (The eBay feedback profile includes a rating number for the bidder and the seller, as well as written comments about either.) Because not everyone uses their real name in these types of communications, you might not have any luck finding information about your subject, but it's worth a try.

eBay Feedback Profiles

Background information can show up in all sorts of places on the Internet, such as comments that buyers can leave on a seller's eBay feedback profile (and the seller's responding comments). In an unpublished California case, a buyer (plaintiff Grace), left negative comments on the feedback profile of the seller (defendant Neeley). In response, Neeley left negative comments about Grace. Grace asked eBay to remove the comments about him. When eBay refused, Grace filed a libel suit against Neeley and eBay. The Appellate court agreed with the trial court, and held, under 47 U.S.C. section 230(c)(1), that eBay was immune from a libel suit because it was an interactive computer service provider under 47 U.S.C. § 230(c)(1) *available at* **http://tinyurl.com/http-tinyurl47usc230** (which provides: "No provider or user of an interactive computer service shall be treated as the publisher or speaker of any information provided by another information content provider.") and could not be treated as the publisher or speaker of any information provided by another information content provider. *Grace* v. *EBAY*, No. B168765, unpublished op. (CA App February 5, 2004) *available at* **http://w2.eff.org/legal/ISP_liability/CDA230/grace_v_ebay_1.pdf.**

Using "publicly available" resources, the following information about a person might be found for free on the Internet:

- Address
- Phone number
- Education
- Occupation
- Place of employment
- Publications by or about the subject found in books, articles, e-newsletters, blogs, and Web sites (such as an employer's site)
- Biography or profile
- Image
- Hobbies
- Interests
- Civic and volunteer work
- A PowerPoint presentation, Excel spreadsheet, or Word document created and posted on the Internet by the subject or about the subject
- Postings to, from, or about the subject (found in the ongoing discussions or archives of online communities)

The following information is generally found in public records on the Internet usually (but not always) for free:

- Social Security number
- Date of birth
- Date of death
- Cases
- Dockets
- Assets (real property, planes, boats, trademarks, copyrights, patents, stocks, business ownerships, and so on)
- Liens, judgments, and bankruptcies
- Lawsuits
- Political party membership
- Campaign contributions
- Marriages and divorces
- Professional or occupational licenses

The public records and some of the publicly available information noted above can often be found in one place by using a pay investigative database.

*CHAPTER*TWO

Finding Missing People

Locating the Dead

When trying to locate someone, we recommend first seeing if the person is dead. You can save a lot of time if you first verify whether they are alive or dead. Otherwise you might waste time and money searching for someone who is dead. The first site to ascertain whether someone is dead is the Social Security Death Index (SSDI) located on RootsWeb's site.

People often ask us how to locate where a particular relative has been buried. This is after they have been unable to verify the death through the SSDI. People who ask this question are always certain that the relative died, and that the relative left them a fortune, even though they'd been out of touch with the decedent for a good long time. There are some other options besides the SSDI for the hopeful heir trying to verify a death. For instance, locating the gravesite or an obituary can help establish the place of death. From there you can narrow down the search to a specific jurisdiction and begin your phone and letter inquiries. Also, look for state and local death and obituary records by using links at the USGenWeb Project (see page 115).

While you can use RootsWeb SSDI to discover a dead person's SSN and to discover if someone is illegally using a dead person's SSN, you will need to use U.S. InfoSearch to verify whether someone has provided you with a completely made-up SSN.

Death Records

Lawyers often need to verify deaths for many reasons. Recently, a lawyer trying to locate an heir asked for our assistance. Before doing any extensive investigating, we first check to see if a missing heir (or witness) is deceased. National death records can be found in the Social Security Death Index (SSDI), searchable at several free sites, such as Ancestry.com (**http://www.ancestry.com**) and RootsWeb (**http://ssdi .rootsweb.ancestry.com**). There are also other death indexes found at the state and local level.

RootsWeb SSDI Search

http://ssdi.rootsweb.ancestry.com

Purpose: For genealogy research primarily, but useful to verify a death in the Social Security Death Index (SSDI) and to find Social Security numbers (of dead people).

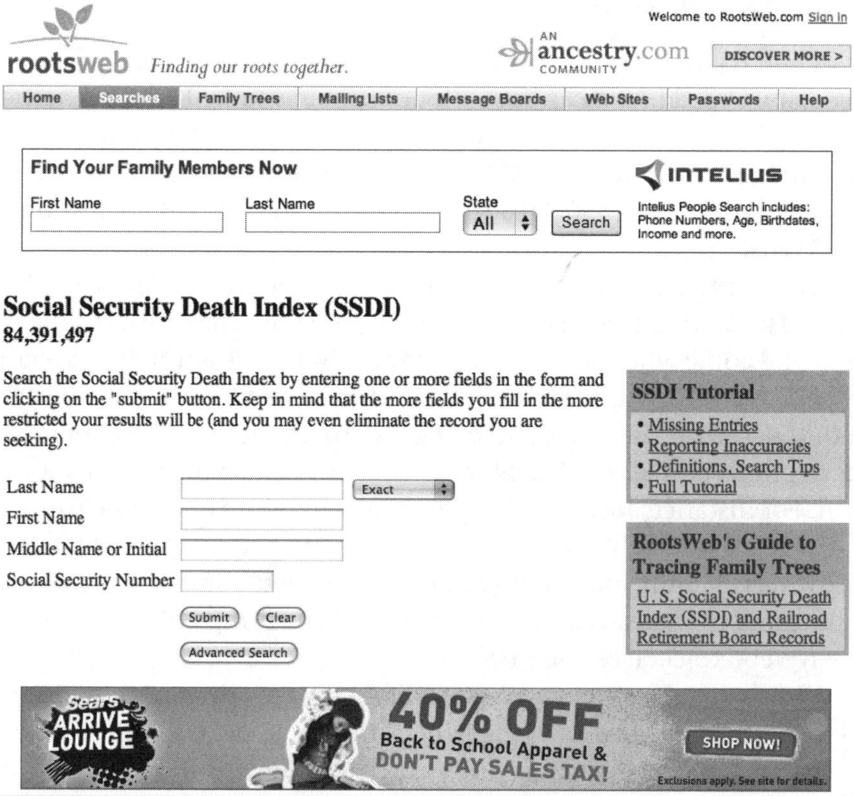

Welcome to RootsWeb.com Sign in

rootsweb *Finding our roots together.* AN ancestry.com COMMUNITY DISCOVER MORE >

| Home | Searches | Family Trees | Mailing Lists | Message Boards | Web Sites | Passwords | Help |

Find Your Family Members Now INTELIUS

First Name   Last Name   State [All ▲▼] [Search]   Intelius People Search includes: Phone Numbers, Age, Birthdates, Income and more.

Social Security Death Index (SSDI)
84,391,497

Search the Social Security Death Index by entering one or more fields in the form and clicking on the "submit" button. Keep in mind that the more fields you fill in the more restricted your results will be (and you may even eliminate the record you are seeking).

Last Name [_____] [Exact ▲▼]
First Name [_____]
Middle Name or Initial [_____]
Social Security Number [_____]

[Submit] [Clear]
[Advanced Search]

SSDI Tutorial
• Missing Entries
• Reporting Inaccuracies
• Definitions, Search Tips
• Full Tutorial

RootsWeb's Guide to Tracing Family Trees
U. S. Social Security Death Index (SSDI) and Railroad Retirement Board Records

Sears ARRIVE LOUNGE **40% OFF** Back to School Apparel & DON'T PAY SALES TAX! [SHOP NOW!] Exclusions apply. See site for details.

Figure 2-1. Unless you have the subject's Social Security number, be sure to click on the **Advanced Search** button on this page where more search options are provided to assist you in pinpointing the correct person.

Content: The site contains death records for over 83 million deaths occurring after 1962 that were reported to the Social Security Administration. The index is updated monthly. While records include the decedent's name, birth and death dates, last known address, and Social Security number and place of its issuance, not every record contains all of this information.

Although there are many ways to access the SSDI from the RootsWeb home page, the easiest and most direct route is to avoid going to the home page and use the URL noted in the previous page. However, if you do find yourself on the home page, do not enter any information into the **Search RootsWeb Search Ancestry** query boxes on the home page. It's simply a diversion. Some summary results will be displayed and then an offer to sign up for Ancestry.com's pay service will be displayed.

Also, don't enter the decedent's name into the search boxes displayed on the Death Index's main search page (noted in the previous page). Instead, click on **Advanced Search** and then search by any of the following criteria, or combinations of them: name (for the last name you can choose exact, or if unsure of the spelling, choose soundex, which is the "sounds like" feature); last residence; last place benefit was sent to; Social Security number; birth date; and death date.

Our View: Although RootsWeb and Ancestry.com have similar data, including the SSDI, we prefer RootsWeb because it does not require registering (Ancestry.com does) and some of the same data that is fee-based at Ancestry.com (some state public records) is free at RootsWeb.

Tip: Once you locate the record, you may decide that you want a copy of the decedent's original Social Security application for further background information. To do this, click on **SS-5 Letter** in the right-hand column of the search results. The decedent's information is automatically placed into a letter to the Social Security Administration, which you can print out and mail with a $27 check to obtain a copy of the application. The following valuable information will be found once you

Figure 2-2. The Advanced Search menu for the Social Security Death Index offers more search fields to narrow down your results.

receive a copy of the decedent's original application: full name; full name at birth (including maiden name); present mailing address and current employer's name and address (at the time of application); age at last birthday; date of birth; place of birth (city, county, state); father's full name (regardless of whether living or dead); mother's full name, including maiden name (regardless of whether living or dead); sex; race; whether the decedent ever previously applied for a Social Security number or Railroad Retirement; date signed; and the applicant's signature. If you require additional records, such as birth, death, marriage, or divorce, click on the shopping cart icon in the **Order Record?** column. This will take you to VitalChek—a pay service.

Although we usually suggest that you enter as much information into a database about a person in order to narrow a search, if you receive no results from the SSDI (or any database, for that matter), start backing out information. Not all records contain the person's middle name, or place of death, for instance.

Validating Social Security Numbers

U.S. InfoSearch

http://www.free-ssn-id-verification.usinfosearch.com

Purpose: For Social Security number validation.

Content: This search shows whether a Social Security number is valid and whether it belongs to someone alive or deceased. To use this site, enter a Social Security number into the search box and then enter your e-mail address. Results will be e-mailed to you almost instantly.

Our View: This site's service is limited because it does not tell you who is linked to the number. Nevertheless, it has some value because it does tell you if someone is using a deceased person's Social Security number or an invalid (made-up) number, indicating that someone is concealing his true identity. But, if someone is misusing a live person's actual number, then this site is of little value since it doesn't show names.

Tip: Since this service is free, it's useful as a preliminary check because it can show that the Social Security number is invalid or belongs to a deceased person. If the number is valid, you'll need to search a pay database sooner or later to verify that the Social Security number belongs to the person who is claiming it or you can register for free use of the Social Security Business Services Online (BSO) service (**http://www.socialsecurity.gov/ bso/bsowelcome.htm**). The BSO offers two options to verify that employees' names and Social Security numbers match their Social Security records. Online verification of up to ten names and SSNs is the first option for those who wish to receive immediate results. Uploading batch files of up to 250,000 names and SSNs is the second option. Results are typically provided the next day. Both services are available to all employers but may only be used to verify current or former employees and only for wage reporting (Form W-2) purposes (**http://www .ssa.gov/employer/ssnv.htm**).

Over the phone verification is also another option but there is a limit of five names/SSNs. Call toll-free for phone verification at 1-800-772-6270. The hours are weekdays only, from 7:00 a.m. to 7:00 p.m. EST. You must provide: your company name and EIN and the employee's SSN, last name, first name, middle initial, date of birth, and gender (**http://www.ssa.gov/employer/ssnv additional.htm**).

Using Obituaries to Locate the Dead and to Uncover Other Information (Names of Relatives and Potential Heirs)

While it can take up to six weeks after a death occurs to be able to verify it at the Social Security Death Index (**http://ssdi.rootsweb.com**), you might be able to verify a death much quicker through an obituary since they typically show up within just a few days of the death in sites like the Obituary Daily Times (**http://obits.rootsweb.com/cgi-bin/obit.cgi**), NOA (**http://www.arrangeonline.com**), and Legacy (**http://www.legacy.com**), all discussed below. Obituaries are also a rich source for finding names of living relatives in case you need to contact them for a quiet title action, an inheritance, or even to try to collect a debt. They are also useful for finding a missing person if that person is mentioned in someone's obituary as a surviving relative.

Legacy

http://www.legacy.com

 (to search and access recent obituaries)

 (to view older obituaries)

Purpose: To locate obituaries.

Content: Founded in 1998, the site provides a searchable, master database of millions of obituaries from more than 700 newspapers across the United States and Canada (including major chains such as Tribune, Advance [Newhouse], Hearst and others). Newspaper obituary information is updated daily.

Its search engine, ObitFinder™, searches newspaper obituaries dating back to as early as February 2001. Search results display the text of the obituary and photo (if available). Results may also include a link to a **Guest Book** (if available) where friends and family can post remembrances, etc., about the departed individual. Searches also include results from the Social Security Death Index back to 2001.

Newer obituaries are available to view, full text, for free. Older obituaries (those marked **Archived Notice**) cost $2.95 each. The charge can be billed to a credit card, and the obituary is made available immediately after payment. You might find enough information in the older obituary's brief annotation (or annotations if the obituary appears in more than one outlet) to avoid paying to read the full obituary. There were four brief annotations for our subject and by piecing them together we learned the date of death, the date of birth, names of family members, names of newspapers and dates where the obituary was published, and the place and time of the funeral service.

The basic search on the site's home page allows for a **By Person** search or a **By Newspaper** search. If **By Person** is selected you would enter a name into the **First Name** and **Last Name** search boxes (entering a **First Name** is optional). The search can be narrowed by selecting a country from the drop-down menu (**United States**, **Canada**, or **All U.S. and Canada**) and/or by selecting a date or date range (e.g., **All records**, **Past 3 days**, etc.). Clicking the **More Search Options** link gives you the ability to narrow down your search further, by adding a **Keyword** or limiting your search to a specific **Newspaper** or to a specific state (or province if Canada was selected).

You can also browse obituaries from more than 700 individual newspapers in North America, Europe, and Australia, by linking directly to the paper you're interested in (**http://www.legacy.com/NS/about/newspapers.aspx**).

Our View: This site is most useful in researching those who may have died recently, because no source goes back beyond 2001 and with many offering information back only to late 2007. The geographic coverage of the Web site is a bit confusing. On its home page, there is a reference to obituaries "from 700 newspapers in the U.S. and around the world," but the drop-down menu on that same page only provides for a U.S. or Canada selection. We think the international reference is only for the browsing feature noted above.

Tips: Be sure to check the list of coverage dates for each of the participating newspapers (available by selecting the **By Newspaper** tab and clicking the **700 newspapers** link; **http://www.legacy.com/Obituaries.asp?Page= ObitFinder**).

The **Guest Book** can be a good source for names of surviving family members or business associates.

Remember to visit your public library's Web site to see if the obituary is available for free in one of the newspaper databases the library allows you to access remotely. For information about remote library databases, see chapter 12, Using Expensive Pay Databases for Free.

Tributes.com

http://www.tributes.com/

Purpose: Tributes.com provides a searchable death notice and obituary database of 84 million deaths, dating back to 1930 (and possibly earlier).

Content: Searching is by one or more of the following criteria: last name, first name, or date. If a search retrieves too many results, only the first 100 will be displayed and an advanced search will be offered to add in more information, such as city, state, or keywords. To visit the advanced search directly, see **http://www.tributes.com/ search/obituaries**. Although a search by only a first name is possible, there will probably be too many results. Try narrowing down by date, city, state, or keywords. There is also a location browsing feature. Searching is free, but to create a tribute, one must register (also free). To add photos and multimedia, a pay account must be set up (from $3.99 per month to $7.99 per month).

Our View: In our test searches, we did not see any tributes or any of the features that one could pay to create. Typically, we saw a statement as to the decedent's age, date of death, and place of death.

Tips: Tributes provides an alert service to inform you when someone has died. This requires a registration (free). One must provide an e-mail address and create a password.

Obituary Daily Times

http://obits.rootsweb.com/cgi-bin/obit.cgi

Purpose: To discover in which newspaper an obituary is published when you don't know where to begin your search.

Content: The site is an index of published obituaries (15,009,208 as of December 13, 2009). While the actual obituary is not online, the index tells you in which newspaper it was published. To learn which newspapers participate in this index, see **http://www.rootsweb.ancestry.com/~obituary/publications.html**. To receive an e-mail alert (often twice a day) of new obituaries, see **http://www.rootsweb.ancestry.com/~obituary/#sub** or to volunteer, see the instructions at **http://www.rootsweb.ancestry.com/~obituary**.

Our View: This free index of published obituaries, which adds over 2,500 entries a day, is a good place to start a search if you don't know where someone died. Volunteers are responsible for monitoring each newspaper's obituaries and then adding them to the index, but not all newspapers have been adopted by a volunteer. With so many newspapers online, it should not be too difficult to obtain an obituary from a specific newspaper either at the newspaper's Web site or by using your remote library databases that may include that newspaper (see Chapter 12, "Using Expensive Pay Databases for Free").

Tips: Another obituary index is the National Obituary Archive (NOA), with almost 55 million obituaries (**http://www .arrangeonline.com**). By clicking on the **Search** button (toward the top and center of the home page next to **Find An Obituary**), an advanced search menu will pop up. Fill in the last name of the decedent and any (or all) of the following criteria: first name, city, state/province, country, or approximate date of death. If unsure of the spelling of a name, a "wild-card" search can be performed. The percent sign is used as the wild card. For instance, a search for bosl* will find bosley, boslin, and so on. There is no need to register to search this site. Only those who want to create memorials, tributes, and picture albums would want to consider registering. With funeral directors across North America serving as contributing members to this site, it contains very recent data.

If you know where someone died, check the Web to see if the local library or historical society has a site because they often have local obituaries online. To find library Web sites, see Libweb (**http://lists.webjunction.org/ libweb/**), which offers keyword searching by location, library type, and name, or browsing by library type or by region for foreign countries' libraries. To find links to many local historical societies, see RootsWeb.com (**http://www.rootsweb.ancestry.com/roots-l/usa.html**) and select the state you are interested in. You might find useful Web sites under one of the following headings in the state lists: (1) **Archives, Libraries and Special Collections**; (2) **Cemeteries**; (3) **Societies, Historical and Genealogical**; and (4) **Local**.

Cemeteries and Graves

Find A Grave

http://www.findagrave.com

Purpose: To locate gravesite locations of 38 million people.

Content: The site contains information on gravesites of both the celebrity and the mere mortal. Search by name, (**http://www.findagrave.com/cgi-bin/fg.cgi**) or date, or browse by location. Name searching can be further limited by date of birth or death or by the state in which the person is buried. Other search options allow you to check off an **Include maiden name(s) in my search** box or a **Do partial name search on surname** box. It even includes noncemetery burial sites, such as cre-

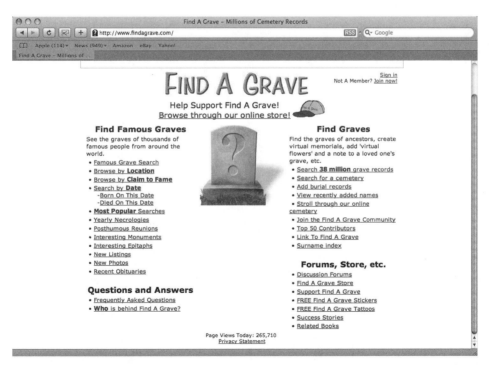

Figure 2-3. FindAGrave.com's searchable database of more than 38 million gravesites includes location of burial, as well as birth and death date information for many entries.

mation "sites." A link to the SSDI's advanced search page is also offered.

Our View: While over 350,000 contributors to this site have more free time than most of us, we're happy to take advantage of their work. Although more than 26 million people have been added to the site between 2003-2009, we still did not find a name we searched for back in 2003 when we tried again in 2009.

Tip: If you don't find your decedent at this cemetery site, try one of the obituary sites noted in the previous pages.

*CHAPTER*THREE

Proper Name Searching

War Story: Finding Someone Without Having a Name

Sometimes lawyers have the name of the person they are trying to find and sometimes they don't. Even when you don't know the name of the person you seek, the Internet can be the answer to your problem. Lawyer and law librarian Cathy Pennington Paunov tells this story:

One of my favorite examples is the case where someone in Ohio was working on a salmonella ice cream case. She was desperate. She needed additional information. We only wanted to get hold of practitioners that had worked on cases like this. So I went to AltaVista (**http://www.altavista.com**), which is my favorite search engine on the Internet, and searched the Internet for the following three words: "salmonella" and "ice cream." I got something like three hundred hits. One of them, and it was in the first batch—the nice thing about AltaVista is it ranks the stuff in order of probable relevance—the third or fourth hit down, was some law firm in Chicago. Their Web site said that one of their senior litigation partners had handled the largest salmonella ice cream case in the country. I actually picked up the phone because I knew how desperate this poor lawyer was. I picked up the phone and called the lawyer in Ohio and said, "Listen, here's someone in Chicago." I also called the Chicago lawyer and warned him I was doing this—and he said, "Fine, I'd be happy to help her out."

I don't think I would have found the salmonella ice cream guy but for the Internet. There's no way I could have found him anywhere else. That was the most incredible story. I've got one very happy small-town lawyer and she's got the name of the top legal expert in the field.

Free Is Sometimes Best

If Paunov had tried searching for this information before we were using the Internet for research, she might have racked up a huge bill by running a nationwide search looking for court opinions in a commercial database about salmonella ice cream cases. And to boot, she may have come up empty-handed if there were only state trial-level opinions on the topic, since trial-level cases are not usually published. The beauty of the Internet is you might find a story about an unreported trial-level case right on point on some firm's Web site as Paunov did, or in a posting in an online community—information resources that the commercial databases don't index (yet).

Search for the Expertise

When you don't have the name of an expert, you often need to search by the expertise to discover names of potential experts. See Chapter 11, "Finding and Backgrounding Expert Witnesses," for various places to find and background experts.

The Internet is an excellent source for finding people if you know something about the individual. For example, if you're looking for a lawyer, there are two lawyer directories available for free on the Internet: FindLaw's Legal Directory and Martindale Hubbell. FindLaw's Directory (**http://lawyers.findlaw.com/lawyer/lawyer_dir/search/jsp/adv_search .jsp**) has an advanced search that allows you to search by **Legal Issue**, **Location**, **Language**, and **Payment** (**Credit Card accepted** or **Free Consultation Offered**). You will need to choose whether you want your results to include only law firms or only lawyers. Another option is to search by lawyer or firm name (**http://lawyers.findlaw.com/lawyer/ lawyer_dir/search/jsp/name_search.jsp**). For the lawyer name search, only a last name is required, but you can also narrow your search by entering a **First Name**, **City**, **State**, or **Legal Issue**. Martindale Hubbell (**http://www.martindale.com**) can be used for searching by practice area, name, language spoken, and more.

If you are looking for someone whose employer typically posts an employee directory on the Internet, such as private companies, universities, and government agencies, you might be able to use the Internet to find a way to contact that person even when it's after normal business hours and nobody's answering the telephone at the main number. Professional associations often post their members contact information online, so if you're looking for an American physician, for example, the American Medical Association provides a database that can locate over 690,000 doctors by name, specialty, and location who are licensed to practice in the U.S. To begin a search visit **http://webapps.ama-assn.org/doctorfinder/home.jsp** and select **Patients and consumers Search for a physician**.

Reverse Searching

If you don't have the name of the person you are trying to locate (or if you are unsure of the spelling or there has been a name change), but you do have other clues about the person, reverse searching is a possible option. The following clues about a person can be turned into a reverse search and lead you to that person (sometimes a combination of these clues needs to be employed):

- Social Security number
- An alias
- Phone number or address (current or past)
- Date of birth
- Age range
- Occupation

Problems with Name Searching

Even if a lawyer has the name of the person he is trying to find or background, the search can prove difficult if any of the following events have occurred:

- Address or phone number change
- Name change due to marriage or divorce
- A misspelled name
- Death

Another problem with name searching is you can't always be sure that you have the right person since many people share the same name. Also, because many people refer to themselves in various ways, it's hard to be certain that you've done a thorough search. Name searching requires finding all the various names (and variations) that the subject uses and then searching using all of them. You need to discover what name your subject uses:

- First and last name only?
- First and last name, with a middle name or middle initial?
- Nickname?
- Aliases?
- Married name?
- Maiden name?
- Middle name as a first name?
- Initials instead of a full first name?

Lessons Learned About Proper Names in Our Search for a Missing Subject

A client asked us to locate someone named Gregg Harwick (the name has been changed to protect the true subject's privacy). The only information we had, besides his name, was that he lived in LaJolla, California.

First, we ran a basic Google search using the first and last name. One of the results showed an address in the Los Angeles area. Our satisfaction with hitting pay dirt with just one search quickly dissipated as we learned from our client that this was not our subject, but the subject's son.

- Lesson number one: Don't think you'll find someone <u>that</u> quickly!

Although our client had no budget for us to use pay databases and had asked us to only use free resources, we decided to use a pay database anyway because our subscription to Merlin is "use it or lose it." If we don't use Merlin in any given month, $10 is deducted from our deposit account. Since we hadn't used the full $10 on Merlin that month, it made sense to run a report on our dime (or in this case twenty-five cents).

Splurging on a twenty-five cent address search, we found a record for Gregg Harwick, but it only included his city and state—Pauma Valley, California. Perhaps Pauma Valley was near LaJolla? To confirm that Pauma Valley was near LaJolla, we searched Mapquest.com and learned that it was.

- Lesson number two: Sometimes it pays to spend some money on searches because you might find a new clue, such as a different city name; and

- Lesson number three: if someone tells you a subject lives in a specific city, don't discount a result that shows the subject's name attached to a different city. Instead, use Mapquest (or a similar resource) to see if it's close to the city where the client thought the subject lived.

We decided that if the client was mistaken about the subject's city, perhaps the client was also mistaken about the subject's first name. We started to wonder if the name "Gregg" could be spelled "Greg" or could be short for "Greggory" or "Gregory." So we decided to revisit Google to search with the new city name, Pauma Valley, and delete the first name entirely from our search, using only the last name, "Harwick." That led to an obituary for "Roy Harwick," which listed someone named "Marvin Harwick" as a surviving brother . . . and he lived in Pauma Valley. Some people use their middle name as their preferred name. Perhaps Marvin Harwick was really Marvin Gregg Harwick but preferred to be called Gregg?

- Lesson number four: Clients who seem certain about their information sometimes make mistakes. Drop a first name from your search and just search by last name (and other identifying information you have, e.g., a city) to look for variations of the first name or to learn if the subject uses his middle name as his first name; and

- Lesson number five: Obituaries can be very helpful because they often list the names of surviving relatives and the cities in which they live.

Since we still did not have a street address or phone number, we decided to look through a few more Google search results. One of the results was a link labeled WIP Case List which brought us to an Excel spreadsheet at the California Secretary of State's Web site. Even after looking at the Excel spreadsheet, we had no idea what WIP stood for. We then used Google's Advanced Search page to search for *WIP* and to avoid getting irrelevant results we restricted the domain to *swrcb.ca.gov*. We found that WIP refers to Well Investigation Program.

Instead of scrolling through the long spreadsheet, we invoked the "Find" function (CTRL+F) and entered *Harwick* into the Find search box. We quickly located a reference to M.G. Harwick and his city was listed as Pauma Valley. Could the "M.G." stand for "Marvin Gregg Harwick" as we had surmised while perusing the obituary mentioned above?

Unfortunately, only a post office box number was listed so we still lacked an exact street address or phone number.

- Lesson number six: Use Google's Advanced Search page and the Search within a site or domain function; and

- Lesson number seven: You can often find useful information in Excel spreadsheets (or even PowerPoint presentations or Word documents) that have been uploaded to Web sites.

We decided to search the home page of the Web site where we had found the Excel spreadsheet. This turned out to be the California EPA, Los Angles Regional Water Quality Control Board. Using the internal search engine at the site, we once again searched for *Harwick* and found three references—which led us to another WIP Case List. This one was labeled, "California Regional Water Quality Control Board—Los Angeles Region Case List—San Gabriel and San Fernando Valley Cleanup Program dated 9/30/07."

Since Harwick's name was noted on a cleanup list, we wondered if he had once owned a company that had contributed to some sort of environmental problem now requiring cleanup. Assuming he still owned the company, or was still connected to it, we decided to search the California Secretary of State's Web site using the name *Harwick*. In California, the Secretary of State's business records database can only be searched by company name, so we hoped that his company name included his last name. (In many other states, the Secretary of State Web sites don't limit you to searching only by company name but also allow you to search by an officer's name or a registered agent's name.) Luckily for us, there was a company that included Harwick's last name. The agent for service of process was listed as: "Marvin Greggory Harwick." In addition, the record included a street address in Pauma Valley, California.

- Lesson number eight: If your subject owns a company or is an officer or registered agent at a company, search the Secretary of State's Web site.

Armed with the subject's correct first name and correct city, we returned to Merlin to conduct another twenty-five cent address/telephone search and found our subject's record, which included his street address in Pauma Valley, California, and also a phone number.

- Lesson number nine: Don't give up. Think of alternative ways to spell names or search only by a last name. Consider that your subject is using his middle name instead of his first name.

- Final lesson: Cross-check, cross-check, and cross-check your results using multiple sources to ensure you have found the correct person.

Tips for Name Searching

If you think the person uses only a first and last name, enter the name into a search engine as a phrase by surrounding it with quotation marks ("*carole levitt*"). This will help narrow your search.

If it's possible that the subject uses a middle name or initial (either regularly or sporadically) or if you don't know the middle name, use a Boolean connector between the first and last name (*carole AND levitt*) to find any document with the name "carole" and the name "levitt"—and anything in between those two names. This can give you many irrelevant results, though—you might find a Carole Brown and a Robert Levitt in the same document, which is technically a correct result but not the one you're looking for.

Or, better yet, visit Yahoo! (**http://www.yahoo.com**) and enter your subject's first name followed by a space, an asterisk, another space, and their last name <u>and</u> enclose the entire string in quotation marks. (The asterisk replaces one word (e.g., a middle initial or middle name), but can only be used within a phrase.) In addition, add a space, an OR, and your subject's first and last name enclosed in quotation marks. Be sure to capitalize the OR. Your search would look like this: "*carole * levitt*" OR "*carole levitt*." We think this search strategy is unique to Yahoo!. The search results will include the name *carole* within one word of *levitt* and/or the name *carole* adjacent to *levitt* (in that exact order with no intervening words). Thus, your results will include: *Carole Levitt, Carole A. Levitt, Carole Ann Levitt, Carole B. Levitt,* and so on. This search will not bring back *Levitt, Carole* because the quotation marks indicate to Yahoo! that you wanted the first name first and the last name last.

*CHAPTER*FOUR

Finding Telephone Numbers and Addresses

Transitioning from Print to Free and Pay Web-Based Telephone and Address Directories

To find and background people, researchers used to rely extensively upon print materials (such as directories and phone books), CD-ROMs, microfilm, microfiche, and proprietary databases. These resources would often be inaccessible to many researchers because they were expensive, cumbersome to use, cumbersome to store, or geographically inaccessible.

But as more and more of these traditional research resources have been converted to Web-based resources, they have become much more accessible in every way and thus much more useful for finding people. Take print phone directories that are now Web-based, for example: since many are free, the expense of buying and storing them is no longer an issue; since they are searchable in a digital format, there is no longer a need to manually search through multiple directories so they are no longer cumbersome to use; since they are stored on the Internet, they are no longer cumbersome to store; and since they can be accessed by anyone with a computer and an Internet connection, there is no longer an issue of geographical inaccessibility.

Free Telephone Directories on the Web

The most common (though often overlooked) way to find people is to use the most common reference book there is—the telephone book, now found free in Web-based phone book directories. The thousands of U.S.

regional phone directories are perfectly suited to the quick lookup speed of computer databases. Results usually include street address, telephone number (home and business landlines), and sometimes an e-mail address, a map to the address, and more. At present, there is no comprehensive directory for cellular phones. Later in this chapter, we'll provide some limited assistance for finding cellular phone numbers and even records of calls made from both cellular and landline numbers—for a fee.

While some years ago a number of CD-ROM publishers seized the opportunity to issue national phone directories on disk, Internet-based phone books are a step ahead of CD-ROM phone books in some ways. The Internet makes databases easier to update and distribute, so they can be more current than a CD-ROM, although it's hard to tell how often the Web-based directories are actually updated. Using the Internet avoids the need to change disks. Internet phone books are accessible from anywhere (assuming you have an Internet connection, of course) and Internet phone books are free.

On the flip side, if you want to print large phone lists, CD-ROM is superior because Internet-based directories generally allow you to display only a few names and phone listings at a time. Karen Olson, an independent information specialist (**karen@koinfopro.net**), still finds that phone directories on CD have several advantages over the Web directories. Olson explains:

> The CD has an auto-type-ahead feature, which the Web lacks. This makes it possible to see the list of query results fill in as you type the search terms. Often with both individual and business names, the searcher is trying to find a name and is handicapped with an incorrect spelling. The auto-type-ahead feature lets you see the possible answer set at each character stroke. Secondly, although it is true that the CD is not up to the minute in currency, the product at least lets the user know what release date they are working with whereas the Web directories don't provide any date information at all. Finally, the CD directories search faster. Not only does the CD have a faster search response time, but it saves you the time from going from one phone Web directory to the next since the CD is more comprehensive than any one Web directory site.

Unpublished and Unlisted Phone Numbers

Many of the Web phone directories draw data from the same sources—published White Page or Yellow Page directories and other publicly available sources. If a phone number is unpublished or unlisted, you most likely won't find it in one of these Web phone directories. (There is some debate about whether there is any difference between an unpublished and an unlisted number. Some say "no" while a law librarian/former telephone company employee says there are some similarities and some differences. For example, both unlisted and unpublished numbers are similar to each other because neither appears in the phone book and neither is sold to other companies. However, an unpublished number is different from an unlisted number because it is also not included in the directory assistance database while an unlisted number is (and may be given out when one phones directory assistance). But sometimes people with unpublished or unlisted phone numbers do provide their phone numbers to sources other than the phone company. You might be able to find the number in those sources, especially if it's in a public record or private database.

Discovering an Unpublished or Unlisted Phone Number Through a Domain Registry

Sometimes people with unpublished or unlisted phone numbers do provide their phone numbers to sources other than the phone company. You might find the number listed on a Web site, a blog, a social networking site (see Chapter 8), a pay database (see Chapter 12) or even in an Internet Domain Registry application found at one of the "Who is" directories (such as **http://whois.com/** or **http://www.betterwhois.com/**). To *try* to discover who is behind a Web site and to obtain their contact information, type the site's URL into a registry such as Better-Whois (**http://www.betterwhois.com**) or Allwhois (**http://www.allwhois.com**). The reason why we emphasized the word "try" is because no registry, for a variety of reasons, seems to be "completely complete." A registry may claim to be the "most complete 'whois' service on the Internet," but this doesn't mean complete as in "comprehensive"—just the most complete that it can be, given all the obstacles. It's difficult to create a comprehensive registry because registries may receive less-than-complete records when a domain is registered, and most registries only cover the most popular TLD types such as .com, .net, or .org, thus leaving out many records from the less popular TLDs such as .biz or .museum. Even if you do find the registration statement, it's hard to say whether you have found the actual site owner because anyone can list themselves as the contact person on the registration statement—the site owner, the IT manager, or the Web site's outside designer. It's also hard to say whether you have found the correct contact information, because the information is not verified by the domain registry.

More Information?

Nearly all of the phone book sites are advertiser-supported, with enticements labeled **More Info** or **Public Record Click Here**. For example, after finding Carole Levitt's name, partial address, and phone number in a free Yahoo! People Search (**http://people.yahoo.com**), we clicked on her name and were brought to a page that included her full address and a **Find More Information** link. Upon clicking the link, we were brought to Intelius' Web site (**http://www.intelius.com**), which is a pay site that you will see over and over again—at various telephone directory sites and other people finding sites. We were informed that for $49.95, Intelius could find "Criminal Report, Lawsuits, Judgments, Liens, Bankruptcies, Property Ownership, 30 Year Address History, Relatives & Associates, Neighbors, Licenses, Marriage records, and more." At that price, we weren't willing to bite. If you need this type of information, you might be better off with a subscription to Accurint.com or Merlindata.com, where this information is less costly. Another pay site (similar to Intelius) that the free telephone directories link to is 1.800.US.SEARCH. (See Whitepages.com below for more information about 1.800.US.SEARCH.)

Free Web-Based Telephone Directory Searching by Name and Reverse Searching by Telephone Number or Address

For finding phone numbers, addresses, neighbors, maps, e-mail addresses, and so on, we used to prefer Infospace out of all the Web phone directories because it had so many useful features to locate people and businesses through both traditional searching and reverse searching. However, Infospace eliminated some of its useful features and then, on June 9, 2008, Infospace.com was replaced by Superpages.com. Now we are favoring Whitepages.com.

Reverse phone number or address searching is the perfect tool when you are uncertain of someone's name (or the spelling), but you know that person's phone number or address. With a reverse phone search (or address search) the person's name (and correct spelling) should be retrieved. Reverse phone or address searching is also the perfect tool for business searching when you don't know the company name (or its correct spelling), but do have its address or phone number. Address searching is also useful when you want to be certain you are naming all relevant parties and you suspect that multiple businesses owned by the same person are operating out of one address. The reverse address search results may show you all the company names related to that one address. If Whitepages.com doesn't bring any results, try using a phone directory metasite, such as theultimates.com (see below), to identify other phone directory sites, and if the free sites there fail, then see the information on pay sites below.

Whitepages

http://www.whitepages.com (for basic contact information)

 (if you click on certain links that lead to pay services)

Purpose: To find phone numbers, addresses, area codes, ZIP codes, maps, and driving directions to homes and businesses and to conduct reverse searching (by phone number, address, area code, and ZIP code). Also, see the *Tip* section on page 33 to learn how to find someone's neighbors.

Content: To search **Whitepages.com**, select one of the tabs at the top of its home page:

- **People Search:** Only the **Last Name** is a required field, but the more fields you fill in (such as **First Name**, **City or ZIP/Postal/State/Prov**), the more assured you are of finding the correct party.
  - If there is only one result, the listing will display the person's address, phone number, and map of their location. Also displayed are links to many free features such as: **Find Neighbors**, **Driving Directions**, **Send/Save** (to your: **cell phone**, **email**, **address book**, or **Outlook**), and **Print**.
  - If there is more than one result, you must select **Listing Details** under the person's name you are interested in and then you will see the links to the above mentioned free features.
  - There is an **Advanced Search** option, where you can search using the **Begins With** feature if you are unsure of how a first or last name is spelled. You can also select **Include surrounding area** which is useful if you are searching for someone who you think lives in a specific city but actually lives in a nearby city.
  - See *Our View* (on the next page) for a warning about the links that lead you to pay sites.
- **Business Search:** Into the **Name** or **Category** box, enter the business name or category you are seeking. (You can also select from a drop-down menu of busi-

ness categories.) With either search, it's optional to add a city, state, or ZIP code. The displayed results will show an address and also a **map** and a **phone** link. You can also save the contact information to Outlook or to a Whitepages.com address book.

- **Reverse Lookup:** You can perform a phone or address reverse search. When someone has left a phone number on your voicemail, but failed to leave their name, or if your caller ID only displays a phone number, use the **Phone Reverse Lookup** to identify who called you before deciding whether to phone them back. The **Address Reverse Lookup** is useful if you need to link a name and/or phone number to a known address. To search by address, enter the house number and street name (required) and city or ZIP code (required) and state (optional).

- **Area & ZIP Codes:** Use the **Area Code** feature to search by city (required) and state (optional) to find a city's area code. You can also search by area code to find the correlating city. This is useful when someone has left their area code and phone number but not their name. If you can't remember who they are, some-times finding out the city will trigger your memory.

- A tab located underneath the main tabs, labeled **International Resources**, will link to a database of **International Calling Codes** and **International Directories**.

Our View: Like most of the other free telephone directory sites, Whitepages.com's result page displays contact informa-tion for free, but also displays links that take you to pay sites—without clearly warning you. For instance, on the results page for **Mark Rosch**, in addition to his contact information (displayed for free) there are also links (such as: **View More Records**, **Background Records**, **Criminal Records**, **All Public Records**, **Court Records**, **Get Home Values**, and **Address History**) that bring you to the pay site US Search at **http://www.ussearch.com** (see Chapter 16). Although we understand that Web sites need to make money to stay in business, we'd prefer seeing a statement that clearly designates these links as leading to pay sites.

On the other hand, if you do click on the links, you might find some of the "teaser" information useful. For instance, when we clicked on **View More Records** for **Mark Rosch**, his correct age was listed, six cities were listed (five of which were cities where he had once lived and his current city) and two relatives were listed—each correct.

Tip: If you are searching for someone who has moved or is being evasive, the **Find Neighbors** feature is especially useful. By clicking on the **Find Neighbors** feature, you will be armed with the names and contact information of the missing/evasive person's neighbors. One of them might be able to help track them down.

Other Free Phone Directories' Features

While Anywho.com's free site includes many of the same search features as Whitepages.com described above, you can also type in a company name to discover its toll-free number (**http://anywho.com/tf.html**).

Like many of the other phone directory sites, links on the Anywho .com results pages, such as **Phone Number**, **Address & Public Records Available** or **Instant Background Check**, bring you to the pay site Intelius (mentioned in the current chapter). Our usual admonition: Read about less expensive sites in Chapter 16, such as Accurint and Merlin, etc.

Free International Phone Directory

Infobel (formerly teldir)

http://www.infobel.com/en/world

Purpose: To link to the White Pages, Yellow Pages, business directories, and other people-finding directories in more than 216 countries.

Content: There are two ways to search for available telephone directories. While the first way allows you to select from the drop-down menu any country from the alphabetical list, we prefer the second way, which is to click on the icon of one of the continents or countries listed to the right of the continent icon. The second way is preferable because it offers an annotation about the types of phone directories available and whether any are in English.

Our View: We found this site to be a wealth of information and easy to use. For example, when we searched for a listing in Denmark and couldn't recall the exact spelling of the city we wanted, all we had to do was click on **City list** and type in part of the name ("Hel"). This brought us to a city list showing three cities beginning with "Hel" (ours was Helsingor).

Tip: Because each country's telephone directory is hosted by a separate site, search functions will vary at each of the country directory sites. The Denmark phone directory, for example, allows you to click on **Extended Search** to add in first names and postal codes to refine the search, and you can also click on **Reverse Search**.

Pay Site Directory Searching

In addition to all sorts of traditional or reverse phone and address searching functions, most of the pay investigative databases we discuss in Chapter 16 have the ability to search databases that are updated daily and to search by an old address or phone number and get an updated result. You won't find these options at the free phone directory sites noted in this chapter.

Using Google to Search by Name for a Listed Landline Phone Number or Address or to Reverse Search by a Listed Phone Number or Address

Another method for finding listed telephone numbers and addresses is to simply run a search engine search at Google. From Google's homepage's search box, one can use Google as a telephone or address directory and even a reverse directory. If a searcher enters a person's name and their city (or state abbreviation, ZIP, or area code) into the search box, Google will display the phone number and address of that person. The information will display above the results list and will be preceded by a telephone icon. To obtain these results, Google has licensed a phone book database so these results include only publicly listed U.S. street addresses and phone numbers.

To find listings for a U.S. business, type the business name into the Google search box, along with the city and state or ZIP code. Google can also be used for reverse searching (e.g., If you type a phone number or address into the search box at Google's home page, a name tied to the number or address (with a telephone icon to the left) will be displayed above the regular Google results list).

Notice the regular search engine results that appear below the licensed phone book results. These results are often quite helpful if someone has placed their number or address anywhere on the Internet (e.g., on their Web site, in a blog, on a social networking site, etc.).

> Users can fill out Google's online form (**http://www.google .com/help/pbremoval.html**) to request removal of their own personal listing information from the online Google phone book directory. That page also contains an address where one can send a hard copy request to remove one's own business information from the Google phone book. The request must be signed and on company letterhead.

Cellular Phones and Facsimile Numbers

There is no comprehensive cellular phone or facsimile number directory (for free or pay). Finding fax or cell numbers is not as straightforward as finding phone landline numbers. Despite claims made by some Web sites that they can uncover cellular or facsimile numbers, their claims can sometimes turn out to be misleading, at best. For instance, a researcher recently reported that she attempted to use Intelius' reverse cell phone directory (**http://www.intelius.com/people-search-phone.html**) to ascertain the owner of a cell phone number. She was lured in by the "No

Figure 4-1. A Google search for a person's name and the city and state where he lives can return a "phonebook" result that includes his listed phone number and address. Google™ is a trademark of Google Technology Inc.

results, no charge!" guarantee. The results page informed her that her transaction WAS successful, but in the name field all that was listed was "U.S. Cellular"—the cellular phone service provider. To the researcher, this was NOT a successful result because she was looking for the name of the person who owned the phone number, not the provider. While she was charged for this "result," her later request for a refund from Intelius was promptly honored. The reply e-mail she received from Intelius stated, "We apologize for the lack of information in your phone search. The public record only contains carrier information for the telephone number." Intelius' description of its reverse cell phone directory stated that it was "[a]n online caller ID service, which provides available information associated with cell . . . numbers. Reports may include information such as name, address, phone company, connection status, and more." Notice the use of the word "may"—indicating that Intelius isn't necessarily going to include the name of the cell phone owner. But to most researchers, anything short of the name wouldn't be considered a result at all.

Since there is no comprehensive directory (free or pay) for cellular or facsimile numbers on the Internet and Web sites that claim to offer this type of information do not always deliver, what can an Internet researcher do?

The following section offers some tips on how to use general search engines to find cell or fax numbers for free. After that, we'll discuss a free site for determining whether a phone number is a wireless phone number (see FoneFinder). We'll then discuss a free self-reporting directory that allows one to search by name (see MobilephoneNo.com) and a pay site for conducting a reverse wireless phone number search to discover who owns the specific cellular number (see Cell-Phone-Numbers.com).

Finally, we'll discuss other pay databases that may be less expensive than Cell-Phone-Numbers.com.

How to Use Search Engines or Google Groups to Find Cellular Telephone Numbers and Facsimile Numbers

Believe it or not, people do (sometimes purposely but other times inadvertently) post their unlisted or unpublished telephone numbers and addresses, cell numbers, or fax numbers to their Web site or in an e-mail discussion posting (such as Google Groups). It's also possible that a third party could post another person's contact information to the Web, without the owner's knowledge or permission. We've found lists of phone numbers and addresses in a PDF or Excel spreadsheet that someone had uploaded to the Web, probably unknown to the various owners of those numbers and addresses.

- To find someone's fax number, type their name into the search engine search box and add the word *fax* and then the Boolean connector *OR* and the word *facsimile*.

Your search would look like this: *mark rosch fax OR facsimile*

- To find someone's cell phone number, use the same search strategy as above but replace the words *fax* and *facsimile* with the words *cell* and *cellular*.

Your search would look like this: *mark rosch cell OR cellular*

- To find the owner of a particular cell or fax number, conduct a reverse search by typing the number into a search engine search box (with and without the dashes between each segment).

To test how well the above searches work, one of the authors of this book, who does not post her fax number on her Web site, tried searching her name and the keyword word *fax* using Google. She found her fax number listed on a State Bar of California biography that she had posted on the Law Practice Management Section's Executive Committee page. She had no memory of including the fax number, but apparently she must have included it.

In another example, we tried to locate a cell number for a staff person at the New Mexico State Bar's Web site, but we only found a staff directory with landlines. But, by using Google to search the person's name with the word *cell*, we hit pay dirt. The cell number was included as part of an advertisement in a PDF of the State Bar's *Bar Bulletin*. The advertisement instructed those who were interested in setting up attorney Web pages to contact the staff person at her cell number (and proceeded to include it). To find a fax number for a person at his place of employment, you can also try locating the employer's Web site to see if it is listed there.

Is It a Landline or a Cell Phone?

FoneFinder

http://www.fonefinder.net/

Purpose: This site can be used free to discover if a specific phone number is for a landline or a wireless phone and it displays the carrier, which can be useful information in case one needs to subpoena the carrier to learn the identity of the telephone number's owner.

Content: Search by the area code, prefix, and the first number following the prefix of a phone number. The results do not
show the name of the person who owns the phone number but show the type and name of the phone company
that "owns" the prefix (a wireless company or a regional
Bell operating company, like Pacific Bell or Bell Atlantic).
It also displays the city and state connected to the prefix.
This site can be used for U.S., Canada, and international
phone number searching. Reverse searching by city or
ZIP code will bring back prefix results for that city or ZIP
code. This site also allows one to search by name of
country to find the country's phone code.

Our View: This can be very useful when you're having trouble tracing a phone number, because you are tipped off right
away whether it's a wireless number. And, if it's wireless,
you won't be able to use the same avenues to find out
who owns it as you would for a landline. Although we
ported over our business landlines to our cellular phones
several years ago, FoneFinder still shows the number as
a landline. According to FoneFinder, it cannot track
ported over numbers because the administrator of the
Number Portability Administration Center/Service
Management System, NeuStar, has a nondisclosure
agreement that prohibits releasing porting information
(unless compelled by law). See Merlin (later in this chapter), which informs you if a landline has been ported
over to a cell number.

Tip: Once you've identified the number as wireless, see the
next two listings that follow for further tips on how to
identify who owns the wireless number.

Free Web Site for Name Searching to Discover a Cellular Number

MobilephoneNo

http://www.mobilephoneno.com

Purpose: Searching by name to discover who owns a wireless
number.

Figure 4-2. The content at Mobilephoneno.com is accessible to only those who have chosen to self-register at the site.

Content:	This site offers free listings to people who choose to register their wireless number here. Searching (by name) is also free.
Our View:	Though it's nifty to be able to find the name and address of a wireless owner, the content is very limited—to those who have chosen to self-register. In our test searches, we often received this message, "Your search result did not return any results in the free MobilePhoneNumber.com database. However, you may find full results instantly at ReversePhoneDetective.com." ReversePhoneDetective.com is a pay database that offers, "Full Phone Report + Unlimited Reverse Phone Lookups for 1 Year" at $39.95 or one lookup for $14.95.
Tips:	If you want others to be able to locate you by your wireless number, you might want to register it here. A cell number is kept online for one year only, so you need to remember to renew your registration (for free). If you provided this site with your e-mail address when you initially listed your cell number, they will notify you two weeks prior to your listing expiration. Just as with the initial listing, there is no cost to re-list.

If you need to discover the carrier, use FoneFinder (above) or enter the phone number into **http://www .411.com/reverse_phone** and then select **Listing Detail**. The carrier (provider) will be displayed and so will the type of telephone service (landline or cellular).

> If you know that your subject uses a cell phone number but you are unable to find it, it's possible that your subject might be changing her cell number frequently by using a prepaid cell phone service. Or, your subject may simply be using a friend's (or family member's) cell phone. If that is the case, the cell phone number would not be in her name.

Pay Telephone Database

Reverse Cellular Number Searching to Discover the Owner's Name

Cell-Phone-Numbers

http://www.cell-phone-numbers.com   **$**

Purpose: Reverse searching by a phone number to discover who owns a wireless number.

Content: For $57 you can request a reverse wireless number search to discover the name and address of the person who owns the number.

Our View: We haven't used this service, but there was an interesting story in the *Chicago Tribune* on December 13, 2002 about Eric Smith, a 21-year-old student at the University of New Orleans, who used it when he needed to find the name and address of someone who had defrauded him of $3,000 on eBay. It worked!

Tip: You wouldn't use this service until after discovering that the number is wireless and after being unable to locate it at MobilephoneNo.com.

The search is priced at $5. The database is updated continuously with almost one half-million, real time daily updates. Where does the information in this database come from? Merlin tells us, "it is provided by over 20 million daily transactions by consumers who purchase products either online or over the telephone."

Search results include the phone subscriber's name and address, and the names of both phone companies if the number has been ported. Once the phone number search is linked to an address, a reverse address search is run. The report will display other names and phone numbers listed at the subscriber's address.

We tested our current cell number that we ported from our landline several years ago. The results showed our company name as "Internet For LA" although the name is actually Internet For Lawyers. The partial name was displayed because that is all our cell phone company displays when a name is too long. Also included was our former address (but not our current address), the names of our landline and cell phone companies (and the fact that the landline had been ported to a cell number), the history of the number (which included Carole Levitt's name), and several of our neighbors' names. Despite having different unit numbers from our five other neighbors, they are often incorrectly attached to our records probably because we share the same street address and street name. The report showed our neighbors' phone numbers in addition to their names and addresses.

Pay Database Phone Directory

MasterFiles

http://www.masterfiles.com/index.html   **$**

Purpose:	Its Reach411 product provides real time access to over 130 million listings.
Content:	Listings of U.S. residences, businesses, and government agencies for all fifty states (since the last edition of this book, Hawaii and Alaska have been added). Data is from Ameritech, Bell South, Cincinnati Bell, PacBell, QWEST, Southern New England Telephone, Southwestern Bell, and Verizon.
Our View:	Considering you can search by name, phone, or address for twenty cents to forty-five cents (based on search type and volume), and that the content is refreshed continually, this may be useful to find someone who has recently

moved or who is continually on the move. However, you will be billed even if no record is found or if there are too many records found to be displayed. There is a $60 start-up fee to fund your debit account.

Tip: Make sure the coverage fits your needs. If you're searching for international listings, this won't do much good.

Using Pay Investigative Databases for Cell Phone (and Landline) Searches

The pay databases, Accurint and Merlin (and various similar databases), can be used to search for cell phone (and landline) numbers with varying degrees of success (but you will need a subscription to each vendor's services, which also requires successfully completing a preapproval process). Accurint's cell phone database, Phones Plus (**http://www.accurint.com/**), is searchable by name. However, the last time we searched by a person's name, we had no luck finding that person's cell number (although we know that person has one). Accurint does not post the cost to search Phones Plus because rates will vary depending on your individual subscription with Accurint.

Figure 4-3. Merlin's Cell Phones database can be searched by name or address and is updated in real time.

Merlin offers a seperate cell number database searchable by name or address. A name search requires at least a last name and a city and a state or just a ZIP code. An address search requires a street number and a street name and a city and a state or just a ZIP code. This search is priced at $2.50. If there is no result, the fee is waived. We have not had much luck with either Accurint's or Merlin's cell phone searching by name, although we know that our subjects have cell numbers. In one case, the results displayed our subject's old cell number instead of his current one. We had better luck using Merlin's Reverse Phone Number Lookup database, which is a database of landlines combined with (what the site claims is) over 60 percent of all cellular phone numbers in the United States, as well as 65 million U.S. unlisted phone numbers (**http://www.merlindata.com**).

Bestpeoplesearch (**http://www.bestpeoplesearch.com**) offers to find a cell phone number by name, but you are hiring a private investigator to perform the search for $147. Bestpeoplesearch requires that you supply the subject's name, address (if available), city, and state. If you have a subscription to Accurint or Merlin, you might find that this search is less costly at those sites.

CHAPTER**FIVE**

Can You Obtain Records of Phone Calls?

Phone records can be useful to divorcing spouses, identity thieves, or criminal lawyers looking for ties between people to show evidence of a conspiracy, or a myriad of other people in a myriad of other scenarios. The record shows the phone number of the recipient of the phone call and the day, time, and duration of the call. Whether a call has been made from a landline, cell phone, or voice over IP, it once had been possible to obtain records listing all phone calls made from that number. Using Mark Rosch's cell number, in November 2005, we tested out whether a third party would be able to obtain Mark's most recent cell phone bill. Within hours we received a fax of Mark's bill with a record of his calls. The fax also had a cover page showing Mark's home and office landline numbers and a statement that his landline numbers were listed as belonging to Carole Levitt. But, is any of this legal?

Until it was shut down by the Missouri Attorney General in January of 2006, Locatecell.com provided a list for $110 of the outgoing calls from your subject's phone, up to 100 calls of the last billing cycle. All that was required was your subject's name, address, and phone number. One could place an online order and get results within hours. How did Locatecell.com obtain these records? Law enforcement surmises that either telephone company employees were violating their companies' rules and simply selling customers' phone call records to independent information brokers and investigators, or that information brokers and investigators were using age-old pretexting (pretending to be the customer) to obtain records from the phone companies. Both Verizon and Cingular Wireless have sued companies who have sold their customers' cell phone records to third parties.

Pretexting and Telephone Records

As discussed on page 210, pretexting financial institutions is illegal, but in 2005, it was a gray area as to whether it was illegal to pretext non-financial entities (such as telephone or other utility companies or even a private individual), although Joel Winston (Associate Director of the Federal Trade Commission's Financial Practices Division) was quoted in a July 8, 2005 *Washington Post* article (**http://www.washingtonpost.com/wp-dyn/content/article/2005/07/07/AR2005070701862_pf.html**) as saying, "The FTC views pretexting as a deceptive practice even without a specific ban on its use for telephone records."

The Electronic Privacy Information Center filed a complaint (*available at* **http://www.epic.org/privacy/iei/ftccomplaint.html**) on July 7, 2005 with the Federal Trade Commission against a data broker, Intelligent e-Commerce Inc., of Encinitas, California, which hosts the Web site noted earlier, Bestpeoplesearch (**http://www.bestpeoplesearch.com**). This site advertised the sale of cell phone records, among other personal information.

In a January 17, 2006 press release (*available at* **http://hraunfoss.fcc.gov/edocs_public/attachmatch/DOC-263216A1.doc**), FCC Commissioner Jonathan S. Adelstein stated that he was, "[a]larmed by reports that data brokers are obtaining and selling customers' personal telephone records without the customers' consent or knowledge." Further, he stated, that "[a] petition for rulemaking on enhanced consumer data protection standards filed by the Electronic Privacy Information Center (EPIC) in August 2005 could be an appropriate vehicle for tightening our rules."

When we visited the Bestpeoplesearch site on January 20, 2006, we learned through their January 18, 2006 press release that, "Due to controversy surrounding the availability of phone records via the [I]nternet we have decided to discontinue offering these searches. We apologize to anyone with a legitimate need for these searches." When we visited the site on August 29, 2008, the word "discontinued" was displayed next to the **Cell Phone Record Searches** link and we found a different press release from the one we originally found in 2006. This press release claimed that obtaining someone else's phone records was a service that had been available for years and that Bestpeoplesearch had always confirmed that the request was for a legitimate business purpose before giving out the information to a third party (**https://secure.bestpeoplesearch.com/pdf/**

Press_Release_1-16-06.pdf). The press release also claimed that other vendors were not as conscientious as Bestpeoplesearch about confirming whether a customer had a legitimate business purpose.

On January 12, 2007, the Telephone Records and Privacy Protection Act of 2006 became law, making it a federal crime for data brokers or others to pretext to obtain telephone records. (Public Law No: 109-476 *available at* **http://frwebgate.access.gpo.gov/cgi-bin/getdoc.cgi?dbname= 109_cong_public_laws&docid=f:publ476.109.pdf**). The Act, (now codified at 18 U.S.C. 1039 (2008) *available at* **http://www.law.cornell.edu/ uscode/html/uscode18/1039.html**), does not apply to "any lawfully authorized investigative, protective, or intelligence activity of a law enforcement agency of the United States, at State, or political subdivision of a State, or of an intelligence agency of the United States."

The following language from the Act explains: why Congress passed the Act; what "pretexting" is; and how telephone records have been obtained by pretext:

Congress finds that—

(1) telephone records can be of great use to criminals because the information contained in call logs may include a wealth of personal data;

(2) call logs may reveal the names of telephone users' doctors, public and private relationships, business associates, and more;

(3) call logs are typically maintained for the exclusive use of phone companies, their authorized agents, and authorized consumers;

(4) telephone records have been obtained without the knowledge or consent of consumers through the use of a number of fraudulent methods and devices that include—

    (A) telephone company employees selling data to unauthorized data brokers;

    (B) "pretexting", whereby a data broker or other person represents that they are an authorized consumer and convinces an agent of the telephone company to release the data; or

    (C) gaining unauthorized Internet access to account data by improperly activating a consumer's account management features on a phone company's Web page or contracting with an Internet-based data broker who traffics in such records; and

(5) the unauthorized disclosure of telephone records not only assaults individual privacy but, in some instances, may further acts of domestic violence or stalking, compromise the personal safety of law enforcement officers, their families, victims of crime, witnesses, or confidential informants, and undermine the integrity of law enforcement investigations.

*CHAPTER***SIX**

Using Search Engines, Summarization Search Engines, and Meta Search Sites for Investigative Research

Using a Search Engine

To locate a person and to find information about him or her, first enter the name into a search engine (such as Google). You never know what you're going to find on the free Internet and sometimes it's more than you would find using a pay database. The second step is to run their name through a discussion site (like Google Groups at **http://groups.google.com**).

War Story: A Search Engine Finds Fraud Convictions

"Not using the Internet [to find people or find out about them] is malpractice," asserts Steve Whiteside, J.D., from Sheppard, Mullin in San Diego, California:

> I'm a law firm librarian . . . and an incident the other day pointed out the importance of Internet research. I was asked to find information on a person believed to be involved in tax fraud schemes. I happened to be on Westlaw at the time, so I searched their news database. Only one hit came up on the name and that was some insignificant committee the person was on. Without the Internet, the guy checked out OK. I then ran the name on the Internet and received dozens of hits on his multiple convictions for tax fraud and various news items on schemes he was involved with. The main difference was the PDF files that I could access through Google from the Treasury Department and attorneys general sites.

PDFs

Lucky that Whiteside knew to choose Google as his search engine, which at the time was one of the few general-purpose search engines (aside from AltaVista) that indexed PDF files. If he hadn't, he would have missed these documents. He also may have had luck at USA.gov, a government site that indexes PDFs, considering that some of the PDF documents Google found were from government sites. These days, most all general-purpose search engines, from MSN.com to Yahoo.com to Excite.com, etc., index PDFs.

War Story: A Search Engine Leads to a Settlement

Charlie Cochran, a lawyer in Northern California, relates this story of how using the Internet as an investigative tool allowed him to settle a case the day before the trial, for a fraction of the original settlement demand:

> Anyhow, after attending your seminar I tried to implement some of your research tools to a trial I had scheduled in March 2003. The Plaintiff was a well-known musician and producer who claimed he had brain injury from an auto accident and could no longer play the piano. My search began with a Google "I'm feeling lucky" which sent me to the Plaintiff's home page. On the home page he was selling an album that he had recorded after our auto accident. The Google search naturally hit many online sites where his albums were being sold. One of the Google hits had him giving an online interview with an entertainment reporter where he discussed his auto accident, that he could not play piano for a few months but after that he was back to playing and writing with a new spirit and inspiration. Google Image hits are amazing. It's fascinating what people post on the Internet. One image of the Plaintiff was a concert he did about a year after the accident where he was shown playing piano in front of a class of graduate level pianists. The look on their faces showed that they were really impressed with his abilities. We ended up issuing a trial subpoena to the woman that held the concert and [also issued a subpoena for the entertainment reporter who had] interviewed the Plaintiff for the online interview. The case settled the day before the trial for a fraction of the original settlement demand because, in my opinion, we were going to confront the Plaintiff with the photo of him playing the piano, the words from his online interview, and albums that he was selling over the Internet.

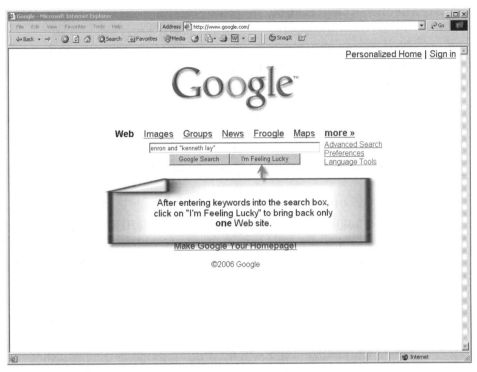

Figure 6-1. Using the I'm Feeling Lucky search button returns just one site; it's often the most relevant, especially when searching by a person or company's name. Google™ is a trademark of Google Technology Inc.

I'm Feeling Lucky

The **I'm Feeling Lucky** search button returns one Web site only and, as illustrated here, often it's the most relevant. Using Google's **I'm Feeling Lucky** search button quickly led lawyer Cochran directly to the plaintiff's own Web site. To obtain more results, Cochran returned to his original search page and merely clicked on the **Google Search** button. This search led him to an online interview of the musician and to sites selling his recent albums, information that he probably would not have found without the Internet. Finally, using Google's Images feature, Cochran proved that a picture is indeed worth a thousand words.

Summarization Search Engines (and Meta Search Sites)

While we frequently search someone's name or company name through a search engine (e.g., Google or Yahoo!), we find that we often get overwhelmed by the number of results. Instead, you might consider trying a summarization search engine (also called a meta search site because it sends your search to many search engines to collect results) that creates a summary sheet about a person or company from information gathered from various sources of the Web.

ZoomInfo

http://www.zoominfo.com/

Purpose: ZoomInfo describes itself as a summarization search engine. It locates, collects, and categorizes information on people and their business, personal, and university affiliations, and allows users access to their own biographical data, which they can update, correct, or supplement.

Content: Formerly known as Eliyon.com (before a name change in March 2005), ZoomInfo creates a summary information sheet for about 45 million people and more than 5 million companies gleaned from a variety of outlets, such as electronic news services, SEC filings, press releases, corporate Web sites, and other online sources.

The ZoomInfo Web site offers both free and subscription-only options.

To conduct a free people search, you can enter an individual's name into the box and click find, or you can click on the advanced search option. This will allow you to enter either a company or a university along with the person's name. The free service requires you to search with a person's name while the paid service allows you to search for a person that meets criteria that you designate. For example, if you didn't recall Mark Rosch's name, but you remembered that he was the vice president of an Internet research company in New Mexico, you could enter that information into the criteria fields labeled: **Title**, **Industry**, and **Geography**. Your search results will be listed ten to a page, ranked by Web popularity. Clicking on any of the results brings

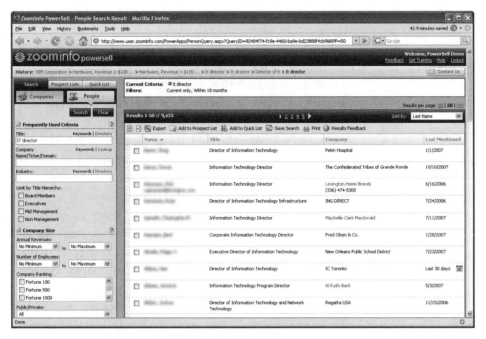

Figure 6-2. ZoomInfo.com's database contains information about more than 45 million people and 5 million companies. Its paid PowerSearch and PowerSell (above) products offer more options than the site's free search.

up the summary sheet. For instance, a search for Mark Rosch offered five results for individuals named "Mark Rosch." Four of those results did refer to the coauthor of this book. By clicking on the first result, a summary sheet with information populated by 104 Web sources provided a summary of Mark, from his title to his board memberships, education and work history (past two companies only), and full biographies about Mark Rosch (taken from various conferences where he has spoken, in addition to his company Web site).

Users may also access their own Web information by clicking on the **This is Me** link to the right of their name, but it is necessary to register first. Once registration is completed, ZoomInfo creates an online location for you to store your information. They will continue to add to this page as they find information about you on the Web.

ZoomInfo also has various subscription-based services including:

- **ZoomInfo PowerSearch** (This service allows you to search by numerous fields such as **Industry**, **Company Size**, **Public/Private**, **Geography**, and others.)
- **ZoomInfo PowerSell** (This service provides information on professionals at all levels and companies of all sizes from the Fortune 1000 to small businesses.)

Our View: ZoomInfo's data can be useful in recruiting, client development, backgrounding individuals, competitive intelligence, and other general business research. Valuable intelligence can be gained gathering background information on business people and companies, to prepare for a meeting, or perhaps just for a better business relationship. Because ZoomInfo collects and compiles all of this data automatically, it is not always completely accurate. For example, one result for our search for information about Mark Rosch indicated that he was both a "Contributor" and a "Principal" at a magazine for which he had written a few articles but never owned. However, the information can be a good point to begin or continue one's research.

Tips: Subscribers can export ZoomInfo's information results to a spreadsheet, address book, or save them to an online folder. You can view a demonstration of Zoominfo online, or request a live one-on-one demonstration.

A Narrower Summarization Search Engine

Zabasearch

http://www.zabasearch.com/

Purpose: A narrower summarization search engine than Zoominfo because it only retrieves people's addresses, phone numbers, and birth month and birth year free, and then links to fee-based people backgrounding sites.

Content: ZABA, a derivative from the Greek word "tzaba" which means "free," searches available public records and publicly available information, including, but not limited to: court records, phone listings, subscriptions, and real property records. However, they are not all free! The search box asks for a name and the pull-down menu lists the states. We typed in the name of our research assistant, Kristine K. Pike, and then chose California with the pull-down menu—an "all-states" option is available, too—and were shown two exact matches in the first result group, three matches for a K.K. Pike, and eight matches for a Kristine Pike.

After clicking **Search**, "Premium" results are listed on top—linking you to a pay background-check database, Intelius (you will also link to Intelius if you click on the link **More info for a fee**). Scroll down past the premium results to view your subject's address, phone number, and birth month and year. If you click on the person's name, another window opens with choices to run the person's name in a variety of search engines, such as Yahoo!, Yahoo! Image, Highbeam, Dogpile, Lycos, A9, AltaVista, or AltaVista Image. This new window also allows you to link to Google Maps and Mapquest.com for maps and/or directions.

Our View: What makes ZabaSearch different from some of the other free people-search engines on the Web is that it offers month and year of birth for free. If you were looking to discover that bit of information, this would be the engine to use. Otherwise, ZabaSearch's free results are not too helpful.

*CHAPTER***SEVEN**

Online Communities

Definitions of Online Communities

- Usenet (also called newsgroups): a global online electronic bulletin board of Usenet newsgroups, covering thousands of topics. They are different from mailing lists because one cannot post to a Usenet group via e-mail (as one can with a mailing list). Instead, messages reside on central newsgroup servers where they can be read and commented upon like a community bulletin board. However, Usenet users can receive and read Usenet group messages via e-mail.
- Mailing lists (also called LISTSERVs or discussion groups): a group discussion via e-mail. To actively participate, members first must e-mail a subscribe request to the list manager. Then, the subscriber can both post and receive messages. All messages are e-mailed to a central server where they are then distributed to each subscriber's e-mail inbox. Some lists distribute messages automatically while others are moderated. If the list is moderated, then the e-mails are reviewed by an actual person—the moderator—to be sure the discussion stays on topic, and so on, before being distributed. Some people mistakenly use LISTSERV as a generic term for all mailing lists. It's not. LISTSERV is a type of mailing list software.

- Message (or bulletin) boards: messages are posted to a Web-based bulletin board where visitors can read, comment upon, or leave new messages (or files). Requires users to visit the site.
- Forums: Same as message (or bulletin) board.
- Blogs (Web logs): a Web site "light." Blogs have been compared to an online diary. They are easy to create and to update. They can be educational, entertaining, or frivolous, depending on the person who set up the blog. Blogs are indexed and searchable at such sites as Technorati.com (**http://www.technorati.com**), which searches "112.8 million blogs and over 250 million pieces of tagged social media" (**http://technoratimedia.com/about/**), and Blogstreet.com (**http://www.blogstreet.com**). Google's Web search engine and Yahoo!'s will both return results that include blogs. But, to display blog-only results from Google, use its Blog Search at **http://blogsearch.google.com/** or choose the link to the *Advanced Blog Search* (**http://blogsearch.google.com/blogsearch/advanced_blog_search**) to narrow your results by searching for words in the **Post title** or the **Blog title**. You can also search for a blog or post by **Author**, by **Date** or by **Language**. You can be alerted to new blog postings on your subject by subscribing to the Atom or RSS feeds. The link to these services is found at the bottom of the blog search results page. Yahoo! (**http://www.yahoo.com**) does not have a blog-only search.
- Blawgs: same as blogs, but topics are law related only. (See Theblogsoflaw at **http://www.theblogsoflaw.com** for an annotated list of law-related blogs and podcasts. To keyword search law-related blogs, see Justia.com (**http://www.justia.com**) and click on the **Law Blogs** link above the search box. You can also keyword search law-related podcasts by clicking on the **Legal Podcasts** link above the search box.
- There are numerous sites offering tools to create blogs, such as Blogger.com (**http://www.blogger.com**), **Journal Space** (**http://www.journalspace.com**), or **Moveable Type** (**http://moveabletype.org**).

> • Social (and Professional) Networks: the latest and fastest growing online community. Unlike traditional online communities, members of social networks first create profiles about themselves and then they begin communicating. And, unlike traditional online communities, social network profiles can include a multimedia aspect, such as photos and videos. Like traditional online communities, networks can be either private or public. This topic will be discussed in Chapter 8, "Using Social Networking Sites for Investigative Research."

Searching Online Communities

The ease of communicating over the Internet has fostered the creation of a countless number of online communities (which focus on countless topics) used for the public exchange of ideas. There are various types of (and labels for) online communities, such as LISTSERV lists, mailing lists, discussion groups, Usenet newsgroups, forums, message (or bulletin) boards, blogs, and social (and professional) networks. There are various ways that people join and participate in a community on the Internet. Despite the variances, we'll discuss them generically (except for social and professional networks which will be discussed in more detail) and focus only on those that are public, have been archived, and are searchable by anyone.

There are various ways to participate in an online community:

- You can initiate the discussion.
- You can respond to someone else's discussion.
- You can "lurk," which means you simply read the discussions posted by others and do not join in the discussion.
- You can visit the group's archives (if the group has one and it's public) and search the archived postings by keyword (or by a person's name or e-mail address) to see what has been discussed in the past (and by whom).

Joining Online Communities

Some groups have strict membership rules for joining (for example, to join the Los Angeles County Bar Association's Family Law Section group you first would need to join and pay your dues to the association and the section). Some types of groups require registration before you can join (but place no restrictions on who can join), while others may not require registration at all. Some groups require you to visit the group each time you want to participate (or even to lurk) while others "visit" you via e-mail. For instance, each time you want to participate in a message board, you need to visit that board by typing its URL into your browser's address box and then either read messages, answer a message, or post your own message. On the other hand, to participate in a mailing list, you only need visit once—to subscribe. Once you've done that, you'll automatically begin receiving e-mails from other participants. You can then respond to the entire list (or just to the individual sender) if you want to join the discussion and you can also initiate a discussion by sending an e-mail to the list. Once again, for convenience's sake, we'll label any online community communication a "posting."

Using Online Community Postings for Investigative Research

Why do we care about online communities? Because, from the on-going discussions in the online community to the postings that are archived, online communities can contain a treasure trove of information. Reading a posting might help you to find someone or to find out about someone. From a person's hobbies, to opinions, to concerns, it's all available to any Internet researcher who knows where to look. Many people use their actual names and e-mail addresses when posting to an online community, failing to realize that their postings are being archived and can be searched. This is a boon to the researcher (assuming the postings have relevant information). A further boon to a researcher is when a subject has configured his e-mail with an automatic signature block (with all his contact information) that attaches to any e-mail sent.

On the other hand, online communities can be a complete black hole. For instance, in your quest to find someone (or find out about him) you may come up empty-handed if that person has joined a community using an alias or using an anonymous e-mail address. There is always the chance that even if the subject has joined an online community, he joined one that has restricted membership or one that lacks a searchable archive. Additionally, information found in online communities may be completely false, as was the case for Mathew Firsht, who sued an old school friend for libel and misuse of personal information after the so-called friend created a false Facebook profile for Mr. Firsht. In this English case, Firsht was awarded close to $35,000 in damages (Times Online, July 24, 2008, **http://technology.timesonline.co.uk/tol/news/tech_and_web/ article4389538.ece**). For this reason, it's best to cross-check your information with other print or online sources (or even the person being investigated when appropriate) to confirm its veracity.

Google Groups

Google Groups (**http://groups.google.com**) is one of the best-known online communities. Google Groups is a feature separate from Google's general-purpose search engine, Google.com. Although Groups results will be included in a regular Google.com search, they may be buried so far down the results list that you might miss them. To hone in on Groups postings only, focus your search by visiting **http://groups.google.com**. To visit the Groups database from Google's home page, select the **more** tab which will reveal the link to **Groups.** Using Google Groups, one can anonymously search through over 1 billion postings. There is no need to subscribe to a Google Group to be able to search and lurk. The postings are from the archives of thousands of Usenet newsgroups, dating back to 1981. To create Google Groups, in 2001 Google purchased 500 million messages dating back to 1995 from Deja.com. In addition, Google acquired messages from other groups, some dating back to 1981. Subsequently, Google Groups has added (and continues to add) millions (and possibly billions) of messages to the original archive of messages. While the Google Groups' archive is full text keyword searchable, there is an even more useful feature available on the advanced search page for finding information about a specific individual: the ability to search for a specific person's message by their name or their e-mail address. (See section later in this chapter titled, "Google Groups People Finding Search Strategy Tips.")

War Story: Online Community Search Finds Hobbies

If you know something about the person, add a descriptive keyword (such as the name of his city, his company, or his profession) to the name search when searching through an online community's archives (or search engine). For example, one of this book's authors, Carole Levitt, was looking for background information about the president of Elite.com because she had to introduce him at a conference. She decided to search Google Groups and because he had a very common name, she searched using his name in conjunction with the name of his company and came up with some interesting information, including his hobby—he's a Trekkie.

When else might these types of tidbits come in handy? Sometimes it's useful to find out a potential client's hobby before your first meeting. Or, according to Texas lawyer Craig Ball, he uses these tidbits of information at deposition to show the deponent that Craig Ball knows all! Ball swears deponents are more forthright when they think he already knows everything—even information about their hobbies. He also uses information found on the Internet about a deponent to "bond" with the deponent and help him feel more comfortable.

Google Groups People Finding Search Strategy Tips

To find a specific person's messages, users should conduct a few different types of searches on Google Group's Advanced Groups Search page (**http://groups.google.com/advanced_search?=&**).

First, search the name in the **Return only messages where the author is** field. However, keep in mind that some people surf anonymously by using pseudonyms, so you may find nothing.

Second, search the specific person's e-mail address in the **Return only messages where the author is** field. After all, besides a Social Security number, what other identifier is more unique than an e-mail address? Since many people share the same name, searching by a unique e-mail address will help you verify that you've found the correct person.

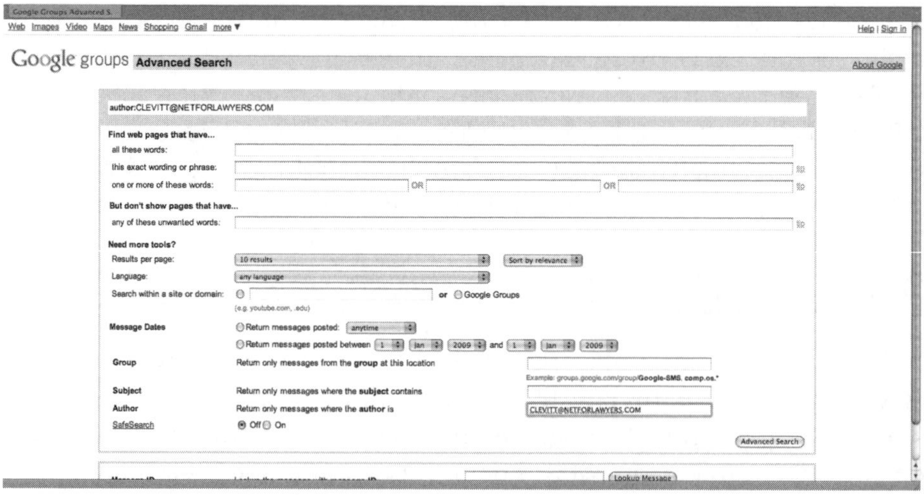

Figure 7-1. The Google Groups Advanced Groups Search allows you to search for group postings by the name or e-mail address of the person who posted the message. Google™ is a trademark of Google Technology Inc.

Because some people have more than one e-mail address, try to discover all of them to conduct a complete search of their postings. There are various ways to discover someone's e-mail address, from simply asking them (whether informally or through discovery) to "Googling" their name through Google and Google Groups.

After performing a search through Google Groups and displaying results, the author's e-mail address used to be displayed, but Google is now masking the author's e-mail address. Although there is a work-around for unmasking the address once someone's posting is displayed, there are several steps to take before it can be displayed: First, click on the **Show Options** link on the posting. A partial address will be displayed. It will have ellipses inserted between the first part of the e-mail address and the domain ("m ...@aol.com"). Click on the ellipses. Then, enter the characters in the picture to "unlock" the full e-mail address. The posting is shown again but the e-mail address is still masked. Click **Show Options** once more and it will be unmasked.

The third search method is to search for the specific person's name in one of the keyword fields of the Advanced Groups Search page (either in the **with all of the words** field or the **with the exact phrase** field). This may disclose other people's messages that contain your sub-

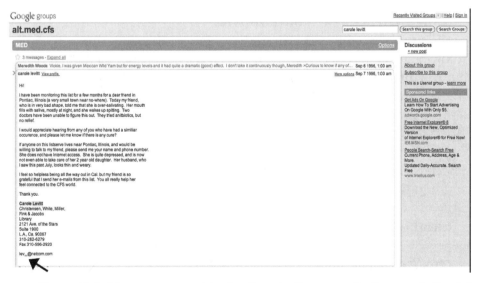

Figure 7-2. Messages stored in the Google Groups collection mask the full e-mail address of the sender. You can unlock the full e-mail address by clicking on the ellipses. Google™ is a trademark of Google Technology Inc.

ject's name. You might learn about someone's opinion of your subject or the message may disclose some contact information about your subject. You can also attempt to e-mail the author of the message to learn more.

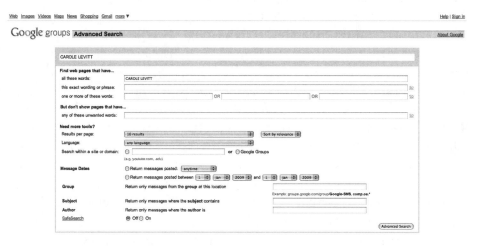

Figure 7-3. Is someone else discussing the person you're interested in finding out about? You can also use Google Group's Advanced Groups Search page to search using your target's name as a keyword (or as a phrase). Google™ is a trademark of Google Technology Inc.

Finding Other Online Communities

To find other online communities to join or to search through, aside from Google Groups, visit CataList (**http://www.lsoft.com/lists/listref .html**), a directory and search engine of 52,406 public LISTSERV lists that can be searched by keywords found in the list name, list title, or host name or browsed by host countries, country, or by number of subscribers. Topica (**http://lists.topica.com/**), a newsgroup directory and search engine that you can either keyword search or browse by categories and subcategories to find the right group, is another site for finding online communities.

CataList

http://www.lsoft.com/lists/listref.html

Purpose: To find a LISTSERV list that will meet your purposes.

Content: CataList is the official catalog of LISTSERV mailing lists, covering 53,563 public lists out of 550,686 LISTSERV

L-Soft

CataList, the official catalog of LISTSERV® lists

Last update: 10 Aug 2009

53,563 public lists
out of 550,686 LISTSERV lists

CataList
Swedish mirror

Welcome to *CataList*, the catalog of LISTSERV lists! From this page, you can browse any of the 53,563 public LISTSERV lists on the Internet, search for mailing lists of interest, and get information about LISTSERV host sites.

The *CataList* service is operated by L-Soft, the company that develops LISTSERV. L-Soft's solutions are used for email newsletters, discussion groups and opt-in email marketing campaigns.

List information

- Search for a mailing list of interest
- View lists by host country
- View lists with 10,000 subscribers or more
- View lists with 1,000 subscribers or more

Site information

- Search for a LISTSERV site of interest

Figure 7-4. The official catalog of LISTSERV mailing lists includes more than 53,000 public lists.

lists. There are several ways to use this catalog of lists: view lists by host country; view lists by number of subscribers; search the list by keyword, with the option of limiting your keyword search to list name, host name, or list title; and search lists that only have a Web archive interface.

Our View: A search for "research" returned 829 mailing lists. Results included the name of the list, a one-line description, and the number of subscribers. A search for "legal research" provided two results. Clicking on the title provided additional information, including host name and some features of the lists. The amount of information in the annotation for each list varied considerably. While it was useful that some of the lists had an Eye icon indicating access to archives, some of those archive links worked and some of them didn't.

Tip: If you don't find what you need at CataList, use a search engine and type in keywords that describe the type of list you are seeking and the word "listserv" (or "list") or try searching a newsgroup directory and search engine such as Topica (**http://lists.topica.com/**). At Topica, you can either search by keywords or browse categories and subcategories to find the right group.

CHAPTER**EIGHT**

Using Social Networking Sites for Investigative Research

What Is Social Networking?

One of the most-talked-about areas of content growth on the Internet is "Social Network" sites such as MySpace (**http://www.myspace.com**). The term "social network" was coined in the mid-1950s by sociologist J. A. Barnes to describe interactions between people in the real-world who have similar personal and/or professional interests. On the Web, it describes interactions between people in the "virtual" world who have similar personal and/or professional interests.

While social networking sites were developed as a way for people to interact with others who might have similar personal interests, they have also evolved into a marketing tool used by numerous professionals including lawyers, consultants, and experts. However, our interest in the information posted in these profiles is primarily for investigative research purposes.

Friendster (**http://www.friendster.com**) was one of the first sites referred to as a "social network." However, later arrivals such as MySpace (**http://www.myspace.com**) and Facebook (**http://www.facebook.com**) have become better known. Classmates.com (**http://www.classmates .com**), which offers many of the same functions, was launched long before the "social network" label was applied to Web sites. To a lesser degree, even video sharing sites like YouTube (**http://www.youtube.com**) include many of the social networking aspects of these other sites and can be sources for useful information.

One of the mantras of our live seminars has long-been, "don't underestimate the type or the volume of information people will post about themselves online." Social (and now professional) networking sites are the perfect illustration of this point. Even though they were originally the domain of the 20-and-under crowd, a December 2008 survey by the Pew Internet & American Life Project found that 57 percent of Internet users ages 25-34, 30 percent ages 35-44, and 19 percent ages 45-54 have at least one social network profile. The survey also found that over 60 percent of adult users reported annual household income above $50,000 (Pew Internet Project Data Memo: Adults and Social Network Web sites, *available at* **http://www.pewinternet.org/pdfs/PIP_Adult_social_networking_data_memo_FINAL.pdf**). So now, users of all ages, professional strata, etc., post a surprising amount of personally identifiable information and private information about themselves in their profiles. The study also found that more than one-third of these adults (36 percent) "allow anyone to view their profiles online," with no restrictions. But only 20 percent of adults thought "that it would be difficult for someone to find out who they are," based on the information in their profiles. Because of the penchant people seem to have about sharing explicit details with others on social and professional networking sites, online investigative researchers can have a field day.

Youtube Video and Family Law

When Broadway producer Philip Smith began divorce proceedings against his wife Tricia Walsh-Smith, she replied by posting a scathing six-minute video on YouTube. In the video, she made numerous claims about her relationship with Smith, including "I signed a prenup and he paid for the lawyer who did the prenup and apparently there's some clause in this prenup that he's got a thing that he can throw me out in 30 days . . . he's got no grounds for divorce but he's still trying to throw me out of our apartment in 30 days for no reason. I don't know why"; (almost off-handedly) "oh, another thing . . . we never had sex"; describing his older daughter as "evil" and a "bad, bad, bad person"; and leading viewers around their apartment. She can even be seen on the video telling an assistant at her husband's office (he's president of the Shubert Organization), via speakerphone, about their lack of a sex life and other intimate details.

The video received millions of views on YouTube and generated coverage in traditional media like CNN (transcript *available at* **http://edition.cnn.com/TRANSCRIPTS/0804/29/sbt.01.html**), Good Morning America (transcript *available at* **http://abcnews.go .com/GMA/story?id=4694121**), and *New York Magazine* (*available at* **http://nymag.com/news/features/47389/**).

The presiding judge, Justice Harold Beeler of New York County, N.Y., Supreme Court, was reportedly "appalled" by the video and ensuing coverage. He found for Mr. Smith and upheld the terms of the prenuptial agreement.

See the video that started it all at **http://www.triciawalsh smith.com/The_Videos.html**.

For more coverage of the Smith divorce see **http://tinyurl .com/c5dqxk** and **http://tinyurl.com/csh7tf**.

How Individuals Participate in the Social Networking Craze

To participate in a social networking site, one typically creates an online "profile" to share information about themselves. Most sites give users the ability to post text, images, sound, and other information to their profiles. Users can add as much or as little information to their profiles as they wish. They usually post all types of information about their personal, professional, and educational backgrounds; interests; hobbies; friends; etc. These social networking sites might also include the ability to create a blog where users can easily post information about their personal/professional activities. Most sites give visitors access to a list of the member's (online) "friends" and sometimes even those friends' comments to the user.

People are very forthcoming with information about themselves when the information is intended for a specific audience. These social networkers forget that, in many instances, the information they include in their profiles is not just visible to their intended audience (of online friends), but can be read by anyone who views their profile. The profile owner can take steps to limit who can see the information in their profile, but many do not. This is particularly true if they are using these sites as a professional marketing tool and want their profiles to be accessible to the widest possible audience.

While some lawyers have found social networking sites useful for marketing and referrals, in this chapter, we will focus on how lawyers can use social networking sites to investigate people's backgrounds and to find missing people.

Investigative Uses of Social Networking Sites

- Companies, associations, and even judges and law firms use social networking sites to mine the wealth of information that people post about themselves (or their friends post about them). Some have used this information to learn about the background of a person they are considering hiring. Other employers even contact the candidate's "connections" from LinkedIn (see below) to obtain references.
- Lawyers and law enforcement use social networking sites to locate missing heirs, potential witnesses, escapees, etc.

Ethics Alert

Lawyers conducting investigative research by viewing/collecting information contained in social networking profiles should be careful not to cross the line into having contact with the targets of their research. Exchanging messages with an opposing party, or even just sending a message to an opposing party could be viewed as an *ex parte* communication.

The Philadelphia Bar Association, in Opinion 2009-02 of its Professional Guidance Committee (*available at* **http://tinyurl.com/ cgwgwr**) advised that a lawyer who used a third party to contact a witness who was "not a party to the litigation, nor [was] she represented" by sending a **Friend** request on Facebook would be in violation of the states rules governing attorney misconduct and truthfulness in statements to others.

While this opinion is "advisory only" and "not binding upon the Disciplinary Board of the Supreme Court of Pennsylvania or any other court," attorneys would be wise to read the opinion for themselves in the event their own jurisdictions might be influenced by the committees' arguments.

The full text of the opinion is located in the Appendix at the end of this book.

How Information Clients Post About Themselves in Their Social Networking Profiles Has Made a Difference in the Outcome of Their Case

Many lawyers have discovered that the information in social networking profiles has made a difference in the outcomes of their cases. For example, in a drunken driving case where the defendant's actions caused the death of her passenger, a Santa Barbara, California, defense lawyer was reportedly, "'blindsided' by a presentencing report from prosecutors that featured photos posted of his client on MySpace after the crash."

Published reports indicate that defense attorney Steve Balash was aware of the negative effect social networking profiles could have on his client's case. These reports indicate that, "the day he met his client Jessica Binkerd, a recent college graduate charged with a fatal drunken driving crash, he asked if she had a MySpace page. When she said yes, he told her to take it down because he figured it might have pictures that cast her in a bad light." Unfortunately for Balash and Binkerd, she did not take her profile down, leading to photos from that profile being included in the prosecutor's presentencing report. The reports describe some of the photos posted after the date of the crash as, "show[ing] Binkerd holding a beer bottle . . . [and another in which she is] wearing a shirt advertising tequila and a belt bearing plastic shot glasses."

Blinkerd was sentenced to five years in prison (although it is reported that her sentence was later shortened for reasons unrelated to the photos).

See **http://tinyurl.com/bbg9fm**, **http://tinyurl.com/bop66c**, and **http://tinyurl.com/dclpcn** for additional reporting on this case.

War Story: Information People Post in Their Own Social Networking Profiles Comes into Play During Child Custody Proceedings

Blake Boyd, a Senior Trial Consultant based in San Antonio, Texas (**http://www.dlstx.com**), relates this story:

One of our attorney clients was representing a father going through a child custody battle. During a conversation I heard the attorney mention that the child had a MySpace page, but no one had looked at it. Using the child's name, age, a known online alias, and a picture for reference, we were able to find her profile in ten minutes while sitting in the attorney's conference room.

From her profile we were able to determine that she was involved in a very alternative religious group that she had previously denied any involvement with. After ten more minutes of searching her online friends' profiles, we found a picture of her smoking what appeared to be marijuana at a New Year's Eve party. After consulting with his client, we also learned she had possession of the child on that New Year's Eve. It was all very damning evidence.

There are lots of little tricks here and there that you can use to find people. I by no means consider myself an expert in this area. Is there such an expert? But if you have a little bit of basic information about the person, and they have a social networking profile, anyone can be found. And it's pretty easy, just takes time. It's absolutely amazing how many people expose their lives on social networking sites.

Ethics Alert

> Before advising clients to delete, purge, or otherwise alter their social networking profiles, lawyers would be wise to consider whether this could be construed as spoliation of evidence by the court.

Facebook

http://www.facebook.com

Purpose: Although the purpose of this site is to allow people who were in the same "network" (e.g., all students or alumni of a particular university) to socialize over the Internet, legal professionals have found another purpose for this site: to find and background people.

Content: Facebook claims more than 400 million active members around the world (as of January 2010), broken down into "networks" based on their attendance at specific schools, employment at specific workplaces, etc. The Pew Internet Project's December 2008 survey reported that 22 percent of adult social network users had a Facebook profile and the median age of these adult users was 26-years old.

When you visit Facebook.com, it appears that the only way to use Facebook is to register and create a profile of your own. However, if you visit **http://www.facebook .com/srch.php** instead, you will be allowed to search without registering for your own account. Facebook warns you that if you search without first registering (and logging into your account), "Search results will only give you a preview of results that will include the users' profile photo and registration name." Even with the limited information displayed, it can be useful to quickly establish that a particular individual does have a Facebook profile. The results also include links to: **Add as Friend**, **Send a Message**, or **View Friends**. Unfortunately, without being logged into your own profile, you will not be able to take advantage of any of those links. Registering requires you to enter a name and an e-mail address. The e-mail address that you register with determines which network you are a member of and allows you to view profiles in that particular network. For example, if you have a University of Illinois student or alumni e-mail address and you register with it, you automatically

Figure 8-1. Facebook users can include information about their personal, educational, and professional backgrounds in their profiles.

become part of that network. If you lack a "network" e-mail, you can still register, but you are restricted to a regional network such as **Los Angeles**.

When you register, you also have to provide a date of birth which, along with your name and e-mail address, will be displayed on your profile. The rest of your profile content is up to you. You can add as much or as little additional information to your profile as you wish. You can add photos and videos, contact information, and any information about your personal life, work life, education, etc. Your profile also displays messages from other Facebook users you have designated as your "**Friends**."

Regardless of what network(s) you're assigned to when you register, you can still search through all the Facebook profiles (use the **Search** feature on the left side of the screen once you're logged into your account) to see if a particular person you're interested in has created a Facebook profile for themselves, and learn which network they belong to. In addition, you will be able to see their photo and a list of their Facebook **Friends**. You can send any person in Facebook a message (but they will then be able to view your profile for a month) or you can "**poke**" anyone, which means you are asking to be added to their list of friends and they will then be able to view your profile for a week.

Our View: This site is more useful if you can get access to a specific network. For example, if you did not attend the University of Illinois, but want to view the profile of a Facebook member who did (and was part of the University of Illinois network), you could not do so on your own. You would have to find another Facebook user who is a member of that network and ask them to "loan" you access to his Facebook account. You might be able to find a colleague who has the ability to be a member of that particular network who would be willing to create a Facebook profile that you could "borrow." Also, many people have the access settings for their profiles set to be viewable by **Friends of Friends**. If your research target has done so (and there's no way to determine this in advance), you can identify your target's Facebook **Friends** and then **poke** them (see *Tips* on the next page), requesting to be their **Friend**. This would give you access to their **Friends'** profiles (who have set their access to **Friends of Friends**), perhaps including that of your target. Be sure to review the Philadelphia Bar Association Professional Guidance Committee's Opinion 2009-02 located in the Appendix to decide whether "borrowing" someone else's account is ethical. It's a gray area.

Be Mindful of the Information You Share in Your Own Social Networking Profile(s)

If you're joining social networking sites to locate information about people (through their public profiles or if you are in their network), consider how much (or little) information you include in the profiles you set up to gain access to the information of others. It may be advisable to include as little identifiable information in your own profiles as possible to protect your privacy and to avoid offending a potential client, for instance.

Tips: Sometimes the information in the friend's messages can be more useful than the person's profile. For example, as we read through a person's profile in the Los Angeles network, we learned, through her friend's message, that she was a student at the University of California at San Diego—something she had not included in her own profile. So, instead of concentrating our search for her in Los Angeles, we could now shift to the San Diego area.

While it's not obvious, you can conduct more advanced searches by logging in at **http://www.facebook.com/srch.php** instead of at facebook.com. You will be offered a search menu that allows you to search by: (1) **Person's Name or E-mail**, (2) **Classmate Search** (you can enter a **School Name** only or you can narrow the search down by adding a **Class Year** or a **Person's Name**), or (3) **Search by Company** (you can also narrow this search by adding in a **Person's Name**). To narrow your search even further, see the discussion on page 87 (**Using Google's Advanced Search Page to Limit Your Search to Facebook**).

How Information in Social Networking Profiles Has Made a Difference in the Outcomes of Cases

In another Santa Barbara, California, case of a drunken driver's actions causing the death of her passenger, the prosecutor said that information a woman posted about her partying lifestyle on MySpace.com was the difference between seeking a prison sentence rather than probation.

In published reports, Prosecutor Danny Perlin indicated that, "he was willing to recommend probation for [defendant] Lara Buys for a drunken driving crash that killed her passenger." That was until he uncovered her MySpace profile in preparation for sentencing.

The profile reportedly contained photos of the defendant "holding a glass of wine as well as joking comments about drinking," taken after the accident. Rather than seek probation, as would have been customary in similar cases involving first-time offenders, Perlin used the photos as part of his argument for a jail sentence—winning a two year sentence in jail for the defendant.

"Pending sentencing, you should be going to (Alcoholics Anonymous), you should be in therapy, you should be in a program to learn to deal with drinking and driving," Perlin said in interviews after the sentencing. "She was doing nothing other than having a good old time."

See **http://tinyurl.com/dhg8ff**, **http://tinyurl.com/bop66c** and **http://tinyurl.com/chcek9** for additional reporting on this case.

MySpace

http://www.myspace.com

Purpose: Although the purpose of this site is to allow people to socialize over the Internet, legal professionals have found another purpose for this site: to find and background people.

Content: MySpace claims that over 260 million profiles have been self-created by people around the world with 100 million being active monthly users as of January 2010. The Pew Internet Project's December 2008 survey reported that 50 percent of adult social network users had a

Figure 8-2. Information that people post in their MySpace.com profiles can be useful to attorneys.

MySpace profile and the median age of these adult users was 27-years old. The basic profile includes predefined categories of information into which members can add their own information. These are:

- **Headline**
- **About Me**
- **I'd Like to Meet**
- **Interests**
- **Movies**
- **Music**
- **Books**
- **Heroes**

Users can also add audio, video, or pictures to their profiles, as well as posting information about schools they have attended (middle schools, high schools, and universities).

Creating an online calendar or adding a blog to their profile are also options. There is no cost to create a profile or to search through the profiles' contents. Members can add as much or as little information to their profiles as they wish.

MySpace members create their own network of contacts by selecting other members as their **Friends**. (Once selected, these other members must accept the other's invitation to be a **Friend** before that relationship is established.) Members can also choose to make their profiles "private"—so that only their Friends can view its contents. By default, all profiles of members under the age of 16 are set to "private."

The minimum age to create a MySpace profile is 14. (Note that this is self-reported by the user when they create the profile, and there is no independent verification.)

It is not necessary to create a MySpace account to be able to browse or search through the "public" profiles on the site. Any information a member adds to their "public" profile would be visible to anyone who visits that profile—including the list of their **Friends** and **Comments** those **Friends** have sent to the member. Because the majority of profiles are not "private," any researcher can access a large number of profiles to see if a particular person they're interested in has created a MySpace profile for themselves, and learn who their "friends" are.

MySpace provides a **Search** box, located at the top of each MySpace page. It includes a number of limiters (listed above the **Search** box or in a drop-down menu on the right-hand side of the **Search** box) to help you narrow in on the types of information you're looking for in the profiles. The two most useful to online researchers are probably **MySpace** (which seemingly searches full text through all visible content contained in public MySpace profiles) and **People** (which seemingly searches through MySpace's registration database by the first and last names or the e-mail members used when they created their account). Note that the **People** search is the default search. If you instead want to search using descriptive keywords (e.g., matt chicago "farmington hills") or a display name (matt), you will need to select **MySpace** from the drop-down menu. The first search brought back 98 results while the second brought back 500. Lucky for us, in the first search, our target happened to be the very first result. If you want to continue conducting **MySpace** searches, be careful because the search defaults back to the **People** search after completing each search.

You can also click the **Find Friends** tab (located beneath the MySpace logo in the blue bar). You will ONLY see this choice if you are NOT logged in. (If you are logged in, you will see a **Friends** tab, which is not the same search as a **Find Friends** search.) **Find Friends** is actually an advanced search because it allows you to search all public MySpace profiles by: **All Name Fields**, **Name**, **Display Name**, **or E-mail**. The **Friends** tab displayed after you log in to your account also allows you to advance search, but only within your list of friends.

Our View: MySpace profiles are the perfect illustration of our point to not underestimate the type or the volume of information people will post about themselves online. MySpace has outgrown its original demographic of the 20-and-under crowd, to the point where users of all ages now post a surprising amount of personal and otherwise private information about themselves in their profiles. For an example of one attorney's profile, see "It's Not Just Kids Posting Embarrassing Information in Their Social Network Profiles" (on the next page).

Unfortunately, the **Search** functions described above do not do as good a job uncovering information contained in those profiles as one would expect. In some test searches, we have been able to locate an individual's profile using their last name as a search term and limiting our search using the **People** limiter. Other times, similar searches have failed to yield a profile even when we know an individual does have a MySpace profile, and has used his correct name to set it up.

We find it extremely helpful that MySpace posts the date on which a profile was last updated by its owner.

Tip: Because MySpace allowed you to only search with keywords (and not phrases) and the Boolean connector *AND*, we used to advise you to use the **Advanced Search** page at Google to create a sophisticated search mixing keywords, phrases and Boolean connectors, and using the Advanced Search's Domain limiter to return only results found at the MySpace.com domain. This is no longer necessary because it seems that MySpace now allows you to search with all the Boolean connectors and also with phrases.

It's Not Just Kids Posting Embarrassing Information in Their Social Network Profiles

Before you say, "That couldn't possibly happen to a professional like a lawyer," consider the case of Nevada criminal defense lawyer Jonathan MacArthur.

In August 2007, the Las Vegas Review Journal (*available at* **http://www.lvrj.com/news/9121536.html**) reported that MacArthur lost his Judge pro tem position, "with the North Las Vegas Justice Court last week because of hostile comments aimed at prosecutors on his MySpace page." After seeing comments that he felt were hostile and biased against prosecutors, the County District Attorney, "went to the North Las Vegas Justice Court administrator and asked that MacArthur be recused from criminal cases," the paper reported. In an attempt to defend his postings, MacArthur told the paper that, "People who know me and interact with me socially know I'm constantly trying to say things in a funny, provocative manner."

Taken at their face value however, the comments, as MacArthur posted them, cost him his bench and, according to the paper, possibly damaged his intended campaign for a full-time Judge's position in 2009. In summation, MacArthur told the paper, "Being I never expected the DA was going to go searching for something like that, I was perfectly comfortable [posting the comments I posted]." MacArthur returned to his private law practice, reportedly with the intent of seeking election to the bench in 2009.

Lawyers should remember that any of the profiles they create online, either at the popular social networking sites like MySpace and Facebook, general professional networking sites like LinkedIn, or specialized legal professional networking sites like LawLink and Legally Minded, are part of the publicly available information clients might use in determining whether to hire them or that the opposition might use against them.

Separately, jurors have also been reported to read lawyers' profiles, resulting in possible bias for or against the lawyer and their client.

Using MySpace's People Search to Locate Public and Private Profiles Even if the Member's Real Name Does Not Appear on the Profile Itself

A little-known feature of MySpace's **People** search (accessed via the pull-down menu on the right-hand side of the search box found at the top of every page and profile on MySpace) is that it appears to search through the site's registration database to return its results—not just the visible text of public profiles (as the **MySpace** search does). Because of this, we have been able to locate the private profiles of minor children on MySpace; they used their full, real name when they registered to create their profile.

When we ran a **People** search for *Sarah Jones*, we were able to locate the private profile of a Southern California teenager. Even though her profile was private and we could not view the profile because we were not her **Friend**. Her full name did not appear in the (limited) view we did have of her private profile, but because she had a photo of herself as the profile's primary image and listed her age and the city and state where she lived, we were able to determine that this profile belonged to the person we were researching. It was retrieved by our **People** search because she used her full name when registering to create her profile on MySpace. Note that users can change their registration information after-the-fact. So MySpace users could begin to replace their names with pseudonyms or delete their last names entirely if they become aware of this search capability.

Classmates

http://www.classmates.com

 (for basic profile and networking)

 $ (for premium level service)

Purpose: Although the purpose of this site is to allow people to reconnect with old friends via the Internet, legal professionals have found another purpose for this site: to find and "background" people.

Figure 8-3. People tend to include a lot of useful and correct information about themselves in profiles at Classmates.com since the site's stated purpose is to reconnect with high school and college classmates.

Content:　　As of March 2010, the site's database boasted over 60 million people from 130,000 high schools located in the United States and Canada; over 5 million members identified with over 34,000 colleges; nearly 2.5 million members identified with nearly 2.4 million companies; and, over 1.4 million members identified with more than 66,000 military units. More than 4 million of these members have paid accounts allowing them to post additional information and directly contact other members. The Pew Internet Project's December 2008 survey reported that only 1 percent of adult social network users had a Classmates profile.

Users can add a wide variety of information to their profiles, including:

- **Name**
- **Birthdate**
- **Photos (then & now)**
- **Narrative description/ story about themselves**
- **Mailing Address**
- **E-mail Address**

- **K-12 School(s) attended**
- **Colleges/Universities attended**
- **Jobs**
- **Military duty stations**

Users can even opt to have a map included in their profile showing their location (based on addresses provided by the user).

You must register and create your own (free) profile before you can access any of the site's search functions. You can enter as much or as little information about yourself as you wish. Remember that Classmates has a built-in mechanism to let paid members "know how many people have stopped by and if someone's left their name." If you're doing more "covert" types of research about people see *Tips* regarding covering your tracks as you view others' profiles.

Many investigators have told us that they maintain profiles under assumed names to cover their tracks or better elicit information from their targets. Note that this is a violation of Classmates.com's **Terms of Service**. (Section 1 B reads "For your part, you agree that all Your Information that you provide to us or post on the Web site is complete, accurate and up to date." *available at* **http://www.classmates.com/cmo/reg/terms.jsp# registering**.) The Terms of Service also indicate that, ". . . if all or part of Your Information is (or appears to be) untrue, inaccurate, or incomplete we may suspend or terminate your membership and refuse any and all current or future use of our Web site and Services, without refund to you of any fees paid."

Ethics Alert

Lawyers should remember that contacting people online, either through their social networking profiles or otherwise, is akin to contacting those people in the "real" world.

Rule 4.2 of the ABA's *Model Rules of Professional Conduct* states that, "In representing a client, a lawyer shall not communicate about the subject of the representation with a person the lawyer knows to be represented by another lawyer in the matter, unless the lawyer has the consent of the other lawyer or is authorized to do so by law or a court order." (See **http://www.abanet .org/cpr/mrpc/rule_4_2.html**.)

This rule should apply regardless if the contact is made through one of these online resources or via phone, mail, or in person.

The simple search box at the top of each page allows you to search by **People** (name), **K-12 Schools**, **Colleges**, **Workplaces**, **Military**, or **Neighborhoods**.

The **Advanced Search** functions allow you to refine your query by offering separate fields for a person's **First** and **Last** name, separate fields for **City** and **State/Province**, as well as a combined search of **K-12 School**, **College**, **Workplace**, **Military Assignment**, or **Neighborhood**.

Our View: Because people using Classmates.com want to be found (by fellow classmates, etc.), they tend to use their real names. This makes the site popular with private investigators.

Some information can be obtained free with registration, but to take full advantage of this site requires a $39 annual fee. Registration specials are frequent. Recently we were offered a $59/two year and $17/4 month option in addition to the regular $39 annual membership.

Tips: Regardless of what school, company, etc. is listed in your profile, you can search through the entire database. You're not limited to searching just through the **Communities** that you've indicated you're a member of.

Set your account to **Quiet** mode to view other members' profiles without them knowing who was there. To do this, click the **Your Account** link in the blue navigation bar near the top of each page (once you're logged in). Then click **Profile Visit Settings** from the list of links on the left-hand side. Then select the **Quiet (anonymous visits every time)** option from the list.

Friendster

http://www.friendster.com

Purpose: Although the purpose of this site is to allow people to socialize over the Internet, legal professionals have found another purpose for this site: to find and "background" people.

Content: The content of Friendster profiles is very similar to those found at MySpace, including photos, information on K-12 schools, colleges/universities attended, etc.

Profiles also include lists of the user's **Friends** with profiles (and links to those profiles), comments from those friends, and other content that can be useful as part of the investigative research process.

Similar to MySpace, Friendster's name searches return results from the site's registration database—not just the names displayed in the profiles. So, as long as an individual created their profile using their real name, it is discoverable by clicking the **Search** link in the blue navigation bar near the top of the page. This defaults to the **Friends** search tab where "you can search by name, email, location or a combination of these." This is the only search tab available to non-Friendster users. However, even non-registered searchers can view profiles if the profile owners have opted to make the profile public.

Other search tab options—**College Search** and **School Search**—are only available to registered users who are logged into their account.

Our View: We like the openness of the Friendster model that allows even those without accounts to view the profiles of Friendster members, as long as the members have opted to allow such wide access.

Tip: Similar to Classmates, Friendster users can be informed who has been viewing their profile by clicking the **Who's Viewed Me?** link when they are logged into their account. So to conceal your viewing of other people's profiles while logged into your own Friendster account, you must change Friendster's default settings so you can view profiles anonymously. To do so, click the **Who's Viewed Me?** link (in your profile) and then, next to the **Viewing profiles anonymously** entry, click the **Change Settings** link to access a long list of customizable settings for your account. Scroll down to the setting labeled **View profiles anonymously**. Selecting **Yes** for this setting allows you to visit other users' profiles without alerting them to who you are.

How Information Others Post About Your Client in Their Own Social Networking Profiles Can Make a Difference in the Outcome of a Case

MySpace isn't the only source of photos that have lead to stiffer sentences for convicted criminals.

Rhode Island Prosecutor Jay Sullivan reportedly used pictures of Joshua Lipton that had been posted on Facebook by Lipton's friends to paint Lipton as unrepentant and unremorseful after causing a three-car collision that left one person hospitalized for weeks. Lipton was unhurt and, according to published reports, attended a Halloween party only two weeks later dressed in a black-and-white striped shirt, covered by an orange jumpsuit with the words "jail bird" stenciled on the front.

Sullivan assembled this and other photos into a PowerPoint presentation that he screened during sentencing. In an interview, Superior Court Judge Daniel Procaccini said, "I did feel that gave me some indication of how that young man was feeling a short time after a near-fatal accident, that he thought it was appropriate to joke and mock about the possibility of going to prison."

It's important to note that Lipton did not post these images in his profile himself. The images were posted in the profile(s) of one of Lipton's Facebook friends, but were apparently "tagged" with Lipton's name. "Tagging" allows users to identify individuals in the photos they post to their own profiles. If those individuals in the photo also have Facebook profiles and are "friends" with the individual who posted the picture, then that photo becomes visible in the profile of the person whose name was tagged onto the photo. From published descriptions, this sounds like what happened in Lipton's case. Users like Lipton have the power to remove photos like this from their profile—apparently, Lipton did not know that.

Lipton was sentenced to two years in prison. His sentence was later reduced by six months.

See **http://tinyurl.com/cmpzgn** and **http://tinyurl.com/chcek9** for additional reporting on this case.

Using Google's Advanced Search Page to Limit Your Search to Facebook (or any Web Site)

Although Facebook does allow for ways to narrow your search down, it does not allow you to connect your keywords and phrases with Boolean connectors, nor does it allow for phrase searching. However, you can use the **Advanced Search** page at Google (**http://www.google.com/ advanced_search**) to create a sophisticated search, mixing keywords, phrases, and Boolean connectors entering facebook.com into the **Search within a site or domain** box, to return only results found at the Facebook.com domain. For example, if you are looking for an expert with a certain expertise, you can search for *expert electronic evidence,* or if you are looking for background information about a person, you can search for their name as a phrase (*carole levitt*) and also add keywords that you think might appear in their profile (e.g., *internet speaker MCLE*) to avoid irrelevant results. The only caveat is that this will only display results of Facebook profile owners who have set their privacy settings to **Everyone** (which means they make their information available to search engines). You can Superimpose the power of Google's advanced search features over any Web site indexed at Google. MySpace, as noted earlier, now allows you to search with Boolean connectors and phrases, so there is little need to superimpose Google over MySpace.

This is just a sampling of some of the major social networking sites. There's a large collection of similar sites where information can be gathered. These include general sites like Google's Orkut (**http://www.orkut .com**), AOL's Bebo (**http://www.bebo.com**), NPR's Gather (**http://www .gather.com**), London-based Badoo (**http://www.badoo.com**), and Tagged.com (**http://www.tagged.com**) among others.

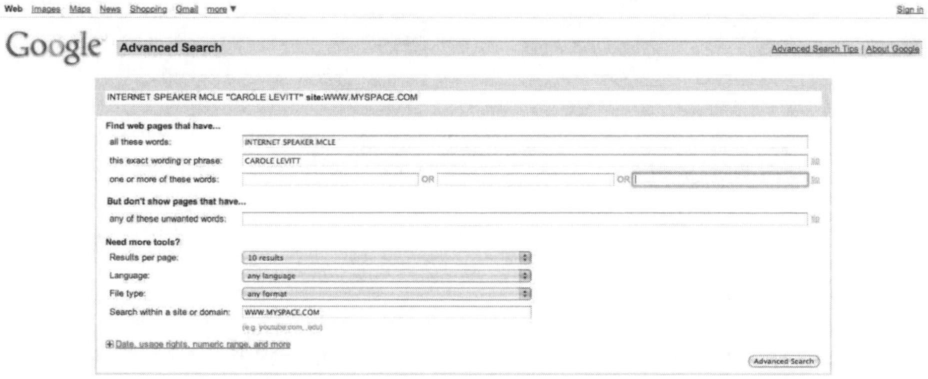

Figure 8-4. You can superimpose Google's search power onto any Web site, including social networks, by entering its Web address into the **Search within a site or domain** box on Google's **Advanced Search** page. Google™ is a trademark of Google Technology Inc.

There are even more narrow social networking sites targeted at individuals of specific:

- Religions:
  - Muslims—Muxlim (**http://www.muxlim.com**)
  - Christians—MyChurch (**http://www.mychurch.org**)
  - Catholics—Xt3 (**http://www.xt3.com**)
  - Jews—Schmooze (**http://www.shmooze.ning.com**)

- Ethnic or cultural segments:
  - African-Americans—BlackPlanet (**http://www.blackplanet.com**)
  - Native-Americans—Native American Passions (**http://www.nativeamericanpassions.com**)
  - Latino-Americans—MiGente (**http://www.migente.com**)
  - Asian-Americans—AsianAve (**http://www.asianave.com**)

- Sexual preference
  - Showtime Television's Our Chart (**http://www.sho.com/site/lword/community.do**)
  - Glee (**http://www.glee.com**)
  - OUTeverywhere (**http://www.outeverywhere.com**)

Social networks are being developed for any social niche imaginable. Try a Google search for a social, demographic, ethnic, hobby, related keyword you're interested in and the phrase *social network site* and see what you come up with.

And that doesn't even take the professional networking sites (see below) into consideration.

Social Networking Sites Provide New Method of Service of Process

Avid social networkers update their profiles often. The Pew Internet Project's December 2008 survey found that 37 percent of adult social network site users visited their profiles at least once per day, with another 23 percent reporting that they visited their profile "every few days." Some visit their profiles multiple times per day to add new information or to read comments from friends, etc. Some may even spend so much time logged into their profiles that lawyers would be able to serve papers on them through notice posted to that person's profile.

While it might sound off-the-wall, that's exactly what Canberra City, Australia lawyers Mark McCormack and Jason Oliver, of Meyer Vandenberg Lawyers, were able to convince a judge of the Australian Capitol Territory Supreme Court (trial court). Their client, a mortgage lender, had won a default judgment against two debtors. The debtors were not available at any of the residence or business addresses they had listed. After exhausting all of the usual methods of personal and substitute service, the attorneys got the idea to not just locate the debtors' profiles as a means to track them down in the "real-world," but to actually serve notice on them through their profiles.

The attorneys were certain that they had located the right profiles because, "the Facebook profiles showed the defendants' dates of birth, e-mail addresses and friend lists—and the co-defendants were friends with one another," McCormack said in an interview. "This information was enough to satisfy the court that Facebook was a sufficient method of communicating with the defendants," he added in the same interview.

Somewhere between substituted service and service by publication, "service by Facebook" hasn't been approved in any U.S. jurisdiction . . . but stay tuned.

For more information about this case see **http://tinyurl.com/6ny7o2** and **http://tinyurl.com/5hu28y**.

Professional Networking Sites

Professional networking sites are similar to social networking sites in their form and function, but as the name implies, they are used primarily for business-related purposes. Because they are business-centric, professional networking profiles tend to contain more useful background information and less embarrassing information than social networking profiles.

Like Classmates.com, those using professional networking sites want to be found, thus, they tend to use their real names, which makes these sites ideal tools for finding people. These sites are also useful to help you learn how people are connected to each other since that is one of their main functions. If you can't locate your subject, you might learn the names of friends or professional associates who you could contact for help locating the subject.

LinkedIn

http://www.linkedin.com

 (for basic profile and networking)

$ (for premium level service)

Purpose: The stated purpose of this site is to allow people to connect, via the Internet, with colleagues, business acquaintances, and other professionals for business networking purposes. While legal professionals have found that purpose useful, they can also use the site to find and "background" people.

Content: LinkedIn includes profiles for over 60 million professionals, world-wide (as of March 2010), from over 150 industries—including executives from almost every Fortune 500 company. Forty-two thousand new members reportedly join daily. LinkedIn members earn an average of $108,000 and their average age is 41. Nearly two-hundred thousand of its users are attorneys. The Pew Internet Project's December 2008 survey reported that 6 percent of adult social network users had a LinkedIn profile.

There are three types of paid LinkedIn accounts beyond the more common free account—$24.95/month, $49.95/month, and $499.95/month. Discounts are available for annual prepayment.

You can search a person's name even if you don't have a LinkedIn profile of your own. However, the amount of information you can see in the returned profiles depends on whether or not you are logged into your own LinkedIn account. For example, some users allow their full profiles to be viewed by other LinkedIn users (accessed by clicking on the **View Full Profiles** button). If you do not have a LinkedIn account (or are not logged into your account) you can't see those full profiles. However, some users allow the majority of their profiles to be visible to anyone who searches, whether or not the searcher has a LinkedIn account.

Since 2007, LinkedIn has allowed users to upload photos. This can be useful to help jog your memory of a person. Users can also opt to use the **TripIt** tool to post information about trips they are taking—allowing viewers of their profile to track their whereabouts. For example, on a recent visit to a connection's profile we knew that at that moment, "Tom is in Portland, or and has traveled 47,019 miles to 35 locations," because he had added the Portland trip to his TripIt calendar.

In addition to simple name searches, once you're logged into your LinkedIn account you can use the **Advanced** search page to search for people by **Title**, **Company**, or **School**. LinkedIn also allows you to search by **Keywords** (e.g., electronic discovery); **Industry** (e.g., law practice, legal services, etc.); user type, located behind the **Interested In** drop-down menu (e.g., consultant, potential employees, industry experts); **Location**; and so on. The results show you the person's name, some background information, and offer you the ability to get introduced. You can click on any name in the results list to see that user's public profile. The amount of information in the public portion of the profile can vary greatly depending on how much information the user allows to be included.

If you want to contact someone displayed in your results list, you can send them a request by clicking the **Add [user] to your network** link in the upper right-hand portion of their profile page, or you can request an introduction through one of your own connections if the LinkedIn user is two or three degrees away from you. Your connection will, in turn, decide whether to forward your request for an introduction onto the desired recipient (if in your 2nd degree) or to a shared connection (if in your 3rd degree).

LinkedIn sends account holders regular updates via e-mail about their connections' LinkedIn activities. For instance, when we recently received an e-mail update about our connections, we learned: (1) one connection had uploaded a new profile picture, (2) the names of other LinkedIn users our connections were newly connected to, and (3) which groups our connections had recently joined.

Searching for Employees of a Particular Company

When we searched LinkedIn for the keywords *State Bar*, employees of many state bar associations were included in the results. When we chose the *Wisconsin State Bar*, it showed that of the 50 current Wisconsin State Bar employees who have LinkedIn profiles, more than 30 were already "in my network" based on either direct connections or mutual connections with other users.

Tip: When looking for information from LinkedIn profiles, be sure to narrow **Company** searches down to **Current only**, **Past only**, or **Past & Current** to locate a more precise list of individuals who may be of interest to you.

Our View: Because people tend to use their real names on professional networking sites like LinkedIn this can be an excellent source of background information about people whose identity you already know, or to identify people who fit specific criteria (e.g., worked at a particular company during a particular time frame, hold specific degrees, graduated from certain schools, etc.).

LinkedIn is one of the best-known, general professional networking sites, but there are numerous others. While their search capabilities might be different, most include similar types of information. Some of the other popular professional networking sites include:

- Ecademy—**http://www.ecademy.com**
- Networking For Professionals—**http://www.networking forprofessionals.com**
- Plaxo—**http://www.plaxo.com**
- Ziggs—**http://www.ziggs.com**

Social & Professional Networking Sites for Marketing & Referrals

You or your law firm might try to use a social or professional networking site, such as LinkedIn, for marketing and referrals. Start out by sending invitations to attorneys and other professionals you know personally who already have profiles, and then go from there.

Google recognizes the power of LinkedIn and so you might find that having a LinkedIn profile for yourself (or your law firm) helps you rank higher in Google's search results when someone "googles" you (or your law firm).

You could also advertise on LinkedIn by targeting a specific segment of LinkedIn professionals based on: industry, seniority, job function, company size, geography, number of connections, or gender.

Some attorneys who use Facebook claim they are using it to take the place of their address book or contact relationship management (CRM) database.

Professional Networks for Lawyers

It was only a matter of time before the launch of networking sites targeted towards the legal profession. More professional than social, these sites, like LinkedIn, fall into the category of professional networking sites. Searching through legal professional networking sites may prove fruitful when you need background information about an attorney or need to find an attorney with whom to associate or to whom to refer a case.

Lawlink.com claims to be the first online network exclusively for licensed attorneys. It was launched in September 2007 by Steven Choi, a trial attorney with over 24 years in practice (he is still practicing in Northern California). However, the Texas State Bar might actually be able to lay claim to offering the first online network exclusively for licensed attorneys. It launched **The Texas Bar Circle** on June 1, 2007—a few months earlier than LawLink. While LawLink is open to all licensed attorneys in

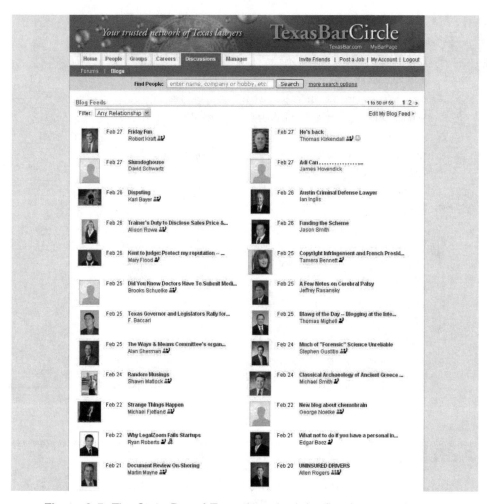

Figure 8-5. The State Bar of Texas launched the first lawyer-only social networking site for its members in June 2007.

the US, UK, Australia, and Canada, The Texas Bar Circle (**https://texasbar.affinitycircles.com/sbot/auth/login**) is a closed site—open only to licensed Texas attorneys.

By July 2009, The Texas Bar Circle had over 10,000 members—with new members joining at the rate of approximately 500 per month. According to information provided by the Bar, an attorney's profile can include their contact information, their resume, a list of friends and groups joined (there are nearly 250), news, announcements, a calendar, and photos. Attorneys who have created blogs outside of The Texas Bar Circle can integrate those RSS feeds into their Texas Bar Circle profiles. In addition, attorney members can keep a journal on their page; browse the **Careers Page** for jobs; or use the **Opportunities** feature to browse or post a job opening, office sharing or rental, volunteer opportunities, etc. In early 2009, Affinity Circles (which provides the platform for Texas Bar Circle) launched a Facebook application that allows users to view their Texas Bar Circle opportunities from within Facebook. Other state Bar Associations, including California and Oklahoma, are also planning professional networks of their own.

LawLink

http://www.lawlink.com/

Purpose: LawLink's misson is "to help attorneys build professional relationships with other attorneys." It serves as a professional networking site, like LinkedIn, but targeted strictly at licensed attorneys and Bar Associations.

Content: As of February 2010, over 7,000 attorneys joined LawLink. (The site is free to join.)

     Like the other social and professional networking sites we've already discussed, attorneys can post biographical details, professional background, and other information about themselves in their profiles. These profiles can also include embedded video or links to the attorney's blog. Attorneys can also post legal documents (which can be shared with everyone, a select group, or just for the attorney's own use) or they can create groups with other attorneys to discuss legal topics. The groups can be open, private, or even secret. There are now over 150 law groups. Additionally, attorneys can post free job ads.

     During the month of February 2010, LawLink reported an average of 80,000 unique visitors per month.

Our View: The site is easy to use and we like that it is full text keyword searchable (once you are logged in as a member). It has a reasonable number of profiles, but there is a dearth of documents posted for sharing.

Tip: You can post a banner advertisement at LawLink for free if you are a bar association or a law firm with five or more attorneys.

LegallyMinded

http://www.legallyminded.com

Purpose: A professional networking site, like LinkedIn, but is open only to legal professionals—not just lawyers. While the site is sponsored by the American Bar Association, it is open to non-ABA members.

Content: The ABA describes its site as "an online community serving the legal profession. [Their] goal is to create an unparalleled resource that gathers law school students, academics, firm administrators, legal support staff, judges, paralegals, attorneys, law librarians and other professionals to contribute, network, and collaborate online."

As of March 2010, the site was still in beta mode (open to the legal community, but still being fine tuned). Some of the features listed on the site include:

- **Connect with Peers**—the primary networking "features to connect, like-minded professionals. Find mentors, research employers, or meet new friends"

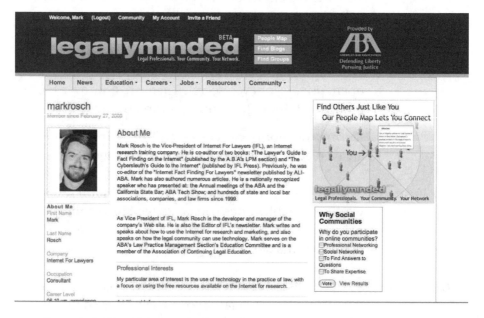

Figure 8-6. The ABA's Legally Minded online community is open to all legal professionals.

- **Share Knowledge**—creating and posting files, or schedules within blogs, wikis, discussion groups, etc. to share with other members
- Resources news and other information aggregated from various Web sources about **Careers**, **Education**, **Practice Management**, and **Diversity**, among other topics
- **Schedule Meetings** with other Legally Minded members
- **Voice Your Opinions**—rate and comment on content found on LegallyMinded

Our View: Overall, LegallyMinded has promise, but (as of this writing) is a work in progress. The site is still in beta mode and has a number of weaknesses that offset some of its strengths, but is still worth considering.

The site offers very detailed search capabilities for locating other members via the **Search People** link located by hovering over the **Community** tab near the top of each page. Criteria include **First Name**, **Last Name**, **Company**, **Legal Practice Area**, **Office Size**, **Location**, and more. This can be very helpful in locating specific (kinds of) people.

Surprisingly though, the site does not allow one to build a "network" in the same way that LinkedIn or MySpace do. While the site automatically creates a "Community" for you based on interests, etc., which you define in your profile, LegallyMinded does not support the concept of "Friends" or "Connections" that LinkedIn or MySpace do. You can add any of the individuals' profiles you locate to your **Contacts**, or **Send a message** to them, or **Request a meeting**, but that seems to be the extent of the interaction. Once added to your contacts, those profiles just sit on that contact list. There are no updates on their activity, etc. This is apparently by design, as the site's FAQ notes that "Contacts do not work like other social networking sites. Contacts in LegallyMinded are for you and you only. Consider them bookmarks to individual profiles in LegallyMinded. At this time there is no hand-shake or acceptance of you adding someone to your contacts or others adding you to theirs."

The site does has an interesting **People Map** feature where you select the type of people and topics you are interested in (and other criteria such as location, etc.) and then a map is created with icons representing individual users. By hovering over the icons, the screen names of people who match your criteria are displayed. You can then click on their name to visit their profiles. (Disturbingly, when Mark Rosch, coauthor of this book, created his profile, coauthor Carole Levitt was not included in his **Community**, despite both of them listing the same company name, Web site address, book titles, etc. in their respective profiles.)

Oddly, the ABA allows new users to login to Legally-Minded using their existing ABA Web site username and password; however, none of the user's information (e.g., name, address, etc.) already on file with the ABA is pre-populated.

Martindale Hubbell (and others) Join the Professional Networking Trend

Not to be left behind in the social/professional networking frenzy, in the Summer of 2008 the venerable legal directory, Martindale-Hubbell (**http://www.martindale.com**), announced its intention to build a professional networking site for the legal community, as well as a partnership with LinkedIn.

Through the partnership with LinkedIn, the connections that an attorney makes through their profile on LinkedIn can be accessed as part of that attorney's Martindale.com entry. When users search Martindale .com the profiles of attorneys who are LinkedIn members will include a LinkedIn icon. Similarly, Martindale.com profiles for law firms whose attorneys are LinkedIn members will also carry the LinkedIn icon. If the researcher has their own LinkedIn profile, they can click the LinkedIn icon in the attorney's Martindale.com profile to "**Allow LexisNexis to access your LinkedIn account**" to see common LinkedIn connections. (This requires the researcher to log into their LinkedIn account via the Martindale.com interface.)

Martindale-Hubbell's own professional networking site—Martindale-Hubbell Connected (**http://www.martindale.com/connected**)—"offers members the ability to expand their professional network with authenticated contacts, to uncover new relationships and trusted referrals, to share information and insights, and to efficiently collaborate in a virtual community," according to a description on the site. The site officially launched in March 2009 with 3,000 members. (The site had been in development since June 2008.) By July 2009, the site had grown to over 9,000 members. One of the keys to the site is its ability to "authenticate" profiles using Martindale.com's existing database of, "more than one million lawyers and law firms around the world." Initially, the site is only open to lawyers. However, "law school faculty and students, law firm marketing directors, paralegals and other qualified legal professionals will be invited to join the network . . . as the network continues to evolve," according to a LexisNexis press release announcing the site's launch (*available at* **http://www.lexis nexis.com/about/releases/1094.asp**).

Legal OnRamp (**http://www.legalonramp.com**) is an invitation-only network targeted at, "in-house counsel and invited outside lawyers and third party service providers." The site reportedly allows members to post messages to each other and create open forums and closed groups for discussion. Members can also post documents for sharing and post projects or jobs for which they can receive proposals from other members (firms or attorneys). As of November 2008, the site reportedly had 6,000 members (see **http://kmspace.blogspot.com/2008/11/legal-onramp-and-wired-gc.html**).

Will online professional networking sites be the future of legal marketing and collaboration? Ralph Calistri, CEO of Martindale-Hubbell and senior vice president of Global Client Development at LexisNexis seems to think they will. In a press release announcing Martindale's relationship with LinkedIn he said, "Online professional networking is a growing area of importance in the legal industry" and continued that LexisNexis would be developing "a global network for the legal community through Martindale-Hubbell for launch later this year" (*available at* **http://www.martindale.com/xp/legal/News_Events/Press_Releases/2008/2008_0710.xml**).

Calistri's prediction was presumably based on LexisNexis' 2008 Networks for Counsel Survey (**http://www.leadernetworks.com**) which stated that, "almost 50 percent of attorneys are members of online social networks and over 40 percent of attorneys believe professional networking has the potential to change the business and practice of law over the next five years."

We don't discount the importance of social/professional networking sites as marketing tools for lawyers—or as investigative research tools. We just don't think these statistics paint an accurate picture of the legal profession at large, because the survey was administered only to large companies and to large law firms (those with 100 to 10,000 plus employees). It ignored the majority of attorneys—those who practice as solos or in small firms. And, those are the attorneys who often seem less willing to embrace technology.

Networks for (Nearly) Every Profession

While we have focused on some of the better-known professional networking sites geared toward legal professionals, there are also a number of other sites targeted at other specific professions, including:

- Doctors & Medical Students; Doctor's Hangout— **http://www.doctorshangout.com/**
- Emergency Medicine; JEMS Connect—**http://connect.jems .com**
- Finance/Accounting; Finance and Accounting Professional Network—**http://www.fandapros.ning.com/**
- Hispanic Engineers; Society of Hispanic Professional Engineers— **http://network.nshp.org/**

Blogs

Blogs (short for weblogs) are Web sites, but their content is often more like a personal journal or diary—usually with an attitude. Blogs are typically made up of short, frequently updated posts that are ordinarily arranged chronologically, with the newest posts at the top of the page.

The contents and purposes of blogs vary with the personalities of the people who create them—known as "bloggers." Blogs contain everything from links and commentary about current events, to news about a specific topic or company. More personal blogs might constitute online diaries, and include photos, poetry, mini-essays, project updates, or fiction. Often blogs are no more than a chronicle of what's on the mind of the blogger at any given time. The ease of developing and creating a blog makes it extremely easy for anyone, even those with limited technical ability, to create, host, and update their own Web site.

Blogs give their owners an unfettered opportunity to express themselves, vent frustrations, espouse a particular point of view, discuss important issues, or spread rumors for their own purposes. Blogs can range from the off-beat humor of **Davezilla (http://www.davezilla.com)** or straightforward information sharing like **TechForLawyers (http://www.techfor lawyers.net)** to opinion pieces, such as Stanford Law School Professor Lawrence Lessig's discussion of Internet Law (**http://cyberlaw.stanford .edu/lessig/blog/**), and everything in between.

Law-related blogs are often referred to as "blawgs." Los Angeles intellectual property and appellate lawyer Denise Howell is generally credited with coining the term on her blawg (**Bag & Baggage**, at **http://bgbg .blogspot.com**). Blawgs may cover a single legal practice area such as intellectual property, or they may cover a broader topic, such as how to manage your practice. Many respected blawgs are maintained by lawyers who are experts in a particular area of practice and use their blawgs to track pertinent case law and legislative and regulatory developments, while others are maintained by journalists, librarians, or vendors with a particular area of interest or expertise. Ernest Svenson's **Ernie the Attorney** (**http://www.ernietheattorney.net**), Tom Mighell's **Inter-Alia** (**http://www.inter-alia.net**), and Monica Bay's **The Common Scold** (**http://www.commonscold.typepad.com**) are some of the more well-known blawgs. Each of these blawgs also has links to numerous other blawgs that their respective owners find useful. The news, information, and commentary provided by blawgs can provide informational support to lawyers who practice in the same areas of law. You can sample some of the most popular blawgs by visiting **The ABA Journal's Blawg Directory** (**http://www.abajournal.net/blawgs**), **The Blogs of Law** (**http:// www.theblogsoflaw.com**), or **Blawg.org** (**http://www.blawg.org**).

So, "How do blogs fit into my search for facts on the Internet?" you might ask yourself. For lawyers who represent companies that manufacture products or provide services to the public, periodic reading of posts from certain blogs could help provide early warnings of product liability issues or shareholder unrest that could later lead to individual or class action lawsuits.

Many bloggers include links to breaking news, magazine stories, or other Web sites that interest them. Because blogs are updated often (e.g., throughout the day), they can be rich sources of current news or information on a specific topic.

A more personal blog might give you valuable information about the opposition or one of their witnesses—or even your own client. Have a look at a few of the diary-style blogs available at some of the sites mentioned below. You will probably be surprised at the volume and kinds of information people post about themselves on the Internet.

Locating and Searching Blogs

Searching blogs is almost like listening in on someone's phone conversation—except the blogger expects people to be listening. If bloggers are unhappy with a company, its financial performance, or the performance of its products, they may discuss it in their blog. Additionally, if someone was particularly upset, they might set up a blog devoted to bashing the company. Conversely, a blogger might offer praise for a company (it could happen). Monitoring blog posts about a company or product could help avoid greater unrest, or legal action, in the future. Knowing about it early, you can advise your client of steps to help minimize the damage or avoid the confrontation altogether. If you are representing disgruntled shareholders or an individual injured by a company's product, locating others with similar opinions or experiences can be helpful. Locating the right phone line to listen to is easier than you might think. Blogs can be an excellent way to gauge consumers' perception of a client company or product.

Google Blog Search

http://blogsearch.google.com/

Purpose: To locate information contained in blogs—using the search power of Google.

Content: Google has created a separate search engine to locate information posted to blogs. The interface will look familiar to anyone who is currently using the Google Web search engine. Google's blog search includes the familiar, standard search box with a link to the **Advanced Blog Search** appearing on the first page.

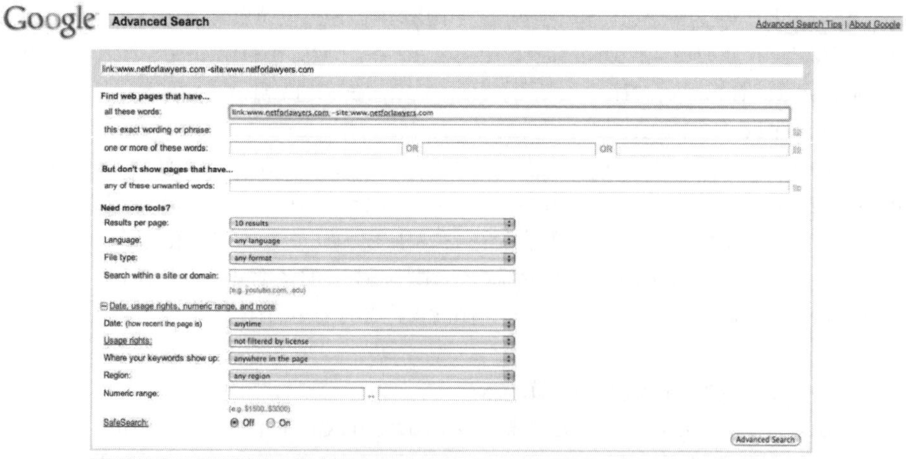

Figure 8-7. This is the Google "Advanced Blog Search" page where a more precise keyword or author search can be conducted. Google™ is a trademark of Google Technology Inc.

Type the keyword(s) for which you want to search into the search query box and click the **Search** button. The Advanced search will allow users to define more specific criteria for their searches, including: the **Language**, **Author**, **Dates**, and **Title** of the blog they are searching for. A **Safe Search** is available as well, which allows users to filter "explicit sexual content" from search results. The default display mode for results is **Sorted by Relevance**; users can also choose to **Sort by Date** by clicking on the **Sort by Date** link above the results list.

Our View: Blog posts are likely to turn up in a "regular" Google Web search, but limiting results just to blog sources can be useful. Blogs can be an excellent source of news (compiled from various sources by others), as well as commentary on hot topics, public opinion, or rumors regarding products or companies. Google does a good job of keeping up with the frequently updated blogs it indexes. In test searches, we have found blog posts in Blog Search results within 20 minutes of their being posted.

Tip: Google Blog Search also gives you the option of being updated automatically about new results for your search terms via an RSS feed or e-mail via the **Blogs Alert** or **RSS** on the left-hand side of the results page.

The Google Blog Search (like the Google Web search) allows users to limit their search with very specific criteria. For example, you can search for blog postings where your search term appears in the page's title by typing *intitle: search term* in the search box. All of the other standard Google Search limiters are also supported in Blog Search. These include:

- link:
- site:

Additionally, there are a number of search limiters that are exclusive to the Blog Search service:

- inblogtitle:
- inposttitle:
- inpostauthor:
- blogurl:

Technorati

http://technorati.com

Purpose: To locate current information contained in blogs.

Contents: Technorati is a blog-only search site. Searches conducted using the simple search box on the home page will return a list of results that point only to blog sources. Similar to "regular" Web search results lists, each result includes a link to the source and its Web address. Unlike other searches, the text that accompanies each entry is the first 30-50 words of the blog post. Additionally, each entry has an **Authority** rating that lists the number of different blogs that have linked to the source of that particular result in the last six months. The higher the **Authority** rating a source has (presumably) the higher its reliability. Clicking the **Authority** link displays the list of sites that have linked to the site it accompanies. You can then follow those links to read the entries that linked to the site you're considering. (Note that these **Authority** sites may not necessarily be linking to the blog post(s) you're interested in—just to some page on the site at which it is posted.)

Once an initial search results list is displayed, four drop-down menus appear in a green bar above the results to help you further filter the results. You can opt to **Search Posts** (the full text of the actual blog entries), **Search Blogs** (the names of blogs), **Tags Only** (the category identifiers/keywords assigned by the post's author), and other criteria.

The advanced search page offers the usual Boolean search options (**All of the words, At least one of the words, The exact phrase**, and **None of the words**). Additionally, you can choose to search **Blogs about** a specific topic or indicate **This blog URL** to limit results to a single blog source. Using the **URL Search** box you can enter any Web site address to see what blogs link to the site you've entered and click to read the blog posts that link to it.

Our View: We like the inclusion of the **Authority** figure and the ease with which we can see other sites that find the information from the source we're reading to be useful. While Technorati is often considered the frontrunner in blog-only search, in a number of test searches we have found blog results in a Google Blog Search that were not returned in the same Technorati search (and vice versa—to be fair). Perhaps, more importantly, we have found results sooner after they were posted by conducting a Google Blog Search than the same search at Technorati. This may be caused by a regular difference in how the two search engines update their indices, or it may be a temporary situation where Technorati's "search indexing hit a snag" as it did on April 2, 2009, when it's indexing was "behind 24 hours." (Technorati informed users of this delay in a post on its own blog at **http://technorati.com/weblog/2009/04/489.html**.)

Tip: If you only want to search blog posts you can go to **http://search.technorati.com**.

Justia's Blog Search

http://blawgsearch.justia.com

Purpose: To locate information in law-related blogs (aka blawgs).

Content: Justia's Blawg Search lists nearly 7,000 law-related blogs on topics ranging from **Administrative Law** to **Worker's Compensation**.

You can browse through the topics to locate a blog of interest to you, link to the **Most Popular** or **Recent Posts**, or you can use the **Search** box to keyword search through all of the blogs included in Justia's index simultaneously. You can also click on any of the **Recent Search Terms** to see the results of searches previously performed by others or you can click on one of the **Blawg Post Tags** to see all of the posts that authors have "tagged" with a particular subject heading.

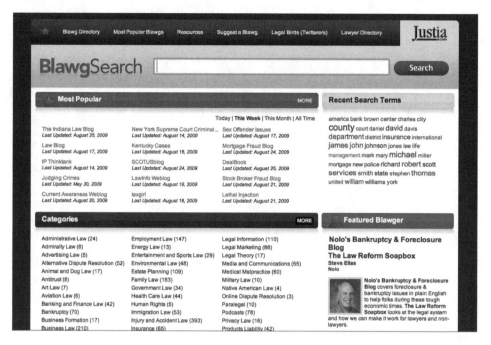

Figure 8-8. Justia's BlawgSearch offers easy access to nearly 7,000 law-related blogs (aka blawgs).

Our View: Justia's collection of law-related blogs is easy to navigate. We appreciate the variety of means by which to extract information from the collection. We think the addition of an Advanced Search page or some documentation would make the keyword search even more useful.

Tips: While there is no documentation for the search functions, you can use some familiar search operators such as enclosing your search terms in quotation marks to perform a phrase search. However, Justia's Blawg Search does not recognize the minus sign ("-") to exclude a word or phrase from results or the *OR* or *AND NOT* Boolean connectors.

The larger a subject heading is in the **Blawg Post Tags** section, the more blog posts you'll find on that subject.

Microblogging and Status Updating Sites

As the description implies, micoblogging sites limit users to short posts—very short. The most popular, Twitter (**http://www.twitter.com**), limits posts (known as "tweets") to just 140 characters. (This limit is based on the 160 character limit of cellular-phone-sent text messages.) Micro-blogging sites are even easier to update than the "traditional" blogs discussed above. These posts often address the answer to the question, "What are you doing?" and can include detailed information about the individual poster's daily activities. Increasingly, users are posting links to, and commentary about, news stories and current events. All of this information, freely shared by the poster, can help researchers develop a profile about the individual, as well as a schedule of their daily routines.

According to a February 2009 Pew Internet & American Life Project survey on Twitter and status updating sites, 11 percent of online American adults said they used a service like Twitter to share updates about themselves or to see the updates of others (*available at* **http://www.pewinternet.org/PPF/r/276/report_display.asp**).

The Pew study also found that adults who use other social networking sites are more likely to also use Twitter (and similar services) than those who don't. Nearly one quarter (23 percent) of [adult] social network users say they have ever Twittered or used a similar service. In comparison, just 4 percent of those who reported not using social networks have ever used Twitter or similar sites to update their status online.

Neilsen media research (Neilsen NetView February 2009 *available at* **http://tinyurl.com/dbzxgx**) indicates that 42 percent of Twitter's users range in age from 35-49 monthly. Neilsen also found that the majority of people (62 percent) visit Twitter from work. Additionally, Neilsen found the site's growth is beyond exponential—1382 percent from February 2008 and February 2009 growing to 3 million unique monthly visitors. Continuing this meteoric growth, Neilsen reported in its "Social Media Quick Take: May 2009" (*available at* **http://tinyurl.com/kqbgvz**) 1448 percent growth for Twitter in May 2009 over May 2008, boasting 18.2 million unique visitors.

In addition to Twitter, other popular microblogging sites are **Jaiku** (**http://www.jaiku.com**) and **Plurk** (**http://www.plurk.com**). Neither Jaiku nor Plurk have the search capabilities of Twitter.

Blogging. Texting. Tweeting. Coming to a Courtroom Near You?

Colorado Court Okays Texting, Computers, and Realtime Blogging During Trial

In early 2009, Boulder, CO Judge Lael Montgomery ruled that cell phones and computers would be allowed in the courtroom during a local man's child abuse trial.

Both sides argued against the real time blogging that had been allowed during the trial of the man's wife—which had been held previously. (She was found guilty and sentenced to 16 years in prison.) In published reports, defense attorney Paul McCormick went so far as to warn that the practice could, "contaminat[e] our jury in some way."

In approving access, a report quoted the judge as saying, "I think there are other manageable options and less restrictive options than shutting down the flow of information during the trial." The report also noted that she would "give clear instructions to the jury to refrain from reading or viewing any media accounts of the case," etc.

For more information about this case see The Boulder Daily Camera **http://tinyurl.com/96gzeh**.

Michigan Supreme Court Bans Electronic Communication for Jurors on Duty

In Michigan however, judges were concerned that jurors who had access to texting, blogging, tweeting, etc. were not focused on their task at hand. At a minimum, judges seemed concerned that jurors were merely distracted from their duties. At worse, jurors could share information regarding the cases they were hearing, or conduct their own online investigations of information presented at trial using their cell phones, PDA's, or other electronic communications devices.

Beginning September 1, 2009 the Michigan Supreme Court ordered sitting jurors to turn off their handheld electronic devices while in court. Once outside the courtroom, jurors can turn the devices back on—but they still must be careful not to send or receive any information about the cases they're hearing until after the trial concludes.

Twitter

http://www.twitter.com

Purpose: A microblogging site that allows people to post short updates, comments, etc.

Content: Millions of Twitter users post short updates, comments, etc. They are retrievable by user name or real name (if the user has used their real name when they registered their account), as well as being keyword searchable.

Clicking the **Search** link at the bottom of the home page accesses Twitter's simple search box. With this search form you can keyword search through the millions of individual posts. To create more sophisticated, specific searches, click the **Advanced Search** link underneath the search box.

Similar to Google's Advanced Search page, Twitter's **Advanced Search** page includes numerous Boolean search options to locate posts with **All of these words**, **Any of these words**, **None of these words**, and **This exact phrase**.

Further down the page are the **People** search options. Here you can limit results **From this person**, **To this person**, or **Referencing this person**. These are a bit misleading because you have to know the username that an individual posts under. You cannot search by their real name. (A number of people however, post under some form of their real names; one of the authors of this book posts as **MarkRosch**.)

Additionally, once you've located the username of a person you are interested in, you can click their username and see a list of all their most recent posts—if they haven't "protected their updates." (In many cases, we have been able to browse through a user's entire list of posts dating back nearly two years.)

Our View: Twitter posts are another prime example of our admonition not to underestimate the type or volume of information that people willingly post about themselves online. Since these tweets are intended for a limited audience of friends, or other online followers, this is especially ture. However, if the information is posted on a non-password protected Web page (as most Twitter accounts are), the information is available to anyone who knows how to find it.

We would like to see a first name and last name search option.

Tip: See **http://search.twitter.com/operators** for a list of advanced search instructions you can type into the simple search box. Note that all of these can be accomplished via the **Advanced Search** page.

Note too that users have the ability to **Protect my updates** that gives them the power to shield their Twitter posts from public view (as mentioned in the *Content* section above).

*CHAPTER*NINE

Using Genealogy Sites as Investigative Tools

How many times have you tried to get information from your bank or a credit card company and the first security question they ask is, "What's your mother's maiden name?" In Operation Detect Pretext (see Chapter 15), it's likely that the inquiring female fiancé provided her fiance's mother's maiden name to the information broker, but it's also possible to obtain this type of information from a family tree, many of which are published freely on the Internet.

Family Trees

RootsWeb

http://worldconnect.rootsweb.com

Purpose:	Primarily for genealogy research, but the family trees may be useful for finding relatives of missing witnesses, missing heirs, and so on, who may be willing to assist you in finding the missing person. Searching through family trees by a woman's maiden name may uncover whether a subject now uses a married name. The search can then be redirected using the married name.
Content:	There are nearly 600 million names on file in the Family Tree database. For a more targeted search, use the Advanced Search at **http://wc.rootsweb.ancestry.com/**

Figure 9-1. The Advanced Search menu of RootsWeb's Family Tree database offers numerous fields by which you can search the nearly 600 million names it contains.

cgi-bin/igm.cgi. You can narrow your search by: (1) selecting **Exact** if you are certain of the surname's spelling or selecting **Metaphone** or **Soundex** if uncertain of the spelling; (2) adding a **Birth** or **Death Place;** (3) adding a **Birth** or **Death Year;** or (4)adding a **Marriage Place** or **Year.** For detailed instructions on other ways to narrow your search, see **http://helpdesk .rootsweb.com/FAQ/wcsearch1.html**.

Our View: You'll learn more than you can imagine. Some family trees include, along with family members' names, dates of births, deaths, marriages, links to the family's home page, with pictures and contact information. During our search for Jordan Sanders, we even found pictures of his ancestor's headstone and a relative's will.

Tip: Check for your own family tree in case your third cousin twice removed put one up—it has more information than you want publicized.

War Story: A Random Google Search, a Family Tree Result, and a Social Networking Profile Find a Missing Person

In a search for a missing Illinois attorney, we searched by first name/ last name through the Illinois Attorney Registration and Disciplinary

Commission (ARDC) database (**http://www.iardc.org/lawyersearch.asp**), but found nothing. We dropped the attorney's first name in our ARDC search, but still found nothing. The husband was a former Illinois state court trial judge; so, we also tried a first name/last name search of ARDC for him (he had a different last name than his wife). We ruled out dropping the judge's last name because it was too common and we were so sure of his first name. We assumed they weren't listed because they were both retired. We knew the couple when they lived in Illinois and last heard they were living in Ruidoso, New Mexico. We also knew they had a daughter. One last clue was that the wife was originally from Oklahoma. We had no luck using pay investigative databases.

A simple Google search pointed to an article about the judge's retirement. The article included his first, middle, and last name and that is how we learned that we had been searching for him by an incorrect first name. Unknown to us, he used his middle name as his first name, which is how we were introduced to him years ago. That's why most of our searches had been fruitless. Returning to the ARDC database, we entered the judge's correct first name and last name and found a result, but it did not include any contact information.

We decided to search Ancestry for a family tree in an attempt to find names of family members. Perhaps those family members' contact information would be easier to locate than the attorney and judge. Maybe they'd be willing to lead us to the attorney. While we didn't find a family tree at Ancestry, we did come upon a family tree listing in our Google results, which included the judge's name, his wife's name, and their daughter's name (with middle names included for all). That's when we realized we had been spelling the attorney's last name incorrectly and that's when we decided to try a different tactic—to search for the attorney through her daughter.

We knew their daughter was probably in high school or college; so, we ran her name through Facebook and MySpace and found what looked like matches at both. Her MySpace profile listed her by her first and middle name only, but we read the MySpace entry in the Social Networking Chapter to learn how we found her by searching her first and last name. At MySpace, we learned the daughter had graduated from Ruidoso High School (where we knew they had once lived), was enrolled at Tulane University, and her current hometown was Okalahoma City (where we knew her mother was originally from). The Facebook search results showed 27 people with the same name, but only one listed Oklahoma City. Both profiles provided pictures of the daughter and they both looked like the attorney we were searching for.

Through Facebook, we emailed the daughter, who promptly forwarded our e-mail to her mother, who promptly e-mailed back with her phone number. Without the random Google searches and the family tree result, we're not sure we ever would have found our missing attorney. Of course, this only works so easily when the person wants to be found. If the attorney was purposely evading us, at least we now had enough clues to narrow our search to Oklahoma City.

Genealogy Library and Online Databases

Godfrey Memorial Library

http://www.godfrey.org/   **$**

Purpose:	Godfrey Memorial Library is located in Middleton, Connecticut, and specializes in genealogical materials. Its Godfrey.org Web site offers users remote access to its online databases 24/7.
Content:	The library's mission has been to collect genealogical materials, with the majority of its information from pre-1900. Its list of titles consists of a number of reference books, genealogies, and indexes, including the 226-volume *American Genealogical-Biographical Index* (*AGBI*)— the largest reference set ever published.

For free, you can search the library's catalog by selecting the **Search** tab on Godfrey.org's home page and clicking on the **Online Catalogue** link. Notice that there is an **Advanced Search** option on the basic search page. If you are in need of a more in-depth search, the **Godfrey Scholar Program** offers remote access to Godfrey's various pay databases. There are four subscription levels, ranging from $35 to $110 (**http://www.godfrey.org/ subscribe.html**). The $110 subscription also includes access to NewspaperArchives.com and World Vital Records U.S. Collection. Another research option is to request that the library conduct your search for you. They can perform a "Quick Search" (**http://www.god frey.org/search.html**), where they will only spend 30 minutes on each search and charge $10 per name, or they can perform more in-depth research (**http://www .godfrey.org/agbiform.pdf**), where the cost will vary depending on the results.

Our View: Godfrey.org is a very specific library database, and the fact that we can now access it online is pretty phenomenal.

Tip: Whenever she needs to work on a quiet title action, Tamara Thompson, a private investigator from Oakland, California, makes use of Godfrey.org by using its older genealogical and census records.

State Genealogy Records Metasite

USGenWeb Project

http://www.usgenweb.org/

Purpose: USGenWeb.org is a genealogical Web site that provides links to all the free state genealogy Web sites. The state sites then link to individual counties' free genealogy Web sites in each state. This site could be useful to lawyers who are searching for a missing person, verifying a death, or researching offspring in a quiet title action.

Content: USGenWeb.org is completely volunteer-driven, and it is the responsibility of the individual volunteer to maintain each site. Thus, each state and county Web site

Figure 9-2. The USGenWeb Project is a volunteer-run organization whose Web site catalogs hundreds of genealogy-related resources by state. Genealogical resources can be helpful for investigative and background research.

varies to a certain degree. Many states also have different ongoing projects as diverse as reuniting families with lost photos, or transcribing Civil War regiments. All of the counties provide links to access the archives, the state's home page, and to post queries.

On the left-hand side of the home page, there is a list of the fifty states. Clicking on California to start a search, we found ourselves on the CAGenWeb home page. Scrolling down to the bottom of the page, we found the following nine options: **Counties Table; Counties Map; Archives; Mailing List; California Research Help; CAGenWeb Supporters; About CAGenWeb Project; History of California;** and **Search CAGen-Web.**

To search for documents within the counties of California, click on **Search CAGenWeb.** The traditional search box will appear. You may choose to match **ANY** or **ALL** of the search terms in the box, and there is a pull-down menu of the counties available to the right. (If you have any trouble with the search, scroll down and there are helpful directions to aid the user. Once again, this help section may not be found on all Web sites since different volunteer workers create the sites.) We typed the name *Pike*, chose to match **ALL** the search terms, and pulled Los Angeles County from the menu. We received six documents from cemetery records and a 1923 Society Blue Book to links to death records.

Our View: USGenWeb is an extremely useful start for any investigative research you might be conducting. For instance, because there are links to every state and county, the user would be assisted in a search for a missing person or for an individual's death records. And the states do vary tremendously. We took a peek at Arkansas—their home page offered twice the links that California did.

CHAPTER**TEN**

Searching Through News and Magazine Articles to Find and Background People

Search Engines for News

Newspaper and magazine articles can be useful for finding and backgrounding people. Many articles are free online. For recent news articles, try Google News, Yahoo News, or AltaVista News. Even though you could use their general search for news, searching these discrete news databases allows you to quickly hone in on just current news. For older news, try Google News Archive, discussed later in this chapter.

Google News

http://news.google.com

Purpose: Search engine for news.

Content: This site uses Google's search and page-ranking technologies to gather stories from over 25,000 news sources around the world, ranging from the BBC, CNN, and the Boston Globe to press releases from selected companies. News stories displayed on the Google News home page or in News search results are updated continuously throughout the day. (On a recent visit to the site, the "freshest" story was only five minutes old.) Headlines and abstracts are prominently displayed on the main

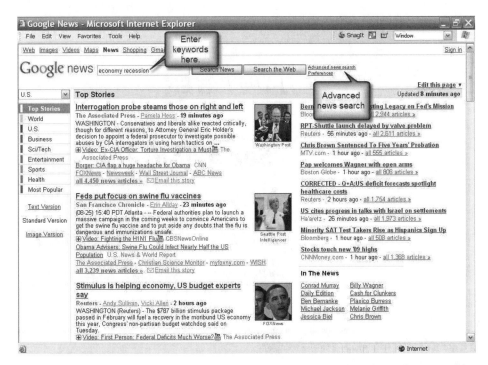

Figure 10-1. Search Google News to limit your search only to the past thirty days of news or to browse today's top stories. Google™ is a trademark of Google Technology Inc.

page under Top Stories. Users can also perform keyword searches for links to news stories on particular subjects. Returned results can include stories up to (approximately) thirty days old. There is also an **Advanced news search** (located on the top right-hand side of the page) to limit the search by **Date**, **News source**, **News source location**, **Location** (about a local area), in addition to the regular advanced Google Boolean and Proximity search menu.

Unfortunately, the **News Alerts** and **RSS** links have been removed from the left-hand column. The RSS feed, while still displayed, is at the bottom of the page and may now go unnoticed. These features can be used to keep up-to-date on any topic or person and will be discussed later in this chapter.

Our View: The search results page lists news in a variety of categories (including **Top Stories, World, U.S., Business, Entertainment,** and more) in a direc-

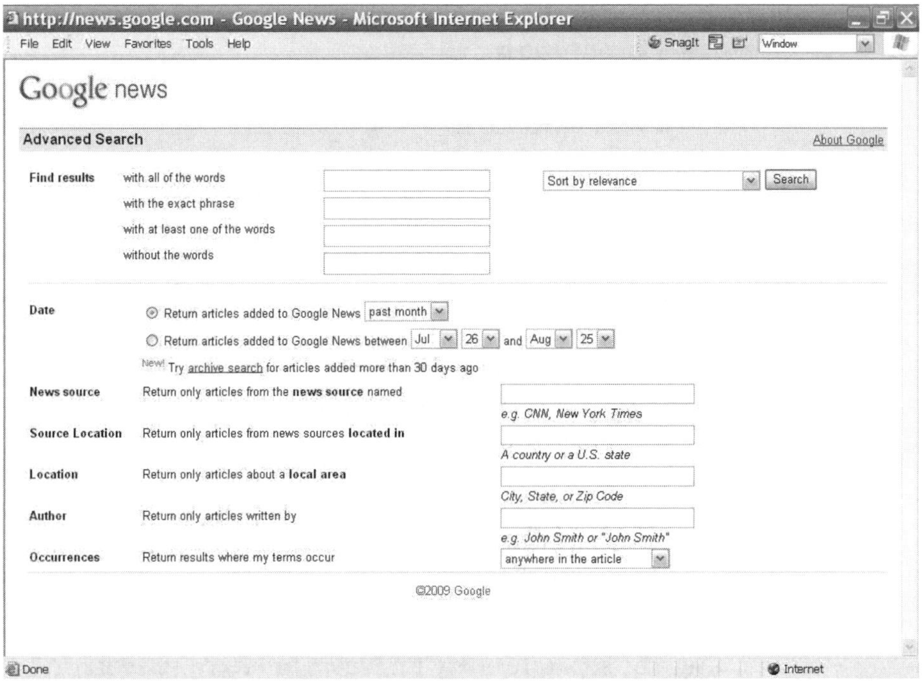

Figure 10-2. The Advanced search page also allows you to narrow your search by **Author** or even by **Occurrence** (to limit results only to where your keyword appears in the headline or in the body of the article). Google™ is a trademark of Google Technology Inc.

tory style. Within those categories, stories are grouped together by subject, with stories from multiple sources—covering the same news subject—in subgroups.

A recent search for *Somalia pirates* returned over 29,400 results. In Google's ordering of the stories by relevance, the first result linked to a story from Reuters that was thirty minutes old, while the second result from the Associated Press was a video clip of the president of a shipping company whose captain had just been rescued by the Navy (after having been taken hostage by Somalian pirates), indicating the up-to-date nature of the search results. Under the third result were related news stories from other publications around the world.

A sampling of other sources included:

- The BBC
- *Christian Science Monitor*
- CNN
- *Hindustan Times*

- *Miami Herald*
- *Jordan Times*
- *San Jose Mercury News*
- WPTV (Florida)

It is important to take note of a story's source, since Google may also include company press releases in its news search results, which may at times be biased or include puffery.

Tips: Use the site's **Sort by date** function (on the top right-hand side of the results page) to put the most current results at the top of the list.

Unfortunately, the links to **News archive search** on the top right-hand side of the Google News home page have been removed. Instead of recent stories, this database contains older stories, even back as far as 1910. See the separate entry for **News archive search** on page 125.

AltaVista News

http://www.altavista.com/news/default

Purpose: Search engine for news.

Content: The AltaVista News search includes millions of articles from thousands of sources, worldwide. Running the same *Somalia pirates* search that we did at Google News retrieved fewer results than Google did.

Our View: In addition to conducting standard keyword and phrase searches, you can limit your search with user-definable parameters in drop-down menus. You can select

- Dates ranging from **Today** or **Yesterday** to **Any-time** or you can enter a specific **Date Range**
- Topic category
- Geographical region

Tip:　　　　While there is no Advanced Search option in the AltaVista News search, it supports all search commands also used on its Web search. If you enter multiple words, AltaVista returns only articles that have all of the words.

- To exclude words, put a minus sign (-) in front of them
- Use quotation marks for phrase searches
- Use Boolean commands including *AND, OR, AND NOT, NEAR*
- To return results from a specific source, use the "host:" command to indicate its Web site. For example *host:latimes.com presidential election* will return results containing the words *presidential* and *election* found at the *Los Angeles Times* Web site.

News Metasites

There are several metasites that link to general newspapers and magazines, business newspapers and magazines, and wire services, with the Drudge Report (profiled below) being one of the most useful.

Drudge Report

http://www.drudgereport.com

Purpose:　　To search for news and information through various links to news organizations.

Content:　　The Drudge Report site offers a comprehensive set of links to major news organizations around the world. The site also includes a list of American columnists (listed alphabetically), Chinese, Japanese, and English language wire services, and even the *National Enquirer*.

Our View:　　While best known for the "shoot-from-the-hip" muckraking style of his own reporting, Webmaster Matt Drudge provides a good list of links to more established news organizations on this site. Along with the links comes Drudge's own (conservative) opinions on the news stories he chooses to highlight.

Tip: For links to many of the same news resources, and thousands of other resources in dozens of other categories, see the Refdesk.com site (discussed in Chapter 11, Finding and Backgrounding Expert Witnesses) maintained by Matt Drudge's father, Robert Drudge.

Free Remote Access to News and Magazine Databases Via Public Library Web Sites

Many public libraries offer their patrons free remote access to various full text searchable databases, such as Newsbank with its full text content of the *Los Angeles Times, Christian Science Monitor, USA Today, Orange County Register, Riverside Press-Enterprise, San Diego Union-Tribune,* and *San Francisco Chronicle.* All a patron needs is a library card. The National Newspaper Index, offered remotely by some libraries, provides access to an index of the *New York Times,* the *Wall Street Journal,* the *Christian Science Monitor,* as well as to news stories written by the staff writers of the *Los Angeles Times* and the *Washington Post.* Local libraries may also offer other local and regional databases that provide full text searchable archives of various papers. In addition, many libraries offer free remote access to various directories, encyclopedias, and magazines, all of which can be excellent sources for investigative research. For more information on how to access your public library's databases remotely, see Chapter 12, Using Expensive Pay Databases for Free.

Tracking People (or Other Information) Automatically By Setting Up Alerts

Are you spending money for a pay database to track or set up alerts about a specific company, individual, case, event, or product? Since there may be information unique to the Web (such as blogs, groups, video, and recent news), you might also want to track the same data on free sites that you're currently tracking on a pay site. Or you may be able to discontinue the pay alert altogether if you can locate the same service on the Web for free. For example, some legislatures and some courts allow you to sign up for an e-mail alert every time there is any action affecting a pending bill or taken in a case. Just visit the site and see if they offer the service, then specify what to track (such as "senate bill 213" or "docket number 2002-98"). If you're paying for an alert like this, consider canceling it. Or, you might want to track a specific page on a Web site, such as a client's company site or the opposition's company site. You decide how often you want to be alerted to changes. You also decide whether you want an e-mail alert or whether you want to visit the tracking service and check for changes at your convenience. The best known free alert service is Google Alerts. Additionally, Chris Sherman of SearchEngineWatch (**http://www.searchengine watch.com**) recommends the following alert services:

- WebSite-Watcher (**http://www.aignes.com**): It's powerful and highlights all changes, but is desktop-based. A free thirty-day trial is offered. Thereafter, the cost is $38.25 for personal use and $126.42 for corporate use.
- WatchThatPage (**http://www.watchthatpage.com**): It's Web-based, so you can access it from anywhere and it's free to individuals. (It requires registration.)
- InfoMinder (**http://www.infominder.com**): It highlights changes, is Web-based, and offers a variety of page-mining options at a variety of prices. The "Pro" version of the service tracks the pages you indicate once per day and offers five volumes of service, tracking from twenty pages ($9/year) to one thousand pages ($179/year). The "Premium" version tracks up to four times per day tracking from one hundred pages ($65/year) to one thousand pages ($499/year). An in-house, server edition is also available that can monitor higher volumes of Web pages as often as once per hour.

Setting Up Alerts

Google Alerts

http://www.google.com/alerts

Purpose: Google Alerts sends you up-to-the-minute e-mail Alerts so you can monitor the Internet (using keywords you specify, such as a person's name or a topic), via Google's search engine **Web**, **News**, **Groups**, **Blogs or Video** databases or you can run a **Comprehensive** search.

Content: To create a **Google Alert** you need to enter your keywords into the first box and then answer three simple questions: (1) the type of alert you would like (**Web**, **News**, **Video**, **Blogs**, **Groups**, or **Comprehensive**); (2) how often you would like the alerts e-mailed (daily, weekly, or as they occur); and (3) your e-mail address.

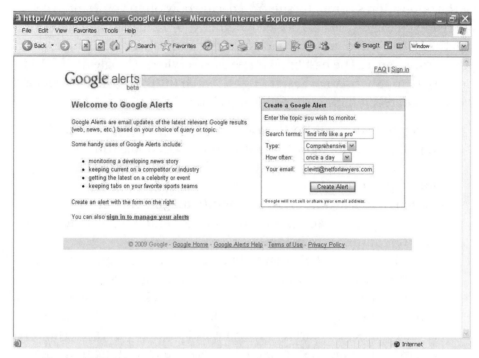

Figure 10-3. We set up an alert to track any mention of this book by entering the book title as a phrase (*find info like a pro*) and choosing **Comprehensive**. Consider setting up alerts with your name, your firm's name, or a client's name. Google™ is a trademark of Google Technology Inc.

On the bottom left of this same page, Google asks if you would like to manage your Alerts. If you click on this link, Google will then require you to sign up and register with an e-mail address and password. The benefit of this process is that every time you log on to Google Alerts you can view your list of Alerts that you have created, as well as edit or delete them easily. For example, we originally created a **Web** Alert for the topic Iraq that we wanted sent to us daily. Later, it was simple to revise the Alert to add **News** to have the Alert also monitor Google's **News** database, in addition to the **Web**. We also revised the Alert to request the Alert be sent as it happens, instead of just daily.

If you decide to forgo this option, you will not be able to edit your search queries at all. You will have to delete the Alert entirely (by clicking on a link at the bottom of an Alert e-mail) and then create a brand new Alert to your new specifications.

Our View: Google has created a simple way to keep you in touch with the information you need, when you need it. When we signed up for the Iraq **News** Alert, our first e-mail arrived within two hours. Granted the topic was pretty newsworthy, but Google Alerts still deserves kudos for their speedy entry of our information and queries.

Although the Alerts home page technically says it is still in its Beta stage, that doesn't mean it hasn't been around for a while. Google seems to keep their services in Beta mode longer than most other companies, apparently so they can continue to add and "play" with their products. We found this to be a really good service, and one of the few free ones of this type on the Internet.

Tip: For those who can't wait to receive their automatic alerts, another neat option of the **Manage** page allows you to click on your Alert to run your search on the spot.

Locating Historical Information

Google recently extended the date range of its news search with the launch of the **Google News Archive Search** (**http://news.google.com/archivesearch**).

Google News Archive Search

http://news.google.com/archivesearch

 (some articles are free)

 (some articles and all cases from Loislaw, Versuslaw, and Fastcase have a fee attached)

Purpose: Google states that the purpose of the News Archive is to, "[s]earch and explore historical archives" and to "[a]utomatically create timelines which show selected results from relevant time periods.

Content: The News Archive retrieves major newspaper and magazine articles and news archives back to 1910 and earlier,

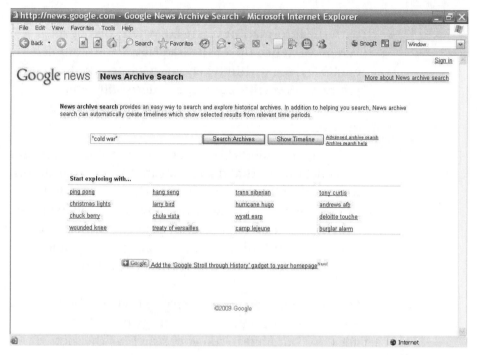

Figure 10-4. To search older stories, such as stories about the Cold War, search Google's News Archives. Google™ is a trademark of Google Technology Inc.

primarily from U.S. sources (but also from international sources for more recent time periods). While access to many of the articles is free, the price to access other articles varies from source to source. The News Archive also indexes a variety of case law databases (Loislaw, Versuslaw, and Fastcase) and links to the databases where researchers must pay (with a credit card) to retrieve full text cases. (Google states that, "We do not receive payment when users purchase articles.") The Google News Archive can be searched by entering keywords into the search box and selecting either **Search Archives** or **Show Timeline**. The **Search Archives** results are displayed by relevancy or date (from **Last Hour** to **All Dates**) while the **Show Timeline** results are shown in reverse chronological order. Google is partnering with the copyright holders of various newspapers to scan newspapers that have not yet been digitized.

Our View: We're pleased to see historical information being added to the Internet. The **Advanced News Archive Search** (**http://news.google.com/archivesearch/advanced_ search**) is useful to limit your search by **Date**, **Language**, **Source**, **Price**, and **View** (the **View** feature allows one to select **Search Articles, Show full timeline**, or **Show news timeline**).

Tips: Before paying for an article, check your library to see if it's available for free when you access the library's remote databases. (See Chapter 12, Using Expensive Pay Databases for Free, to learn more about free remote library databases.) Also, before paying for a case, check your state bar association to see if they offer free case

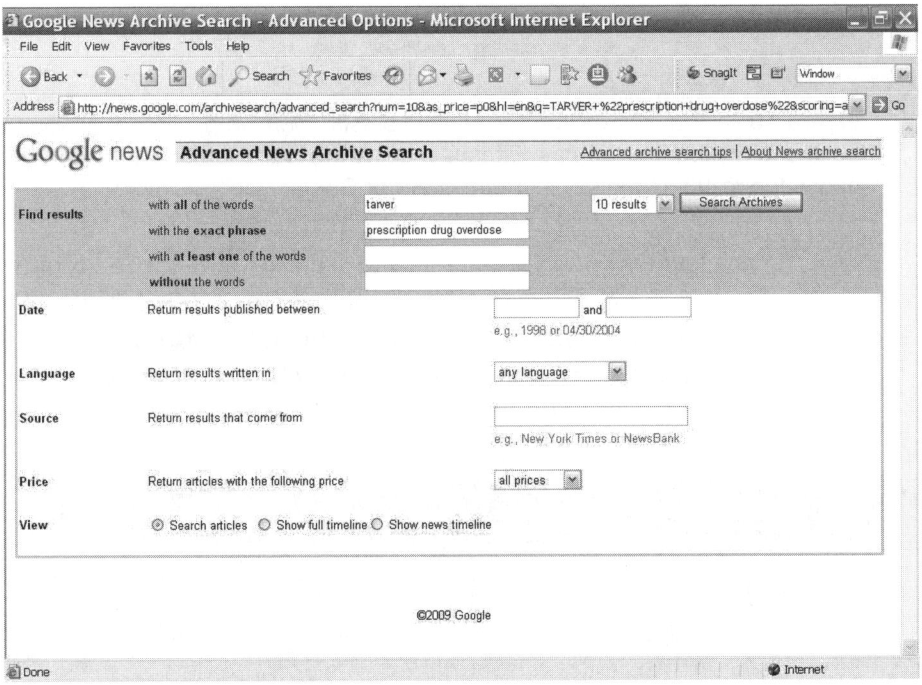

Figure 10-5. You can even search for case law at Google's News Archive. Using the Advanced Search menu, we entered the case name *Tarver* into the **with all the words** search box and entered the phrase *prescription drug overdose* into the **with the exact phrase** search box. Google™ is a trademark of Google Technology Inc.

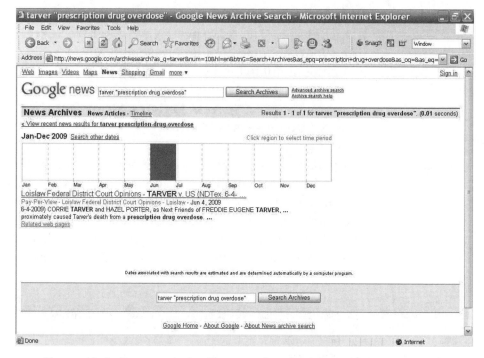

Figure 10-6. Our search for *Tarver* and *prescription drug overdose* brought back one result from the pay database, Loislaw. Notice the timeline displayed above the result. Google™ is a trademark of Google Technology Inc.

law through Casemaker or Fastcase, or visit the myriad of free case law databases such as the Public Library of Law (at **http://www.plol.org**), Justia (at **http://www.justia.com**), LexisONE (at **http://www.lexisone.com**), or FindLaw (at **http://www.findlaw.com**).

News Flash! Free Case Law at Google Scholar

On November 17, 2009, Google launched a database of free federal and state case law and legal journal articles at its Google Scholar page (**http://scholar.google.com**). For more details, see **http://www.netforlawyers.com/content/google-makes-free-caselaw-search-available-scholar**. For ease of searching, we recommend using the advanced search at **http://scholar.google.com/advanced_scholar_search?hl=en&as_sdt=2000**.

*CHAPTER*ELEVEN

Finding and Backgrounding Expert Witnesses

There are plenty of low-tech traditional ways to find experts, such as telephoning colleagues or one of the numerous brokerages (not unlike Hollywood talent agencies) that represent experts. These companies can pump résumés and curriculum vitaes (CVs) through your e-mail or fax machine to satisfy every esoteric expert need you can think of. They also often charge fees in advance of providing any expertise. You'll find scads of ads for these companies, as well as for individual experts in the back pages of most legal periodicals, especially those targeted at trial lawyers. Usually, these companies charge a representation fee in addition to the fee you'll pay to the expert. Another low-tech way of searching is to look through an expert witness directory (in print). This is time consuming and often means a trip to a library. Also, the print directory's arrangement is not always helpful. If you want to search for an expert by both location and expertise, but the directory is only arranged by expertise, or only by location, or only by expert's name, you'll be out of luck.

The Internet, however, has expedited the traditional searching for expert witnesses by providing easy and free access to so many resources, from online expert witness directories to online library catalogs, periodical indexes, and databases that contain full text articles (to satisfy your search for articles or books relevant to the subject or authored by the expert).

The Internet also lends itself to creative ways to find experts (and to help you learn enough about the subject matter and the expert to be able to make an informed decision about the qualifications of a potential expert). These creative ways vary from taking advantage of the professional association community, to reviewing jury verdicts, to finding mailing-list postings and the like, to searching through the expert's own site. Many of the traditional searches and creative searches can be done on the Web and usually for free.

War Story: Enhanced Collaboration

Insurance defense lawyer Jim Walter relates this collaborative use he made of a free online expert witness directory, JurisPro (see page 138 for a detailed discussion):

> In one case, we needed to find an expert witness who could testify regarding premises liability issues. From the JurisPro Web site, I downloaded the experts' full curriculum vitae, reviewed the experts' background as a witness, (including the number of times they have testified, and whether it was for the plaintiff or defense), and read their articles that discussed their expertise. Most impressively, I was able to get an idea how the various experts *presented* themselves—by viewing their photos and hearing them speak through streaming audio on the site. I then got on the phone with the insurance adjustor and we simultaneously reviewed the qualifications of potential experts online on JurisPro. JurisPro allowed my firm and the company to agree to hire an expert witness in one telephone call. We did not have to fax résumés back and forth, play "phone tag" for several hours or days on potential hires, or have an adjustor simply rely on my judgment in hiring a witness. The hiring process was easy and fast, allowing both of us to make a decision swiftly and move on to other cases.

Checklist for Finding and Verifying Experts

  ❑   1.   Develop a working knowledge of the expertise by reading books and articles. This can also lead you to the experts in the field or help verify credentials for the experts you already have.

  ❑   2.   Review the expert's writings.

  ❑   3.   Search free expert witness directories.

  ❑   4.   Use online directories to find trade or professional associations.

  ❑   5.   Find the expert's conference presentations.

  ❑   6.   Join an online community to find experts' postings or to learn about the topic.

  ❑   7.   Review the expert's own Web site.

❑   8. Determine if the expert has ever been disciplined.

❑   9. Find experts via jury verdict reporter databases.

❑ 10. Find the expert's deposition testimony.

❑ 11. Find briefs and cases that refer to the expert.

❑ 12. Locate academic experts through university sites.

❑ 13. Find government experts through government reports.

❑ 14. Use pay referral sites.

Checklist Item 1: Develop a Working Knowledge of the Expertise by Reading Books and Articles

Before seeking an expert, it's useful to first familiarize yourself with the area of expertise by reading an article or two, or scanning a book on the topic. Searching a library's catalog (via the Internet, of course) by subject can lead you to some of the literature in that area of expertise. A comprehensive listing of public library Web sites can be found at Libweb (**http://lists.webjunction.org/libweb/**). As you browse through the book titles, you may spot certain authors who have written several books on that specialty and this may assist you in identifying some of the top experts in the field to contact. In addition to sifting through online card catalogs for books, you should also conduct an online search for articles; articles tend to be more current than books and are certainly easier to digest than a lengthy book. This search for books and articles can also assist you in finding materials authored by an expert you have already been referred to.

Online Library Catalogs

Libweb

http://lists.webjunction.org/libweb/

Purpose: To find library URLs to search their online catalogs.

Content: Use Libweb to link to 7700 library home pages of all types in 146 countries by browsing by location or type of library, or by keyword searching using the library name, a location, a type of library, or a combination of these. From the library's home page, link to the catalog and search by author, subject, or title.

Our View: It's useful to begin with your own public library in case you want to borrow the book or have them arrange an interlibrary loan for you.

Tips: However you do a thorough search, don't overlook the mother of online library catalogs—the Library of Congress (**http://catalog.loc.gov**). Finally, don't discount online bookstore catalogs such as Amazon (**http://www.amazon.com**) or Barnes & Noble (**http://www.barnesandnoble.com**) to find leading authors in a subject area. Results at those retail sites may include a synopsis, the author's name, Table of Contents, a note from the publisher about the work, and, in many cases, reviews of the book.

Has the Expert Been Published?

Although someone may have provided you with a name of an expert, it's your job to independently verify the expert's expertise. One way to do this is to discover if the expert has been published in his or her area of expertise. You will need to uncover the expert's authored materials (and not by just by reading the materials featured on the expert's own Web site). Reading authored material will also show you the expert's opinions and help you to discover any inconsistencies. Uncovering the opposition's expert's authored materials is also in order—for the very same reasons. This research will assist you to better prepare for direct or cross-examination.

Checklist Item 2: Review the Expert's Writings

You cannot depend on experts to have posted all of their published works on their Web sites, and therefore an independent literature search is in order. To conduct a nationwide search of newspaper or periodical articles written by (or about) your expert, pay databases such as Lexis, Westlaw, or Ingenta Connect (**http://www.ingentaconnect.com**) are best, especially for scholarly articles. Ingenta Connect is useful for those who do not have a subscription to Lexis or Westlaw because you can search, at no cost, the summaries of more than 24 million articles from over 31,000 publications and purchase the full text online. To obtain articles from consumer magazine articles, at no cost, use FindArticles.com, where you can search a database of full text articles from hundreds of magazines and journals dating back to 1998. (Articles from other periodicals are also available for a fee.) For more specialized topics, such as toxic mold and stachybotrys, a search through medical literature at the government's National Library of Medicine (NLM) gateway site is in order (**http://gateway.nlm.nih.gov/gw/Cmd**).

Online Periodical Indexes and Full Text Articles

Google Scholar

http://scholar.google.com/

Purpose: To locate articles written by expert witnesses (and others).

Content: The Google Scholar search applies the familiar Google search interface and ranking system to scholarly literature. Its search returns results only from peer-reviewed papers, theses, books, abstracts, and articles. These sources come from a variety of academic publishers, professional societies, preprint repositories, universities, and other scholarly organizations.

Figure 11-1. The Google Scholar search retrieves results from academic publishers, professional societies, preprint repositories, universities, and other scholarly organizations. Secondary results from the same source (marked by a green triangle) can link to a review of the book noted in the main result or even a free copy of the article referenced. Google™ is a trademark of Google Technology Inc.

To read the full text of any referenced search result you will usually have to purchase access to it from the Web site that hosts the article, or use the citation information provided in the search result to locate a copy from a library or other "real-world" source. Some results are accompanied by a green triangle that points to a secondary link for a particular search result, which might be a review of a book listed in the main search results (but not the book itself) or it might be a link to a copy of the full text article listed in the main search results.

The **Library Search** link that accompanies many results makes locating a library that has a copy of that particular source a bit easier. The link retrieves a list of libraries that own a copy of the book from the online library catalogs of WorldCat. The **Related Articles** link returns a list of other articles related to the topic you selected.

Our View: Google Scholar is an excellent finding tool for the writings of experts and others. It would be even more useful if we could click directly to the full text of those writings, but this is an example that not everything is available for free on the Internet.

It's also useful that many results include a link labeled **Cited by XXX** where the **XXX** indicates the number of other publications the Google Scholar search is aware of that have cited back to that particular article. Clicking the **Cited by XXX** link displays the list of those articles.

The **Related Articles** link can be useful for locating articles from different experts on the same topic.

Tip: Use the **Advanced Scholar Search** (**http://scholar .google.com/advanced_scholar_search**) to search for articles by author's name, to limit results to a particular publication, or to create other sophisticated searches.

What an Expert Writes Can and Will Be Used Against Them

Tom Baker, a Kansas City lawyer, represented a manufacturer in a product liability trial in which the plaintiff claimed that the defendant's riding lawnmower was defectively designed.

When the plaintiff named an expert who was an editor for a magazine that rated the safety and efficiency of products, I ran an Internet search of the expert's articles on riding lawnmowers and discovered an article written several years earlier praising the exact same design. Needless to say, the page containing the praise and a photo of the "safe" riding mower design was enlarged to "billboard size" for the jury to follow during cross-examination. Moral to the story: Run an Internet search of your own expert—the other side will.

FindArticles

http://www.FindArticles.com **$**

Purpose: To conduct a literature search for the articles written by (or about) an expert to ascertain their expertise and their opinions; to obtain basic knowledge about the subject before hiring an expert.

Content: FindArticles.com is a database of published articles that can be searched for free. It is continually updated, and contains millions of articles dating back to at least 1984 from thousands of trade publications covering major industry sectors and companies.

Our View: Being able to read and print the full text of an article at no cost is very useful, especially if you need an overview of a topic or need to find an expert. Many of the articles contain quotes by experts.

Ingenta

To search: (to view and print full text)

http://www.ingentaconnect.com

Purpose: To conduct a literature search for the articles written by (or about) an expert to ascertain expertise and opinions; to obtain basic knowledge about the subject before hiring an expert.

Content: Search over 25 million articles from more than 31,000 academic and professional publications and read the abstracts—for free.

Our View: Being able to read abstracts and purchase the full text of the articles online without having to figure out which library may carry a specified article is very useful when time is of the essence. If time is not important, you might be able to locate the article for free at a local library because Ingenta Connect provides the complete citation.

Tips: Be sure to click on **Advanced Search** to refine or narrow your search. You can e-mail the first two hundred results on your list to someone so they can choose the articles they want, download your results list as a text file, or bookmark your results to return to them with a single click.

Check the Library

Before paying for an article, check your library's online databases to see if the full text of the article is offered there for free (see Chapter 12, Using Expensive Pay Databases for Free). Also, run the article title through a search engine in case it has been posted free on someone's Web site (such as the author's).

If you need to only access an individual newspaper or magazine, the Internet is a perfect source. For links to thousands of publications from around the world, see sites such as CEOExpress (**http://www.ceo express.com**).

Many trade associations publish online newsletters, and some provide either full text articles or extracts. For example, the Accident Reconstruction (ARC) Network (**http://www.accidentreconstruction.com**), a professional organization for those in the accident reconstruction industry, has a monthly newsletter with experts' articles available for free at its site. This site also has an active discussion forum that includes opinions posted by various accident reconstructionists, as well as a searchable directory of experts in this field.

Use Dictionaries and Encyclopedias

Sometimes you just need a brief introduction to a subject area and an encyclopedia article or dictionary will do the trick instead of a book or journal article. Check out Refdesk.com for links to medical and drug dictionaries, technology encyclopedias, and more (**http://www.refdesk.com**). There's even an **Ask an Expert** section (found by scrolling down the right-hand column).

War Story: Finding an Expert—Fast

Ben Wright (Ben_Wright@compuserve.com) is a lawyer in Dallas, Texas, and an expert on digital signatures and electronic contracts. He described how Julian Ding, a lawyer in Malaysia, arranged for his expert services.

Julian Ding needed to find an electronic commerce expert—fast. Julian is a partner in Zaid Ibrahim & Co., a large law firm in Malaysia, a developing country determined to leapfrog itself into leadership on the information highway. The Malaysian Parliament was in the process of adopting digital signature legislation, and Julian's firm wanted to convene a public seminar to examine the topic. To add the requisite cachet, the firm invited the Minister of Energy, Telecommunications and Post to open the seminar.

Unfortunately, the Minister could only confirm the invitation rather late due to his busy schedule. That left Julian in a bind. He was forced to organize the seminar in thirty days, and he needed to find, among other experts, a foreign lawyer having special experience with digital signatures. So, he turned to Yahoo! (**http://www.yahoo.com**) and searched for "digital signature," which yielded the Web page for Ben Wright's book, *The Law of Electronic Commerce* (**http://www.aspenpublishers.com/Product.asp? catalog_name=Aspen&product_id=0735516480**). Julian dashed off an e-mail invitation to Ben, and the two soon negotiated an arrangement for Ben to be present at the event.

Finding an Expert's Book

Had Ding searched Barnesandnoble.com or Amazon.com for the keywords *electronic* and *commerce and law*, Wright's book would have been included in the results list along with the works of other experts on the topic. Tip: to find the most recent books, sort results by date. If Wright had not been available to present at the conference, Ding might have had better luck inviting one of the other author/experts.

Checklist Item 3: Search Free Expert Witness Directories

There are many expert directories on the Internet. While most of them charge experts to be listed, they provide free search access to everyone. All the directories are searchable by expertise, while many are also searchable by expert name, geographic location, and a few other methods. The directories that offer geographic searching are useful, especially when a lawyer wants to hold down travel expenses by finding a local expert. The directory listings vary from the very brief to the very detailed.

Lawyer Jim Robinson founded the JurisPro Expert Witness Directory (**http://www.JurisPro.com**) after experiencing frustration over trying to locate expert witnesses for his cases. Robinson noted:

> There are a lot of "white page telephone" types of expert witness directories that just include an expert's contact information, with very little information about their background. Attorneys rely on experts to make them look good to the client; therefore, attorneys want to be as comfortable with that expert as possible. We have not met an attorney yet who said they want to know *less* about the expert they were going to hire. We designed the features of JurisPro from an

attorney's point of view. Attorneys want to know the expert's full range of experience within their field of expertise, and their background as an expert witness. They want to be able to read the expert's actual résumé (not just some blurb), and know how the expert presents him or herself. They also wanted to be able to find out this information from a place that was free and convenient to use. With this in mind, we set up JurisPro as a free, content-based directory for finding and researching expert witnesses.

Free Expert Witness Directories, Searchable by Keyword, Name, and Location

Jurispro

http://www.jurispro.com

Purpose: To find experts, view their pictures, listen to their audio, and read their CVs and articles.

Content: Search for an expert witness by name or area of expertise, or by selecting from a list of expert categories. As each expert is displayed, you will first see a narrative summary

Figure 11-2. JurisPro provides lawyers with an invaluable tool by allowing them to see the experts' pictures and listen to their audio clips.

of the expert's background, contact information, photo, and an audio clip to listen to his or her voice. Then, select any of these tabs for more data: **Background** (in the form of questions and answers), **CV**, **Publications**, **References**, **Web Page**, and **E-mail**.

Our View: A jury survey found that jurors sided with one expert over another because one expert more clearly communicated her expertise. JurisPro provides lawyers with an invaluable tool in this regard by allowing them to see the experts' pictures and listen to their audio clips. If it sounds like the expert can clearly communicate his expertise on the audio clip, this can help lawyers decide whether to even bother phoning the expert in the first place.

Tip: Once you pull up a list of results searching by expertise, you can further refine the search by selecting a state.

Experts

http://www.experts.com

Purpose: To find experts and consultants.

Content: Search by clicking on the **search** tab at the top and then search by **Keywords**, **Category**, **Name**, **Company**, **Location**, or a combination. You can also browse by clicking on the **directory** tab and then choosing a category (some will have subcategories). To refine the directory search, choose **Categories** or **Experts** from the pull-down menu on the Directory page, then type in a keyword and click on one of the directory categories. Results will display a summary of the expert's background and a link to the expert's e-mail and Web site. Some experts have their picture displayed.

Our View: An interesting feature is the ability for the lawyer to let the experts know he's interested in hearing from them by placing check marks next to the experts'

Figure 11-3. Search the Experts.com directory by area of expertise, or by name of expert, company, or other criteria.

names and clicking the **SynapsUS** online inquiry button at the bottom of the page.

While the site indicates that it also gives experts the ability to add an audio recording to their profile, we could not find any experts listed at Experts.com who have taken advantage of this feature.

Tips: You have a choice of refining your search on the Search page by choosing **all words**, **is exactly** or **any words**. Experts.com members are entitled to a discount at the Daubert Tracker database (**http://www.daubert tracker.com**).

ALM (American Lawyer Media) Experts

http://www.almexperts.com

Purpose: To find experts and consultants.

Content: ALM has a directory with over 15,000 experts, expert witnesses, investigators, court reporters, litigation support professionals, and consultants in more than 3,000 categories. While free to users, experts who wish to list themselves in the database pay for inclusion. Users can search by **Keyword**, **Area of Expertise**, **or Expert/ Company Name** to find a list of national experts. Users can also choose to browse through the directory of expert categories. Once an expert is selected, the site makes it easy to determine if the expert has posted a **Resume**, **Profile**, **Image**, **Web**, or **E-mail** link.

Our View: A very useful feature is the link (on the left-hand side of the expert's listing page) that allows you to check **Verdict Search** for cases involving the expert you've selected. A summary of the verdicts is displayed, and you can buy them for $35 each (see Verdict Search later in this chapter or at **http://www.verdictsearch.com** for more information). We like the handy chart that appears with the resulting list of experts. If you can't figure out what the icons stand for, just hover over them—they indicate whether the expert has an online profile, photograph, or CV; a Web site; or an e-mail address.

See Expert's Prior Cases

The ALM Experts directory provides a useful feature: links to a pay site that displays the expert's prior cases. The Expert Witness Profiler site (**http://www.expertwitnessprofiler.com**; see page 171) also provides similar information.

Tip: Click on the **Advanced Search by State** link, on the left-hand side of the page below the search box, to further refine your search by state or keywords.

Society of Expert Witnesses

http://www.sew.org.uk/database/

Purpose: To locate potential expert witnesses in the European Union.

Content: The Society of Expert Witnesses provides a browseable directory of what the site describes as only "a small sample" of their "over a thousand members," as only those members who request it are added to the online database. Database categories range from "Accident" to "Woodworm" specialists. Of most interest to U.S. lawyers will probably be those categories related to international business (e.g., contracts, valuations, taxation, pensions, etc.). The Society is a private, non-profit membership organization run by and for expert witnesses, established to "promot[e] training for expert witnesses and those aspiring to become expert witnesses."

Our View: The alphabetical list of areas of expertise is easy to browse. The clickable links take you directly to contact information for each expert listed, including their e-mail and Web site addresses (where applicable), in addition to their postal mail address and phone number.

Free Expert Witness Directories, Searchable by Category Only

National Directory of Expert Witnesses

http://national-experts.com/Members2/search.html

Purpose: To locate expert witnesses.

Content: The National Directory of Expert Witnesses is an extensive print directory of experts and a free searchable online database of 2,000 technical, scientific, and medical experts arranged into 400 categories. It is published by the Claims Providers of America and is designed to be used by law firms and insurance professionals. Search by keywords (partial or complete), phrases, category, name of expert, or name of company.

Our View: While not the largest of the directories discussed here, The National Directory of Expert Witnesses still contains listings for many knowledgeable expert witnesses that might not be found in others.

Tips: To limit the search to a certain state, use its postal abbreviation, followed by an ampersand (e.g., "IL&"). You can also e-mail this site and ask for a referral (for free) to an expert in a specified field.

Hieros Gamos Directory of Expert Witnesses

http://www.hgexperts.com

Purpose: To locate expert witnesses.

Content: Hieros Gamos' database lists experts in nearly 1,200 categories. It is searchable by any name, or keyword in the expert's description. The database is also browseable by subject.

Our View: While Hieros Gamos' directory listings offer the experts the ability to include a great deal of information, much of it is displayed on one long page that requires much scrolling to get through. This is one place the superior organization of directories like JurisPro are appreciated. In its favor, we think that Hieros Gamos' inclusion of a category for **Legal Speakers** can be helpful for attorneys needing to locate presenters for programs they might be planning. While it may seem like a small distinction (between "expert" and "speaker"), this can be an important one, as not every expert witness (no matter how knowledgeable or effective at trial) makes a good seminar presenter.

Tip: Even though there is no expert-name field, you can search for an expert's name in the description field (using it as a keyword).

Expertclick
(formerly Yearbook of Experts, Authorities and Spokespersons)

http://www.expertclick.com

Purpose: A very extensive searchable database of experts designed primarily for journalists, but anyone can search it for free.

Content: The database contains information on more than 900 experts in over 12,000 topic areas. Once a search is conducted for a particular area of expertise, you can read a summary about the expert, link to the expert's site, and link to press releases posted by the expert.

Our View: While the Expertclick database is smaller than some of the others discussed here, because it is targeted at journalists, rather than lawyers, there's a good chance that searches will yield different results than some of the others. This site also makes it easy to search for experts and to access additional information about them. The **Contact** link is a useful shortcut that will help you get a message or question to the expert quickly. In some cases, you will be informed that you must be a registered journalist. However, you can easily contact the expert on your own—from the information listed on the profile or by linking to the expert's site.

Tips: By clicking on **View Releases** you can read the expert's press releases. But remember—this is what the expert wrote, not what an objective third party wrote.

Some expert listings include a **View Daybook** link to view the expert's calendar of events (such as seminars).

An electronic version of the site's print directory is accessible for download at **http://www.scribd.com/doc/ 4060189/Yearbook-of-Experts-28th-Final-July-2008**.

Free Expert Witness Directories, Searchable byCategory and Location

ExpertPages

http://www.expertpages.com

Purpose: To locate expert witnesses.

Content: Founded in 1995, ExpertPages is one of the oldest online directories of expert witnesses. Experts are arranged in hierarchical categories and subcategories of expertise. The categories are further distinguished with **Medical Experts**, **Non-Medical Experts**, and **Experts by State** links at the top of the home page. The directory is

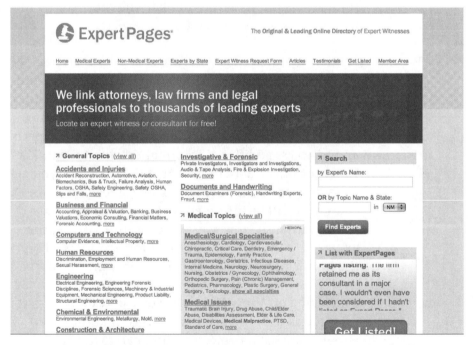

Figure 11-4. Expertpages.com allows you to browse for experts by topic, or to search by name, or area of expertise.

also searchable by **Expert's Name** or **Topic Name & State** using the search form on the left-hand side of the home page.

Our View: The information for each listing is very brief, but does include links to the expert's Web site, e-mail, or phone number.

Tip: If you don't find an expert who suits your needs in the database, click the **Expert Witness Request Form** link at the top of the home page and the site will attempt to locate an expert who does—free of charge.

FindLaw Expert Witness Directory

http://marketcenter.findlaw.com/expert_witnesses.html

Purpose: To locate expert witnesses.

Content: Findlaw's expert witness database is browseable by category or first by state and then by category. The results might include listings of individual experts or links to some of the referral sites we note below. Some of the expert listings offer a bit more information than those at ExpertPages—including descriptions of services offered—if the expert has chosen to add it (or presumably to pay for an expanded listing). Many listings we browsed offered only name, address, and phone number.

Our View: The amount of information varies wildly from listing to listing. While some have expanded descriptions, etc., as noted above, the others that include only a name, address, and phone number are much less useful than the more detailed listings at sites like JurisPro. Another downside, even when browsing by state first, many of the results are for "nationwide" experts.

Tip: There's no need to use the pull-down menu labeled **Expert Witnesses** when searching this directory. It will take you to other searchable vendor databases, such as **Court Reporters** and **Investigators**. While those databases can be useful if you're looking for vendors in those areas, they are distracting if you only need to find an expert witness.

Finding an Expert in Your State

Although several sites allow the user to narrow down the expert witness search to a particular state, it should be noted that no matter what state is chosen, the results may still include experts from outside your requested state. This is because experts can ask to be listed in states other than the one in which they reside.

Does Your Bar Association Have an Expert Witness Database?

When you need to keep expenses to a minimum, but still need an expert, it's helpful if you can target local experts. To do this, consider turning to your local bar association's Web site to see if they have created an expert witness directory. For instance, in Los Angeles, lawyers can consult the Los Angeles County Bar Association's online expert database, Expert4law.org (**http://www.expert4law.org**), and lawyers in the Bay area can consult the Bar Association of San Francisco's online directory of expert witnesses (**http://www.sfbar.org/register/**).

Checklist Item 4: Use Online Directories to Find Trade or Professional Associations

Lawyers who need an expert in an uncommon field or who simply do not know where to begin their search for an expert should consider consulting with an association that deals with that particular field. According to the American Society of Association Executives (ASAE) and Gale Research (publishers of the Encyclopedia of Associations), there are over 147,000 associations in the United States (127,340 local, state, or regional; 20,285 national; and 2,409 international associations headquartered in the United States—see **http://www.asaecenter.org/General Detail.cfm?ItemNumber=8247**). Another way to find an association's Web site is to simply enter its name into a Web search engine (like Google); however, this assumes you know the name of the association. If you don't know the name, you can enter a descriptive keyword and the word *association*. One more easy way to find an association's Web site is to access one of the free online association indices or directories discussed in the upcoming pages.

As an example, lawyers very often need to find translators or interpreters. A useful site for finding one is the American Translators Association's site (**http://www.atanet.org**). Like many association sites, it includes an online directory searchable by name, language, location, and various other criteria.

War Story: Chewing Gum Expert

There are associations for nearly every profession and interest group, as we learned when asked to find a chewing gum expert (for a personal injury case). The case involved a plaintiff who slipped and fell on a hard piece of chewing gum and the issue was one of notice, which could only be answered by figuring out how long that piece of chewing gum was on the floor. This, in turn, called for a chewing gum expert who could tell us how long it takes chewing gum to become hard. We knew it would be a waste of time to search a traditional expert witness directory and immediately thought of the Encyclopedia of Associations (also called Associations Unlimited). Seconds after logging into my public library's Web site, and locating the free Associations Unlimited remote database, we found the Association of Chewing Gum Manufacturers. We turned the contact over to the lawyers.

The Encyclopedia of Associations is free to use only if your public library provides remote access to it (otherwise, it is a pay database). If your library does provide access, you are in particular luck because it is one of the largest of the association directories. It indexes and provides detailed information on more than 155,000 organizations worldwide, and has Internal Revenue Service (IRS) data on 300,000 nonprofit organizations with 501(c) status. The Encyclopedia provides numerous search functions—keyword, acronyms, location, subject, and more. If the Encyclopedia entry for the association has a URL listed, go there to scour the site for a list of research links to learn more about the topic. Also, take note of the executive director's name or the names of any of the association's officers. Typically, their e-mail addresses or a link to them will be included. Lawyers can then contact the director or one of the officers for a referral to an expert. If you don't have access to the Encyclopedia of Associations, see below for some free alternatives. For more information on remote online resources offered by public libraries, see Chapter 12, Using Expensive Pay Databases for Free.

Online Directories of Associations

The Internet Public Library Associations on the Net

http://www.ipl.org/div/aon

Purpose: To browse or search for information about prominent organizations and associations.

Content: The Internet Public Library provides this collection of hundreds of descriptions and links to associations on the Internet. Categories include **Arts & Humanities**; **Business & Economics**; **Computers & Internet**; **Education**; **Entertainment & Leisure**; **Health & Medical Science**; **Law, Government & Political Science**; **Reference**; **Regional & County Information**; **Science & Technology**; and **Social Sciences**.

Our View: The descriptions are helpful in determining if a particular association will yield useful information before linking to the association's Web site.

Tip: To perform a keyword search of this Associations list, select the **Advanced Search & Help** link underneath the search box in the upper right-hand corner of the page. On the subsequent page, you will be able to conduct keyword and phrase searches to help locate specific associations. Note however, that this is a search of all of the Internet Public Library's resources and not just the associations list.

GuideStar

http://www2.guidestar.org/AdvancedSearch.aspx

Purpose: To search for data on nonprofits; geared to donors, grantors, and nonprofits.

Content: GuideStar provides annual reports and IRS Form 990s filed by nearly 1.8 million nonprofit organizations, and also provides direct links to nonprofits' Web sites. The free "GuideStar Basic" registration allows users to search **Organization Name**, **Keyword**, **City**, or **State**. Users who opt for the paid "GuideStar Premium" ($40/5-day, $100/month, or $1,000/year), get even more search options, including **ZIP Code/ZIP Code Range** and **Income Range**.

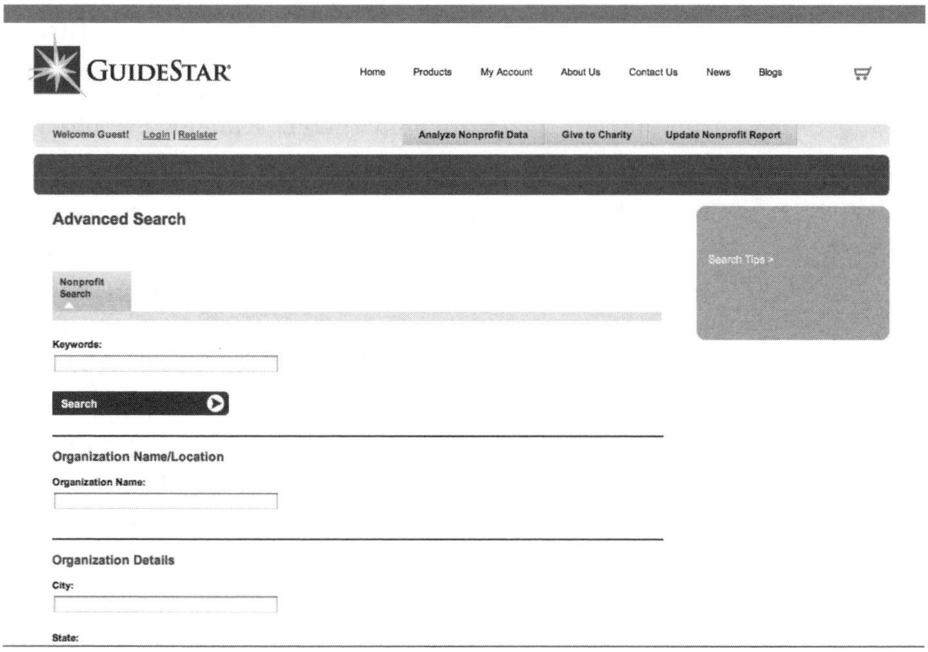

Figure 11-5. GuideStar provides annual reports and IRS 990 forms filed by nearly 1.8 million nonprofit organizations, and also provides direct links to the nonprofits' Web sites.

Our View: If you are looking for financial data on a specific organization (and you know the organization's name), the free, Basic registration will get users much of the information they need. However, if you're looking for data on organizations using more general search criteria (e.g., organization type, ZIP code, or income range) it'll be necessary to opt for one of the Premium subscriptions.

Tips: While address searching is limited to Premium subscribers, Basic subscribers can use street names as keywords. For example a search for the phrase "Mark Twain" limited to organizations in California returned a number of results with the keyword in the name of the organization, but also "The International Possibilities Foundation" on Mark Twain Drive in San Rafael, CA. A similar strategy can be used to search for organization directors/contacts.

Note that the inclusion of EIN and e-mail information is only included in the Premium subscriber's report. However, the EIN and phone number for an organization is included in the Form 990 which is available even to Basic subscribers.

If you don't find the charitable organization that you are looking for, check the list of charitable organizations in IRS Publication 78, Cumulative List of Organizations, and its Addendum. To search this list, type "Publication 78" into the **Search Forms and Publications for** query box at **http://www.irs.gov**, or go to **http://apps .irs.gov/app/pub78**. You can search by full or partial organization name, city, or state. Returned results include only the name of the charity, its city and state, and its IRS deductibility code.

Be sure to also check the alphabetical addendum to the list at **http://www.irs.gov/charities/article/0,,id= 96291,00.html**. The addendum, an alphabetical list, is not searchable.

The Foundation Finder

http://lnp.fdncenter.org/finder.html

Purpose: To search for information about nonprofits.

Content: Search the Foundation Finder—a listing of 92,000 private and community foundations in the U.S. Other information on this site includes a list of the top funders by type or state (hover over **Find Funders** at the top of the home page and then select **Top Funders** from the drop-down menu that appears).

Our View: It's an easily searchable database, and one more source for PDFs of each organization's filled-in and filed IRS Form 990. Additionally, phone, fax, e-mail, and Web site contact information are all included in the search

Figure 11-6. Search the Foundation Finder by foundation's name (or partial name) or its EIN, and add a city, ZIP code, or state to narrow the search.

results. So, at Foundation Center you don't have to dig through the Form 990 to find this information—like you do when performing searches at Guidestar.org. However, Foundation Center, does not offer the keyword search available at Guidestar.

Specialized Association Directories

While the above directories cover a wide spectrum of areas, there are directories that are more specialized. For example, in the health care industry, the Joint Commission on Accreditation of Healthcare Organizations has a site that includes a database of thousands of health care organizations accredited by the Commission. Searchable by ZIP code or organization name, the database includes ambulatory care facilities, assisted living facilities, behavioral health care facilities (such as chemical dependency centers and developmental disabilities organizations), HMOs, home care organizations, hospitals, laboratories, long-term care facilities, and office-based surgery facilities, among other types of facilities (**http://www.qualitycheck.org**).

Physician Directories

AMA Doctor Finder Select

http://webapps.ama-assn.org/doctorfinder/home.jsp

Content: The AMA provides the primary physician directory available to the public. For information on individual doctors, choose **Doctor Finder**. All 814,000 accredited doctors (MDs and DOs) in the U.S. are represented. To conduct a search you will need to read and accept the disclaimer at **http://webapps.ama-assn.org/doctor finder/disclaimer.jsp**. You can search by the doctor's name but you must enter their state or ZIP code. You can also search by a specialty and location. Information provided includes address, phone number, specialty, where degrees were obtained, where residencies were served, and American Board of Medical Specialties certifications. No discipline information is provided.

Our View: Of course, we'd all rather have access to the government's National Practitioner Data Bank (**http://npdb-**

hipdb.hrsa.gov/) to access a doctors disciplinary record. Start lobbying.

Tips: Use the asterisk (*) as a wild card when uncertain of a doctor's first name spelling (for example, to search for Jeffrey Smith, type "J* Smith" in case "Jeffrey" is spelled "Jeffery" or in case the doctor goes by "Jeff").

You can also perform a sounds-like search (click the **Perform a sound-like search** box under the ZIP code entry field) if you're not sure how to spell the doctor's last name or city. Note that this only works for last names, not first names. The sound-like search can be employed when searching by physician specialty if you are unsure of the spelling of a city.

Deceased physicians will not be found online, but contact the AMA—they keep some limited history.

eCare UPIN Lookup

http://upin.ecare.com

Content: Federal law provides for the creation of a Unique Physician Identification Number (UPIN) for every doctor who provides services for which payment is made under Medicare, and requires the publication of a directory of those numbers. At this site, you can search for a doctor's UPIN, or determine a doctor's name if you only know the UPIN. For each physician, the database provides medical specialty, state, ZIP code, and identification number only. For a full address, you will have to use the AMA database noted above.

Other Health Profession Sites

Here are some sites for more health profession associations:

- American Chiropractic Association at **http://www.acatoday.org**. (Click **Find a Doctor** under the **Patients** heading.)

- American Dental Association at **http://www.ada.org**. (To find a dentist, visit **http://www.ada.org/public/directory/index.asp**.)
- American Health Lawyers Association at **http://www.health lawyers.org**. (The list of members can only be searched by registered members.)
- American Nurses Association at **http://www.nursingworld.org**. (The American Nurses Association (ANA) is the only professional organization representing the nation's 2.9 million registered nurses.)
- American Optometric Association at **http://www.aoa.org**. (Visit **http://www.aoa.org/x5428.xml** to find an optometrist.)
- American Physical Therapy Association at **http://www.apta.org**. (Select the **Find a PT** link on the top bar of the home page to search by ZIP code or ZIP code and expertise.)
- American Psychiatric Association at **http://www.psych.org**.
- American Academy of Nurse Practitioners at **http://www.aanp .org**.

Reliability and Revelance of Experts

Harold J. Bursztajn, MD, is an Associate Clinical Professor of Psychiatry at Beth Israel Deaconess Medical Center, Harvard Medical School. He also has broad courtroom experience as a medical and psychiatric expert witness in civil and criminal litigation. In his forensic practice, he has consulted to plaintiff and defense counsel and to state and federal agencies as an expert in medical-legal decision-making, forensic psychiatry, and evaluating the methodological reliability of expert testimony. Dr. Bursztajn's Web site (**http://www.forensic-psych.com**) focuses on the nexus of forensic psychiatry, medicine, and the law. He is often consulted by attorneys as an expert on experts for referral to experts in a range of medical and psychiatric specialties. He offered the following insights regarding using the Internet to find medical experts:

With its emphasis on judicial discretion, and on the judge as "gatekeeper" for admitting expert testimony, *Daubert v. Merrell Dow Pharmaceuticals, Inc. 509 U.S. 579 (1993)*, has been slowly but steadily transforming how lawyers seek experts. With the increasing likelihood that an expert's testimony will face judicial scrutiny, the reliability and relevance of an expert's analysis and evaluation need to be established long before trial, ideally prior to retaining an expert. While the specific guidelines enumerated by the Supreme Court for scientific testimony are most often used in the quantitative sciences, the more general criteria of reliability and relevance are increasingly used by judges to evaluate the admissibility of applied science-based expert medical opinion. One of my most common forensic consultations is to evaluate another "expert's" opinion. When I analyze a proffered expert opinion as unreliable or irrelevant on medical-decision analytic grounds, the lawyer or court that has retained me can rapidly move to dismiss either the questionable testimony or the entire claim or defense which is founded on such testimony (*Mayotte M. Jones v. Metrowest Medical Inc.* [CA-96-10860-WD]).

By researching via the Internet, a lawyer seeking an expert can avoid both false starts and subsequent disappointments. The Internet offers the following advantages for evaluating the potential usefulness of a medical expert in light of the general principles of *Daubert:*

1. *Reliability:* The medical expert needs to be both a practicing physician who consults to other physicians and patients, and well published in refereed medical journals. This information can be gleaned from the expert's Web page more easily than from the CV alone. The Web page will often include not only a complete CV, but also selected case citations and authored publications. Moreover, the expert with a resource page on the Web is more likely to be able to do computer-aided literature searches. Such research can provide the foundation for the reviews and analyses needed to corroborate the reliability of another expert's opinion. In addition, such research can identify alternative opinions in the medical community. Since reading CVs on the Internet can be like picking out a needle in a haystack, if in doubt about an expert's specific strengths one can send the prospective expert an e-mailed inquiry.

2. *Relevance:* The medical expert needs to show ability to teach not only other medical professionals, but also other professionals and educated laypersons, e.g., judges, lawyers, and jurors. The lawyer can have some sense of how the expert teaches in a public context by reviewing the expert's Web page. A content-filled, yet user-friendly Web page can itself be an indication that

an expert has the competence, confidence, and sensitivity to present work in a public context with authority rather than arrogance, and in a relevant and meaningful manner. Along these lines, it is advantageous to select an expert with a demonstrated capacity to work on a multispecialty team. An expert who has published a variety of multiauthored papers, and not always as the first author, promises to be a team player rather than a *prima donna*.

For more detailed guidelines for selecting an expert in the post-Daubert environment, see Bursztajn HJ, Pulde MF, Pirakitikulr D, Perlin M. "*Kumho* for clinicians in the courtroom: Inconsistency in the trial courts." *Medical Malpractice Law & Strategy* 2006 (Nov); 24(2):1-7. (*Available at* **http://www.forensic-psych.com/articles/artKumhoClinicians.php**.)

Daubert on the Web

See Peter Nordberg's site, Daubert on the Web, to read the *Daubert* decision and hundreds of post-*Daubert* cases—indexed by circuit and by area of expertise through September 2006 (**http://daubertontheweb.com**). For more current updates see Nordberg's blog at **http://www.daubertontheweb.com/blog702.html**. Nordberg is a shareholder in the Philadelphia-based Berger & Montague, specializing in complex and environmental litigation.

Checklist Item 5: Find the Expert's Conference Presentations

One way to locate an expert in a specific area of expertise is to enter the search term *expert witness* (in quotation marks) along with any other search criteria, such as *child custody*, into a search engine.

When you know an expert's name (either the opposition's or one you're considering retaining), it can be useful to run their name through a search engine as a way to capture any extra nuggets of information—such as links to the expert's personal Web site, discussion group messages sent by the expert, or any references to the expert on a discussion group or a Web site other than his or her own.

It can often be important to learn if an expert's opinion has been consistent in public forums, such as conferences. An expert's conference papers can sometimes be found on the Web by typing the expert's name into your favorite search engine. Very often, experts post their own papers. Other times conference sponsors might post them without the experts' knowledge. To limit your search to an experts' PowerPoint presentations only, go to Google or **http://search.yahoo.com** and click on **Advanced Search**. Enter your search term (the expert's name) and then select **Microsoft PowerPoint (.ppt)** as the file format.

PowerPoint Presentations from Government Entities

USA.gov also indexes PowerPoint presentations that have been posted, but they are limited to presentations posted on government Web sites only.

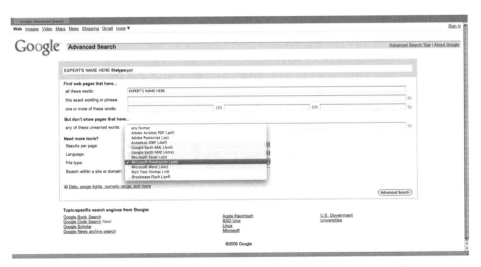

Figure 11-7. Using Google's Advanced Search page, you can limit a search to a PowerPoint presentation by clicking in the file format drop-down menu. Google™ is a trademark of Google Technology Inc.

Checklist Item 6: Join an Online Community to Find Experts' Postings or to Learn About the Topic

Online discussions can take place in a variety of places on the Internet: in Usenet newsgroups, mailing lists, forums, blogs, and message boards. Though very hit or miss, searching through online communities' current discussions and archives can sometimes be excellent strategies for identifying and contacting experts. For any topic you can imagine, there is an online community discussing it.

Some online communities require that you subscribe in order to participate, and some limit their subscriptions to those with particular credentials. But many lists have no subscriber limitations at all. Once you locate an appropriate community, the best thing to do is lurk around a bit. In other words, read the postings prior to submitting your own, or simply browse through the archives. In this way, you may come across an expert or another lawyer with whom you wish to correspond. You can then send private e-mail messages to those individuals, rather than letting all of the list's subscribers know your intentions. If the community has an archive, search it for your expert's name or the expertise you are seeking (not all archives are keyword searchable, however).

To determine whether an online community in a particular subject area exists, or to find out about any subscriber limitations, or to simply find out how to subscribe, consult a LISTSERV list directory such as Cata-List (**http://www.lsoft.com/lists/listref.html**) or a newsletter directory like the one maintained by Topica (formerly Liszt) (**http://lists.topica.com**).

While some Listservs like LAWLIB have remained active over time, others like PSYLAW-L have ceased to exist entirely. Even after a list ceases being active, its archive of old messages can still yield useful information. Unfortunately, PSYLAW-L's archive has disappeared from the Internet as well.

In its time, EXPERT-L was an active Internet mailing list for those individuals engaged in expert witness activities associated with litigation. It was inspired by the need for experts to communicate with each other about issues related to the expert witness profession and for networking between experts and lawyers. In recent years, the list has been supplanted by other means of online communication and information sharing. Since the Fall of 2005, its available archive (**http://lists.digilogic.com/archives/expert-l.html**) does not list any new postings. However, the old postings, dating back to 1998 can still yield information on experts who are still active. For example, a search in the archives (where you can search without subscribing) found a request from a lawyer for an "expert in tensile strength and fractile characteristics of cast metal machinery components."

At Topica, you can either search by keywords or browse categories and subcategories to find the right group. Browsing through the category **Health & Fitness**, we found many subcategories and chose **Diseases & Conditions**, then **Autoimmune & Immune Disorders**, and then **CFS (Chronic Fatigue Syndrome)**. Reading some of the recent posts, we found one that included the name, e-mail address, and mailing address of a staff member of the National CFIDS Foundation, Inc., and a reference to a case involving long-term disability benefits for a plaintiff suffering from chronic fatigue syndrome. It would be easy to contact her for follow-up.

One of the phenomena that have reduced the role of Listserv discussions is the rise of social and professional networking sites as a means to share information. See Chapter 8, Using Social Networking Sites for Investigative Research for more information.

Using Google Groups to Find or Background an Expert

As discussed earlier, Google Groups (**http://groups.google.com**) allows for anonymous searching through over one billion postings of the archives of thousands of Usenet newsgroups dating back to 1981. For a thorough discussion on how to use Google Groups, see the "Using Online Community Postings for Investigative Research" section in Chapter 7, Online Communities. Searching Google Groups by keyword, you may come across an expert who is relevant to the matter at hand. Searching by an expert's name, you may come across a posting made by your own expert or your opponent's expert. This is an excellent way to attempt to undermine the opponent's expert and to evaluate your own expert.

To find the expert's postings, users should conduct a few different types of searches on Google Group's Advanced Groups Search page (**http://groups.google.com/advanced_group_search**). First, search for the expert's name in the **Return only messages where the author is** field. However, keep in mind that some people post anonymously by using pseudonyms, so you may find nothing.

Second, search for the expert's e-mail address in the **Return only messages where the author is** field. Since many people share the same name, searching by a unique e-mail address will help you verify that

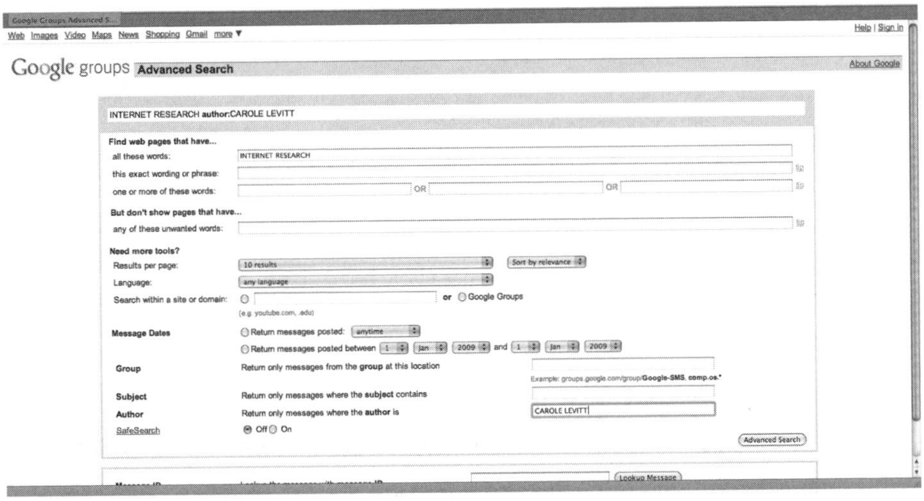

Figure 11-8. Search for the expert's name in the **Return only messages where the author is** field of Google Groups' Advanced Search page. Google™ is a trademark of Google Technology Inc.

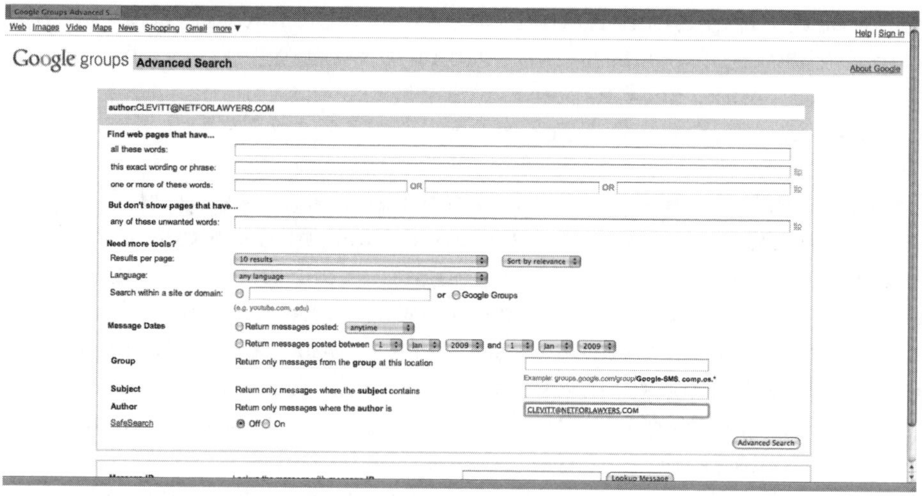

Figure 11-9. Search for the expert's e-mail address in the **Return only messages where the author is** field of Google Groups' Advanced Search page. Google™ is a trademark of Google Technology Inc.

you've found messages from the correct person. Because some people have more than one e-mail address, try to discover all of them to conduct as complete a search as possible for a person's postings.

The third search method is to search for the expert's name in one of the keyword fields of the Advanced Groups Search page (either in the **with all of the words** field or **with the exact phrase** field). This may disclose other people's postings that contain their opinions about the expert.

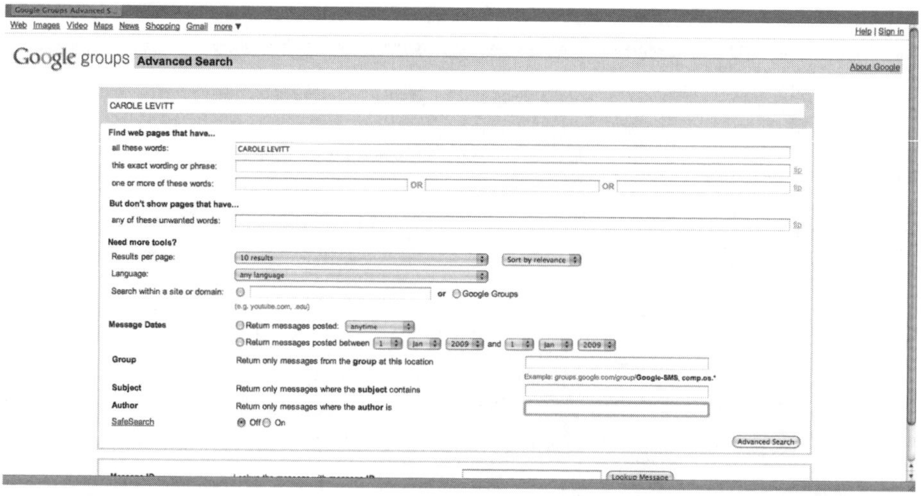

Figure 11-10. Search for the expert's name in one of the keyword fields of Google Groups' Advanced Search page. Google™ is a trademark of Google Technology Inc.

Fourth, Google Groups can also be used to search by topic to find experts in a certain specialty when you don't already have a name of an expert. For example, if you are representing a client who was seriously injured when the treads of his Firestone tires separated, causing his vehicle to overturn, searching Google Groups for the phrase *Firestone tires* might lead you to an expert who has testified in prior tread-separation lawsuits. Additionally, the same search may identify people who have also been seriously injured when the tire treads on their vehicles separated. They might mention their expert's name or their lawyer's name (which can be a lead for you), or they may express their opinion about the expert.

Checklist Item 7: Review the Expert's Own Web Site

An expert's own Web site should be carefully reviewed prior to retaining him or her. If a search engine did not locate the expert's Web site, try simply entering the expert's name or company name followed by .com (expertname.com). Many experts post their full CV, prior litigation experience, speaking engagements, references, memberships and professional organization affiliations, and articles and newsletters on their Web sites. When reviewing an expert's Web site, keep in mind that opposing counsel can do so as well. Be aware that experts' Web sites are sometimes little more than self-promotion, so tread carefully. Is there anything embarrassing or contradictory on the site? Does the expert pronounce that he or she is "the leader in the industry" or put forth similar bravado that could affect how the jury perceives the expert? Imagine how the jury would react if the pages of the expert's Web site were displayed as exhibits at trial—because they very well could be.

Checklist Item 8: Determine If the Expert Has Ever Been Disciplined

It is also important to determine if an expert has been reviewed or disciplined by their jurisdiction's licensing boards. You may be able to find this discipline information by conducting a free public records search if this type of information is public record. Although not a free search site, Idex.com has created a searchable database of experts who have been reviewed or disciplined by their jurisdiction's licensing boards (**https://idex.lexisnexis.com/about/index.html**). Also see the description of the Expert Witness Profiler service (**http://www.expertwitnessprofiler .com**) on page 171 for information on a similar service. It is also worthwhile to check with any voluntary or mandatory membership professional organizations of which the expert is (or might be) a member to gather this information.

Checklist Item 9: Find Experts via Jury Verdict Reporter Databases

Another way to find experts is by way of jury verdict reporters. While most lawyers search jury verdicts to assess the worth of a case, the astute lawyer knows that jury verdicts are also useful in finding experts who testified in specific types of cases. By searching for an expert's name in a jury verdict reporter, you may discover whether the expert has given opposing opinions in similar cases, appears more often as a defense witness, or has usually testified for the winning side. The lawyers involved in the cases are also listed in the jury verdict database. You might consider contacting them for information about their experience with their own expert or the opposition's expert (for example, how the opposition's expert came across during cross-examination). Free online jury verdicts (and settlements) can be found at MoreLaw.com. Lexis and Westlaw offer pay jury verdict databases, as do the National Association of State Jury Verdict Publishers (NASJVP) and VerdictSearch.com.

Free Jury Verdict Reporter Databases

MoreLaw.com

http://www.morelaw.com

Purpose: To find experts by way of jury verdict reports.

Content: MoreLaw.com is a free online legal information resource with a jury verdict reports database (where experts can be found), a lawyer directory, and an expert witness database. MoreLaw.com's verdict database has thousands of verdicts, all hand selected and summarized by Tulsa, Oklahoma, lawyer Kent Morlan, who reviews verdicts by searching Google, legal newspapers, and hundreds of appellate court Web sites. The database is searchable by keywords describing the expertise involved, by the facts of the case, or by lawyer, expert, or party name.

Our View: This might be the only free verdict site you'll find. It's a useful site for searching for experts; you may discover whether the expert has given opposing opinions in similar cases, appears more often as a defense witness, or has usually testified for the winning side. The lawyers involved in the cases are also listed in the verdict database and may provide you with information about their experience with the expert if you contact them directly.

Tips: We have found experts through MoreLaw.com's jury verdict database who did not list themselves on the expert witness database. Check both.

To begin searching verdicts, first click on **Search Database**, (under **Verdicts & Decisions** in the left-hand column) then click on the drop-down menu titled **Select Field to Search**. Select **Case Description** as the field to search if looking for a case similar to your case and then enter your keywords. If you are looking only for cases where a specific expert served as a plaintiff's expert (or defendant's expert), select the **Plaintiff(s) Expert(s)** or **Defendant(s) Expert(s)** field and enter the expert's name into the search box.

Pay Jury Verdict Reporter Databases

VerdictSearch

http://www.verdictsearch.com

Purpose: To find verdicts and settlements in order to identify experts.

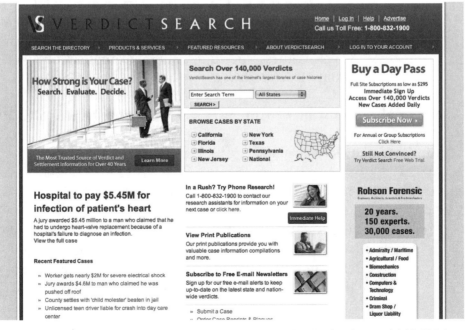

Figure 11-11. VerdictSearch.com offers a searchable database of 140,000 jury verdicts from various jurisdictions.

Content: VerdictSearch is a division of Incisive Media, the new corporate parent of ALM (formerly American Lawyer Media). Its database includes over 140,000 jury verdicts from the VerdictSearch National, VerdictSearch California, VerdictSearch Florida, VerdictSearch Illinois, VerdictSearch New Jersey, VerdictSearch New York, VerdictSearch Pennsylvania, VerdictSearch Texas, and New York Judicial Review of Damages, among other sources.

Our View: This is a useful service for those who frequently need to find experts and want to read about the cases that the experts were involved in. The cost for an annual subscription is dependent upon the size of the firm, with solo lawyers paying $1,195 and larger firms up to $1,795 (there is a limit of 250 cases e-mailed and/or viewed within any 24-hour period). A 24-hour subscription for $250 has a limit of 100 cases e-mailed and/or viewed within the 24-hour period. A free limited subscription is also available.

Tip: Instead of subscribing to VerdictSearch, the occasional user might try searching the expert or expertise at the ALM Expert Directory site (**http://www.almexperts.com**). Then, from the ALM Expert Directory, a user can link to that expert's list of cases at VerdictSearch and purchase a single verdict for $19.95. (See the above section, "Free Expert Witness Directories," for more information about ALMExperts).

National Association of State Jury Verdict Publishers (NASJVP)

http://www.juryverdicts.com

Purpose: To find experts via jury verdict or case testified.

Content: The NASJVP site does not offer a searchable database of verdicts. It offers an alphabetical listing of nearly 40,000 experts. Entries include their expertise and the name of the jury verdict publication where they are referenced.

Our View: Although users can browse free at NASJVP, after clicking on the expert's name, they are simply referred to the third-party company that has published the verdict related to that expert (e.g., VerdictSearch) where the user can obtain detailed information about the verdict, for a fee.

Tip: If you don't have the luxury of time, you'll probably be better off using one of the pay databases where the verdicts are readily available online and full text.

Checklist Item 10: Find the Expert's Deposition Testimony

Reading an expert's deposition testimony can provide an abundance of information about how the expert may perform. Currently there is no free, centralized database for expert witness transcripts, but there are several commercial sites and professional association sites that gather this information for members.

Deposition Testimony Databases

TrialSmith

http://www.trialsmith.com (formerly known as DepoConnect)

Purpose: For plaintiff lawyers only—to find expert's deposition testimony to determine possible performance.

Content: TrialSmith is an online database with nearly 400,000 depositions, and other documents that include briefs, pleadings, seminar papers, verdicts, and settlements. It also includes an expert witness database and e-mail discussion lists where lawyers discuss and recommend experts.

Our View: If you're a member of one of the dozens of "partner" trial lawyers associations to which TrialSmith offers free "Basic" memberships, there's no reason not to sign up. (Free members pay $49 per document to print or save a transcript.) Even the paid annual subscription beginning at $379 per year and $30 per transcript seems reasonable.

Lawyers may find the private discussion groups useful for sharing information about experts. For individuals who are not members of a "partner" association, subscription prices to access the depositions start at $399 per year.

Tip: Paid subscribers can instantly view or download any transcript.

While TrialSmith is for the plaintiff's bar, the Defense Research Institute (DRI) site, as its name implies, is only for defense lawyers who are DRI members (**http://www.dri.org**). Idex has built its database of deposition transcripts (and trial testimony by experts) by submissions from its own members (**http://www.Idex.lexisnexis.com**). Electronic versions of some documents can be viewed and downloaded directly from this site at a reduced price. According to its Web site, 6,000 records are added each month to Idex's database of over 2.2 million records of expert involvement. Subscription pricing for access to the Index database is $375 for the first year (and then $185 per year thereafter), plus $40 per transcript in their collection. Pricing is also available for retrieval of transcripts not already in their collection.

AAJ

Also, see the **Exchange** section of the American Association for Justice (AAJ) site at **http://www.atlanet.org/**, which makes available to its members a database of thousands of expert witnesses, and over 155,000 searchable transcripts. This database is developed by submission from its members. AAJ posts the contact information for the member who provided information about that expert.

Defense Research Institute (DRI)

http://www.dri.org   **$**

Purpose: To find expert's deposition testimony to determine possible performance.

Content: The DRI Expert Witness Database includes information on over 65,000 expert witnesses. Information on an expert may include text searchable depositions, trial transcripts, CVs, articles, and other miscellaneous documents, such as motions, affidavits, or orders.

Our View: DRI offers its Expert Witness Database as an exclusive benefit to its members. The $225 annual DRI membership fee (for individual defense attorneys) seems quite reasonable to access this database, even when compared to the free "Basic" membership at TrialSmith, because all documents downloaded or requested via e-mail are free to DRI members. Only documents requested in either CD-ROM or hard-copy format are charged a per document handling fee.

Tip: The DRI has other member benefits, such as a magazine, a newsletter, and seminars.

Checklist Item 11: Find Briefs and Cases That Refer to the Expert

Briefs

Daubert Tracker

   (to search)

   (to access full text of documents)

http://www.dauberttracker.com/

Purpose: To locate information about challenges to specific expert witnesses.

Content: The Daubert Tracker's database contains "all reported and numerous unreported cases from both state and federal jurisdictions" related to expert witness challenges. Key documents related to the challenges, including briefs, motions, and responses are available for purchase from the site. The site's research staff actively searches for unreported case information from a variety of sources including dockets, news reports, jury verdicts, and court Web sites. Additionally, visitors to the Daubert Tracker site are invited to submit information regarding unreported cases via an online form (**http://www.dauberttracker.com/caseReport.cfm**).

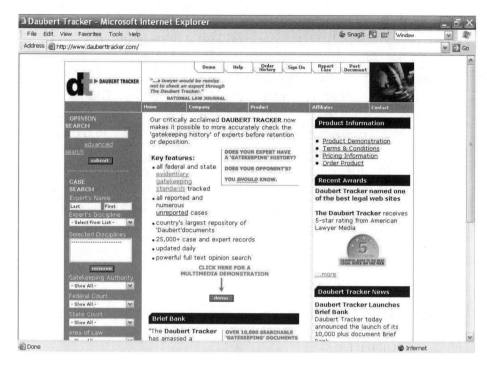

Figure 11-12. Daubert Tracker aggregates "gatekeeping" challenges to expert witness testimony from multiple disparate sources.

Case information is searchable by numerous criteria including: Expert **Name**, **Discipline**, **Court**, **Judge**, etc., all located in the left-hand column of the home page. A date range (from 1993 to the present) can also be set.

The site's collection of "over 10,000 briefs and other supporting documents" can also be keyword searched to retrieve sample documents for cases you may be handling. The search is free and "the first 10 percent of the document you may have interest in purchasing" is viewable for free. Prices for the full text of the documents is the same as noted below.

Individual annual subscriptions are $295. A two hour and a half hour individual subscription are also available for $25 and $10 respectively. Annual subscribers pay $7.50 per brief, motion, transcript, etc. from the site's collection; two hour and half hour subscribers pay $15. Multiple-user/law firm subscriptions are also available.

Our View: Checking for previous challenges (whether successful or not) to the opposition's experts, and even to your own experts before retaining them, can be an excellent strategy. While much of the information in the site's database can be located from various free sources on the Internet, Daubert Tracker can save you time by doing the leg work for you by aggregating all of it in one place. This is particularly true in the cases where their staff researches the names of those referred to in motions only as "plaintiff's expert" or where their staff corrects an expert's name that was misspelled in a document.

Expert Witness Profiler

As this volume was going to print, we learned about a new service offering due diligence services for expert witnesses. The Expert Witness Profiler is a joint venture between the principals of The Daubert Tracker (**http://www.dauberttracker.com**) and the JurisPro Expert Witness Directory (**http://www.jurispro.com**).

The Expert Witness Profiler (**www.expertwitnessprofiler.com**) will provide comprehensive expert witness background reports detailing references to specific experts from a variety of sources. These include: case opinions, Daubert Tracker Case Reports, jury verdict reports, briefs, and other case-related documents (including access to transcripts where available). The Profiler will also include personal information such as the expert's political persuasion, interests, and opinions posted on various Web sites. Attorneys could use the Expert Witness Profiler to research an expert's professional background, including an expert's disciplinary history, licenses, and certifications.

Ask a Lawyer for Help

An alternative to joining one of these associations in order to search their deposition transcripts would be to contact lawyers directly to see if they will supply you with transcripts of the experts. You would either have to know of a case similar to yours to do this (which you might through your case law or jury verdict research), or you might find that the experts themselves have listed, on their Web sites, the names of the lawyers with whom they have worked in the past. Of course, you can simply ask the expert for a list of lawyer references and case names. Most lawyers keep their own expert witness transcripts, and would be willing to share (provided, of course, the favor is returned some day).

Case Law

An expert's name may also appear in a reported opinion. Fortunately, many reported opinions can be searched for free through one of the many free case law databases, such as the Public Library of Law at **http://www.plol.org**, Justia at **http://www.justia.com**, LexisOne at **http://www.lexisone.com**, or FindLaw at **http://www.findlaw.com**. To conduct retrospective or nationwide searches, you'll usually need to use a pay database, such as major players Lexis or Westlaw (which both also have a variety of other tools for finding experts, including expert witness directories and jury verdicts), or some of the newer case law sites, such as Casemaker, Fastcase, LoisLaw, or VersusLaw, some of which may be

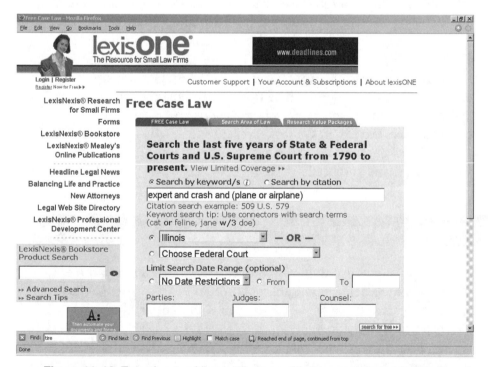

Figure 11-13. Type the word "expert" along with the expertise sought using relevant keywords that describe the expertise (e.g., plane crash). Reprinted with permission of LexisNexis.

offered free through your bar association as a member benefit. Searching for experts in reported decisions is similar to the technique used in a general search-engine search for experts as noted above. To find cases using a known expert's name, type in the name alone; if their name is common, add keywords that describe the expertise. If trying to locate an expert in a specific area of expertise, type the word *expert* along with the expertise sought, using relevant keywords.

Checklist Item 12: Locate Academic Experts Through University Sites

If you plan to hire or depose experts who happen to be professors, go to the college's or university's Web site for a look at their CV, courses they've taught, and articles or books they have published. Links to college and university home pages can be found at the American Universities site, described below.

Index of American Universities

http://www.clas.ufl.edu/CLAS/american-universities.html

Purpose: To locate for academic experts who are teaching in universities and colleges.

Content: The site provides an alphabetical list of links to Web sites of universities and colleges in the Unites States granting Bachelor or advanced degrees.

Our View: Having to link to individual schools college by college, and then search for faculty who may make good experts at each one can be time consuming.

Tips: Start out with institutions nearby. A list of links to U.S. community colleges can be found at **http://www.mcli .dist.maricopa.edu/cc/**. A list of links to Canadian universities can be found at **http://www.uwaterloo.ca/canu**. A list of links international universities can be found at **http://www.findaschool.org**.

Checklist Item 13: Find Government Experts Through Government Reports

Former government employees may make good experts and so may nongovernment experts who have testified before a Senate or House committee hearing, or have been quoted in a Senate or House report. Current

USC Experts

USC Experts Directory is a directory provided by the University of Southern California of over a thousand USC scientists, scholars, administrators, and physicians who are able and willing to comment on issues in the news. Although primarily for the media, this could be another avenue to find academic experts. (See **http://www.usc.edu/uscnews/experts/**.)

government employees may be able to answer your questions or point you to a former government expert. But, it can take time to cut through the layers of government to find the right person. If you persevere, you're likely to be rewarded with someone who understands exactly what you're talking about. A good starting place to locate potential experts is at a government agency's Web site because it often includes personnel directories. To find a specific state government agency's Web site, see State and Local Government on the Net (**http://www.statelocalgov.net**). To browse through an alphabetical list of all federal agencies, a visit to USA.gov is in order (**http://www.usa.gov/Agencies/Federal/All_Agencies/index.shtml**).

USA.gov can also be searched using keywords to locate testifying experts by name or by the specialty you are interested in (**http://www .usa.gov**). USA.gov indexes millions of Web pages from federal and state

Figure 11-14. Browse through USA.gov's alphabetical list of agencies to link to one that deals with the subject area for which you are seeking an expert.

governments, the District of Columbia, and U.S. territories. Most of these pages are not available on any commercial Web site.

To search House and Senate committee reports, full text dating back to 1995, use Thomas (**http://thomas.loc.gov/home/thomas.html**). At the state level, the legislative history of a bill may include references to government and nongovernment experts. Use FindLaw (**http://www.findlaw .com/casecode/#statelaw**) to link to any state's legislative information.

Here is an example of how we found experts by searching California legislative history. We searched the bills for the keywords *seat belt and school bus and safety and children*. This led to a 1999 bill requiring that seat belts be installed in school buses by 2002 (**http://www.leginfo.ca.gov/ bilinfo.html**). The Analyses (California's equivalent of legislative history) section of the bill listed several committee reports. We reviewed the Senate committee report from July 12, 1999 and its staff comments and learned that "this bill is the latest in a series of efforts . . . [that] have been largely unsuccessful . . . [A] study to determine the appropriateness of requiring lap belts . . . determined that the existing research . . . weigh(ed) *against* new lap belt policies for . . . school buses." Listed in these staff comments were specific references to several studies, the names of associations in opposition to the bill, the name of the chair of the committee, and the name of the consultant for the study. Contacting any of these people or groups could be fruitful in finding an expert to testify that requiring lap belts in school buses is unsafe.

Checklist Item 14: Use Pay Referral Sites

If you haven't had luck finding the appropriate expert with any of the above sources (or if you want someone else to do the legwork for you), consult a referral site.

The California-based ForensisGroup (**http://www.forensisgroup.com**) provides referrals to "over 1,000 consultants, experts, expert witnesses, forensic experts, and investigators in construction, engineering, medicine, science, and other technical disciplines, throughout the United States." While you can search their database by expertise and geographic area, and view very short blurbs about selected experts, you'll need to contact this referral company to retain that expert or to learn of other experts in that field. (Note that no expert names are displayed in search results, only an identifying **Expert No.** and the brief description mentioned above are displayed.)

For referrals to medical experts who will review a case or testify in all types of health-care related malpractice, personal injury, and other tort litigation cases (and criminal law), go to medQuest (**http://www.med questltd.com**). It provides referrals to testifying medical experts (physicians, dentists, osteopaths, podiatrists, chiropractors, optometrists, nurses, pharmacists, therapists, and others) in every region of the country. MedQuest does not offer even the briefest descriptions for you to preview as there are at ForensisGroup.

TASA (**http://www.tasanet.com**), a site with more than 10,000 areas of expertise represented, is one of the best known of the expert witness referral companies. When you search TASA's online Directory of Expertise you are offered many categories to choose from, plus subcategories. Once you make your selection, the number of experts in the selected field and their geographic locations are shown. Users are then required to call or e-mail TASA for the experts' names and contact information. There is no fee until the expert is engaged. The expert's fees and expenses, as well as a one-time (per-case) $175 fee are billed by TASA.

CHAPTER TWELVE

Using Expensive Pay Databases for Free

Remote Internet Access to Expensive Pay Databases Free Through Your Library

Libraries have come a long way in terms of providing access to library resources over the Internet. At first, libraries only uploaded their catalogs to the Web.

Oh, how far we've come; libraries are now providing library patrons with *free* remote access over the Internet to selected pay databases that contain a wealth of factual information that we can use for investigative purposes. To say that the addition of free remote access to pay databases is a valuable resource is an understatement. In fact, it's invaluable. It not only saves you a commute to the library, it opens up amazing amounts of expensive and useful information to you, free—saving you from investing in database subscriptions that you might need only occasionally. What better way to gather background information about people than by reading articles from newspapers and magazines?

Whether a library offers remote access at all varies widely from library to library. To find out if your local public library does, visit their Web site. Don't know your public library's URL? You can locate it at the Libdex site (**http://www.libdex.com**). Here are links to three library remote access databases: Chicago Public Library (CPL) at **http://www.chipublib.org/cpl booksmovies/research/online_research.php**, Los Angeles Public Library (LAPL) at **http://databases.lapl.org**, and New York Public Library (NYPL) at **http://www.nypl.org/databases/**. If your library does have remote access, you'll need to have a library card. Some libraries allow you to apply online and then pick the card up in person. Once you have your card, you'll need to enter your library card number into the library's remote access database Web page. You may have to also enter a password or your ZIP code.

For those libraries that offer remote access to databases, the number and type of databases vary widely. The following are examples of the types of databases that can be accessed at NYPL. Many of these can also be accessed at LAPL and CPL, among other libraries:

- Academic Search Premier: 4,000 scholarly publications (full text) covering social sciences, humanities, education, computer sciences, engineering, medical sciences, and more
- Biography Resource Center: information on over 275,000 people
- Business and Company Resource Center (Gale): subjects include finance, acquisitions and mergers, international trade, money management, new technologies and products, local and regional business trends, investments, and banking
- Business Source Premier: 2,470 scholarly business journals (full text) covering management, economics, finance, accounting, international business, and more
- Encyclopaedia Britannica: Also includes Merriam-Webster's Collegiate Dictionary and the Britannica Book of the Year
- National Newspaper Index (1977–present): Simultaneous search of *The New York Times, The Wall Street Journal, The Christian Science Monitor, Los Angeles Times, USA Today* and *The Washington Post*
- *New York Times* and *New York Post* (Gale): full text newspaper articles from 2000 to the present
- Newspaper Source: full text of more than 170 regional U.S. newspapers, 20 international newspapers, newswires, and television and radio news transcripts

You will find that some of the databases that are available at one library on a remote basis may be completely unavailable at another library (remotely or in-person). For example, CPL has remote access to *ABI Inform* while the other two libraries don't carry this database at all. And the *Associations Unlimited*, which has detailed descriptions of over 135,000 international and U.S. national, regional, state, and local associations covering a multitude of subjects, is available remotely (free) at LAPL and NYPL, but not CPL. This title is extremely useful for locating experts— especially those in unusual fields. See Chapter 11, Finding and Backgrounding Expert Witnesses, for our quest for a chewing gum expert.

Other times, you will find that one library's remote database is another library's in-person database only. There's no rhyme or reason. For example, at LAPL, *Reference USA* (used to search 120 million U.S. households by name to obtain phone numbers and addresses) and the Oxford Dictionary are remote access databases, but not so at NYPL. They can be accessed only by an in-person visit to NYPL.

As you peruse any of these libraries' lists of remote databases, you should have one foot out the door—heading over to visit your local library to pick up your library card. These databases have truly remarkable information. If your local library does not provide access to databases, some states (e.g., Ohio) provide this service to anyone in the state who has a library card. (See Ohio Public Library Information Network (OPLIN) at **http://tinyurl.com/rnqkd**.) Also, some libraries will offer free library cards even to those outside their jurisdiction. For example, Los Angeles Public Library (**http://www.lapl.org/about/borrower.html**) offers cards to residents of Orange and Ventura Counties, in addition to Los Angeles County. However, one has to pick the card up in person. Finally, some libraries allow non-residents to access their libraries and remote databases for a fee. NYPL charges non-residents $100 for this service (**http://www.nypl.org/about/faq.html**).

The convenience of being able to search remotely (and for free) through the full text of so many databases for information, and to read and print the full text of the materials from your office or home computer, surpasses anything we imagined just a few years ago. The usefulness of browsing through a library's online catalog to locate books or journals probably now pales in comparison to the actual full text information you can access via remote library databases.

> For those still paying for articles found in a Google News Archive search or found at various newspaper and magazine Web sites, be sure to first check your library remote databases to see if the same article is available there for free.

Free Public Library Virtual Reference Services

Many public libraries offer free virtual reference services. For example, the New York Public Library's Ask Librarians Online service (**http://www.nypl.org/questions**), allows public-library patrons the option of asking librarians questions online and then receiving answers via e-mail (within 24 hours) or through chat 24/7. A patron can also choose to chat with a Spanish-speaking librarian. The reference staff at NYPL will answer questions over the telephone, Monday to Saturday, from 9:00 am to 6:00 pm, EST. One does not have to be a NYPL patron to take advantage of these services. Locate your local public library's Web site at the Libdex site to find out if they offer a similar service (**http://www.libdex.com**). Use the LiveRef directory to link to various types of libraries (government, university, or special libraries) that offer free chat reference services (**http://www.public.iastate.edu/~CYBERSTACKS/LiveRef.htm**). While some of the links no longer work, this site gives you an idea of the wide variety of libraries that offer virtual reference service.

Pay Library Virtual (Chat) Reference Services

Many libraries also offer pay reference services in a virtual (chat) mode. With the advent of the Web, you don't even need to be restricted to your *local* library, but can make use of any library's services remotely. For example, the New York Public Library's pay reference service can assist you in "locating a discrete fact to compiling a report." See NYPL Express at **http://www.nypl.org/express/index.html** and for pricing, see **http://www.nypl.org/express/fees.html**. Fees for research range from $60 to $140 per hour and fees for document delivery only range from $18 to $50, depending on the turnaround time requested. Academic libraries and county law libraries also may offer pay reference services and document delivery.

Other Reference Assistance

The Association of Independent Information Professionals offers a free referral service at their site to obtain contact information for fee-based reference assistance (**http://www.aiip.org/MemberDirectory?&tab=1**). To find the right informational professional for your needs, search by name, business name, city, subject expertise, service type, or business description. Finally, take a look at Chapter 11, Finding and Backgrounding Expert Witnesses, for ideas on where else to find subject specialists. Often, a professional or trade association has a staff person (or even a library) where you can make inquiries about research assistance.

*CHAPTER*THIRTEEN

Finding Altered or Removed Web Pages

Isn't the Most Current Information Better?

You might wonder why you'd want to find old information that has been altered or removed from the Internet completely. After all, aren't we supposed to be looking for the most current information?

- What if your client asks you to conduct due diligence before the client invests in a business, but when you review the business owner's Web site to review past press releases, there are only recent press releases. You'd like to review past press releases but they aren't in your Google search engine results either.
- What if a potential client is being sued for theft of trade secrets by his former employer? The potential client swears he got the information off their public Web site, but when you visit the site, the information is nowhere to be found. How can you find out if the former employer took the information down and that this potential client is telling the truth?
- What if you'd read an article on an opposing expert witness' Web site that ends up contradicting a point the expert made during their deposition and you now want to find that article to impeach the expert at trial but the article has been taken down from the site when you go back to look for it?

There may still be a way to find the information you need: by locating older versions of Web pages that have been altered or removed using

Google Cache, **Yahoo! Cache**, and **The Wayback Machine** (also referred to as **Internet Archive** or **Archive.org**).

War Story: Using Archive.org's Wayback Machine

Marcia Burris, library manager at Ogletree, Deakins, Nash, Smoak & Stewart, P.C., in Greenville, South Carolina, tells this story:

> I needed to confirm the contents of a two-year-old news article that appeared on the Internet. The story was about a mugging and was needed to verify an individual's date of injury in a litigation matter our firm was involved in. The story had appeared in the *Daily Star*, "The First Bangladeshi Daily Newspaper on the Internet," but the archives from that year were no longer online. My e-mail to the editor may have gone through, but I got no response. My e-mail to the Webmaster bounced back. I also tried looking in other sources on Westlaw and Lexis for coverage of the same story, but found nothing. After posing the question on a research LISTERV, a number of people suggested the Wayback Machine. I was able to find the archived version of the online paper for the date I was looking for and printed out the article I needed.

As we have mentioned many times in this book, material on the Internet changes constantly. This can be a boon or bane to a lawyer searching for information. While Web page changes usually result in more information being available, the opposite can also be true.

For a variety of reasons, a Web site owner might remove information from a Web site. Just because information has been removed from a site does not (necessarily) mean that it is gone forever as illustrated by the earlier war story. Here are details about the Wayback Machine to help you retrieve that information after it has been removed from the site owner's Web server.

Internet Archive (the Wayback Machine)

http://www.archive.org

Purpose: To retrieve older versions of Web pages.

Content: In 1996, the Internet Archive set about building a permanent historical record of that ephemeral new

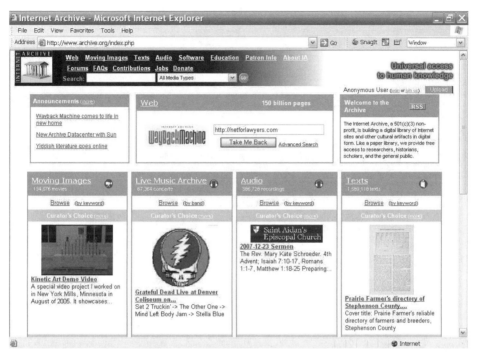

Figure 13-1. The Wayback Machine at Archive.org has archived versions of many Web sites dating back to 1996.

medium, the World Wide Web. Since then, the Internet Archive has been collaborating with the Library of Congress, the Smithsonian Institution, National Science Foundation, and others to store and record Web pages. The Internet Archive made its collection available to the public via its Wayback Machine Web site in October 2001. In August 2006, the site boasted more than 55 billion Web pages in its archive, up from 10 billion only three years earlier. As of May 2009, there were 150 billion pages.

Type the URL of any site you are interested in viewing into the search box on the Archive.org home page to comb the archive's hundreds of terabytes of data. Results are returned in a table listing the target site's stored pages by the date they were modified and added to the archive.

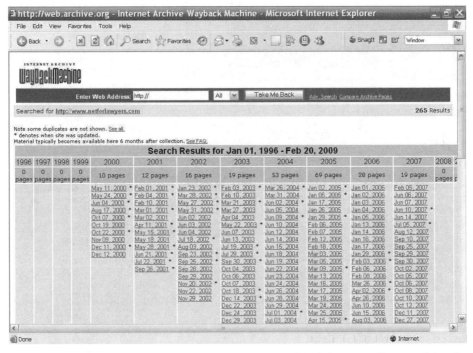

Figure 13-2. Click on any date listed in the table of dates to discover how the Web page looked on that day.

There are some instructions in the upper left corner of the table of results informing you that:

- Some duplicates are not shown (but a **See all** link is provided to view duplicates)
- An asterisk to the right of a date denotes that the site was updated on that date
- Web pages will be available 6-14 months <u>after</u> collection (so this site might not help you if you need to see Web pages that were changed within the last 6-14 months)

Clicking on any of the returned links brings up the stored version of that page as it appeared on the date indicated.

Clicking on the **Advanced Search** option underneath the **Take Me Back** button on the site's home page gives you additional options for honing in on the pages you want from the target Web site. You can request results be returned only within a specific date range. (If you don't select a date range, the results will include links to all of the versions of your target site in the Wayback Machine's archive.) You can also request that the results show check boxes to allow comparison of two versions of a page. A new (still in Beta) feature on the Advanced Search Page links to **http://www.2convert.com**, a service that will convert a Web page that you are viewing to PDF. This is useful for saving a page to your hard drive for later use for those of you who do not own the full version of Acrobat (or other PDF creation software).

Another handy feature is the ability to restrict results to a specific file type (**Images**, **Audio**, **Binary**, **Text**, or **PDF**). The default is all file types. If one is searching for a PDF document once located at someone's Web site (and now no longer there) enter the URL into archive.org's **Advanced search** box and limit the results to PDF. We've tried it and it works. Notice that the PowerPoint file type is not an option in the drop-down menu. We

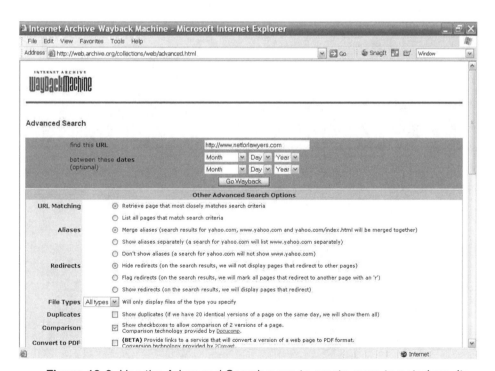

Figure 13-3. Use the Advanced Search page to create more targeted results.

have, however, found PowerPoint presentations stored in the Internet Archive. If we have the exact URL for the PowerPoint presentation, it's an easy task. But if we are simply fishing around to ascertain the existence of a PowerPoint presentation, that's a more time consuming task. We would enter the domain's URL into the Internet Archive's search box and click on random dates listed on the table of results until we chanced upon one.

It is important to note that the Internet Archive displays the exact date and time (military time) that it captured each Web page. This information is found in the address bar of each page stored at Archive.org. For example, **http://web.archive.org/web/20010201152800/http:// netforlawyers.com**, shows that the page was captured by Archive.org on 02/01/2001 at 15:28:00 (3:28 PM). However, there is a caveat about dates. Archive.org explains that,

> The date assigned by the Internet Archive applies to the HTML file but not to image files linked therein. Thus images

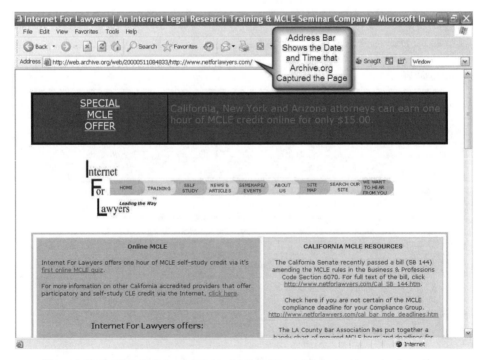

Figure 13-4. The address bar shows that the netforlawyers.com page was captured by Archive.org on 02/01/2001 at 15:28:00 (3:28 PM).

that appear on the printed page may not have been archived on the same date as the HTML file. Likewise, if a website is designed with "frames," the date assigned by the Internet Archive applies to the frameset as a whole, and not the individual pages within each frame.

When would Archive.org's display of each page's exact dates be important: when trying to prove certain facts, such as who had "first use" to a trademark in a "first use" trademark opposition or infringement proceeding. By displaying older versions of each party's Web site (stored at Archive.org), one could show the exact date each party used the mark. The senior user would probably prevail.

Our View: While the Wayback Machine's archive is not complete, it does offer a rare opportunity to view Web site content that has been changed or removed from the Internet.

Tip: The archive preserves many (but not all) of the embedded hyper-links in Web pages that it stores. For example, if you were to click on the **May 11, 2001** link in the results list of an Archive.org search for the netforlawyers.com Web site, you would see the home page of the site as it appeared on May 11, 2000. You would also be able to click on the hyperlinks on that page to jump to different pages on that older version of the site. It's important to note that the archive does not capture every page of every Web site on every visit. If you click a hyperlink to request a page that was not captured on the same day as the page you've started on, Archive.org will deliver the next available date of the page you requested. For example, if you click the **About Us** hyperlink on the **May 11, 2001** version of netforlawyers.com's home page, you would be taken to the May 20, 2001 version of the **About Us** page, because the Archive did not capture the **About Us** page on May 11, 2001. To complicate the issue of dates even more, "If the requested page has not been archived, but [is] still available on the live web, the Wayback Machine will grab the live page and it will be displayed with today's date code."

Review the Internet Archives' FAQ at **http://www .archive.org/about/faqs.php** for more detailed information on how the Archive works and how to obtain an affidavit to authenticate Internet Archive pages that you need to rely upon for litigation. See the appendix to view the affidavit that Molly Davis (the Internet Archive's Administrative Director) provided in 2004 to the court during the *Telewizja Polska USA v. Echostar Satellite* litigation.

The site's **Compare Archive Pages** feature allows you to select two dates from your search results lists. Clicking the **Compare two dates** button displays the newer text in one color while the text from the earlier version that it replaced is struck-through and in another color. While this is handy for a quick comparison while researching, if comparing two versions of a site for a jury, it might be better to display clean versions of both side-by-side and point out (or otherwise highlight) the differences you want jurors to focus on.

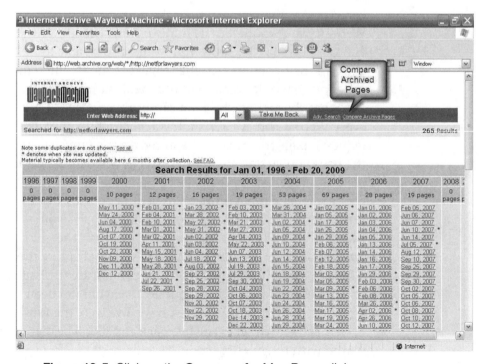

Figure 13-5. Click on the **Compare Archive Pages** link.

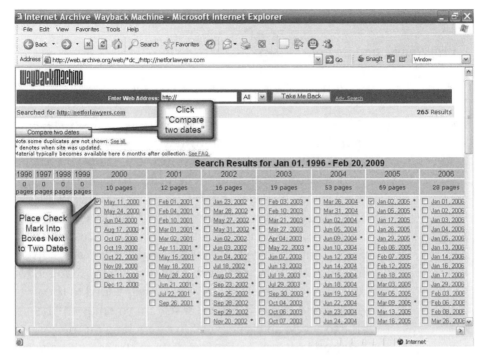

Figure 13-6. A new table of results offers check boxes to the left of each date. Enter check marks into the boxes next to two dates and then click **Compare two dates**.

Not All Sites Are Indexed at Archive.org

The **Robots.txt Query Exclusion**, "means that the site is blocked by the site owner. The Internet Archive was not contacted and has no record of when the exclusion took effect." Thus, the Internet Archive does not crawl the site and the site's pages are not stored at the Internet Archive.

The **Blocked Site Error**, "means that the Internet Archive was contacted by the site owner and asked to remove the site from the Wayback Machine. Pursuant to its document retention policy, the Internet Archive keeps the original request for [one] month." If a site is unavailable at Archive.org, for either of the reasons noted above, this might indicate the site owner is hiding something. Try subpoenaing the site owner directly.

Ethics Alert

If a site owner requests that their site be removed from the Wayback Machine after litigation has begun, would this be considered spoliation of evidence?

Google Cache

http://www.google.com

Purpose: To retrieve older versions of Web pages.

Content: When Google adds most pages to its index, it also takes a snapshot of the page, adding it to Google's cache of stored Web pages. This allows Google to show you where your keywords appear in the returned page, or to display the page in the event that it later becomes unavailable. This can serve as a viewable record of the page before it changed or became unavailable. The date on which Google captured its "cached" version of the page is displayed at the very top of the page. If a page is changed (or removed from the Internet) after it was added to the Google index and before your search, you may still be able to access an earlier version by clicking on the **Cached** link (see Figure 13-8). When the cached page is displayed, each search term is highlighted in a different color on the page.

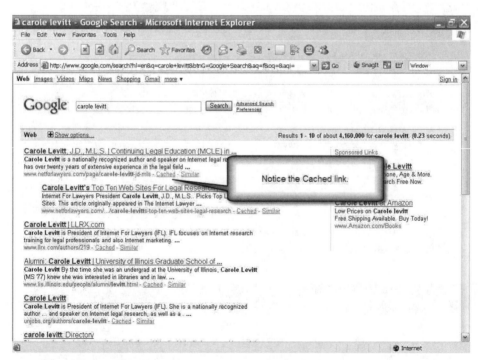

Figure 13-7. Cached links are found in most Google search results (to the right of the URL). Google™ is a trademark of Google Technology Inc.

The Google cache stores only the HTML content of a Web page on Google's servers (the actual HTML code that makes up the page, including any text visible on the page). One major drawback of the Google cache is that it does not store non-HTML information, such as images (photos, buttons, banners, and so on), video, audio, or multimedia files (Macromedia Flash files). When displaying the cached page, Google's server retrieves this non-HTML content from its original location on the Web server where the cached page was originally stored (in other words, the live site of the specific Web site you are viewing and not the Google cache on Google's server). Therefore you might find large, empty spaces with little red X's in place of the non-HMTL content if those files have been removed from their original locations; or you might be viewing more current, live graphics or video content from the current version of a page along with the archived text content stored in the Google cache.

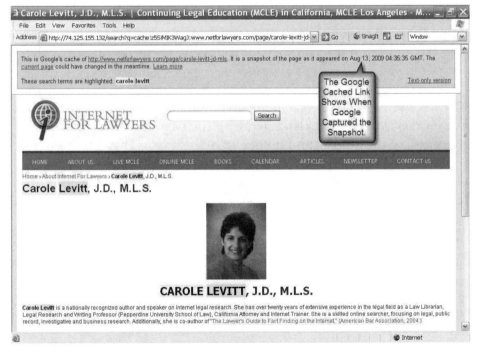

Figure 13-8. Clicking on the **Cached** page link returns a snapshot of the text of the target Web page on the day that Google's robots last visited it (including the date of the visit, which is displayed at the top). Non-text elements, such as images or movies seen in a cached page, are not actually cached on the Google servers, but are fed live from the target Web page's server if still loaded there. Google™ is a trademark of Google Technology Inc.

We can't really be certain how long an archived version of a Web page will remain in the Google cache. On average, Google revisits Web pages once a month (though some are visited on a significantly more frequent basis). The older cached version is replaced by a newer cached version after Google revisits the page and finds a change. This is in contrast to the Internet Archive, which attempts to save as many versions as possible.

Our View: Unfortunately, not every search result is accompanied by a Cached link. In fact, Web site owners can request that Google not cache their pages.

Tip: If the page you are searching for is not available from Google's cache, try searching the cache at MSN Bing or Yahoo! Another option is to search at the Archive.org.

Yahoo! (**http://www.yahoo.com**) and Bing (**http://www.bing.com**) also offer cached versions of many of the sites in their index. Yahoo! and Bing both present their cached material in much the same way as Google except that Yahoo! does not include the date on which the cached version was captured, but it does include a link directly to the Archive.org collection of old versions of the same page.

Like Google, Bing, and Yahoo!, Archive.org also stores primarily the HTML content of the pages it archives, but in many instances, it does also store non-HTML content associated with the pages stored in its archive, but not all of the images, and not for all of the pages. Therefore, you may or may not get to see the full view of the old version of the Web page when viewing these old versions of pages stored in the Google, Bing, or Yahoo! cache or at Archive.org.

CHAPTER **FOURTEEN**

Getting Web Pages from the Internet and Archive.org Admitted into Evidence

Getting Web pages admitted into evidence should be no different than getting traditional sources of evidence admitted. Like traditional evidence, evidence from Web pages must be: (1) relevant and (2) authentic before they can be admissible. While proving relevancy of Web pages rarely seems to be an issue, problems <u>authenticating</u> Web page evidence often arise, especially if the Web pages are no longer available at the original Web site, but are instead stored at the Archive.org.

Authenticating Web Pages for Admissibility

Pursuant to Federal Rules of Evidence 901 (a), an attorney's first step to authenticate Web pages, is to prove that "the matter in question is what its proponent claims." To meet this requirement, the Web page that contains the evidence should be printed, along with any page on the Web site that indicates who owns the site. This is usually found on the **About Us** page. (Searching a domain registry, such as Betterwhois.com, to verify ownership is not necessarily going to yield the true owner of the Web site because domain registries do not verify that real names are used.) The print-out of the pages should include both the URL and the date the page was viewed. Also request that the researcher sign a declaration explaining how, and on what date, the Web page evidence was found on the Internet.

Besides printing the page, some attorneys also save it as a PDF. But if you own the full version of Adobe Acrobat, you know that information in a PDF can be altered and may be subject to objections by opposing counsel. Another (and probably better) way to save a Web page would be to take a screen shot of it because screen shots are not easily altered. To take a screen shot, simultaneously hold down the **Alt** and **PrtSc** keys on your Windows keyboard and then paste (**Ctrl V**) it into a Word, WordPerfect, or Powerpoint document. Mac users should simultaneously hold down the **Apple**, **Shift**, and number **3** keys to take a screen shot. This will save it to the desktop as a .png image (which can be pasted into a Word, WordPerfect, or Powerpoint document).

Asking the Web site owner to authenticate the contents of his or her page is another avenue. If the Web site owner is the opposing party, this can be more challenging, but do try to elicit a stipulation. If trying to authenticate Web pages that are no longer stored at the Web site in question, but which are now stored at the Internet Archive, "judicial notice and stipulation" are suggested by the Internet Archive and if that fails, their standard affidavit is available (**http://www.archive.org/legal/affidavit.php**). (See the Appendix for a copy of the affidavit.)

Case Law Regarding Authenticating Web Page Evidence from Archive.org

The most widely cited "case" in favor of admitting evidence from Archive.org, *Telewizja Polska USA, Inc.* v. *Echostar Satellite*, Memorandum Opinion and Order, Case No. 02C3293 (N.D. Ill. Oct. 14, 2004), actually emanates from a Federal Magistrate Judge's Memorandum Opinion and Order in a *Motion in limine* hearing. The *Telewizja Polska* case is unreported (and thus, not binding on other courts). To read the full text of the Magistrate's Memorandum Opinion and Order, see page 295 in the Appendix. In the *Motion in limine*, Plaintiff *Telewizja Polska* sought to suppress what their Web site pages looked like on various days in 2001 (as displayed at Archive.org). According to the opinion, the pages were potentially damaging to plaintiff's case. In footnote 1, the Magistrate noted, "Coincidentally, Plaintiff claims that it is unable to access any images of its website during the time in question." (Hence, the defendant resorted to relying upon the Web pages stored at Archive.org.)

After the Motion *in limine* hearing, Federal Magistrate Keys rejected plaintiff's claim that Web pages from the Internet Archive Web site were not properly authenticated. He also rejected plaintiff's attack on the Internet Archive Web site as an unreliable source, stating that Federal Rules of Evidence Rule 901 requires only a *prima facie* showing of genuineness and leaves it to the jury to determine the true authenticity. As to admissibility, the Magistrate noted that many prior courts have indicated that hearsay objections to Internet evidence could be overcome. The Magistrate rejected plaintiff's contention that the archived Web pages stored at the Internet Archive constituted hearsay, finding that they were not "statements" but merely images and text showing what a Web site once looked like. (The plaintiff had alleged they were "double hearsay," no less.) The Magistrate also found that the Web site pages were an admission by a party-opponent and were admissible under the "best evidence" rule.

However, those who want to rely on Magistrate Keys' decision will encounter a slight glitch: District Court Judge Ronald Guzman <u>overruled</u> Magistrate Keys' findings in the *Telewizja Polska USA* v. *Echostar Satellite*, case. Judge Guzman's opinion is never cited by any authors writing articles about admitting Internet Archive pages (except for one), nor do any judges, deciding similar cases, cite to it. They only cite to the Magistrate's decision. The only article to inform us that District Court Judge Ronald Guzman overruled Magistrate Keys at trial, is from Wikipedia (**http://en.wikipedia.org/wiki/Wayback_Machine#Telewizja_Polska**), not necessarily considered the most trusted of sources. The Wikipedia article offers no citation to back up its assertion that Judge Guzman overruled Magistrate Keys. In fact, the only citation is to an article in the *Journal of Internet Law* and that article cites to the <u>Magistrate's</u> decision.

After sifting through many documents at PACER, we were unable to find the judge's overruling opinion. We then e-mailed Phillip Zisook at Deutsch, Levy, and Engel (**http://www.dlec.com/attorneys/phillipzisook.html**), Telewizja Polska's attorney in the case, who confirmed that the Wikipedia article was correct (and was written by someone at his firm). Mr. Zisook also informed us that the ruling was made during trial, thus there was no written opinion or order, and that's the reason no one cites to what actually happened at trial. There's also no trial transcript available because the client did not order one.

The following is what the Wikipedia article (**http://en.wikipedia.org/wiki/Wayback_Machine#Telewizja_Polska**) stated that Judge Guzman held (and confirmed by Attorney Zisook):

> The Internet Archive employee's affidavit and underlying Web pages (at Telewizja Polska's Web site) were not admissible as evidence.
>
> The employee's affidavit contained hearsay and inconclusive supporting statements.
>
> The purported Web page printouts were not self-authenticating.

In another unreported federal Internet Archive.org admissibility case, *Novak* v. *Tucows*, No. 06-CV-1909, 2007 U.S. Dist. Lexis 21269 (E.D.N.Y. March 26, 2007), the court explained, in its Memorandum and Order, that plaintiff Novak, "obtained a printout through a web site called the Internet Archive." The court described the Internet Archive as, "[a] digital library of Internet sites. . . . The Internet Archive operates a service called the 'Wayback Machine,' which purports to allow a user to obtain an archived Web page as it appeared at a particular moment in time. . . ." The court also discussed Novak's declaration regarding the authenticity of pages printed from the Wayback Machine:

> While plaintiff's declaration purports to cure his inability to authenticate the documents printed from the [I]nternet, he in fact lacks the personal knowledge required to set forth with any certainty that the documents obtained via third-party Web sites are, in fact, what he proclaims them to be. This problem is even more acute in the case of documents procured through the Wayback Machine. Plaintiff states that the Web pages archived within the Wayback Machine are based upon "data from third parties who compile the data by using software programs known as crawlers," who then "donate" such data to the Internet Archive, which "preserves and provides access to it." (Novak Decl. ¶ 4.) Based upon Novak's assertions, it is clear that the information posted on the Wayback Machine is only as valid as the third-party donating the page decides to make it—the authorized owners and managers of the archived websites play no role in ensuring that the material posted in the Wayback Machine accurately represents what was posted on their official websites at the relevant time. As Novak proffers neither testimony nor sworn statements attesting to the authenticity of the contested Web page exhibits by any employee of the companies hosting the sites from which plaintiff printed the pages, such exhibits cannot be authenticated as required under the Rules of Evidence.

It appears that Novak obtained the above explanation about the Internet Archive from Internet Archive's own standard affidavit. (See **http://www.archive.org/legal/affidavit.php** and the Appendix of this book.) Perhaps the affidavit needs to contain a better description of how Archive.org works.

Because *Telewizja Polska* Judge Guzman and Magistrate Keys came to opposite conclusions, and because both *Telewizja* and *Novak* are both unreported opinions, we do not have a binding <u>reported</u> decision as to whether pages from the Archive.org can be authenticated and overcome hearsay objections. However, anecdotal reporting from attorneys attending our seminars indicates that admitting Internet Web pages (from the original site in question and from pages stored at Archive.org) happens all the time <u>and</u> the same can be said for suppressing the pages. In other words, it varies from judge to judge. Much will depend upon their understanding of the Internet. Therefore, depending on whether you need to admit or suppress Web pages, especially from Archive.org, educating the judge (through an expert witness) may be in order.

Educating the Judge about Internet Archive

The *Novak* judge's comments regarding how the Internet Archive works shows a fundamental misunderstanding of its processes and indicates to us that some judges could benefit from Internet education. In particular, the following comment led us to this conclusion: "It is clear that the information posted on the Wayback Machine is only as valid as the third-party donating the page decides to make it." It seems to us that the court is under the impression that the "third-party donating the page" is a human being and that the donation (the text and images of pages from various Web sites), is subject to human manipulation. Another indication that judges could benefit from Internet education is the *Novak* judge's reliance, as late as 2007, on a 1999 case where information from the Internet was dismissed as "Voodoo information" by the judge in *St. Clair v. Johnny's Oyster & Shrimp, Inc.*, 76 F. Supp. 2d 773, 775 (S.D. Tex. 1999). See page xxvii for details about this case and see page 251 of the Appendix for the full text of this case.

In educating judges about the Internet Archive, it's best to focus on the other part of Novak's explanation—that the "third parties" (the Web service, Alexa.com) use "software programs known as crawlers" to gather and archive the Web pages. Crawlers are merely <u>automated</u> software programs, and unlike humans, have no reason to manipulate the pages before Alexa.com "donates" them to Archive.org.

*CHAPTER*FIFTEEN

Consumer Credit Reports and Credit Headers

Some of the "freshest" information about someone's most current address and phone number comes from the credit applications they fill out each time they attempt to obtain credit from a financial institution or pay their monthly credit card statement. Information from the applications is reported to credit bureaus (such as Experian, TransUnion, and Equifax). These bureaus compile the information into a consumer credit report (also referred to as a "credit report" or a "consumer report") that contains financial information, such as the account type, the opening date of the account, the credit limit, the account status, and the payment history. It also contains nonfinancial/nonpublic, personal information such as a person's address and phone number, date of birth, Social Security number, and sometimes even a drivers' license number or employment information.

There are two federal laws to protect people's financial and nonfinancial/nonpublic information from being disclosed to just anyone. The first law, originally passed in 1970, is the Fair Credit Reporting Act (FCRA), 15 U.S.C. §§ 1681 *et seq* (as amended through 2009) *available at* **http://ftc.gov/os/statutes/fcradoc.pdf**, which regulates access to credit reports (relevant portions of FCRA are laid out on pages 200–201). The second law is the Gramm-Leach-Bliley Act (GLBA), P.L. 106-102, 113 STAT. 1338, 15 U.S.C. 6801 *et seq*, *available at* **http://frwebgate.access.gpo.gov/cgi-bin/getdoc .cgi?dbname=106_cong_public_laws&docid=f:publ102.106.pdf**. Our primary focus will be on Section 6821, which concerns pretexting (*available at* **http://www.ftc.gov/privacy/glbact/glbsub2.htm**) and Section 6802 which prevents financial institutions (including credit bureaus) from disclosing (and selling) nonfinancial/nonpublic, personal information to third parties unless they come within Section 6802's general exceptions (*available at* **http://www.ftc.gov/privacy/glbact/glbsub1.htm**). GLBA will be discussed in more detail later (relevant portions of GLBA are laid out on pages 204–206).

Why Consumer Credit Reports Can't be Used to Find or Background a Person

For anyone who wants to use a consumer credit report to simply locate a person or to obtain general and financial information about that person, beware of the Fair Credit Reporting Act (FCRA), particularly 15 U.S.C. § 1681b(a) through 1681(b)(4), as amended through 2009, *available at* **http://ftc.gov/os/statutes/fcradoc.pdf**. Section 1681b prohibits the disclosure of consumer credit reports by consumer credit reporting agencies, except in response to the following kinds of requests (none of which involve locating a missing person or obtaining background information about a person):

1681b

(a) In general

Subject to subsection (c) of this section, any consumer reporting agency may furnish a consumer report under the following circumstances and no other:

(1) In response to the order of a court having jurisdiction to issue such an order, or a subpoena issued in connection with proceedings before a Federal grand jury.

(2) In accordance with the written instructions of the consumer to whom it relates.

(3) To a person which it has reason to believe—

(A) intends to use the information in connection with a credit transaction involving the consumer on whom the information is to be furnished and involving the extension of credit to, or review or collection of an account of, the consumer; or

(B) intends to use the information for employment purposes; or

(C) intends to use the information in connection with the underwriting of insurance involving the consumer; or

(D) intends to use the information in connection with a determination of the consumer's eligibility for a license or other benefit granted by a governmental instrumentality required by law to consider an applicant's financial responsibility or status; or

        (E) intends to use the information, as a potential investor or servicer, or current insurer, in connection with a valuation of, or an assessment of the credit or prepayment risks associated with, an existing credit obligation; or

        (F) otherwise has a legitimate business need for the information—

             (i) in connection with a business transaction that is initiated by the consumer; or

            (ii) to review an account to determine whether the consumer continues to meet the terms of the account.

    (4) In response to a request by the head of a State or local child support enforcement agency (or a State or local government official authorized by the head of such an agency). . .

(Note: There are other conditions one must comply with in relation to using consumer reports for employment purposes—see 1681b(b))

War Story: No Permissible Business Reason Under FCRA § 1681b(a)(3)

In the case of *Phillips v. Grendahl*, 312 F.3d 357 (8th Cir. 2002), *available at* **http://caselaw.lp.findlaw.com/data2/circs/8th/012616p.pdf**, a "concerned" Minnesota mother, Mary Grendahl, hired a private investigator (PI) from McDowell Investigations. She asked him to check out her daughter's fiancé, Lavon Phillips. The PI retrieved Phillips's Social Security Number from a database and then contacted Econ, a company in the business of furnishing consumer reports, finder's reports, and credit scoring to creditors and PIs. Econ provided a "finder's report," showing the fiancé's credit card accounts and child support obligations.

The Eighth Circuit Court held that the "finder's report" was actually a consumer report under FCRA and that none of the actors in this escapade had a permissible business reason under § 1681b(a)(3) for the information. The court remanded the case for trial, ruling that it was an error to grant summary judgment to the defendants (Grendahl, McDowell Investigations, and Econ) regarding Phillips's claim for wrongful disclosure of a consumer report. While the act allows access to consumer reports for decisions bearing on extending credit to, insuring, or employing someone, it does not allow access for decisions about marriage, noted the court. However, the court held that Phillips's invasion of privacy claim relating to disclosure of his child support order (noted in the finder's report) couldn't support this claim. Even though the information was sensitive, it was not considered a publication of a matter that would be "highly offensive to a reasonable person" because it already was of public record. (The daughter ended up not marrying her fiancé, by the way.)

The Fair and Accurate Credit Transactions Act of 2003 (FACTA)

FACTA, Pub. L. 108-159, 111 Stat. 1952 (2003), *available at* **http://frweb-gate.access.gpo.gov/cgi-bin/getdoc.cgi?dbname=108_cong_public_laws &docid=f:publ159.108.pdf**, amended FCRA by adding new sections to FCRA, "to prevent identity theft, improve resolution of consumer disputes, improve the accuracy of consumer records, make improvements in the use of, and consumer access to, credit information. . ."

While FACTA took effect in 2004, the Federal Trade Commission, among other agencies, was responsible for drafting regulations to implement the Act. The adopted regulations can be found at 16 CFR Part 602, *available at* the e-CFR site at **http://ecfr.gpoaccess.gov/cgi/t/text/text-idx?c=ecfr&sid=f30ad747742458d7788c1c36d4d31ced&rgn=div5&view= text&node=16:1.0.1.6.62&idno=16**.

The FTC Penalizes ChoicePoint for Providing Credit Information to Illegal Subscribers

In the continuing saga of identity theft and privacy violations involving the FCRA and consumer reports, in January of 2006, the FTC alleged that consumer data broker ChoicePoint (**http://choicepoint.com/**) violated the FCRA by turning over consumers' sensitive personal information to subscribers who did not have a permissible purpose for the information and whose applications raised obvious "red flags." (On April 16, 2008, ChoicePoint shareholders approved being acquired by Reed Elsevier (parent company of LexisNexis), and on September 19, 2008, the FTC approved the merger.) While it is absolutely correct that sensitive information about approximately 163,000 Americans was obtained by criminals with the intent of perpetrating credit card fraud and identity theft on those individuals, these criminals did not electronically "break into" the ChoicePoint database despite early reporting about hacking. The criminals acquired the information the same way you or I would—they applied for an account with ChoicePoint and purchased the records from Choice-Point. However, there was one small difference between how you or I would have applied for our account and how the criminals applied for theirs: The criminals used stolen identities and credit card information to apply for a ChoicePoint account with assumed business names that passed ChoicePoint's account vetting process.

The FTC alleges that ChoicePoint did not have reasonable procedures to screen prospective subscribers, and turned over consumers' sensitive personal information to subscribers whose applications raised obvious "red flags." Indeed, the FTC alleges that ChoicePoint approved as customers individuals who lied about their credentials and used commercial mail drops as business addresses. In addition, ChoicePoint applicants reportedly used fax machines at public commercial locations to send multiple applications for purportedly separate companies. According to the FTC, ChoicePoint failed to tighten its application approval procedures or monitor subscribers even after receiving subpoenas from law enforcement authorities alerting it to fraudulent activity going back to 2001.

The FTC charged that ChoicePoint violated the Fair Credit Reporting Act (FCRA) by furnishing consumer reports—credit histories—to subscribers who did not have a permissible purpose to obtain them, and by failing to maintain reasonable procedures to verify both their identities and how they intended to use the information. The agency also charged that ChoicePoint violated the FTC Act by making false and misleading statements about its privacy policies. ChoicePoint had publicized privacy principles that addressed the confidentiality and security of personal information it collects and maintains with statements such as:

> ChoicePoint allows access to your consumer reports only by those authorized under the FCRA. . . Every ChoicePoint customer must successfully complete a rigorous credentialing process. ChoicePoint does not distribute information to the general public and monitors the use of its public record information to ensure appropriate use.

The stipulated final judgment and order requires ChoicePoint to pay $10 million in civil penalties—the largest civil penalty in FTC history—and to provide $5 million for consumer redress. It bars the company from furnishing consumer reports to people who do not have a permissible purpose to receive them and requires the company to establish and maintain reasonable procedures to ensure that consumer reports are provided only to those with a permissible purpose. ChoicePoint is required to verify the identity of businesses that apply to receive consumer reports, including making site visits to certain business premises and auditing subscribers' use of consumer reports. The order requires ChoicePoint to establish, implement, and maintain a comprehensive information security program designed to protect the security, confidentiality, and integrity of the personal information it collects from or about consumers. It also requires ChoicePoint to obtain, every two years for the next twenty years, an audit from a qualified, independent, third-party professional to ensure that its security program meets the standards of the order. Choice-Point will be subject to standard record-keeping and reporting provisions to allow the FTC to monitor compliance. Finally, the settlement bars future violations of the FCRA and the FTC Act.

"The message to ChoicePoint and others should be clear: Consumers' private data must be protected from thieves," said Deborah Platt Majoras, Chairman of the FTC. "Data security is critical to consumers, and protecting it is a priority for the FTC, as it should be to every business in America."

ChoicePoint, however, does not admit any wrongdoing. In an interview with the Associated Press, ChoicePoint Chief Executive Derek Smith has been quoted as reacting to the situation with what could be described as the understatement of the decade: "Looking back, I certainly wish the situation hadn't occurred."

ChoicePoint will continue to offer products and services that contain sensitive personal information. In order to access this information, users will need to meet one of three tests:

- Support consumer-driven transactions where the data is needed to complete or maintain relationships, such as insurance, employment, and tenant screening, or to provide access to their own data;
- Provide authentication or fraud prevention tools to large, accredited corporate customers where consumers have existing relationships. For example, information tools for identity verification, customer enrollment, and insurance claims; or
- Assist federal, state, and local government and criminal justice agencies in their important missions.

For a copy of the FTC complaint against ChoicePoint, see **http://www .ftc.gov/os/caselist/choicepoint/0523069complaint.pdf**, and for a copy of the Stipulated Final Judgment and Order for Civil Penalties, Permanent Injunction, and Other Equitable Relief, see **http://www.ftc.gov/os/case list/choicepoint/0523069stip.pdf**.

Credit Headers and the Gramm-Leach-Bliley Act (GLBA)

As mentioned earlier, the second law relating to a consumer's non-financial/nonpublic privacy is the Gramm-Leach-Bliley Act (GLBA), 15 U.S.C. 6801 *et seq*, *available at* **http://frwebgate.access.gpo.gov/cgi-bin/ getdoc.cgi?dbname=106_cong_public_laws&docid=f:publ102.106.pdf**. Our focus is on Section 6802, *available at* **http://www.ftc.gov/privacy/ glbact/glbsub1.htm**, which prevents financial institutions (which includes credit bureaus) from disclosing (and selling) nonfinancial/nonpublic, personal information to third parties, such as Accurint or Merlin, among others, unless they come within one of the "General exceptions" of Section 6802(e)(1)–(e)(8). Thus, financial institutions can extract the *nonfinancial/nonpublic* personal information from credit reports to sell to the investigative pay database vendors and they in turn can sell the information to subscribers who come within the GLBA general exceptions. This nonfinancial/nonpublic personal information is commonly referred to as "credit headers" because the data is found at the "head" of a credit report. (GLBA refers to "nonfinancial/nonpublic personal information" as "nonpublic personal information.") Credit headers are very different from credit reports because they only include a portion of the consumer credit report (the "header"), such as the creditor's name, address, phone number, date of birth, and Social Security number, and not the financial information in the report. (The financial information was never divulged to third parties, such as investigative database vendors and marketing companies.) The vendors aggregate the credit header data with data from other sources, such as public records and publicly available information. Together, this data is used to create, more or less, a dossier about a person.

Each time a lawyer wants to access a pay database that contains nonfinancial/nonpublic personal information, the lawyer must check off one of the GLBA permissible uses listed on the pay databases' search screen. If a search does not fall within a GLBA permissible use, one must check off "no permissible purpose." The lawyer can still use the database, but nonfinancial/nonpublic information from credit headers is not displayed. However, if the same information has been found within public records, publicly available information sources or pre-GLBA credit headers (pre-2000), it will be displayed. The only caveat is that it might not be as fresh as information from a recent credit header.

GRAMM-LEACH-BLILEY ACT

15 U.S.C. § 6802. Obligations with respect to disclosures of personal information

(a) Notice requirements
Except as otherwise provided in this subchapter, a financial institution may not, directly or through any affiliate, disclose to a nonaffiliated third party any nonpublic personal information, unless such financial institution provides or has provided to the consumer a notice that complies with section 6803 . . .

(e) General exceptions

Subsections (a) and (b) of this section shall not prohibit the disclosure of nonpublic personal information—

(1) as necessary to effect, administer, or enforce a transaction requested or authorized by the consumer, or in connection with—

    (A) servicing or processing a financial product or service requested or authorized by the consumer;

    (B) maintaining or servicing the consumer's account with the financial institution, or with another entity as part of a private label credit card program or other extension of credit on behalf of such entity; or

    (C) a proposed or actual securitization, secondary market sale (including sales of servicing rights), or similar transaction related to a transaction of the consumer;

(2) with the consent or at the direction of the consumer;

(3) (A) to protect the confidentiality or security of the financial institution's records pertaining to the consumer, the service or product, or the transaction therein;

    (B) to protect against or prevent actual or potential fraud, unauthorized transactions, claims, or other liability;

    (C) for required institutional risk control, or for resolving customer disputes or inquiries;

    (D) to persons holding a legal or beneficial interest relating to the consumer; or

    (E) to persons acting in a fiduciary or representative capacity on behalf of the consumer . . .

Can Lawyers Claim a GLBA Exception When Using Pay Investigative Databases?

We always assumed that most research conducted by lawyers using investigative databases that included credit header information (such as Merlin, Lexis, Accurint) came within one of the GLBA exceptions listed under 15 U.S.C. 6802(e)(3)(B), 6802(e)(3)(D), or 6802(e)(3)(E). However, over the years, most of the major database vendors declined to provide us with a specific "plain-English" list of the various research topics conducted by lawyers that would come within the GLBA exceptions. Lexis-Nexis once provided a list of research topics that they believed came within GLBA exceptions but it included a disclaimer: "The above list is being furnished for the purpose of setting out examples of reasons for which GLBA regulated data may be used within the GLBA exceptions. By providing this list, LexisNexis is not offering legal advice to its users, and this list should in no way be construed as a definitive interpretation of the GLBA or its regulations." LexisNexis no longer posts this list at any of its pay investigative databases.

Recently, Merlin provided a list of exceptions that guide lawyers as to whether their investigative research would come within GLBA. The following is a list of authorized purposes that Merlin placed on its site (**https://www.merlindata.com/SearchASPs/authorizedpurpose_exp.ASP**).

> The information that this service provides contains information governed by the Gramm-Leach-Bliley (GLB) Act and the Individual Reference Services Group (IRSG). A violation of the privacy laws of the GLB may subject a company, individual or management to civil and/or criminal penalties pursuant to 15 U.S.C. 6821 and 15 U.S.C. 6823. The following are the only Authorized Purposes for which this information may be accessed.
>
> GLB Authorized Purposes
>
> 1. Transactions Authorized by Consumer
>   As necessary to effect, administer or enforce a transaction that was requested or authorized by the consumer.
>
>   This Authorized Purpose is restricted to specific uses. Based on your company's industry classification, options may include some of the following:
>   1(a) Asset Verification
>   1(b) Credit & Collections Activity
>   1(c) Credit & Collections or Skiptracing (Locating Debtors)
>   1(d) Credit & Collections or Skiptracing (Locating References)
>   1(e) Locating Existing Customers for Legal Purposes
>
> 2. Transactions Authorized by Consumer (Application Verification Only)
>   As necessary to effect, administer, or enforce a transaction requested or authorized by the consumer by verifying the identification information contained in applications for employment, housing, or insurance.
>
>   This Authorized Purpose is restricted to specific uses. Based on your company's industry classification, options may include some of the following:
>   2(f) Employment Verification
>   2(g) Pre-Employment Screening
>
> 3. Law Enforcement Purposes
>   To the extent specifically permitted or required under other provisions of law and in accordance with the Right to Financial Privacy Act of 1978, to law enforcement agencies, self-regulatory organizations, or for an investigation on a matter related to public safety.

This Authorized Purpose is restricted to specific uses. Based on your company's industry classification, options may include some of the following:

3(h) Apprehending Criminals

4. Use by Persons Holding a Legal or Beneficial Interest Relating to the Consumer
   For use by persons holding a legal or beneficial interest relating to the consumer.

   This Authorized Purpose is restricted to specific uses. Based on your company's industry classification, options may include some of the following:

   4(i)   Locating Beneficiaries & Heirs

   4(j)   Locating Owners of Unclaimed Goods

[5. Use By Persons Acting In A Fiduciary Capacity On Behalf Of The Consumer]

6. Fraud Prevention or Detection
   For use to protect against or prevent actual or potential fraud, unauthorized transactions, claims, or other liability.

   This Authorized Purpose is restricted to specific uses. Based on your company's industry classification, options may include some of the following:

   6(k)   Fraud Prevention

   6(l)   Insurance Claims Investigations/Subrogation

   6(m) Locating Fraud Victims

[7. Required Institutional Risk Control]

8. Legal Compliance
   For use to comply with Federal, State, or local laws, rules, and other applicable legal requirements.

   This Authorized Purpose is restricted to specific uses. Based on your company's industry classification, options may include some of the following:

   8(n)   Child Support Enforcement

   8(o)   Legal Process Service

   8(p)   Locating Witnesses & Victims

   8(q)   Locating Former Patients

[9. I have no required GLB purpose (IRSG)]
   A violation of the privacy laws of the GLB may subject a company, individual or management to civil and/or criminal penalties pursuant to 15 U.S.C. 6821 and 15 U.S.C. 6823.

Note, if you choose the ninth GLB authorized purpose, you are not prohibited from searching the Merlin database, but information from credit headers will not be displayed in your results.

Merlin users are assigned an Industry Classification, and this determines their use of databases that contain credit headers. The following is Carole Levitt's Merlin profile which shows her Industry Classification (Attorney) and her authorized GLBA purposes for using credit header data:

My Industry Classification(s)

Attorney

For certain Merlin products, you are required to indicate a legitimate Authorized Purpose as defined by the Gramm-Leach-Bliley Act. For these searches, please keep careful records to justify your search, as your account is subject to audit at any time.

Based on your Industry Classification(s), your access to products that contain Experian credit header data is further restricted to the following Authorized Purposes:

Attorney

Transactions Authorized by Consumer

1(b)   Credit & Collections Activity

1(c)   Credit & Collections or Skiptracing (Locating Debtors)

1(d)   Credit & Collections or Skiptracing (Locating References)

Use by Persons Holding a Legal or Beneficial Interest Relating to the Consumer

4(i)   Locating Beneficiaries & Heirs

4(j)   Locating Owners of Unclaimed Goods

Legal Compliance

8(n)   Child Support Enforcement

8(o)   Legal Process Service

8(p)   Locating Witnesses & Victims

Figure 15-1. Prior to conducting a search, Merlin requires attorneys to select an Authorized Purpose (under GLBA) from the drop-down menu.

Note, that if you are using a Merlin database that contains Experian (credit header) data, this detailed GLBA drop-down menu of exceptions (with numbers and letters) will be displayed, but if you are using a Merlin database that does NOT contain Experian data, a shorter list (just numbers without any letters) is displayed:

Pretexting with Financial Institutions: Operation Detect Pretext

We've often been asked to get information about a person's bank account balance. There is no database for this information and if anyone has obtained this information for you after 1999 (without a subpoena), then it was likely done by "pretexting," which is illegal. Pretexting, the practice of obtaining consumers' private financial information under false pretenses, was specifically outlawed in 1999 by Section 6821 of the Gramm-Leach-Bliley Act (GLBA), 15 U.S.C. 6821, *available at* **http://www.ftc.gov/ privacy/glbact/glbsub2.htm**. Under GLBA, it is also illegal to solicit others to obtain financial information via pretext.

In April 2001, the Federal Trade Commission (FTC) filed suit in three U.S. district courts to halt the operations of three information brokers, all of whom allegedly used false pretenses, fraudulent statements, or impersonation to illegally obtain consumers' confidential financial information—such as bank balances—and sell it. The brokers were asked to find out how much money a woman's fiancé had in his bank account. The woman (actually an FTC investigator involved in Operation Detect Pretext) supplied the brokers with her fiancé's name and the name of his bank and other "limited information" (though not stated, it was probably his Social Security number and his mother's maiden name). In each case, the broker used pretexting by posing as the fiancé to obtain the information from the bank (**http://www.ftc.gov/opa/2002/03/pretextingsettlements.htm**).

The FTC and the brokers ended up in settlement. The brokers had to forfeit any money they made while using pretexting to obtain information. Also, they were prohibited from engaging in any activity in connection with the obtaining, offering for sale, or selling of customer information of a financial institution, obtained by:

- Misrepresenting their identities or their right to receive customer information
- Using others who will obtain information using deception
- Selling or disclosing customer information obtained from a financial institution
- Making false and misleading statements

Maiden Names

Finding someone's mother's maiden name, which the information broker in Operation Detect Pretext probably had to do to convince the bank he was the FTC investigator's fiancé, can sometimes be tougher than finding someone's Social Security number. We'd try various pay investigative databases that link people to their relatives and associates (such as Merlin at **http://www.merlindata.com**), Westlaw's PeopleMap at **http://west.thomson.com/westlaw/ public-records/libraries/peoplemap/default.aspx**, or Accurint at **http://www.accurint.com**), and we'd also try a free family tree search at RootsWeb at **http://worldconnect.rootsweb.com** (as discussed in chapter 9, Using Genealogy Sites as Investigative Tools).

Pretexting to Obtain General Information

While GLBA made pretexting to obtain information from a financial institution a federal crime in 1999 and the Telephone Records and Privacy Protection Act made pretexting to obtain telephone records a federal crime in 2006 (see page 46), there is no "general" antipretexting federal law. However, attorneys should check their own state's laws, cases, ethics opinions, and ethics rules to learn if they discuss pretexting. (See the Ethics Alert after the discussion of *Remsburg* to learn how the ABA Rules of Professional Conduct might treat pretexting.) A case in point is *Remsburg v. Docusearch*, 816 A.2d 1001 (N.H. 2003), *available at* **http://www.courts.state.nh.us/supreme/opinions/2003/remsb017.htm**, where the New Hampshire Supreme Court held, "[t]hat an investigator who obtains a person's work address by means of pretextual phone calling, and then sells the information, may be liable for damages under [New Hampshire] RSA Chapter 358-A to the person deceived." The court then remanded the case to the trial court.

In the *Remsburg* case, Liam Youens wanted to find out Amy Boyer's work address. He paid an Internet research company, Docusearch, to find her home address, phone number, and Social Security number, but Docusearch was unable to find her work address. Docusearch then hired an information broker who placed a pretext call to Boyer at her home. The broker lied about her identity and the purpose of her call. She convinced Boyer to reveal her work address. On October 15, 1999, Youens drove to

Boyer's workplace and fatally shot her as she left work. Youens then shot and killed himself. A subsequent police investigation revealed that Youens maintained a Web site containing references to stalking and killing Boyer.

Ethics Alert: Pretexting

Not only is pretexting illegal, it may also be prohibited by Rule 8.4 of the ABA's Model Rules of Professional Conduct (Maintaining The Integrity of The Profession), which states that, "It is professional misconduct for a lawyer to:

(a) violate or attempt to violate the Rules of Professional Conduct, knowingly assist or induce another to do so, or do so through the acts of another;

(b) commit a criminal act that reflects adversely on the lawyer's honesty, trustworthiness or fitness as a lawyer in other respects;

(c) engage in conduct involving dishonesty, fraud, deceit or misrepresentation. . ."

It would also be an ethical violation for a lawyer to hire someone (such as a private investigator or information broker) to pretext because under the ABA Model Rules of Professional Conduct, Rule 5.3, Responsibilities Regarding Nonlawyer Assistants, a lawyer is responsible for the conduct of nonlawyers hired to do something that would be a violation of the Rules of Professional Conduct if engaged in by the lawyer himself and if "the lawyer orders or, with the knowledge of the specific conduct, ratifies the conduct involved."

Banks

As noted earlier, there is no database of where people bank. Sometimes this information can be gleaned from a public record, such as a lien or a mortgage. (See Chapter 16 to learn about pay investigative databases that might include lien or mortgage information.) However, if you need to trace a bank routing number, the next site will assist you.

RoutingTool

http://www.routingtool.com/

Purpose: Routing Tool's site allows you to search their database using only a U.S. routing number to identify bank names, locations, and their phone numbers for funds verification and account validation.

Content: If all you possess is a routing number, then, in a sense, you will need to investigate "in reverse." In the upper-right side of Routing Tool's home page, click on the box that reads **Online Routing Tool FREE**. You will be asked to register your full name and e-mail address. Upon receiving a confirmation e-mail, you then must return to Routing Tools' Web site and provide more contact information. Once you are fully registered, click on **Perform Single Routing Lookups Here**. You may enter either a bank name or the nine-digit routing number.

The results are displayed to you with the following information: Routing number; bank name; address; city, state, and ZIP code that the number was assigned in; and phone number.

Our View: This site worked very simply, keeping clutter down to a minimum. There is a demo on the home page that diagrams where the routing number begins and ends in regards to the account and check numbers next to it.

*CHAPTER*SIXTEEN

Pay Investigative Databases

When to Use Investigative Pay Investigative Databases That Compile Public Records, NonPublic Personal Information, and Publicly Available Information

Before reading this chapter, we recommend you first read chapter 15 as background. While most of the data in this book is about information found at free sites, we are including investigative pay databases because, as we noted earlier, pay databases have their place in research. (While case law and docket databases can also be used for investigative research, we decided to save them for the upcoming companion to this book, which focuses on public records rather than publicly available information.) If you have a lot of clues about a person or if the person has a unique name, you can probably begin your research with free publicly available Web sites and free public record databases. If this is not the case, it's best to begin with a pay investigative database. Beginning your search with a pay investigative database is also best when you need to conduct a national or multi-state search. You should also use a pay database when you need to gather various types of information about your subject gathered from publicly available sources, public records, proprietary databases,and credit headers, which have been compiled into one report that reads almost like a dossier (see the "Consumer Credit Reports and Credit Headers" for details about credit headers). Most of the investigative pay databases described in this chapter are geared to collection agencies, lawyers, private investigators, and law enforcement agencies who are involved in skip-tracing (whether to locate a missing witness, heir, debtor, or criminal suspect), backgrounding people, and marshalling assets (such as a divorce lawyer who needs to search for the other spouse's real property records, boats, planes, patents, trademarks, and so on). While lawyers might be familiar with some of these database companies because they use their legal research databases, such as Reed Elsevier/LexisNexis (**http://www.lexisnexis.com**) and Westlaw (**http://web2.westlaw.com**), which is part of Thomson Reuters, they may not be as familiar with their investigative research databases, such as Reed Elsevier/LexisNexis' ChoicePoint (**http://atxp.choicepoint.com**), KnowX (**http://www.knowx.com**), Accurint (**http://www.accurint.com**), and West-law's PeopleMap (**http://west.thomson.com/westlaw/public-records/libraries/peoplemap/default.aspx**). Then there are some investigative research databases that might be completely foreign to many lawyers, such as Merlin (**http://www.merlindata.com**), LocatePLUS (**https://www.locateplus.com/welcome.asp**), Intelius (**http://www.intelius.com**), US Search (**http://www.ussearch.com/consumer/index.jsp**), People Search Now (**http://www.peoplesearchnow.com/**), and Public Background Checks (**http://www.publicbackgroundchecks.com**), all of which will be discussed in this chapter.

Where Pay Investigative Databases Get Their Data, and How to Become a Subscriber

Before we examine some of these databases, a word about how to gain access to the databases and where they get their information. To gain access to those databases that also include credit header information (see Chapter 15, Consumer Credit Reports and Credit Headers to learn about credit headers), one must become a subscriber and go through an application process to prove that one has a legitimate use of the database. This entails filling out an application (See the Appendix for an example of Merlin's application) and faxing one's business license and law license and other supporting documents. Pay investigative databases that do not contain credit header information, such as KnowX, US Search, Intelius, People Search Now, and Public Background Checks, do not require any application process since they do not come within GLBA. Most lawyers would be approved subscribers, but see the "Consumer Credit Reports and Credit Headers" section to learn about the need to attest to a permissible GLBA purpose each time you use the database. While much of the data in investigative pay databases comes from public records or publicly available information (such as phone directories), some of the information comes from nonpublic personal information found in credit headers. Some of the address/phone data could also come from the address/phone numbers that people voluntarily supply to various companies when they fill out product warranty cards, obtain utility service (such as gas, electricity, and water) and even request pizza delivery service to their home or office.

Relational Investigative Pay Databases

Merlin (**http://www.merlindata.com**), Westlaw's PeopleMap (**http://west.thomson.com/westlaw/public-records/libraries/peoplemap/default.aspx**), and Accurint (**http://www.accurint.com**) are "relational" investigative pay databases. A relational database attempts to link people to their various records. They also try to link people to their neighbors, associates, and relatives—a useful tool for contacting someone who might know the whereabouts of a person who has gone missing. With that said, the relational database is not as powerful as we'd like to see it because it only links people who share the same name and address (or different names but same address). For example, one of the authors of this book who shares the same last name as her parents and brothers, but who hasn't shared an address with them in about thirty years, is not linked to them on her so-called complete Accurint or Merlin report. However, her former father-in-law shows on her 2009 report because they once owned real property together (from 1983–1985).

Pricing and Access to Investigative Pay Databases

Pricing varies among investigative databases. Some offer flat-rate pricing while others offer a per search fee. Some demand a monthly subscription while others don't. Accurint used to offer a per search price and did not require a monthly subscription. All that changed when Lexis acquired Seisint Inc., Accurint's parent company, in 2004 (and paid $775 million in cash for it). We waited for a price increase and, sure enough, in 2005, Lexis instituted a monthly subscription fee for subscribers who are frequent users and want a discounted per search fee. (Fees vary depending on one's contract.) In addition, Lexis clamped down on access to its database and to full Social Security numbers (as did other vendors). For access to Accurint (and most any investigative pay databases) these days, a fairly extensive application and approval process is required to ensure that the vendor is not selling information to identity thieves. For those who need access to full Social Security numbers and not just the truncated numbers, a site inspection at your physical office became another requirement added to the approval process. Merlin charges $60 for the site visit. According to some lawyers we've spoken to (and this was later confirmed by Accurint), at first Accurint only approved full Social Security number access to those lawyers whose primary function was collections work. Merlin, on the other hand, did not have this stringent limitation and Accurint no longer does either. In 2008, we began receiving reports from law librarians, who were Accurint subscribers, about a letter from LexisNexis requesting detailed personal information about the librarian. Also requested was a security check. This would entail a site visit from a third-party security vendor that might include inspection of the librarian's premises and photographs.

> The day before the Seattle, Washington law firm Forsberg & Umlauf was to take the deposition of a person bringing a personal injury claim against their client, the firm's paralegal, Jenny J. Rasmussen called this book's coauthor Carole Levitt. According to Levitt, "Ms. Rasumussen called us to help figure out why the opposing party was using three different Social Security numbers (SSN). The firm was trying to ascertain his credibility. The opposing party claimed that he accidentally used his father's SSN. He didn't seem to have a reason for using the other SSN." Levitt ran a reverse SSN search at Merlin. Levitt reported, "As it turns out, the SSN that he claimed was his father's belonged to someone other than his father. The other SSN was a completely made-up number—so much for credibility."

Merlin Information Services

http://www.merlindata.com   **$**

Purpose: Merlin is a relational investigative pay database, useful for skip-tracing, marshalling assets, and backgrounding people.

Content: Merlin has information from public records, credit headers (live, in contrast to Accurint—which are a month behind according to Merlin), and publicly available information. Merlin includes such information as addresses, phone numbers (including a reverse unlisted phone number feature and cellular phone numbers), bankruptcies, secretary of state records, fictitious business records, dates of birth (sometimes only month and year), crimi-

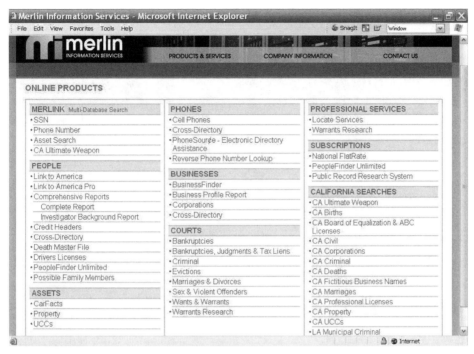

Figure 16-1. The home page of Merlin provides an overview of the various business and people finding databases available, including the new Merlink feature for multidatabase searching.

nal records, real property records, motor vehicle records, UCCs, neighbors, relatives, and more (depending upon the jurisdiction). It covers national data and all states. In addition, it has a heavy California emphasis.

Merlin's databases vary in price. For instance, if you purchase reports from all the databases found in its **California Ultimate Weapon** database, the cost is $20 while a national **Investigator's Background Report** is $3.50. Merlin's **Link to America** feature is a skip-tracing tool that costs $1.00 per search. The Merlin report most similar to Accurint's **Comprehensive Report** is Merlin's **Complete Report**, which costs $7.50 (if you have a GLBA exception it also will include live credit headers and if you have the higher security clearance it will include a full Social Security number and date of birth).

Use the $2 Link to America Pro database to search for your subject by name, date of birth, SSN, address,

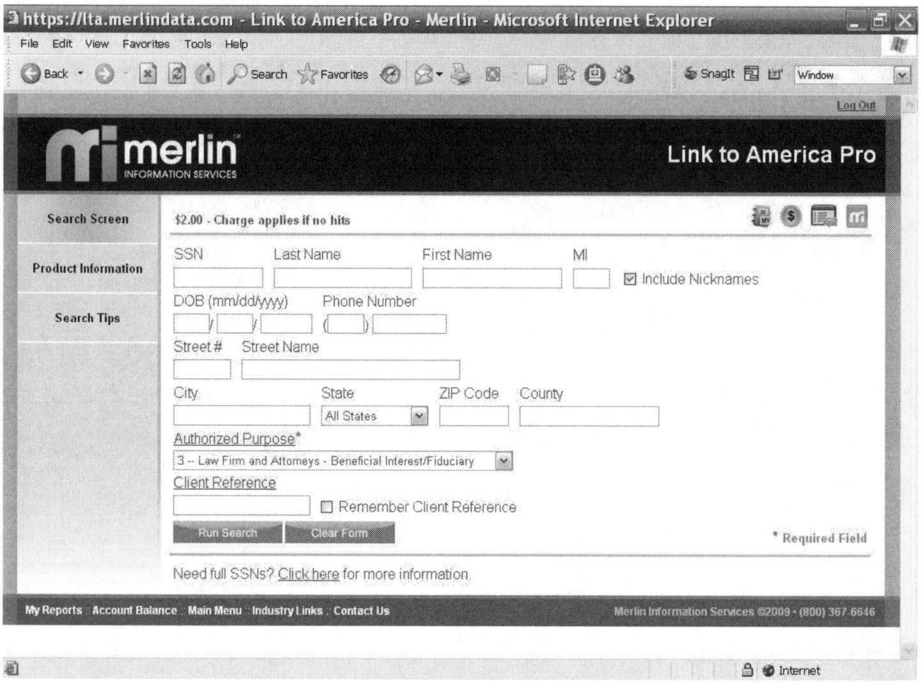

Figure 16-2. A Link to America Pro report will include your subject's name (and aliases), the first five digits of their SSN, current and historical phone listings for each of their addresses, potential relatives in the same geographical area, and up to twenty business and residential neighbors' phone numbers.

phone number, or county. After you receive a results list (which will include the first five digits of your subject's SSN), you can order various reports, such as a Driver's License report or a UCC report. However, to retrieve a Complete Report or an Investigator Background Report, you will need to run a new search at those databases. These databases require that you search by your subject's first/last name and the first five digits of their SSN (which you would have retrieved from the Link to America report).

On July 13, 2009, as we were writing this book, Merlin redesigned its Web site and added three more multi-database searches (MerLink SSN, MerLink Phone Number, and MerLink Asset search), on top of its California Ultimate Weapon search. MerLink SSN searches up to six databases simultaneously (by SSN), MerLink Phone Number searches up to six databases simultaneously (by phone number), and MerLink Asset searches four data-bases simultaneously (by individual or business name).

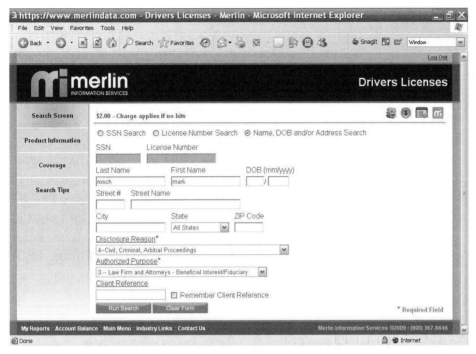

Figure 16-3. Search for a subject's driver license by their last name and first name or add their date of birth and/or address to narrow the search. You can also search just by an address, a SSN, or a license number.

Merlin has a driver's license database with information from 49 states, but only 12 states include current data (Connecticut, Florida, Kentucky, Maine, Michigan, Minnesota, Nebraska, New Hampshire, New Mexico, Tennessee, Texas, and Wisconsin). All 49 states can be searched simultaneously.

Our View: Merlin has long been the private investigator's database of choice for investigative searching, but not the lawyer or law librarian's first choice. Law librarians and lawyers typically use Lexis, Westlaw, ChoicePoint, KnowX, or Accurint. We think Merlin has been overlooked by them because its search engine is not as sleek or fast as the other vendors' search engines. Yet, we think Merlin is worth a shot for the following reasons: (1) Its pricing seems to be lower. Although there had been only a $10 monthly service fee until January 1, 2009, the new fee of $20 per month is still fairly low and is waived if users spend over $35 to search each month or if users have a package or a subscription plan; (2) We also like that

Merlin allows you to sort the columns in your results page to create a customized report; (3) A noteworthy feature in Merlin is its "drill-down feature" that allows the searcher to learn the source behind each record and the date it was last updated.

Tips: Merlin has some proprietary databases that others may not have (especially for California). For instance, California marriage records from 1960–1985 are online at Merlin—records that the State of California no longer sells. Another unique database is its **Western States Evictions** database, covering evictions in all counties in California, Nevada, Oregon, and Washington. Merlin has created a **National Fictitious Business Name** search with over 10 million records—saving you the time of a county-by-county search in each state.

Reed Elsevier/LexisNexis' Pay Investigative Databases

Reed Elsevier/LexisNexis has offered public records at Lexis.com for over twenty-five years. Over time, LexisNexis has acquired many once independent investigative database companies, such as Seisint (Accurint is Seisint's investigative database) and ChoicePoint (with its many investigative databases, such as KnowX, Rapsheets (recently folded into the KnowX database), AutoTrackXP, and ScreenNow).

For now, the various Lexis acquisitions are still accessible as separate databases with their familiar search interfaces. It's possible that the various databases will be integrated at some point into one database. Therefore, we will discuss Accurint, Lexis.com, KnowX, and AutoTrackXP as separate entries. ScreenNow won't be discussed in detail because it's geared to employment screening businesses and not attorneys. Those accessing the data in ScreenNow must comply with the Fair Credit Reporting Act (FCRA).

LexisNexis, a division of Reed Elsevier

http://www.lexisnexis.com **$**

Purpose: To search using more sophisticated search techniques than the free public records sites offer. Lexis is useful for skip-tracing, marshalling assets, and backgrounding people.

Content: Now that Reed Elsevier owns Accurint and, since 2008, ChoicePoint (the parent company of various databases, such as, KnowX, RapSheets, AutoTrackXP, and Screen-Now), expect to see some of these databases integrated over time. From assets to verdicts, the Lexis database contains information garnered from public records, publicly available information, and proprietary sources (e.g., D & B credit reports for companies). For a complete list of public records available at Lexis, scroll down the page at **http://w3.nexis.com/sources/** and click on **Public Records** from the **Publications Types** drop-down menu. For non-U.S. public record data (Canada, France, UK, and Russia), see **http://w3.nexis.com/sources/** and select **Public Records** from the **Publication Types** drop-down menu and then, from the **Regions of Coverage** drop-down menu, select a specific country or **International**. We had no luck finding any public records for most of the countries we selected as we suspected (since foreign countries have more stringent privacy rules regarding access to public records than the U.S.) There were some databases listed for Canada (phone numbers) and the U.K. (company information). When we selected **International**, the list included databases such as **Politically Exposed Persons**.

Our View: The major advantage of Lexis is the ability to conduct multistate and nationwide public record searching and **All Records** searching (searching through a diverse group of records) and having access to the traditional Lexis legal databases (cases, statutes, etc.). However, we have been informed by Accurint that some of the newer features found at Accurint (such as the Contact Card database and the e-mail database) are not integrated into Lexis' public record database. Thus, depending on a researcher's needs, a subscription to Accurint might be in order, instead of (or in addition to) Lexis.

Tip: If you want to find as much information as possible about an individual, it may be worth the money to run an **All Records-All States** type of search instead of running several individual searches in selected states or agencies. Lexis also has all types of **People Finder** databases covering 146 million individuals. The data varies from state-to-state but could include driver's license information, marriage, divorce and death records, voter registration records, and more.

Accurint

http://www.accurint.com **$**

Purpose: To search using more sophisticated search techniques than the free public records sites offer. Accurint is useful for skip-tracing, marshalling assets, linking people together through its "relational" database (informing us about a subject's possible associates, neighbors and relatives, for example) and to discover aliases.

Content: When Accurint was first introduced, it was the least expensive investigative pay site to use, with a basic search (that included address, phone number, and full SSN) costing twenty-five cent and a full report about $6.50. After Lexis purchased Accurint, prices rose. There are various pricing options available, from a transactional "pay as you go" option that offers "per transaction" fees to a "hybrid" option that offers a mix of a flat rate with a "per transaction" fee to a flat rate only. Its database has more than 20 billion records from 1,600 sources.

Search with any clues you have about the person, such as last name, first name, middle name, current address or phone number, old address or phone number, Social Security number, or any combination of these.

The **Comprehensive Report** displays a person's current name (or names), any aliases (AKAs), property ownership, date of birth (usually only the month and year unless you have a higher security status), partial Social Security number (unless you have a higher security status that includes full Social Security numbers), current and historical addresses dating back twenty-to-thirty years, current telephone number, date of death, names of others living at the subject's current address, associ-ates, and relatives. Property and bankruptcy records are also included, among other information, all of which will vary from state-to-state.

Useful Features

- Phones Plus: Back on December 6, 2005, Tamara Thompson, in her PI News Link blog (**http://yourpi news.blogspot.com/2005/12/accurint-unveils-unlisted-and-cell.html**), reported that Accurint was now adding unlisted and cell phone number to its database. Thompson said, "Take a look at the Phones Plus search added to the array of people finder tools offered by Accurint. Here's the official announce-ment, somewhat short on details":

> When traditional phone sources are not enough, Phones Plus provides a new alternative. Access over 50,000,000 phone numbers not typically published, such as non-Elec-tronic Directory Assistance records, including cell phone and unlisted numbers.

Thompson explained how she tried out the new directory:

> I conducted a search entering the first and last name of my subject, with the state and county. The results returned three telephone numbers, one of which was an active Veri-zon cell phone in another state. The cost to you is [fifty] cents, plus your monthly fee.

By 2009, there were 80 million phone numbers in the Phones Plus database, with 30–40 million of them cellular. According to CTIA, The International Associ-ation for the Wireless Industry, as of June 2008, there were 262 million cellular phone numbers in the U.S. and 17.5 percent of households had only a cellular phone number (**http://www.ctia.org/media/index .cfm/AID/10323**). Accurint receives a weekly update if landline phone numbers are ported over to a cellular phone. This information is displayed in Phones Plus reports. (Not all databases provide this information. For instance, in a test search, Westlaw's Reverse Phone database did not show that a landline phone number had been ported over to a cellular phone even though it had been ported over several years earlier.)

- A relational feature "Relavint" that helps you to visualize relationships between people and their possible relatives and associates (and vehicles, property, and even businesses) by allowing you to create diagrams. Relavint costs $2 per diagram. (See Westlaw's People-Map entry in this chapter to learn about their similar feature.)

- Accurint provides access to its records via wireless hand-held devices (such as the Palm, Pocket PC, and BlackBerry), without any extra charge—but only to law enforcement subscribers.

- More criminal court and arrest records or logs from more states and counties have been added to Accurint.

- A new "Phone batch" feature allows you to search for phone numbers in a variety of ways (fees vary depending on the "level" chosen). For example, if you want only directory assistance phone numbers, choose level one, but for a broader search that will attempt to return a "possible" current phone number, choose level four. If you want only the newest phone number, select the **Return Different Phone** option (this is a lower price option).

- The **People at Work** feature added 50 million new records for a total of well over 100 (and possibly close to 200) million individuals. Thus, you might be able to discover the name of your subject's employer.

- The **Instant Identification** database is a validation and verification tool endorsed by the American Bankers Association as a non-documentary verification of a consumer's identification. After you enter all the information you know about the consumer, such as his or her name, address, and Social Security number, the information is searched through numerous databases to be sure it is valid information—that is, in the correct format. It then assigns a verification score of one to fifty to the consumer.

New Accurint features include:

- A Voter's Registration database: This database covers 22 states, but only 18 states are current.
- A Canadian Phones database: This database includes 12 million Canadian residential and 1.8 million Canadian business telephone numbers (out of 33 million people). The person conducting the search must be U.S. based.
- A Driver's License database: This database includes data from 24 states, but only 10 states are current.
- A Vehicle Identification Number database (VIN). This database covers 33 states, but only 24 are current.
- A "Contact Card report" which will list names and contact information of your subject and other people (e.g., relatives and neighbors) who may be able to assist you contact your subject. The named people also include a "relative designation," such as "wife" or "husband." This search will show if a phone number was disconnected and will conduct a relocation search to look for a new phone number.
- A People Alert service: You can be alerted via e-mail if there are any changes to a specified person's report or you can choose to be alerted only to a change of one or more of the following: name, address, phone number, or death. (There is also an option to be alerted if there are no changes.)
- Deep Skip: In addition to contact information for the subject, results will display names of household members. Deep Skip is priced at 20 percent more than a regular Accurint search.
- Feedback: This feature allows the searcher to give Accurint feedback as to whether the phone number provided by Accurint led them to the right party, the wrong party, or to a disconnected number. This information is then integrated into the Deep Skip search results.
- An e-mail database: This database includes 120 million U.S. e-mail addresses. One can search by name or e-mail address or street address. The results will display the person's name, e-mail address, street address, and SSN. The SSN will only be a partial number unless one has the higher security clearance. While Accurint tells

us this database is quite popular, it did not include the e-mail address for a name we tested even though that person's e-mail address is listed on her Web site and various other places on the Internet.

> Accurint's new e-mail database has proven popular with some collections attorneys who find that sending a young debtor an e-mail instead of phoning him or her brings better results.

Our View: We assume that Accurint stands for "accurate" and "current." Is it accurate and current? According to a librarian at Bryan Cave, the answer is "yes" as to its currency; she finds it's the most up-to-date people-finding site. However, lawyers at our seminars report mixed results as to currency and so do we. According to Accurint, addresses, phone numbers, and bankruptcies are updated daily and data from credit bureaus and utility companies are updated weekly. (Merlin informed us that Merlin's credit headers are updated daily, as are death records.) As to accurate, we'd say "yes and no." It is as accurate as the public records and other sources upon which it depends are. Its "relational" ability, which attempts to show relationships between people, can sometimes be inaccurate or incomplete. For instance, a search of Carole Levitt's record linked her to her current husband (but labeled him a mere "associate"). It then linked her to her former husband and his entire family, but as noted earlier, missed her parents and brothers entirely. A search by one of her old phone numbers did not work; however, searching an old address worked like a charm, as did searching by Social Security number. Users must subscribe to Accurint and be approved. The subscriber application requires such information as your bank name and account number, your business license, your law license, and so on. Expect a phone call (or two) to verify your information.

Tips: When dealing with a common name, it helps to have a date of birth. If you don't have that, but are able to estimate the subject's age range, add this information into the **Age Range** field to narrow down the search.

When uncertain of a subject's address, use the **Radius** search box on the search query menu. For example, after you type the subject's suspected address into the **Address** search box, you can type "10" into the radius search box, and the search engine will display addresses within 10 miles of the address you've entered.

Besides home addresses, a full Accurint report will sometimes display work addresses—always a difficult bit of data to locate. Work addresses are getting easier with Accurint's separate People at Work database. Work addresses can sometimes be found for free on a subject's social or professional networking profile.

Basic information about any person found in your subject's report is made available for the price of the original report. You can also link directly to any person listed in your subject's report if you need more information from their separate report (which you will be charged for, of course).

Accurint is planning on releasing a new version of its database by the end of 2009. While its "look and feel" will be different, the search interface and features described in this entry should remain the same.

LexisNexis Accurint Data Breach

In March 2005, Reed Elsevier's LexisNexis unit sent notices to approximately 30,000 people advising them that unauthorized individuals may have accessed their personally identifiable information via LexisNexis' recently acquired Seisint subsidiary and its Accurint database. In early April 2005, LexisNexis said in a press release, "No individual has advised of having experienced any form of identity theft." (See **http://www.lexis nexis.com/about/releases/0789.asp**.)

Also, in March 2005, LexisNexis performed an in-depth audit of data search activity on Accurint covering the past two years. That review found fifty-nine incidents in which "unauthorized persons, primarily using IDs and passwords of legitimate Seisint (Accurint's parent) customers, may have acquired personal-identifying information, such as Social Security numbers (SSNs) or Driver's License numbers (DLNs), of individuals in the

U.S." (See **http://www.lexisnexis.com/presscenter/SanfordTestimony Judiciary.pdf**.) These findings led LexisNexis to notify an additional 280,000 people (approximately) whose information may have been compromised in those newly identified incidents.

Like the ChoicePoint data breach discussed on page 202, there was apparently no "hacking" or other method of electronic eavesdropping or "breaking and entering" into the Accurint database. LexisNexis claims that, "The substantial majority of instances involved IDs and passwords stolen from Seisint customers who had legally permissible access to SSNs and DLNs for legitimate purposes, such as verifying identities and preventing and detecting fraud." (See **http://www.lexisnexis.com/about/ releases/0789.asp**.) So, unlike the ChoicePoint situation where nefarious individuals set up valid accounts using false business identification, the breach at Accurint was caused by the theft (or misuse) of the username and password information of legitimate Accurint account holders. Lexis-Nexis has advised those customers whose usernames and passwords were compromised.

In response to these breaches, LexisNexis began invoking more restrictive access to SSNs for Accurint users. "This included truncating SSNs displayed in nonpublic documents and narrowing access to full SSNs and DLNs to law enforcement and a restricted group of legally authorized organizations, such as banks and insurance companies," the company said in a press release (see **http://www.lexisnexis.com/presscenter/Sanford TestimonyJudiciary.pdf**.). Law firms were not on the list of client categories that could view full SSNs unless the firm's practice was in collections. We heard angry comments from lawyers who could no longer view full SSNs. Eventually, LexisNexis opened full SSN access to those lawyers who successfully passed a site visit.

"Practical Points"

The Accurint situation illustrates an extreme example of improper username and password usage. Any service or technology that requires a username and password can be compromised in the same way—this goes for everything from your e-mail and voice mail to the logon password for your computer.

To help ensure the security of your (and your clients') information, it is important for lawyers to use hard-to-guess passwords and to change them regularly, so that unauthorized individuals do not have access to your information.

ChoicePoint

ChoicePoint (formerly CDB Infotek) is the parent company of various databases, such as KnowX, RapSheets, AutoTrackXP, and ScreenNow. As of October 2008, ChoicePoint is owned by Reed Elsevier/LexisNexis.

Auto TrackXP

http://atxp.choicepoint.com/

Purpose: To search public records using more sophisticated search techniques than the free sites offer; useful for skip-tracing, marshalling assets, and backgrounding people.

Content: AutoTrackXP provides Internet access to millions of current and historical records on individuals and businesses, and allows users to browse through those records instantly. With as little information as a name or Social Security number, users can cross-reference proprietary and public records including identity verification infor-

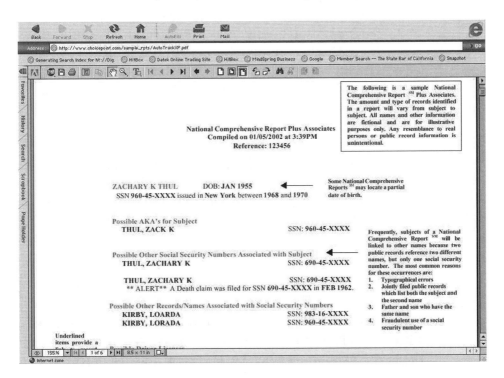

Figure 16-4. A subject's name, partial DOB, and partial SSN are displayed on the first page of a **National Comprehensive Plus Associates** report.

mation, relatives and associates, corporate information, real property records, deed transfers, and much more. In addition, access is available to a staff of field researchers who perform county, state, and federal courthouse public record searches.

Our View: Aside from individual records, one can also retrieve comprehensive reports about people by using the **Info-Probe** or **Discovery PLUS** features. The **Discovery PLUS** report shows an individual's current and previous addresses, relatives, assets, corporate involvement, derogatory information, and vehicle identification number. The **InfoProbe** report searches millions of records simultaneously and shows a list of databases containing records matching your search criteria. From the list, you choose which databases to view and regardless of the number of records viewed, the charge will never exceed $100 per search. The **National Comprehensive Report** searches national and state databases for a subject's assets (e.g., real property and deed transfers and vehicles), professional licenses, current and past addresses and phone numbers, drivers license information, UCCs, bankruptcies, etc. An **Associate** search can also be added to the report, which includes names of neighbors, relatives, and anyone else linked to the subject's addresses.

Tip: If you anticipate that there could be reams of information about your subject, consider an InfoProbe search instead of conducting various individual searches; it might save you time and money.

KnowX

(launched in February of 1997 as Information America, merged with ChoicePoint Inc. in May 2000, and in 2008 became part of the LexisNexis family when LexisNexis acquired ChoicePoint)

http://www.knowx.com   **$**

Purpose: To search public records using more sophisticated search techniques than the free sites offer; useful for skip-tracing, marshalling assets, and backgrounding people.

Content: KnowX searches national and state databases for a summary of assets, driver's licenses, professional licenses, real property, vehicles, liens, business entity filings, lawsuit information, marriage records, birth and death records, associates, relatives and others linked to the same addresses as the subject, and neighbors. SSNs are not available at KnowX. Registration with a credit card is required and searches cost anywhere from $1.50 to $129.50 for a comprehensive report.

Our View: For the occasional user, this may be a better choice than any of the databases that require approval and a subscription because KnowX does not require you to fill out such a personal application and wait to be approved. KnowX obtains its information from "official records," which we assume means public records. They are probably also obtaining information from "publicly available" information, which the individual voluntarily provides, such as when they order telephone service and place their phone numbers in the telephone book. Note, KnowX is not offering the general public access to the "sensitive, personal information" found in credit headers. This means that the information may not be as "fresh" as that found in the databases that do provide access to credit headers (described in Chapter 15).

If you need to perform more than one or two searches you can save some money by purchasing a 24-hour, 30-day, or annual subscription for selected databases, instead of paying per search. For instance, it would cost $2.95 to retrieve one record about one subject from The Ultimate People Finder database and $9.95 to retrieve all of those subject's records. But, by spending $19.95, a searcher could take advantage of 24 hours of unlimited searching and retrieval of records for any number of subjects.

Tip: Some KnowX searches are free (but the results are very summarized).

Even though the free results are very summarized, sometimes that's all you need. For example, a free corporate record search for "Coastal Printworks" returns the result "COASTAL PRINTWORKS, INC. is a business entity in CA." That summarized result just might be good enough if you only wanted to know whether they were registered to do business in California. Those in need of a mailing address and registered agent, however, will need to pay for a more detailed record from KnowX ($6.95), or a savvy searcher can take the information (that the company is registered in California) to visit the Secretary of State site in California, where the full information will be supplied free. However, as noted in the *Our View* section, KnowX's data may not be as fresh as other databases (primarily regarding individuals, not corporations), in which case the free data may be of little or no use.

Acxiom Insight Investigate
(formerly FlatRateInfo.com)

https://www.insightinvestigate.com

InsightAmerica creator of **FlatRateInfo.com** was acquired in 2005 by a public company, Acxiom (**http://www.acxiom.com**). FlatRateInfo no longer exists and Acxiom informed us that they are making changes to their databases and opted out of this book.

Acxiom develops databases for various clients. For instance, the Colorado Judicial Branch hired Acxiom to create CoCourts.com (**http://www.cocourts.com/**), "the first online, real time court records site in the United States." (See **https://www.cocourts.com/public/About.cfm** for more details.) such as a real time court records databases.

Westlaw, part of Thomson Reuters
(Public Records, PeopleMap, and People Finder Report)

http://west.thomson.com/westlaw/public-records/libraries/peoplemap/default.aspx

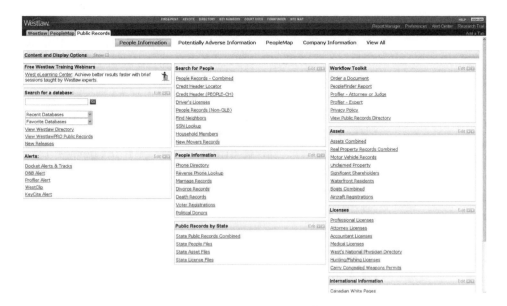

Figure 16-5. This is Westlaw's Public Record page. Researchers can search specific public records from here (such as death records) or they can link to PeopleMap.

Purpose: To search using more sophisticated search techniques than the free public records sites offer. Westlaw's databases are useful for skip-tracing, marshalling assets, and discovering aliases. Its **PeopleMap** database, in particular, is useful for linking people together through its "relational" function (informing us about a subject's possible associates, neighbors, and relatives, for example). While we will briefly explain Public Records and the People Finder Report databases, this discussion will focus primarily on Westlaw's newest product, PeopleMap, launched in February 2009 (**http://west.thomson.com/westlaw/ public%2Drecords/libraries/peoplemap/**).

Content: In addition to its well-known legal research database, Westlaw offers three public record/investigative databases, which Westlaw informs us can be subscribed to on a stand-alone basis. However, Westlaw was unwilling to give us precise pricing.

Tabs for their public record/investigative databases are listed on the home page: (1) **Public Records**; (2) **People Finder Report**; and (3) **PeopleMap**. The Public

Records database is used primarily when a researcher wants to search a name through a specific type of public record or through all public records in a specific jurisdiction, while the People Finder Report database is used primarily for people finding and will include more than just public records (it will include publicly available information and credit headers). PeopleMap, on the other hand, is used to uncover relationships between people (and to link a person to his or her public records), using publicly available information, public records, and credit headers.

Researchers might use PeopleMap for a variety of reasons, from people finding, due diligence (e.g., bankruptcies), antimoney laundering (by checking a name against a U.S. or international watch list), and fraud investigation or for discovery purposes (in preparation for litigation or settlement). In addition to providing the text of a record (and sometimes the actual image), PeopleMap provides visuals to display relationships (using a graphical interface) and pinpoints where your subject might be located (using Microsoft Virtual Earth's mapping feature).

Westlaw explains that PeopleMap is

> a second generation product, and as such is "smarter" about pulling back relevant results, utilizing such features as analysis of name rarity within a geographical area. Additionally, PeopleMap scores relationships with a "confidence level" to indicate the strength of a relationship based on all matching information. Extensive testing has shown the system to be highly accurate and robust against variations in data quality. If a confidence level is under 60 percent, the record won't be displayed.

When conducting a PeopleMap search, a subject's name is first run through the Experian Credit Header database for a match. Experian is a national credit report company whose database is updated daily. (As discussed in Chapter 15, credit headers typically provide the most current information.) PeopleMap then searches through 35 "content sets" (compared to the 24 content sets that

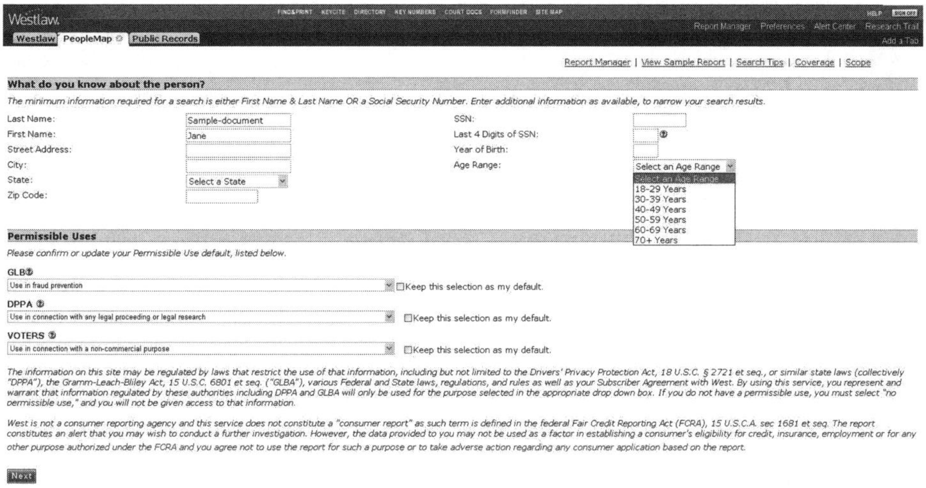

Figure 16-6. In addition to searching PeopleMap by name or SSN, a search can be narrowed down by year of birth, date range, or address. Notice the "permissible uses" drop-down menus.

Westlaw's People Finder Reports searches through). Some of the PeopleMap content sets include civil lawsuit abstracts, dockets, arrest records, World Watch List Profiles, and marriage and divorce records.

To search a subject through PeopleMap, a researcher would input the subject's full SSN, or last name/first name, or last name/last four digits of the SSN into the query boxes. (The **Public Records** database can be searched with terms and connectors (terms can be connected with Boolean connectors such as *AND*, *OR*, *NOT*), while the **PeopleMap** and **People Finder Report** databases cannot be searched with terms and connectors.)

Search results display a citation list with names on the left side of the page and an interactive map on the right side. The full SSN will not be displayed in the results, except to "qualified" government employees (who must re-qualify annually). The map shows connections of people to various documents and to various (up to ten) people. The searcher can click on a person other than the one first searched. Like Merlin, the results can be sorted by name, city, state, and year of birth. The results can also be viewed by type of document.

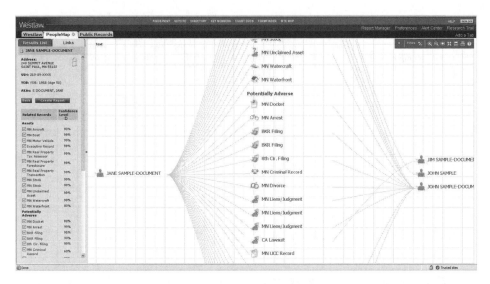

Figure 16-7. PeopleMap's graphical display helps you visualize all of the various records connected to your subject and also various people connected to her.

Once you have honed in on the correct person, customized reports can be created (**Comprehensive**, **Core**, **Assets**, or **Adverse**). As the name implies, the **Comprehensive** report displays all found records. The **Core** report displays all records except for credit headers, criminal records, arrest records, and watch list data. The **Adverse** report includes liens, judgments, evictions, criminal records, arrests, state lawsuit filings (summaries only), and dockets (state and federal). The **Assets** report includes records such as real estate records, boat and aircraft ownership, etc.

The Report will show a summary of results, the underlying records (in full), names of neighbors (at the subject's current and prior addresses), and relatives. Reports can be retrieved for 14 days (without an additional charge) by clicking on the **Report Manager** tab.

Drivers license information is not included in PeopleMap, but vehicle record information is. Vehicle records can be searched by name, VIN (Vehicle Identification Number), or license plate number.

Our View: Because of its "smarter" technology, PeopleMap brings back more relevant results than People Finder. Part of the "smarter" technology includes PeopleMap's ability to recognize inconsistencies in names (or misspellings and typographical errors) and bring back records despite those issues. (People Finder Report is a more literal search and wouldn't bring back records that appear to be inconsistent.) The Confidence Level feature is another aspect of the "smart" technology. Using percentages, it shows researchers how closely related various documents and people are. The PeopleMap visuals are useful to those who prefer visuals to text (or in addition to text).

We'd like to see a separate cellular telephone database instead of a phone database that lumps cellular and landline phone numbers together. When searching a known cellular number through the **Reverse Phone** search database, only a partial company name may be displayed (for instance, our company, Internet For Lawyers, is displayed as Internet for LA because the name is too long for our cellular phone company to display it in full). The number was designated as a landline, even though it had been ported over to a cell phone several years ago. (Some other databases have caught this fact, such as Accurint.) The address displayed was our prior residence. No database is perfect.

Despite PeopleMap's power, if you need to discover full SSNs, PeopleMap (and any other Westlaw public record databases) will not be the right choice (unless you are a qualified government employee). Instead, you would want to use Accurint, LocatePLUS, or Merlin, all of which display full SSNs to subscribers who acquiesce to a site visit and become approved to view full SSNs.

Tips: People Finder Report might serve as a good back-up if PeopleMap is unable to locate your subject because the People Finder Report database takes a different search approach than PeopleMap. Its initial search is not based on Experian Credit Headers, but is based instead on other content sets (mostly publicly available information, such as magazine subscriptions or warranty cards), which could, on occasion, provide a more current address.

Note the **Coverage** tab, which will display the name of the database (state-by-state and county-by-county), the dates of the database (from/to), the date the database was last updated, and the frequency of updating.

A database that is unique to Westlaw is the Pre-Foreclosure database, which includes *lis pendens* or notices of defaults.

LocatePLUS

https://www.locateplus.com/welcome.asp

Purpose: Like other investigative pay databases, LocatePLUS can be used to track witnesses, personal assets, and criminal histories, and create background dossiers. In its **About Us** page, LocatePLUS states its purpose is "to provide commercial and professional users with access to databases of public records and business information . . . offer[ing] nonpublic and public information to those entities who qualify to receive this information under the IRSG Principals and the Driver Privacy Protection Act (18 USC 2721, et seq)."

Content: LocatePLUS claims to have information on 98 percent of the U.S. adult population. The most useful LocatePLUS feature, in our opinion, is that full SSNs are available without a site visit (e.g., business owners, lawyers, private investigators, law enforcement, etc.), but users must still complete an application and become an approved subscriber. This is in stark contrast to Accurint and Merlin (and others), which require a site visit.

Like most of the other pay investigative databases, there is a disclaimer one must agree to, displayed right after logging in with one's password: "You are also representing and warranting that you have a legal right to obtain all information requested from the service, and that you will use all information in compliance with all applicable laws, including without limitation the Fair Credit Reporting Act (15 U.S.C. Sec. 1681 et seq.), the Federal Drivers Privacy Protection Act (18 U.S.C. Section 2721 et seq.), the Gramm-Leach-Bliley Act (U.S.C. Title 15, Chapter 94, Section 6801 et seq.), and similar statues." Note that this list of laws is longer than the one noted on their **About Us** page, which we quoted in the "Purpose" part of this entry and includes GLBA. This leads us to believe that the LocatePLUS database includes credit headers.

Before running each search, one must also check off the reason for needing access to SSNs:

❑ I am conducting work in conjunction with official government business in which SSN is required
❑ I am conducting work in connection with identity fraud
❑ I am conducting work involving a fraud investigation
❑ I am conducting work in a civil or criminal investigation, and the SSN is necessary to my investigation
❑ I am accessing SSN for a legal purpose to which I am legally entitled under FCRA

The following types of searches are available at LocatePLUS:

• Person (by Full or Partial Name or SSN)
• Current and Historical Address
• Common Residence
• Criminal Background (coverage varies from jurisdiction-to-jurisdiction)
• Name-to-Wireless Phone Number (50 percent of all U.S. cell numbers are available.)
• Name-to-Non-published Number
• Reverse Cell Phone and Non-published Number (The search defaults to a $5 enhanced search, but one can override the default and select a $1 basic search. If there are no results, there is no fee.)

- E-mail Address By E-mail address or By Name
- MVR (Motor Vehicle Record) The Motor Vehicle Record search is searchable by **VIN** (Vehicle Identification Number), **Owner's Name**, or **License Plate number**. LocatePLUS' MVR search doesn't always include a state's driver's license database, unlike Merlin which offers a 49-state driver's license database. Neither authors' records were found at LocatePLUS' MVR database, despite their state being one of the 31 included states. (Merlin found both authors' licenses.)
- Corporate Record Search

When searching by name, an **Exact match**, **starts with**, or **contains** feature is offered. To narrow down a name search, enter one or more of the following criteria: the subject's date of birth, a range of years if the exact date of birth is unknown, a city, or a state.

In a 2009 test search for *Carole Levitt*, we entered her last name, first name, state, and a range of years. This narrowed down the results to only one record, "Carole L. Levitt." While it was the correct result, the middle initial of "L" was not technically correct. Her actual middle initial is "A." After she married in 1981, she took her husband's last name and kept "Levitt" as her middle name. Thus, some of her records show "L" as her middle initial, even though she changed her name back to "Carole A. Levitt" in 1985.

After running a search, if there are multiple names listed, select the person of interest. The results page for that person will display information categories, such as **Relatives**, **Associates** (usually people one has shared a residence with), **Vehicles**, **Real Property**, **DOB**, etc. Not every information category contains data for the person being searched.

A **More** link is adjacent to each information category. For example, after selecting the **More** link associated with **Subject's Driver License Information**, you would learn that 13 states provide this information and most include: **Operator Name**, **Date of Birth**, **License Number**, **Sex**, **Height**, and **Address**. (An

available states link is also displayed to show the states.) (Note: Merlin has drivers license information for 49 states, but only 12 are current.)

By hovering one's cursor over the dollar sign adjacent to each information category, pricing is uncovered. If a user wants to view all the information in each category, the **Diamond Package** for $12.50 should be selected. In the **People Search**, the report defaults to **Diamond**, but this can be overridden if less information is needed. The $12.50 price assumes the user is subscribed to LocatePLUS' **Pay-per-click** plan, which requires a $15 minimum monthly subscription. Other packages range in price from $1 to $7.50. LocatePLUS's **Choice Savings Plan** is more like a flat rate plan, with pricing that ranges from $24.99 to $7,999.99. It requires a one year subscription.

Our View: On the plus side, LocatePLUS is quite user friendly and it's one of the only databases we know of to provide full SSNs without requiring a site visit. It's also one of the few databases that found Carole Levitt's childhood home address, but only when we ran a **Common Residence** search.

On the negative side, Carole Levitt's childhood home address didn't show in the **People Search** results. Thus, it seems that the relational aspect of LocatePLUS is not as powerful as we would prefer.

Another negative of LocatePLUS is that some of its data is not as fresh as other investigative pay databases' data. For instance, although the LocatePLUS results showed all the same addresses (dating back to 1983 to the present) as the other database vendors did for our *Carole Levitt* search, it did not show her current phone number (which the other database vendors did). LocatePlus did not find her e-mail address either, while Intelius, for instance, did. LocatePLUS did not find a corporate record for *Internet For Lawyers* although the record was found doing a free search at the New Mexico Public Regulation Commission site, at Merlin for $5, and at Accurint.

According to our LocatePLUS trainer, mortgage details (name of lender, loan amount, etc.), are generally not available at LocatePLUS, although we did find mortgage details in some records.

Pricing can get a bit complicated for some searches and costs could start to add up quickly. For example, it costs $2 for a **Name-to-Wireless Phone Number Search**, but to actually unmask the full number would cost $10 more (for up to three numbers), and to unmask each additional number would cost $2 more.

We'd like to see a cell number search by company name.

Tips: LocatePLUS's database can be accessed on a wireless handheld device to search for people, property, and vehicles.

Non-GLBA Investigative Pay Databases

Although we stated that investigative pay databases are geared to collection agencies, lawyers, private investigators, and law enforcement agencies involved in skip-tracing and backgrounding people, there are some databases geared toward business owners and the general public, such as KnowX (discussed on page 232) and all of the remaining databases in this chapter: US Search, People Search Now, and Intelius. These databases do not require subscribers to be pre-approved because these databases are not including GLBA information (nonpublic personal information from credit reporting agencies, commonly called credit headers). By failing to include credit headers, it's possible that these databases may be missing the freshest address and phone numbers for the person you are researching, but it's also possible that some of the non-GLBA databases can be just as fresh or even fresher than credit headers. It's hard to determine in advance, which is why it's a good idea to have a subscription to more than one database so you can cross-check your findings. You might be familiar with two of the database we'll discuss below, US Search and Intelius, because links to them often pop-up when conducting searches at free telephone directory sites. For example, if you look up a person's name at Infospace.com there may be a link to Intelius. When you click on the Intelius link, free summary information will be displayed, but if you click on the **Background Check**, the cost is $49.95, which seems steep. However, Intelius may satisfy the occasional user who doesn't want to fill out an application, wait for approval, and be boxed into an annual subscription.

US Search

US Search, on the other hand, offered GLBA information to their business clients without any pre-approval, but no longer offers this service.

In 2008, the New York Attorney General's Office completed a one-year investigation of US Search and discovered that US Search sold credit headers (more than 2,385 times) as an "extra benefit" to business clients by falsely attesting its use of credit headers, which came within GLBA's permissible uses (**http://www.oag.state.ny.us/media_center/2008/may/may20a_08.html**). In addition to accessing consumers' names, aliases, current and prior addresses, telephone numbers, and birth dates from the credit headers, US Search also accessed full Social Security numbers. Because most results also displayed information about the consumer's associates, relatives, and neighbors, more people than just the subject of the search had their information compromised. Needless to say, the consumers had not consented to their information being accessed. US Search also failed to maintain records of whose information was accessed and for what GLBA purpose.

"Under the terms of the settlement, US Search.com. Inc., will:

- Immediately suspend its illegal use of credit bureau data;
- Pay $250,000 in penalties, (approximately five times the amount it made from selling the illegally obtained information);
- Require clients to certify that they have a permissible purpose for accessing nonpublic personal information and allow all certifications to be inspected by the Attorney General's Office upon request;
- Train those responsible for accessing, using or disclosing any nonpublic personal information to ensure compliance with terms of the settlement and all applicable laws." (**http://www.oag.state.ny.us/media_center/2008/may/may20a_08.html**)

One year later (2009), US Search is still available online. There is no pre-approval process, which indicates (we assume), that they are complying with the settlement noted above by no longer accessing credit header information, despite their claim to providing "Current & previous addresses" and other data. They are most likely obtaining addresses from records other than credit headers and they may (or may not) be the current address.

US Search

http://www.ussearch.com/consumer/index.jsp **$**

Purpose: US Search, like KnowX and Intelius, is geared to business owners and the general public. US Search describes itself as

> the leading People Search destination. Since 1994, US Search has helped millions of people reconnect with friends, family, classmates, colleagues—anyone. US Search accesses billions of records to provide quick and accurate People Search Results.

Content: US Search includes real estate records, criminal records, court records, marriage/divorce records, maiden name searching, reverse telephone searching, and more.

Our View: As always, we like free summary information and US Search provides that to us. Just running a free summary search, we found that US Search noted the current city and state for Carole Levitt's home and business, eight "aliases" (either common misspellings of her name, her maiden name, and a previous married name), her correct age, past cities where she once lived (back to the 1980s), and one relative (Mark E. Levitt). Carole does not know of a relative with that name. She's guessing it's probably Mark E. Rosch, her husband. Somewhere, in some record, his first name and middle initial were merged with her last name. These are the types of errors that show up on a regular basis in many databases. Accurint also links Carole Levitt to Mark E. Levitt.

Tip: Prices range from $9.95 to $99.95, which seems high to us, but the 24-hour pass may be worthwhile for those who can batch their searches. The pass will only bring back current addresses, phone numbers, and property ownership information, but not other records, such as criminal records.

Intelius

http://www.intelius.com/

Purpose: To search public records using more sophisticated search techniques than the free sites offer; useful for skip-tracing and backgrounding people.

Content: Its database of public records and publicly available information includes the following information about people: address, phone number, real property owner-ship, selected lawsuit information (bankruptcies, marriage and divorce records, criminal records, tax liens, and judgments), licenses, birth and death records, and names, addresses, and phone numbers of neighbors and also of associates, relatives, and others linked to the same addresses as the subject. There are no business name searches available in this database. Registration or filling out an application and being approved in advance are not required leading us to conclude that they are not integrating credit headers into their data-base. Only paying with a credit card is required.

Prices vary depending on the type of data requested. For instance, to find someone's e-mail address will cost $4.95, but can go as low as $1.95 if the searcher agrees to an **Identity Protect** membership. The $1.95 price seems to be a ploy to wring an extra $19.95 each month from the searcher who fails to carefully read the **Identity Protect** membership disclaimer: "After your 7 day free trial, if you do not cancel your Identity Protect membership your credit card will be billed $19.95 and each month thereafter that you continue your member-ship. You may cancel anytime."

After running an e-mail search, the searcher is offered more information about their subject, such as their unlisted and non-published phone numbers ($14.95) and their business records ($7.95). The full background report is priced at $49.95 (or $39.95 for those who agree to the **Identity Protect** membership). For a **People**

Search (priced at $1.95) results include: first name, middle initial, last name, address, city, state, ZIP code, phone number, age, date of birth, average yearly income, and average house price. (The income and home value are compiled from property, demographic, census, and other public record sources and may not reflect the subject's actual income and home value.)

While Intelius seems to be geared more to the general public and small businesses than legal professionals, its Terms and Agreements, (laid out partially, below) give me pause about the general public being able to use it:

> You agree to use our information only for appropriate, legal purposes, and in compliance with all applicable federal, state and local laws and regulations. Additionally, you agree that our databases and information may not be used to bother, stalk, harass, threaten or embarrass any individual. You may not use the service to look up celebrities or other public persons, or to locate individuals under the age of 18. Information shall not be provided or resold to any other person or entity without our prior written consent. All searches of our databases are tracked, and (as noted below) you consent to such tracking and to the provision of all information about your use of our databases to law enforcement and others as may be useful to respond to allegations that our service or information has been misused . . . Intelius is not a consumer reporting agency as defined in the Fair Credit Reporting Act ("FCRA"), and the information in the Intelius databases has not been collected in whole or in part for the purpose of furnishing consumer reports, as defined in the FCRA. You shall not use any of our information as a factor in (1) establishing an individual's eligibility for personal credit or insurance or assessing risks associated with existing consumer credit obligations, (2) evaluating an individual for employment, promotion, reassignment or retention (including employment of household workers such as babysitters, cleaning personnel, nannies, contractors, and other individuals), or (3) any other personal business transaction with another individual (including, but not limited to, leasing an apartment).

Our View: Intelius might be useful to legal professionals if they haven't had any luck with the other databases. It's not our first choice because Intelius does not provide access to information derived from credit headers, which is generally considered the freshest source. However, Intelius was one of the only pay investigative databases that found Carole Levitt's e-mail address. Intelius probably scraped it from her company Web site or one of her social networking profiles, all free and easy ways to find information, so we are surprised that other pay databases did not find it.

While the major pay investigative databases (any Lexis or Westlaw database and Merlin) do not offer any information for free, a preliminary search at Intelius is free. It shows summary information that could prove useful. For instance, by running a **People Search** for "Carole Levitt," we were able to learn her age, her middle initial, and the names of four cities and states where she had lived, all by just viewing the free summary results. Although an incorrect middle initial was displayed among correct ones, the cities and states matched up with our subject. One of the displayed cities was her current city. In contrast, KnowX's free results did not find the same subject's current city. For those who frequently need to access investigative databases, and especially full SSNs, Accurint and Merlin will be better choices than Intelius.

Tip: Intelius offers a 24-hour pass for unlimited people searching for $19.95.

People Search Now

http://www.peoplesearchnow.com/

Public Background Checks

http://www.publicbackgroundchecks.com

People Search Now and Public Background Checks are two more databases that do not place information from credit headers into their databases. Although not evident on their sites, they are both owned by IQ Data, a GLBA database. People Search Now and Public Background Checks allow researchers to conduct a free search that displays summary results (aliases, city, state, and age). While we aren't apt to use non-GLBA databases as a frontline offense, we were impressed that both of these databases found information in a free summary test search that only one other database (LocatePLUS) has ever found (the city where Carole Levitt grew up, but moved away from in 1977). In addition, People Search Now is the only database to note that Carole Levitt has parents and to identify the city where her parents moved to in 1993 (and still live).

Appendix A

76 F.Supp.2d 773 St. Clair v. Johnny's Oyster & Shrimp, Inc.,

S.D.Tex.

F.Supp.2d

76 F.Supp.2d 773

2000 A.M.C. 769, 53 Fed. R. Evid. Serv. 1

United States District Court, S.D. Texas, Galveston Division.

Teddy ST. CLAIR, Plaintiff,

v. JOHNNY'S OYSTER & SHRIMP, INC., Defendant.

No. Civ.A. G-99-594. December 17, 1999.

Seaman brought action for personal injuries sustained aboard a vessel. Upon defendant's motion to dismiss, the District Court, Kent, J., held that information taken off the internet was insufficient to establish that defendant was owner of vessel aboard which seaman sustained an injury.

Motion conditionally denied.

Admiralty k59

774

Kenneth Ross Citti, Citti & Crinion, Houston, TX, for Ross Citti, mediator.

Paul G. Ash, Jr, Attorney at Law, Galveston, TX, David Alan Slaughter, Attorney at Law, Houston, TX, for Teddy St. Clair, plaintiff.

James Richard Watkins, Royston Rayzor et al, Galveston, TX, Marc H. Schneider, Waldron Schneider et al, Houston, TX, for Johnny's Oyster & Shrimp, Inc., defendant.

James Richard Watkins, Royston Rayzor et al, Galveston, TX, Marc H. Schneider, Waldron Schneider et al, Houston, TX, for Shrimps R US, Inc., defendant.

ORDER DENYING DEFENDANT'S MOTION TO DISMISS

KENT, District Judge.

Plaintiff St. Clair brings claims for personal injuries allegedly sustained while employed as a seaman for Defendant Johnny's Oyster &

Shrimp, Inc. aboard the vessel CAPT. LE'BRADO. Now before the Court is Defendant's Motion to Dismiss. For the reasons stated below, Defendant's Motion is conditionally DENIED for the time being.

The Federal Rules of Civil Procedure authorize a court, upon suitable showing, to dismiss any action or any claim within an action for failure to state a claim upon which relief can be granted. See FED.R.CIV.P. 12(b)(6). When considering a motion to dismiss, the Court accepts as true all well-pleaded allegations in the complaint, and views them in a light most favorable to the plaintiff. See *Malina v. Gonzales*, 994 F.2d 1121, 1125 (5th Cir.1993). Unlike a motion for summary judgment, a motion to dismiss should be granted only when it appears without a doubt that the plaintiff can prove no set of facts in support of her claims that would entitle her to relief. See *Conley v. Gibson*, 355 U.S. 41, 45-46, 78 S.Ct. 99, 102, 2 L.Ed.2d 80 (1957); Tuchman v. DSC Communications Corp., 14 F.3d 1061, 1067 (5th Cir.1994).

The basis for Defendant's Motion to Dismiss surrounds the ownership of CAPT. LE'BRADO at the time of Plaintiff's accident, which occurred on August 26, 1999. Defendant alleges that it "does not now, and did not at the time the alleged incident own or operate the vessel CAPT. LE'BRADO." Def.'s Am. Mot. to Dismiss at 1. Defendant notes that on July 1, 1999, ownership was transferred to Oysters R Us, Inc., and on August 1, 1999, Oysters R Us, Inc. transferred ownership of the vessel to Shrimps R Us, Inc. Therefore, because Defendant is not the owner of the vessel, it seeks dismissal under FED.R.CIV.P. 12(b)(6). Plaintiff responds that he has discovered "evidence"—taken off the Worldwide Web on December 1, 1999—revealing that Defendant does "in fact" own CAPT. LE'BRADO. See Pl.'s Resp. to Def.'s Am. Mot. to Dismiss Ex. A at 1-2 (citing data from the United States Coast Guard's on-line vessel data base).

Plaintiff's electronic "evidence" is totally insufficient to withstand Defendant's Motion to Dismiss. While some look to the Internet as an innovative vehicle for communication, the Court continues to warily and wearily view it largely as one large catalyst for rumor, innuendo, and misinformation. So as to not mince words, the Court reiterates that this so-called Web provides no way of verifying the authenticity of the alleged contentions that Plaintiff wishes to rely upon in his Response to Defendant's Motion. There is no way Plaintiff can overcome the presumption that the information he discovered on the Internet is inherently untrustworthy.

775

Anyone can put anything on the Internet. No Web site is monitored for accuracy and nothing contained therein is under oath or even subject to independent verification absent underlying documentation. Moreover, the Court holds no illusions that hackers can adulterate the content on any Web site from any location at any time. For these reasons, any evidence procured off the Internet is adequate for almost nothing, even under the most liberal interpretation of the hearsay exception rules found in FED.R.CIV.P. 807.

Instead of relying on the voodoo information taken from the Internet, Plaintiff must hunt for hard copy back-up documentation in admissible form from the United States Coast Guard or discover alternative information verifying what Plaintiff alleges. Accordingly, Plaintiff has until February 1, 2000 to garner legitimate documents showing that Defendant owns the CAPT. LE'BRADO. If Plaintiff cannot provide the Court with credible, legitimate information supporting its position by February 1, 2000, the Court will be inclined to grant Defendant dispositive relief.

IT IS SO ORDERED.

Appendix B

829 N.E.2d 52 Munster v. Groce

FOR PUBLICATION

ATTORNEYS FOR APPELLANT:

THOMAS D. BLACKBURN
Blackburn & Green
Fort Wayne, Indiana

KARL L. MULVANEY
NANA QUAY-SMITH
CANDACE L. SAGE
Bingham McHale, LLP
Indianapolis, Indiana

ATTORNEY FOR APPELLEES:

MICHAEL D. CONNER
Spitzer Herriman Stephenson
Holderead Musser & Conner, LLP
Marion, Indiana

IN THE
COURT OF APPEALS OF INDIANA

DAVID MUNSTER,	)	
	)	
Appellant-Plaintiff,	)	
	)	
vs.	)	No. 18A02-0409-CV-738
	)	
JOE GROCE and	)	
BUSINESS WORLD, INC.,	)	
	)	
Appellees-Defendants.	)	

APPEAL FROM THE DELAWARE CIRCUIT COURT
The Honorable Marianne L. Vorhees, Judge
Cause No. 18C01-0401-CT-1

June 8, 2005

OPINION—FOR PUBLICATION

BARNES, Judge

Case Summary

David Munster appeals the dismissal of his complaint against Joe Groce and Business World, Inc. ("BWI"). We affirm in part, reverse in part, and remand.

Issues

The restated issues before us are:

I. whether Munster properly effected service of process on Groce; and

II. whether Munster properly effected service of process on BWI.

Facts

On February 25, 2000, Munster and Groce were involved in an automobile accident. At the time, Groce was an employee of BWI, a corporation that later was dissolved in July 2001. On February 15, 2002, Munster filed a complaint against Groce and BWI. Munster attempted to serve both Groce and BWI by certified mail. Both mailings were returned undelivered on March 1, 2002; the mailing to Groce was marked "attempted not known" and the mailing to BWI was marked with a new address. App. p. 2.

No further action was taken in the case until December 2003, when Munster obtained new counsel. Second attempts to serve BWI and Groce by certified mail were again returned undelivered, with the marking on each "forwarding order expired." *Id.* Munster then attempted to serve BWI and Groce through the Indiana Secretary of State, as provided by Indiana Trial Rule 4.10. Munster did not file a praecipe for summons with the trial court, but instead delivered copies of the summons and complaint directly to the Secretary of State. Munster provided the Secretary of State with addresses for BWI and Groce, the Secretary of State mailed copies of the summons and complaint to those addresses, and they were returned undelivered as before.

At least by December 2003, BWI's former insurer learned of Munster's lawsuit and filed an answer on behalf of BWI and Groce, which among other things asserted the affirmative defenses of lack of personal jurisdiction, insufficiency of process, and insufficiency of service of process. On January 22, 2004, counsel also filed a motion to dismiss on behalf of BWI and Groce under Indiana Trial Rules 12(B)(2), (4), and (5), alleging a lack of personal jurisdiction due to insufficiency of process and service of process. The motion also sought dismissal due to failure to prosecute pursuant to Indiana Trial Rule 41(E).

On January 26, 2004, Steve Harris, an investigator hired by Munster's counsel, delivered a copy of the summons and complaint to the residence of George Mikesell, who was listed as a director of BWI in its articles of incorporation. Mikesell was not home at the time, but his wife Lois personally received the summons and complaint. Harris phoned Mikesell the next day and confirmed that he received the summons and complaint. Also on January 26 and January 31, 2004, Harris attempted personal delivery of the summons and complaint at Groce's alleged former places of residence and employment, but could not locate him.

On May 17, 2004, the trial court dismissed Munster's complaint pursuant to Trial Rules 12(B)(2), (4), and (5); it did not dismiss under Trial Rule 41(E). It stated in its order that Munster had not complied with Trial Rule 4.10 allowing for service through the Secretary of State because he had not filed a praecipe for summons with the trial court first. As for the January 26, 2004 delivery of the summons and complaint to Lois Mikesell, the trial court struck the acknowledgment of service she had signed and concluded that she had no actual or apparent authority to accept service on BWI's behalf.

On June 14, 2004, Munster filed a motion to correct error. On the same date, Munster also filed, with the trial court this time, a praecipe for summons for service upon BWI and Groce through the Secretary of State. Using the same addresses as before, the Secretary of State again sent certified mail addressed to BWI and Groce, and the mailings again were returned undelivered. On August 24, 2004, the trial court denied the motion to correct error. Munster now appeals.

Analysis

I. Standard of Review

Technically, Munster is appealing from the denial of a motion to correct error. We generally review a trial court's denial of a motion to correct error for an abuse of discretion. *Principal Life Ins. Co. v. Needler*, 816 N.E.2d 499, 502 (Ind. Ct. App. 2004). Except for pointing out Munster's re-attempt to effect service through the Secretary of State, however, the motion to correct error in this case merely asked the trial court to recon-sider its earlier ruling on the motion to dismiss.

BWI and Groce have not claimed that they lacked insufficient contacts with Indiana for the trial court to exercise jurisdiction over them and base their arguments solely on insufficient service of process. Indiana Trial Rule 12(B)(5) allows for dismissal of a complaint if there is insufficient service of process; Trial Rule 12(B)(2) similarly allows for a dismissal of a complaint if there is a lack of personal jurisdiction. A trial court does not acquire per-sonal jurisdiction over a party if service of process is inadequate. *King v. United Leasing, Inc.*, 765 N.E.2d 1287, 1290 (Ind. Ct. App. 2002).

When a defendant argues a lack of personal jurisdiction, the plaintiff must present evidence to show that there is personal jurisdiction over the defendant. *Anthem Ins. Companies, Inc. v. Tenet Healthcare Corp.*, 730 N.E.2d 1227, 1231 (Ind. 2000). The defendant ultimately bears the burden of proving the lack of personal jurisdiction by a preponderance of the evi-dence, unless the lack of jurisdiction is apparent on the face of the com-plaint. *Id.* The existence of personal jurisdiction over a defendant is a question of law and a constitutional requirement to rendering a valid judgment, mandated by the Due Process Clause of the Fourteenth Amendment to the United States Constitution. *Id.* at 1237. Thus, we review a trial court's determination regarding personal jurisdiction de novo. *Id.* at 1238. To the extent a trial court may make findings of juris-dictional facts, these findings are reviewed for clear error if they were based on in-court testimony. *Id.* at 1238. If, however, only a paper record has been presented to the trial court, we are in as good a position as the trial court to determine the existence of jurisdictional facts and will employ de novo review as to those facts. *Id.* at n.12.

Here, the trial court ruled on the motion to dismiss based entirely on a paper record, consisting of records of Munster's attempts at service and affidavits of Harris and Lois Mikesell. No testimony was presented at the hearings conducted on the motion to dismiss and motion to correct error. Thus, our review of the trial court's personal jurisdiction ruling is entirely de novo. Additionally, we note that although the trial court in dismissing Munster's complaint provided an explanation as to why it was doing so, we will affirm a trial court's grant of a motion to dismiss if it is sustainable on any theory or basis found in the record. See *Minks v. Pina*, 709 N.E.2d 379, 381 (Ind. Ct. App. 1999), *trans. denied.*

II. Service as to Groce

Groce argues that Munster's attempts to serve him with process were insufficient to permit the trial court to exercise jurisdiction over him.[1] This question has two aspects: whether there was compliance with the Indiana Trial Rules regarding service, and whether such attempts at service comported with the Due Process Clause of the Fourteenth Amendment. We conclude that due process required more than was attempted here with respect to service on Groce.

In the seminal case regarding due process and notice, the Supreme Court held that the Due Process Clause requires at a minimum "that deprivation of life, liberty or property by adjudication be preceded by notice and opportunity for hearing appropriate to the nature of the case." *Mullane v. Central Hanover Bank & Trust Co.*, 339 U.S. 306, 313, 70 S. Ct. 652, 656-57 (1950). "This right to be heard has little reality or worth unless one is informed that the matter is pending and can choose for himself whether to appear or default, acquiesce or contest." *Id.* at 314, 70 S. Ct. at 657. "An elementary and fundamental requirement of due process in any proceeding which is to be accorded finality is notice reasonably calculated, under all the circumstances, to apprise interested parties of the pendency of the action and afford them an opportunity to present their objections." *Id.* "[W]hen notice is a person's due, process which is a mere gesture is not due process. The means employed must be such as one desirous of actually informing the absentee might reasonably adopt to accomplish it." *Id.* at 315, 70 S. Ct. at 657. The Court held that alternatives to personal service and actual notice of a suit, such as publication, are permissible

> where it is not reasonably possible or practicable to give more adequate warning. Thus it has been recognized that, in the case of persons missing or unknown, employment of an indirect and even a probably futile means of notification is all that the situation permits and creates no constitutional bar to a final decree foreclosing their rights. . . . [Parties] whose interests or whereabouts could not *with due diligence* be ascertained come clearly within this category.

Id. at 317, 70 S. Ct. at 658-59 (emphasis added). *Mullane* thus clearly indicates that although it is acceptable in some instances to proceed with a lawsuit by using a service method that it is unlikely to give

---

[1] For the sake of clarity, we are referring to Groce as if he has actual knowledge of and has participated in this lawsuit. In fact, there is no indication in the record that he personally has any knowledge of it. Likewise, although we refer to BWI throughout the opinion, it no longer exists as a functioning company.

actual notice to an interested party, this is only the case if that party's whereabouts cannot reasonably, and in the exercise of due diligence, be ascertained.

The textbook example of constructive service and notice of a lawsuit is service by publication, as exemplified by *Mullane*. Indiana Trial Rule 4.13 allows the use of this form of "service" or notice, but only if the party seeking publication files with the trial court "supporting affidavits [showing] that diligent search has been made that the defendant cannot be found, has concealed his whereabouts, or has left the state." This rule, therefore, preemptively requires a party to swear to "due diligence" in attempting to locate an interested party before he or she may seek service by publication.

In the present case, Munster never sought service by publication on Groce. Instead, before turning to the Secretary of State, the CCS indicates that he attempted two certified mailings to Groce, once in February 2002 and once in December 2003. The first mailing was to an apartment address in Muncie, and there is no evidence in the record as to what address was used for the second mailing; the address provided to the Secretary of State was for a street address in Muncie. There is also no evidence in the record as to what information was used to determine Groce's possible whereabouts. In any event, none of these mailings resulted in actual service to Groce, as both mailings were returned to sender. This court has held, "Unclaimed service is insufficient to establish a reasonable probability that the defendant received adequate notice and to confer personal jurisdiction." *King*, 765 N.E.2d at 1290. We have also held, "Service upon a defendant's former residence is insufficient to confer personal jurisdiction." *Mills v. Coil*, 647 N.E.2d 679, 681 (Ind. Ct. App. 1995), *trans. denied*. Additionally, Indiana Trial Rule 4.1(A)(1), which allows for service by certified mail, requires that a return receipt must show receipt of the letter in order for service to be effective.

After the December 2003 failed mailing to Groce, Munster attempted to perfect service through the Secretary of State. Indiana Trial Rule 4.4(A)(2) states:

> Any person or organization that is a nonresident of this state, a resident of this state who has left the state, or a person whose residence is unknown, submits to the jurisdiction of the courts of this state as to any action arising from the following acts committed by him or her or his or her agent: . . . causing personal injury or property damage by an act or omission done within this state. . . .

Trial Rule 4.4(B) goes on to state:

> A person subject to the jurisdiction of the courts of this state under this rule may be served with summons:
>
> (1) As provided by Rules 4.1 (service on individuals), 4.5 (service upon resident who cannot be found or served within the state), 4.6 (service upon organizations), 4.9 (in rem actions); or
> (2) The person shall be deemed to have appointed the Secretary of State as his agent upon whom service of summons may be made as provided in Rule 4.10.

Finally, Trial Rule 4.10 provides:

> Whenever, under these rules or any statute, service is made upon the Secretary of State or any other governmental organization or officer, as agent for the person being served, service may be made upon such agent as provided in this rule.
>
> (1) The person seeking service or his attorney shall:
>   (a) submit his request for service upon the agent in the praecipe for summons, and state that the governmental organization or officer is the agent of the person being served;
>   (b) state the address of the person being served as filed and recorded pursuant to a statute or valid agreement, or if no such address is known, then his last known mailing address, and, if no such address is known, then such shall be stated;
>   (c) pay any fee prescribed by statute to be forwarded together with sufficient copies of the summons, affidavit and complaint, to the agent by the clerk of the court.
> (2) Upon receipt thereof the agent shall promptly:
>   (a) send to the person being served a copy of the summons and complaint by registered or certified mail or by other public means by which a written acknowledgment of receipt may be obtained;
>   (b) complete and deliver to the clerk an affidavit showing the date of the mailing, or if there was no mailing, the reason therefor;
>   (c) send to the clerk a copy of the return receipt along with a copy of the summons;
>   (d) file and retain a copy of the return receipt.

Initially, the parties spent much time arguing as to whether Rule 4.10 required Munster to file a praecipe for summons with the trial court, instead of directly with the Secretary of State, before service could be effected under this rule; the trial court also based its ruling on Munster's not first filing a praceipe for summons with it. It would appear to us that the rule contemplates filing the praecipe with the trial court, which would then forward the necessary materials to the Secretary of State for service. Most tellingly, subsection 1(c) of the rule requires the person seeking service to "pay any fee prescribed by statute to be forwarded together with sufficient copies of the summons, affidavit and complaint, to the agent *by the clerk of the court.*" (Emphasis added.) This seems to say that the clerk of court forwards the summons, affidavit, complaint, and any required fee to the Secretary of State or other government officer, which necessarily means the clerk was provided with those materials in the first place by the party seeking service. We also reject Munster's argument that a party seeking service through the Secretary of State does not have to follow Rule 4.10 to the letter. Subsection (1) clearly states that the party seeking such service "shall" do so as delineated.

Even assuming, however, that it was not fatal to Munster's service attempt that he initially filed a praecipe for summons directly with the Secretary of State instead of with the trial court, there is a fundamental problem in this case. It is evident that attempting to serve Groce through the Secretary of State would, at best, amount only to constructive service and constructive notice of the pending lawsuit. Munster had already twice attempted to mail summons to Groce unsuccessfully. Having the Secretary of State make the mailing instead was not going to somehow give Groce actual notice of the lawsuit.

As noted, the Due Process Clause requires that in order for constructive notice of a lawsuit to be sufficient, a party must exercise due diligence in attempting to locate a litigant's whereabouts. See *Mullane*, 339 U.S. at 317, 70 S. Ct. at 659. A party must provide "notice reasonably calculated, under all the circumstances, to apprise interested parties of the pendency of the action and afford them an opportunity to present their objections." *Id.* at 314, 70 S. Ct. at 657. Rule 4.4(B)(2) does allow for service through the Secretary of State with respect to a defendant "whose residence is unknown," and presumably such service is effective even if the defendant does not receive actual notice of the lawsuit; Rule 4.10 does not expressly require actual notice. We conclude, however, that in order for such service to be constitutionally effective there must be a showing by the plaintiff or party who sought such service that due diligence to ascertain the defendant's current whereabouts was exercised and service through the Secretary of State was reasonable under the circumstances.

We are also aware that neither Rule 4.4(B)(2) nor Rule 4.10 requires a party seeking service through the Secretary of State to provide an affidavit asserting that due diligence to locate the defendant was unsuccessfully attempted, in contrast to service by publication under Rule 4.13. If such service is subsequently challenged by a motion to dismiss or motion to set aside a default judgment, however, we conclude that a plaintiff is required to present evidence of unsuccessful due diligence in locating the defendant, which in turn necessitated the use of constructive notice and service. Otherwise, parties who wished to serve opposing parties whose whereabouts they did not know could always sidestep the due diligence requirements of notice by publication and simply ask for service through the Secretary of State, which is not a proper reading of the Indiana Trial Rules and the Due Process Clause.

With issues as important as due process, notice of a lawsuit, and personal jurisdiction, we will not presume from the scant evidence in this record that Munster used due diligence in attempting to ascertain Groce's current whereabouts. Harris provided the following affidavit describing his efforts to serve Groce: "I duly pursued and exhausted all known information to perfect service upon Joe Groce by attempting to deliver to his possession a true copy of the Summons and Complaint in the above-captioned manner at his former places of residence and employment." App. p. 46. Harris also swore elsewhere that he asked the Mikesells if they were aware of Groce's *current* whereabouts. There is no evidence in the record as to what information was used to ascertain Groce's alleged former places of residence and employment. There is no evidence in the record as to any attempts to locate his current whereabouts, aside from asking the Mikesells.[2] There is no evidence in the record that Groce was or is attempting to hide his whereabouts.

Harris' bare-bones affidavit does not permit the conclusion that due diligence was used to locate Groce's current whereabouts, or that service via the Secretary of State, using an address that apparently was known to be invalid, was reasonably calculated to provide Groce notice of this lawsuit. *Cf. Bays v. Bays*, 489 N.E.2d 555, 557-59 (Ind. Ct. App. 1986) (finding sufficient due diligence to justify service by publication where a husband had spoken to his wife's parents eleven times in three years and her parents

---

[2] At the hearing on the motion to dismiss, counsel for Munster asserted that other steps were taken to ascertain Groce's whereabouts that were not recounted in Harris' affidavit. Arguments of counsel, however, are not evidence that courts may consider in making factual determinations. *El v. Beard*, 795 N.E.2d 462, 467 (Ind. Ct. App. 2003).

stated they did not know his wife's whereabouts, and where husband employed private investigator who searched for wife for three years and provided letter to trial court detailing efforts to locate wife).[3] As such, the trial court never obtained personal jurisdiction over Groce in a manner consistent with the Due Process Clause. Dismissal of Munster's lawsuit as to him for lack of personal jurisdiction and insufficient service of process was proper.

III. Service as to BWI

Next, we address whether Munster effectively served BWI with process. We decline to address Munster's attempts to serve BWI by certified mail and through the Secretary of State, and solely address service at the Mikesell's household. The question of how to serve a defunct corporation like BWI has not previously been addressed by Indiana case law. The trial rules and Indiana Business Corporation Law, however, provide sufficient guidance for how to resolve this issue.

Indiana Code Section 23-1-45-5(b)(5), which governs voluntary dissolution of a corporation and which apparently is what occurred to BWI, expressly provides that dissolution "does not . . . prevent commencement of a proceeding by or against the corporation in its corporate name. . . ." As far as how to serve a defunct corporation with process, BWI points out that subsection (7) of Section 23-1-45-5(b) provides that the authority of the registered agent of a corporation does not terminate with the corporation's dissolution. BWI also notes that Indiana Code Section 23-1-24-4(a) states, "A corporation's registered agent is the corporation's agent for service of process, notice, or demand required or permitted by law to be served on the corporation." BWI essentially argues that pursuant to this statute, Munster was required to attempt to serve BWI's registered agent, Robert Compton, instead of Mikesell, and such attempt never occurred.

Subsection (c) of Section 23-1-24-4, however, plainly states, "This section does not prescribe the only means, or necessarily the required means, of serving a corporation." The Official Comment to this statutory provision of the Indiana Business Corporation Law confirms that methods of service permitted by the Indiana Trial Rules, but not expressly mentioned by Section 23-1-24-4, should be viewed as supplementary to

---

[3] *Bays* does not necessarily establish the minimum that should be required for a showing of due diligence in locating a missing litigant. We do note that there is no evidence in this case of a public records or Internet search for Groce or the use of a skip-trace service to find him. In fact, we discovered, upon entering "Joe Groce Indiana" into the Google™ search engine, an address for Groce that differed from either address used in this case, as well as an apparent obituary for Groce's mother that listed numerous surviving relatives who might have known his whereabouts.

the statute, not inconsistent with it. The Official Comment further cites *Burger Man, Inc. v. Jordan Paper Products, Inc.*, 170 Ind. App. 295, 352 N.E.2d 821 (1976) as an "illustrative" case where this court approved service upon a corporation's "executive officer" rather than the corporation's registered agent, much like what happened in this case. The Indiana Trial Rules and the Indiana Business Corporation Law permitted Munster to attempt service upon someone other than BWI's registered agent.

Indiana Trial Rule 4.6(A) provides that service upon a domestic organization may be made "upon an executive officer thereof. . . ." Trial Rule 83 states, " 'Executive officer' of an organization includes the president, vice president, secretary, treasurer, cashier, *director*, chairman of the board of directors or trustees, office manager, plant manager, or subdivision manager, partner, or majority shareholder." (Emphasis added.) Munster provided BWI's 1986 articles of incorporation to the trial court, which listed George Mikesell as one of its three directors. BWI presented no evidence that Mikesell was not still a director of this closely-held corporation at the time of its dissolution in 2001. As the party seeking dismissal of a complaint on personal jurisdiction grounds, we conclude it was BWI's burden to prove by a preponderance of the evidence that Mikesell was not a director of BWI at the time of its dissolution and to demonstrate that the articles of incorporation's listing of directors was not accurate as of 2001. See *Anthem Ins. Companies*, 730 N.E.2d at 1231. Also, although Trial Rules 4.6(A) and 83 are not crystal clear on this point, we also hold that in the case of a dissolved corporation, it is appropriate to serve process upon a former director of the corporation at the time of its dissolution. See *Warren v. Dixon Ranch Co.*, 260 P.2d 741, 743 (Utah 1953) (holding that service upon former director of defunct corporation was effective service upon the corporation under trial rules similar to Indiana's).

We now address whether Mikesell was adequately served so as to confer jurisdiction upon BWI. Trial Rule 4.6(B) provides that service shall be made upon a proper representative of the corporation, as listed by Rule 4.6(A), in a manner provided for service upon individuals elsewhere in the Trial Rules. Rule 4.6(B) also states that generally such service cannot knowingly be made at the person's dwelling house or place of abode. This restriction, however, clearly is inapplicable in the case of a corporation such as BWI that is no longer functioning and, a fortiori, no longer has a business address. We conclude it was proper to attempt service at Mikesell's dwelling house or place of abode.

Next, we address the effect of leaving the summons and complaint with Lois Mikesell at the Mikesell residence. We find it unnecessary to address whether Lois had the authority to accept service of process on behalf of her husband. Even assuming that she did not, Trial Rule 4.1(A)(3) allows for service by leaving a copy of the summons and complaint at a person's dwelling house or usual place of abode. Thus, even if Lois had not personally been handed the summons and complaint by Harris and he had merely left the documents at the house, this would have constituted service upon Mikesell.[4]

We do observe that there is nothing in the record to indicate that a copy of the summons only was subsequently mailed to the Mikesell residence, which is required as a second step in effective service by Trial Rule 4.1(B) when the complaint and summons has been left at a person's dwelling under Trial Rule 4.1(A)(3). This omission is not fatal to Munster's attempt to serve Mikesell and, hence, BWI, in light of Harris' affidavit recounting that he spoke to Mikesell over the phone the day after delivery of the summons and complaint and Mikesell confirmed that he received them. BWI presented no evidence to refute Harris' memory of events. We have previously held that failure to follow-up delivery of a complaint and summons under Trial Rule 4.1(A)(3) with mailing of a summons under Trial Rule 4.1(B) does not constitute ineffective service of process if the subject of the summons does not dispute actually having received the complaint and summons. See *Boczar v. Reuben*, 742 N.E.2d 1010, 1016 (Ind. Ct. App. 2001).

Finally, BWI argues that service upon it via service upon Mikesell was ineffective because the summons was directed only to BWI, not to Mikesell or any other person, such as a "director" or "officer" of BWI. BWI relies upon *Volunteers of America v. Premier Auto*, 755 N.E.2d 656 (Ind. Ct. App. 2001). There, we held that service upon Volunteers of America ("VOA") was ineffective because none of the initial attempts were directed to a person; instead, the summonses were simply addressed to "Volunteers of America." *Id.* at 660. We also held that this defect in service was not saved by Trial Rule 4.15(F), which provides: "No summons or the service thereof shall be set aside or be adjudged insufficient when either is reasonably calculated to inform the person to be served that an action has been instituted against him, the name of the court, and the time within which he is required to respond." *Id.* We additionally noted that the first time Premier sent a garnishment proceeding notice to VOA addressed to the "Highest Ranking Officer" was also the first time a "proper person" for corporate service received notice of the lawsuit and default judgment. *Id.*

---

[4]BWI has never asserted that Harris did not deliver the summons and complaint to Mikesell's dwelling house or usual place of abode.

Here, the record does seem to indicate that the summons for BWI was addressed only to BWI, and not to any specific individual or title. This case, however, clearly differs from *VOA* because that case concerned mailings to VOA's office that subsequently were never brought to the attention of a high-ranking corporate officer. Here, by contrast, the summons and complaint were delivered directly to Mikesell's residence and he acknowledged receipt of them; there was no chance that the summons and complaint would fail to follow the proper internal corporate channels to a high-ranking officer or director because they were delivered directly to a director. As such, even if there was a technical defect in the summons to BWI, the method of service by delivery at Mikesell's residence still was reasonably calculated to inform BWI of the pending lawsuit and, in fact, did provide such notice. Trial Rule 4.15(F) excuses minor, technical defects in the method of service where actual service has been accomplished. See *Reed Sign Service, Inc. v. Reid*, 755 N.E.2d 690, 696 (Ind. Ct. App. 2001), *trans. denied*. In summary, Munster sufficiently complied with the Indiana Trial Rules so as to effect service upon BWI and give the trial court personal jurisdiction over it. Likewise, as we have indicated the method of service on BWI was reasonably calculated so as to provide it with notice of the lawsuit and, therefore, comports with the Due Process Clause. See *Mullane*, 339 U.S. at 314, 70 S. Ct. at 657. We reverse the trial court's grant of the motion to dismiss with respect to BWI.

Conclusion

Munster has failed to demonstrate that his attempts to serve Groce comported with the Due Process Clause and the trial court was correct to dismiss the lawsuit as to Groce for lack of personal jurisdiction. With respect to BWI, we find sufficient compliance with the Indiana Trial Rules and Due Process Clause regarding service of process to allow the lawsuit against it to proceed. We affirm in part, reverse in part, and remand for further proceedings.

Affirmed in part, reversed in part, and remanded.

KIRSCH, C.J., and BAKER, J., concur.

Appendix C

IN THE DISTRICT COURT OF APPEAL OF THE STATE OF FLORIDA
FOURTH DISTRICT   JANUARY TERM 2005

SONIA DUBOIS and **9060-0677 QUEBEC, INC.,**
d/b/a **AUTOCARS SYMPOSIUM,**

Appellants,

v.

ASHLEY BUTLER, a minor, by and through her mother and
natural guardian **CHRISTINE BUTLER, CHRISTINE BUTLER,**
individually, and **JAMES BUTLER,** individually, **BTM TRAVEL
GROUP, INC.,** and **QUALITY TRANSPORTATION SERVICES, INC.,**

Appellees.

CASE NOS. 4D04-3559 and 4D04-3561

Opinion filed May 25, 2005

    Consolidated appeals of non-final orders from the Circuit Court for the Seventeenth Judicial Circuit, Broward County; J. Leonard Fleet, Judge; L.T. Case No. 03-16918(03).

    Richard M. Gomez of Law Offices of Roland Gomez, Miami Lakes, for appellants.

    Nancy Little Hoffmann of Nancy Little Hoffmann, P.A., Pompano Beach, and Timothy P. Beavers of McFann & Beavers, P.A., Fort Lauderdale, for appellees Ashley Butler, a minor, by and through her mother and natural guardian, Christine Butler, Christine Butler, individually, and James Butler, individually.

    GROSS, J.

    Sonia Dubois and Quebec, Inc., the defendants below, appeal an order denying their motions to dismiss brought under Florida Rule of Civil Procedure 1.140(b)(2) for lack of jurisdiction over the person due to improper service. *See* Fla. R. App. P. 9.130(a)(3)(C)(i) (authorizing appeals of non-final orders that determine "the jurisdiction of the person"). We reverse, holding that service was defective as to both defendants.

To serve Dubois, the plaintiffs used the substituted service procedures of section 48.171, Florida Statutes (2003). "Because the statute allowing substituted service is an exception to the general rule requiring a defendant to be personally served, due process values require *strict compliance* with the statutory requirements." *Monaco v. Nealon*, 810 So. 2d 1084, 1085 (Fla. 4th DCA 2002) (emphasis in original). When using a substituted service statute, "to overcome the primary requirement of personal service, the plaintiff must demonstrate the exercise of due diligence in attempting to locate the defendant." *Wiggam v. Bamford*, 562 So. 2d 389, 391 (Fla. 4th DCA 1990). In *Wiggam*, we indicated what would satisfy the due diligence requirement:

> The test [for determining the sufficiency of substitute service] is not whether it was in fact possible to effect personal service in a given case, but whether the [plaintiff] reasonably employed knowledge at [her] command, made diligent inquiry, and exerted an honest and conscientious effort appropriate to the circumstances, to acquire the information necessary to enable [her] to effect personal service on the defendant.

Id. (quoting *Grammer v. Grammer*, 80 So. 2d 457, 460-61 (Fla. 1955) (quoting *McDaniel v. McElvey*, 108 So. 820, 831 (Fla. 1926))).

Numerous cases involve plaintiffs who fail to exercise "an honest and conscientious effort" to serve a defendant. A common theme of these cases is that the plaintiff fails to follow an "obvious" lead.

For example, in *Robinson v. Cornelius*, 377 So. 2d 776 (Fla. 4th DCA 1979), a plaintiff relied exclusively on an address for the defendant provided by the Department of Motor Vehicles; because the plaintiff did not check the telephone directory or investigate the address disclosed in interrogatories by the defendant's insurer, the court held that the plaintiff failed to exercise due diligence. See also *Cross v. Kalina*, 681 So. 2d 855, 856 (Fla. 5th DCA 1996) (while the plaintiff made an effort to serve the defendant through registered mail, plaintiff had failed to use due diligence: "Here, other than one mailing, there is no evidence that any effort was expended to locate [the defendant]."); *Torelli v. Travelers Indem. Co.*, 495 So. 2d 837 (Fla. 3d DCA 1986) (plaintiff did not demonstrate due diligence in attempting to locate the defendant where he failed to seek information from the defendant's attorney as to his client's whereabouts); *Knabb v. Morris*, 492 So. 2d 839 (Fla. 5th DCA 1986) (plaintiff failed to exercise due diligence when the private investigator, who the plaintiff hired to locate the defendant, failed to utilize obvious and available resources to actually find the defendant).

Here, the record does not demonstrate that the plaintiffs used due diligence to locate Dubois. Other than attempting to serve the defendant at the address listed on a nearly three year-old accident report [the accident happened in December 2000, while the complaint was filed in September 2003], the plaintiffs attested that "attempts were made through information in Canada to obtain a current telephone listing for the correct Sonia Dubois." However, the plaintiffs only tried one method of locating the defendant—calling "Directory Assistance in L'Epiphanie, Quebec, Canada, and request[ing] the telephone number for Sonia Dubois."

While prior case law has not drawn a bright line between efforts that show due diligence in locating a defendant and those that are insufficient, what was done here falls short of "an honest and conscientious effort." *Grammer*, 80 So. 2d at 461. The plaintiffs argue that their attempts were similar to those of the plaintiff in *Bodden v. Young*, 422 So. 2d 1055 (Fla. 4th DCA 1982). In *Bodden*, this court found that a plaintiff had made a good faith effort at serving a defendant where the plaintiff sought to locate a driver through United States Postal authorities, the telephone company, utility company, and other public agencies, and also took discovery from another potential defendant concerning the defendant's whereabouts. The plaintiff in this case utilized only *one* of the five methods used by the plaintiff in *Bodden*. We note that in the 23 years since *Bodden*, advances in modern technology and the widespread use of the Internet have sent the investigative technique of a call to directory assistance the way of the horse and buggy and the eight track stereo.

As to the corporate defendant, Quebec, Inc., the plaintiffs have conceded error. Pursuant to section 48.181, Florida Statutes (2003), the plaintiffs properly served Quebec, Inc. through the Secretary of State. However, the plaintiffs acknowledge that they "did not file a certified mail return receipt of the summons and complaint on Quebec, Inc., or the affidavit of compliance as required by section 48.161(1)."

We therefore reverse the orders denying the motions to dismiss, quash the service of process as to both defendants, and remand to the circuit court where the plaintiffs may seek to perfect proper service.

STEVENSON and SHAHOOD, JJ., concur.

NOT FINAL UNTIL DISPOSITION OF ANY TIMELY FILED MOTION FOR REHEARING.

Appendix D

STATE OF LOUISIANA

COURT OF APPEAL

FIRST CIRCUIT

NUMBER 2004 CA 2734

MICKEY L. WEATHERLY

VERSUS

OPTIMUM ASSET MANAGEMENT, INC. AND
BARBARA F. B. BROYLES AND STEPHEN BROYLES

Judgment Rendered: December 22, 2005

* * * * * * * * * *

Appealed from the Nineteenth Judicial District Court
in and for the Parish of East Baton Rouge,
State of Louisiana
Suit Number 495,255

Honorable Curtis Calloway, Judge

* * * * * * * * * *

Thomas D. Fazio Baton Rouge, LA	Counsel for Plaintiff/Appellee Mickey L. Weatherly
Robert V. McAnelly Baton Rouge, LA	Counsel for Defendants/Appellants Stephen E. Broyles and Barbara F. B. Broyles

* * * * * * * * * *

BEFORE: KUHN, GUIDRY, AND PETTIGREW, JJ.

PETTIGREW, J.

This appeal challenges a trial court's invalidation of a tax sale. We affirm.

BACKGROUND

Most of the facts forming the basis for this lawsuit to annul a tax sale have been stipulated by the parties, and thus are not in dispute. On March 29, 1988, Dr. Leonard A. Buckner, a dentist, purchased an office condominium on Old Hammond Highway in East Baton Rouge Parish ("the property"). The property was encumbered by a collateral mortgage and collateral mortgage note executed by Dr. Buckner in favor of Baton Rouge Bank and Trust Company. The sale and the mortgage were recorded in the mortgage records for East Baton Rouge Parish. The collateral mortgage and the note were later acquired by Whitney National Bank in its merger with Baton Rouge Bank and Trust Company.

In 1996, Dr. Buckner experienced financial difficulties and contacted an acquaintance, Dr. Mickey Weatherly, a Texas resident with a dental practice there for the past 25 years, for assistance. As an accommodation to Dr. Buckner, Dr. Weatherly agreed to pay off Dr. Buckner's debt to Whitney National Bank and accept an assignment of the bank's security interest in the property in return. On September 13, 1996, Whitney National Bank and Dr. Weatherly executed a document styled "Notarial Endorsement and Assignment of Notes and Other Related Security." Therein, Whitney National Bank assigned its security interest in the property to Dr. Weatherly. The document was recorded on February 20, 1997, in the East Baton Rouge Parish mortgage records. Dr. Weatherly is identified in the document by his name, Mickey L. Weatherly, as the holder of a mortgage on the property by virtue of the assignment. There is no other information pertaining to Dr. Weatherly in the document.

In April of 1997, the East Baton Rouge Parish Sheriff's Office sent two notices of an impending tax sale to Dr. Buckner at the mailing address for the property. Both notices were received and signed for by persons other than Dr. Buckner. The sheriff's office also ran two newspaper advertisements as required by law, the first on May 2, 1997, and the second on June 2, 1997. The sheriff's office did not send notice of the tax bills, tax delinquency, or the impending tax sale to Dr. Weatherly.

On June 27, 1997, the property was sold for nonpayment of 1996 property taxes to Optimum Asset Management, Inc., a foreign corporation. On December 21, 2001, Optimum Asset Management, Inc. executed a Quit Claim Deed, transferring whatever interest it had in the property to Barbara and Stephen Broyles.

Dr. Weatherly was not notified by the sheriff's office of the tax sale. In the spring of 2001, he discovered that the sale had occurred. On January 3, 2002, Dr. Buckner and Dr. Weatherly executed a *Dation En Paiement*, extinguishing the debt Dr. Buckner owed and transferring to Dr. Weatherly whatever ownership rights Dr. Buckner had in the property.

Thereafter, on May 13, 2002, Dr. Weatherly filed this suit to annul the tax sale against Optimum Asset Management, Inc. and Barbara and Stephen Broyles. He alleged that as a mortgagee, whose identity was ascertainable at the time of the tax sale, he was entitled to notice of the proceeding, and the failure of the authorities to provide him with such notice violated his procedural due process rights under the United States and Louisiana Constitutions.

In response, the Broyles filed a reconventional demand asking for a confirmation of their tax title. They urged that Dr. Weatherly was not entitled to actual notice of the tax sale because he was not "reasonably identifiable." The Broyles stressed that Dr. Weatherly never lived in East Baton Rouge Parish or maintained an office here, he did not list his name, address or telephone number in any East Baton Rouge Parish directory or registry, and he failed to include any identifying information in the act of assignment other than his name. They submitted that in the absence of additional identifying information in the recorded instrument, notice to Dr. Buckner by publication, was adequate.

Following a hearing, the trial court ran an Internet search on the name "Mickey Weatherly" and, based on the results of that search, found that Dr. Weatherly was "reasonably identifiable." Therefore, the court concluded, the jurisprudence required that the governmental authority make some effort to provide Dr. Weatherly with notice of the tax sale. Finding no evidence that any steps were undertaken to locate the named mortgagee, the court held that the tax sale violated Dr. Weatherly's due process rights. Accordingly, the court decreed the tax sale null and void and declared Dr. Weatherly to be the owner of the property.

This appeal, taken by the Broyles, followed.

DISCUSSION

The trial court correctly observed that the record is devoid of evidence that the sheriffs office made any attempt to notify Dr. Weatherly, whose name appears in the public record as the assignee of the mortgage on the property, of the impending tax sale. Ms. Brenda Edwards, the assistant tax director for the sheriff's tax office, attested that in 1997, the sheriff's office simply did not undertake to identify and send notices to mortgagees of property tax delinquencies. However, she stated, the office currently has a procedure in place for notifying mortgagees of the non-payment of taxes on every tax sale. Ms. Edwards explained that the office does a public records search, and if it were to disclose the name of a mortgagee without an address, further steps would be taken to ascertain an address, including enlisting the aid of the Clerk of Court's research department, as well as a search of the Lexis/Nexis directory.

In their first assignment of error, the Broyles contend that the trial court erred by conducting an Internet search to determine whether Dr. Weatherly's identity was reasonably ascertainable. We agree. A finder of fact may not consider evidence outside the record in making its findings. *Burdis v. Lafourche Parish Police Jury*, 618 So.2d 971, 976 (La. App. 1st Cir.), *writ denied*, 620 So.2d 843 (La. 1993). More particularly, it is well settled that the resolution of disputed issues by judicial notice is improper. *Id.* Nevertheless, we find any error the trial court may have committed by conducting the Internet search is harmless, because the trial court's ultimate conclusion that the tax sale violated Dr. Weatherly's due process rights is legally correct.

The due process clause of the Fourteenth Amendment to the United States Constitution requires that deprivation of property by adjudication be preceded by notice and opportunity for hearing appropriate to the nature of the case. *Mullane v. Central Hanover Bank & Trust Company*, 339 U.S. 306, 313, 70 S.Ct. 652, 656-657, 94 L.Ed. 865 (1950). Thus, an elementary requirement of due process in any proceeding which is to be accorded finality is notice, reasonably calculated, under all of the circumstances, to apprise interested parties of the pendency of the action and afford them an opportunity to present their objections. *Mullane*, 339 U.S. at 314, 70 S.Ct. at 657.

In *Mennonite Board of Missions v. Adams*, 462 U.S. 791, 798, 103 S.Ct. 2706, 2711, 77 L.Ed.2d 180 (1983), the United States Supreme Court recognized that a mortgagee possesses a substantial property interest that is significantly affected by a tax sale, and therefore, the Court held, a mortgagee is entitled to notice reasonably calculated to apprise him of a pending tax sale. In *Mennonite*, the Court ruled that when a mortgagee is identified in a mortgage that is publicly recorded, constructive notice by publication must be supplemented by notice mailed to the mortgagee's last known available address, or by personal service. *Mennonite*, 462 U.S. at 798, 103 S.Ct. at 2711. Constructive notice suffices, the court stressed, only when the mortgagee is not "reasonably identifiable."

Appellants contend that Dr. Weatherly was not entitled to notice of the tax sale because he was not "reasonably identifiable." They submit that it was Dr. Weatherly's inaction, in failing to give identifying information in the assignment, such as an address or Social Security number, and in failing to request written notice of a tax delinquency pursuant to La. R.S. 47:2180.1, that resulted in his lack of notice of the tax sale. Appellants insist that without the proper identifying information in the act of assignment itself, any investigation by the sheriff's office to identify Dr. Weatherly would have been a "vain and useless endeavor," and therefore, the lack of any attempt by the sheriff's office to identify or provide notice to Dr. Weatherly should not serve to invalidate the tax sale.

We disagree. Dr. Weatherly's failure to include identifying information in the assignment, or his failure to request a notice of the tax delinquency under La. R.S. 47:2180.1, did not constitute a waiver of his right to notice under the due process clause. It has long been held that a party's ability to take steps to safeguard his interests does not relieve the state of its constitutional obligation to give notice. *Mennonite*, 462 U.S. at 799, 103 S.Ct at 2712; *Bank of West Baton Rouge v. Stewart*, 2000-0114 (La. App. 1st Cir. 2/16/01), 808 So.2d 464 (holding that a reasonably ascertainable mortgagee does not waive her constitutional due process right to notice of a tax sale by failing to request notice of a tax delinquency as provided for in La. R.S. 47:2180.1); *Parkview Oak Subdivision Corp. v. Tridico*, 95-0604 (La. App. 1st Cir. 11/9/95), 667 So.2d 1101, *writ denied*, 96-0622 (La. 5/10/96), 672 So.2d 921 (holding that the failure of a mortgagee to request notice of a property seizure under La. R.S. 13:3886 is not a waiver of due process notice and does not relieve a creditor of its constitutional obligation if it has reasonable means at its disposal to identify those parties whose interests will be adversely affected by the foreclosure).

Furthermore, the mere fact that the recorded instrument did not contain an address is not fatal to Dr. Weatherly's due process claim. In *Mennonite*, the name of the mortgagee was identified in the public records, but no address was listed. The Court assumed that the mortgagee's address could have been ascertained by "reasonably diligent efforts." The Court stressed, however, that a governmental body was not required to undertake "extraordinary efforts" to discover the identity and whereabouts of a mortgagee whose identity is not in the public record. *Mennonite*, 462 U.S. at 798, 103 S.Ct. at 2711 n.4. Thus, under *Mennonite*, the identification of a mortgagee by name in a publicly recorded instrument triggers a duty on the part of the governmental body to undertake reasonably diligent efforts to give notice of a tax sale to the mortgagee.

Because Dr. Weatherly was identified as a mortgagee in the mortgage records, *Mennonite* required that he be notified of the impending tax sale if his whereabouts could have been ascertained by reasonably diligent efforts. It is undisputed in this case that the sheriff's office made no attempt to identify Dr. Weatherly as an interested party or ascertain his whereabouts. Had the sheriff's office looked into the mortgage records, it would have learned that Mickey Weatherly had a mortgage on the property, and it could have contacted Whitney National Bank, the assignor, or Dr. Buckner, the owner of the property, to obtain an address. Where an interested party's name and address could have been found after a reasonably diligent search, that person is reasonably ascertainable. *Henderson v. Kingpin Development Co.*, 2001-2115, p. 10 (La. App. 1st Cir. 8/6/03), 859 So.2d 122, 130. Under the circumstances of this case, we can only conclude that the sheriff's office failed to undertake "reasonably diligent efforts" to identify and provide notice of the impending tax sale to Dr. Weatherly, and that failure rendered the tax sale an absolute nullity. See also *In re Raz*, 2003-0893 (La. App. 1st Cir. 2/23/04), 871 So.2d 363 (holding a tax sale absolutely null where, despite the presence of a mortgage in the public records, the sheriff's office made no attempt to notify the mortgagee).

CONCLUSION

For the above reasons, the judgment decreeing the tax sale to be a nullity is affirmed. All costs of this appeal are assessed to appellants.

AFFIRMED.

Appendix E

IN THE COMMONWEALTH COURT OF PENNSYLVANIA

Charles Fernandez,	:	
	:	
Appellant	:	
	:	
v.	:	No. 1600 C.D. 2006
	:	
Tax Claim Bureau of Northampton	:	Argued: April 10, 2007
County	:	
	:	
v.	:	
	:	
John Heilman and Mary Ann Heilman	:	
a/k/a Mary Heilman	:	

BEFORE: HONORABLE DAN PELLEGRINI, Judge
HONORABLE RENÉE COHN JUBELIRER, Judge
HONORABLE JAMES R. KELLEY, Senior Judge

OPINION BY JUDGE COHN JUBELIRER   **FILED: May 31, 2007**

This case is an appeal from an Order and Adjudication of the Northampton County Court of Common Pleas (trial court) denying a petition to set aside a judicial sale. The case involves the notice provisions of the Real Estate Tax Sale Law (Law).[1] Prior to the tax sale, Charles

---

[1] Section 607.1 of the Act of July 7, 1947, P.L. 1368, added by Section 30 of the Act of July 3, 1986, P.L. 351, 72 P.S. § 5860.607a. This case involves interpretation and application of Section 607.1 of the Law, which provides:

When any notification of a pending tax sale or a tax sale subject to court confirmation is required to be mailed to any owner, mortgagee, lienholder or other person or entity whose property interests are likely to be significantly affected by such tax sale, and such mailed noti-

Fernandez (Owner) owned the property in question, a vacant lot in Easton, Northampton County (Subject Property). After Owner became delinquent by not paying taxes on the Subject Property, the Northampton County Tax Claim Bureau (Bureau) provided various forms of notice and then sold the Subject Property at judicial sale to John and Mary Ann Heilman (Purchasers). Owner avers that the Bureau did not take sufficient steps to discover his current address, resulting in his not receiving notice of the sale and, so, accordingly, the sale should be set aside. Before the Court are two primary issues: (1) whether the Bureau was required, under the plain language of the Law and in employing reasonable efforts to ascertain the Owner's address, to consult with local, municipal and school tax bureaus;[2] and (2) whether the posting of the Subject Property constitutes actual and sufficient notice to the Owner of the pending sale.

Owner owned both the Subject Property, which is a vacant lot at 204 West St. Joseph Street, Easton, and the single family house immediately adjacent to it at 210 West St. Joseph Street (210 Property). The Subject Property is on the corner of West St. Joseph Street, where it intersects with West St. John Street.[3] Owner used the Subject Property as a yard for the 210 Property. (Trial Ct. Tr. at 26, May 17, 2006.) The deeds to both proper-

---

fication is either returned without the required receipted personal signature of the addressee or under other circumstances raising a significant doubt as to the actual receipt of such notification by the named addressee or is not returned or acknowledged at all, then, before the tax sale can be conducted or confirmed, *the bureau must exercise reasonable efforts to discover the whereabouts of such person or entity and notify him. The bureau's efforts shall include, but not necessarily be restricted to, a search of current telephone directories for the county and of the dockets and indices of the county tax assessment offices, recorder of deeds office and prothonotary's office, as well as contacts made to any apparent alternate address or telephone number which may have been written on or in the file pertinent to such property.* When such reasonable efforts have been exhausted, regardless of whether or not the notification efforts have been successful, a notation shall be placed in the property file describing the efforts made and the results thereof, and the property may be rescheduled for sale or the sale may be confirmed as provided in this act.

72 P.S. § 5860.607a(a) (emphasis added).

[2] Owner frames this as two issues: (1) Did the trial court properly determine that the Bureau in this case made reasonable efforts to learn the correct address of Taxpayer; and (2) Do the reasonable efforts a tax claim bureau must engage in to find an owner's address include contacting local, municipal and school tax bureaus to learn where each mails its tax bill for the property subject to the sale?

[3] There is some discrepancy from Owner as to whether the Subject Property or 210 Property is on the corner. At the hearing, Owner's Counsel stated that "[Owner] lives at Saint Joseph, Your Honor. But it's on the corner of Saint Joseph and Saint John." (Trial Ct. Tr. at 13, May 17, 2006.) In Owner's Statement of Facts and Conclusions of Law filed with the trial court on May 25, 2006, Owner indicates that: "4. The premises of 204 W. St. Joseph Street, City of Easton, Northampton County, Pennsylvania, is on the corner of W. St. Joseph Street and St. John Street." ([Owner's] Statement of Facts and Conclusions of Law, Facts ¶ 4, May 25, 2006.)

ties contain a certification by Owner "that the precise residence of the within grantee, [Owner] is: 50 Kiernan Avenue, Hellertown, PA" (Hellertown Property). (Deed for Subject Property at 3, November 27, 2001; Deed for 210 Property at 3, November 27, 2001.) Owner did not own the Hellertown Property, but rented it from another person.

In May 2003, the Bureau sent notice by certified mail to the Hellertown Property that Owner had unpaid 2002 school real estate taxes on the Subject Property in the amount of $395.36.[4] Owner acknowledged his receipt of the notice by signing for it. The notice indicated that if he failed to pay the taxes the Subject Property could be sold to satisfy the outstanding taxes.

It is not clear exactly when, but at some point subsequent to the recording of these deeds, Owner switched his residence from the Hellertown Property to the 210 Property.[5]

In July 2004, the Northampton County Sheriff's Office (Sheriff) posted the Subject Property to put Owner on notice of the 2002 delinquent taxes. The Sheriff also posted the Subject Property in August 2004 with notice of the tax upset sale.

On August 2, 2004, the Bureau mailed notice of the tax upset sale to the Hellertown Property. The Postal Service returned the notification to the Bureau with a notation that it could not be forwarded.

On September 13, 2004, the Bureau exposed the Subject Property to a tax upset sale as a result of the 2002 delinquent taxes. At the tax upset sale, no one bid on the Subject Property. On November 22, 2004, the Northampton County Court of Common Pleas (trial court) issued a Rule to Show Cause as to why the Subject Property should not be sold at a judicial sale. The Sheriff posted the Subject Property in December 2004, with notice of the upcoming judicial sale.

The judicial sale was held on January 10, 2005, and Purchasers successfully bid on, and were sold, the Subject Property. Purchasers received title to the Subject Property by deed dated February 22, 2005.

---

[4]The amount of the initial bill was $370.36. (*See* Trial Ct. Tr. at 34, May 17, 2006.) The amount in the certified notice seems to include an additional amount for fees and interest, bringing the total at the time of the notice to $395.36. With additional interest and fees that accrued during the time leading up to the sale, the amount the Bureau ended up paying to the District from the judicial sale was $425.56. (*See* Trial Ct. Tr. at 33, May 17, 2006.)

[5]Owner testified that he left the Hellertown Residence in 2001; however, assuming that to be the case, it is not clear why he was there to sign for the notice that was sent to the Hellertown Property in May 2003. It is unclear if he made the county aware of this change, although in 2004 and 2005, the City of Easton's 2004 and 2005 real estate tax bill and the Easton Area School District's real estate school tax bill for 2004/2005 for the Subject Property were sent to the 210 Property.

In March 2005, Owner contacted the tax department about his 2004 taxes, at which time he learned of the judicial sale of the Subject Property for the 2002 taxes. On May 13, 2005, Owner filed a Petition to Set Aside Judicial Sale Nunc Pro Tunc (Petition).[6]

The trial court conducted a hearing on Owner's Petition and heard the testimony of four witnesses: (1) Owner; (2) two representatives from different local taxing authorities; and (3) the Tax Claim Supervisor for Northampton County (Tax Claim Supervisor).

At the hearing, Owner testified that he did not receive notice of the tax upset sale or the judicial sale. He testified that he essentially used the Subject Property as a yard for his house, and that he regularly cut the Subject Property's grass. He also testified that he did not see any signs posted on the Subject Property prior to the judicial sale.

Representatives from two local taxing authorities, the City of Easton (City) and the Easton Area School District (District) testified that their respective tax bills for the Subject Property for the years 2004 and 2005 were sent to the 210 Property.[7]

In contrast, the Tax Claim Supervisor testified that the Bureau's records for the Subject Property *did not* indicate that mail for the Subject Property should be sent to the 210 Property. She indicated that the only information regarding his address was that Owner resided at the Hellertown Property. She testified in detail as to her ultimately unsuccessful efforts to try to obtain Owner's address, but also acknowledged that she did not contact either the City or the District to see what contact or forwarding information either might have had.

The Tax Claim Supervisor testified that she did not check the telephone book and that she was not sure if anyone else in her office checked the telephone book, but that it was standard practice within her office to check the telephone book.[8] She also testified that she conducted a "Google" computer-based search for Owner's whereabouts, which pro-

---

[6] The parties engaged in settlement discussions and reached a settlement agreement that was approved by the trial court. (*See* Trial Ct. Tr. at 2-5, Aug. 30, 2005.) Under the terms, Owner agreed to compensate Purchasers approximately $2000.00 in exchange for the Subject Property. Owner was also to pay Northampton County $2000.00, and Northampton County was to return to Purchasers the excess money they paid at the sale, totaling approximately $1000.00. Owner failed to make the payments set forth in the agreement, and the trial court held him in contempt, fining him $500.00. The trial court also scheduled the case for a hearing on the merits of Owner's Petition.

[7] The first representative was from the Treasurer's Department for the City of Easton. He testified that the 2004 and 2005 tax bills were sent to the 210 Property. The second representative was from the collection agency used by the Easton Area School District (District). She testified that the tax bills for the Subject Property for the 2004/2005 school year were sent to the 210 Property.

[8] Two telephone books (both from calendar year 2004, but in different fiscal years) were introduced into evidence. The telephone books did not identify a Charles Fernandez, and did not list the 210 West St. *Joseph* Street address, but both telephone books did have a "Chuck Fernandez" at 210 West St. *John* Street.

duced a "Chuck Fernandez" living at the Hellertown Property. She dialed the telephone number the Google search provided, and found that the telephone had been disconnected.

The Tax Claim Supervisor checked the recorder of deeds office, which showed that Owner resided at the Hellertown Property. The Tax Claim Supervisor also testified that the Bureau does not change its records without notice from either the tax collector's office or from the owner and that, in this case, it had received no such notice from either that there was a change of address.

The Tax Claim Supervisor also testified that the Subject Property was posted on three occasions. She acknowledged, though, that she had no direct knowledge of the posting, and that "I cannot swear to a posting, no, sir, I cannot swear to that at all." (Trial Ct. Tr. at 36, May 17, 2006.)[9]

At the hearing, during Bureau's questioning of the Tax Claim Supervisor, the trial court asked if Owner's Counsel was going to require that the individuals who posted the Subject Property appear to testify; Owner's Counsel stipulated that the Subject Property was posted, but did not stipulate to the manner in which it was posted.[10]

---

[9]This testimony, placed in context, follows:

A: ... His property was posted after [the notice of the judicial sale was returned] because he did not sign for his notice.
Q: I'm sorry?
A: His property was posted by a sheriff.
Q: But you didn't see the sheriff post it, did you?
A: No, sir. We never see any of the postings personally. He was also posted for the upset sale.
Q: Again, you did not see whether anyone posted that property for an upset sale?
A: I cannot. I cannot say that I saw it no. But it is—he would have been posted three times in the year; once for the notice that was not signed for the 2003 [sic] taxes, that would have been in—most likely in July, then he was posted for the upset sale also in July, and then he would have been posted for the judicial sale in January.
Q: But you didn't see any posting, you didn't drive by the property and see the posting?
A: I cannot swear to a posting, no, sir, I cannot swear to that at all.

(Trial Ct. Tr. at 35-36, May 17, 2006.)
[10]The discussion surrounding this stipulation follows:

Q: Okay. Then you've testified very briefly in reference to the property being posted, and that was posted on a number of occasions to your knowledge?
A: Yes. It was posted on August 12th of 2004 for the upset sale. And that was bought by one gentleman, one person that we the county hires for—
    [Owner's Counsel]: Your Honor, I'm going to object to this, because she can't testify to any type of posting in that on direct examination. They already said she didn't see it. The only way you can have the evidence.
    [The Court]: Do you really want the sheriff's or whoever it is to come in here and say that they actually posted it?
    [Bureau Counsel]: Judge, I was hoping that the Court would take this as a business record exception. We have given Mr. Coffin[, Owner's Counsel,] great leeway with [the Tax Claim Supervisor's] records. What I'm suggesting is that Mr. Coffin is correct, she did not see the posting, but her records would indicate when the posting was done. And I think the Court did rely upon—

The trial court denied the Petition, finding that the Bureau had engaged in reasonable efforts to contact Owner.[11] Additionally, the trial court found the evidence credible that the Subject Property was posted, but found the Owner "incredible" that he did not see the notices, particularly because he maintained the Subject Property and lived next to it. Relying on *In the Matter of Tax Sale of 2003 Upset*, 860 A.2d 1184, 1185 (Pa. Cmwlth. 2004), and based on its credibility determinations, the trial court concluded that Owner received actual notice of the sale. The trial court, alternatively, concluded that Owner received actual notice in May 2003 when he signed and received the certified mail notice indicating that he had delinquent school real estates taxes for 2002. The trial court concluded that since actual notice can cure defects in statutory notice requirements, the sale was not void.[12] Accordingly, the trial court set aside the Petition and Owner appeals that decision.

We first address whether the trial court properly determined that the Bureau made reasonable efforts to learn the correct address of Owner.

The law is well settled in Pennsylvania that a valid tax sale requires strict compliance with all three of the notice provisions of Section 602 of the Law, 72 P.S. § 5860.602: publication, certified mail, and posting. *In re Upset Price Tax Sale of September 25, 1989*, 615 A.2d 870, 872 (Pa. Cmwlth. 1992). If any of the notices are defective, the sale is void. *Id.* Owner's first argument addresses the certified mail notice requirement.[13]

Owner argues that the sale is null and void because Owner never received actual notice of either the upset or judicial sale. Owner argues that, if the Bureau's certified mailed notice is returned to the Bureau, the Bureau is required by statute to contact local tax collectors for contact information

---

[Owner's Counsel]: I would stipulate to it within the records.
[The Court]: Then a business record, very well. So it was posted 8/12 for the upset sale—for the upset sale, and it was posted on December 13th, '04 for the judicial sale.
[Tax Claim Supervisor]: They are by two different people.

(Trial Ct. Tr. at 54-55, May 17, 2006.) We note that the original record does not contain the records of posting to which the trial judge and counsel referred during the hearing.

[11] In doing so, the trial court first found that the Petition was timely because it was brought within the six month statute of limitations under Section 5522(b)(5) of the Judicial Code, 42 Pa. C.S. § 5522(b)(5). This finding is not challenged on appeal.

[12] In tax sales cases, this Court's review is limited to determining whether the trial court abused its discretion, clearly erred as a matter of law or rendered a decision with a lack of supporting evidence. *Rice v. Compro Distributing, Inc.*, 901 A.2d 570, 574 (Pa. Cmwlth. 2006). The trial court is the finder of fact and has exclusive authority to weigh the evidence, make credibility determinations, and draw reasonable inferences from the evidence presented. *Id.*

[13] The certified mail notice requirement of Section 602 provides that:

(1) At least thirty (30) days before the date of the sale, by United States certified mail, restricted delivery, return receipt requested, postage prepaid, to each owner as defined by this act.

72 P.S. § 5860.602(e)(1).

for the owner. Section 607.1(a) of the Law, 72 P.S. § 5860.607a(a). Owner argues the Bureau failed to abide by this requirement. Additionally, Owner argues that the due process clause of the Fourteenth Amendment of the United States Constitution requires additional steps to find a property owner when notice is returned that was sent to the owner to apprise him of an upcoming sale of his property. *Jones v. Flowers*, 547 U.S. 220, 126 S. Ct. 1708 (2006).

In response, the Bureau argues that its efforts, most notably the computer "Google" search and the telephoning of the telephone number the search obtained, was sufficient. Additionally, the Bureau argues that review of the local printed telephone directories would have been fruitless because none of these directories contained a listing for Charles Fernandez, but only had one for Chuck Fernandez. The Purchasers raised arguments similar to those of the Bureau.

In addressing these arguments we note that, under Section 607.1(a) of the Law, the focus of our analysis is on the reasonableness of the Bureau's efforts: "the bureau must exercise reasonable efforts to discover the whereabouts of such person or entity and notify him." 72 P.S. § 5860.607a(a). This section, while listing efforts that must be taken, does not provide an exhaustive list of efforts that could be taken.[14] Reasonable efforts are thus determined, in part, by the facts of the particular case. The Bureau has the burden of establishing that it has complied with the reasonable efforts requirements of Section 607.1 and the notice requirements of Section 602. *Rice v. Compro Distributing, Inc.*, 901 A.2d 570, 575 (Pa. Cmwlth. 2006). A reasonable investigation is one that "use[s] *ordinary common sense business practices to ascertain proper addresses. . . .*" *In re Tax Sale of Real Property Situated in Jefferson Township (Ruffner)*, 828 A.2d 475, 479 (Pa. Cmwlth. 2003) (emphasis added). This ordinary common sense "must go beyond the mere ceremonial act of notice by certified mail," but does not require "the equivalent of a title search. . . ." *Id.*[15] Additionally, the Bureau is required to strictly adhere to the notice provi-

---

[14]Section 607.1(a) provides that:

> The bureau's efforts shall include, but not necessarily be restricted to, a search of current telephone directories for the county and of the dockets and indices of the county tax assessment offices, recorder of deeds office and prothonotary's office, as well as contacts made to any apparent alternate address or telephone number which may have been written on or in the file pertinent to such property.

72 P.S. § 5860.607a(a).

[15]*Jones* similarly holds that the mailing of notice by certified mail that is returned to the governmental body does not, by itself, satisfy due process requirements. In the two cases that this Court has issued since *Jones*, we have placed their holdings squarely within *Ruffner*. *See Miller v. Clinton County Tax Claim Bureau*, 909 A.2d 461 (Pa. Cmwlth. 2006); *Rice*. The focus of the Supreme Court's analysis is that the governmental body must "provide notice reasonably calculated, under all the circumstances, to apprise interested parties of the pendency of the action and

sions of the Law. *Rivera v. Carbon County Tax Claim Bureau*, 857 A.2d 208, 214 (Pa. Cmwlth. 2004).

Applied to the present case, we find that the Bureau failed to strictly adhere to the statutory requirements, and that this failure, by itself, is sufficient to sustain Owner's Petition. Owner focuses on the Bureau's failure to consult with the various county tax assessment offices. Section 607.1 specifies, using the directive, "shall" language, that "the dockets and indices of the county tax assessment offices" be consulted. 72 P.S. § 5860.607a(a). As evidence was presented that the 2004 and 2005 tax bills from the City of Easton and the 2004/2005 school tax bills were sent to the 210 Property, it seems that such a consultation with the tax assessment offices would have been fruitful. Worth noting is that the sale itself arose from a failure to pay school real estate taxes in 2002—yet the District knew to send 2004/2005 tax bills—issued within the same time frame as the upset sale and judicial sale notices—to the 210 Property. The Bureau seems to focus on the reasonableness of its actions, but does not squarely address whether it was actually required to contact the tax assessment offices. When questioned as to why she did not contact the tax collector for the District to find out where the District sent the mail, the Tax Claim Supervisor testified that "I probably made an erroneous assumption because the taxes came from the school district for the following two years." (Trial Ct. Tr. at 49, May 17, 2006.) The Tax Claim Supervisor explained that the county maintains the addresses, which it provides to the various taxing authorities, so she assumed that the authorities would have the same addresses that she did. (Trial Ct. Tr. at 49-50, May 17, 2006.)[16] This failure to consult with these tax assessment offices provides sufficient basis on its own to require the judicial sale to be set aside.[17]

---

afford them an opportunity to present their objections." *Jones*, 126 S. Ct. at 1713-14 (quoting *Mullane v. Central Hanover Bank & Trust Co.*, 339 U.S. 306, 314 (1950)) (quotations omitted). The Court explained that "the State should have taken additional reasonable steps to notify [owner], if practicable to do so" and that "[w]hat steps are reasonable in response to new information depends upon what the new information reveals." *Jones*, 126 S. Ct. at 1718.

[16] She testified that:

> the county is to be the main contact for all changes of mailing addresses. All things are suppose to be coming from our office. And the records that are present here with these addresses on were not provided by the county when they provided the tax downloads. And the county is the one that provides those—those disks. Those addresses were not on those disks that were presented to the school district nor the municipalities.

(Trial Ct. Tr. at 48, May 17, 2006.)

[17] It does not appear that Owner argues this point, but it does seem that the county failed to search the county-wide telephone book, which, by the Law, it was required to consult. The trial court made the following relevant finding: "[The Tax Claim Supervisor] personally did not search the telephone book for Fernandez and [it] is uncertain whether any staff members in her office

We have held that the primary purpose of the Law is not to strip away citizens' property rights but, rather, to ensure the collection of taxes. *Rivera*, 857 A.2d at 214.[18] The United States Supreme Court has noted that "[p]eople must pay their taxes, and the government may hold citizens accountable for tax delinquency by taking their property. But before forcing a citizen to satisfy his debt by forfeiting his property, due process requires the government to provide adequate notice of the impending taking. U.S. Const., Amdt. 14." *Jones*, 126 S. Ct. at 1718. Consistent with these principles, we have explained that, in reviewing whether due process requirements have been met, "the focus is not on the alleged neglect of the owner, which is often present in some degree, but on whether the activities of the Bureau comply with the requirements of the statute." *Smith v. Tax Claim Bureau of Pike County*, 834 A.2d 1247, 1251 (Pa. Cmwlth. 2003).

The Bureau's representative identified the error in this case—a failure to perform statutorily required searches because of an assumption as to what the results of the search would be. Additionally, the assumption does not comport with ordinary common sense business practices. The statutory requirements protect the property rights of citizens and provide

---

did so. [The Tax Claim Supervisor] testified that it is standard practice to search the telephone book for information." (Trial Ct. Adj., Finding of Fact 25.) This finding is supported by the testimony and evidence. Among the specific actions required to be taken is that "current telephone directories for the county" be searched. 72 P.S. § 5860.607a(a). Section 607.1 does not contain the permissive, "may" be consulted, when referring to telephone books, but rather, contains the directive, "shall . . . search . . . current telephone directories." As there was no evidence that this was done, it appears the Bureau did not strictly adhere to the statutory terms.

Additionally, evidence presented before the trial court indicated that, had the telephone books been examined, it would have found a "Chuck Fernandez." The Bureau seeks to diminish this fact, by arguing that the listing contains a different first name, and by also noting that the address listed in the directory is different from the actual mailing address. This argument is undercut by the Tax Claim Supervisor's own testimony as to the computer search that she performed which specifically linked a "Chuck Fernandez" with the Hellertown Property to which the Bureau had sent the notices. Had the Bureau used the telephone number provided for "Chuck Fernandez" in the telephone book, it may have been able to reach him.

In addition, checking the telephone book seems to qualify as an ordinary common sense business practice when one is seeking to obtain an address. Nonetheless, it does not appear that this issue is directly argued before this Court.

[18]In contrast we must call attention to a statement made by the Tax Claim Supervisor that the Bureau's "*goal is to sell the property.*" (Trial Ct. Tr. at 40, May 17, 2006 (emphasis added).) Arguably, this statement can be characterized as a mere comment, or perhaps a misstatement. However, given what is at issue in this case, a deprivation of a person's property interest, and given that this deprivation occurred without following statutorily prescribed procedures, we use this statement to reemphasize the principle that the Law's purpose, and with it, the Bureau's primary purpose, is not to strip away citizen's property, but to ensure payment of taxes. Although selling of the property may end up being the ultimate means used toward achieving that end, it is not the end itself.

a minimum as to what must be accomplished to protect those rights. As noted in *Ruffner* and *Jones*, that minimum may not be sufficient under the facts of a particular case. That minimum was not accomplished here.[19] Accordingly, we conclude that the judicial sale must be set aside.[20]

For these reasons, the order of the trial court is reversed.

RENÉE COHN JUBELIRER, Judge

---

[19] It does not appear that Owner makes this argument, but it seems that the trial court erred in finding that actual notice of *tax delinquency* would suffice as actual notice of the *tax sale*. In *Jones*, the United States Supreme Court reiterated its rejection that notice of tax delinquency satisfied the notice requirements for the *actual sale* of property:

> [T]he common knowledge that property may become subject to government taking when taxes are not paid does not excuse the government from complying with its constitutional obligation of notice before taking private property. We have previously stated the opposite: **An interested party's knowledge of delinquency in the payment of taxes is not equivalent to notice that a tax sale is pending**.

126 S. Ct. at 1717 (quotations omitted) (emphasis added). Under this authority, to the extent the trial court found actual notice from the tax delinquency notice that Owner received, the trial court erred. However, as noted, Owner does not seem to squarely raise this argument.

[20] Based on our resolution of this first issue, we do not reach the issue of actual and sufficient notice.

IN THE COMMONWEALTH COURT OF PENNSYLVANIA

Charles Fernandez,	:	
	:	
Appellant	:	
	:	
v.	:	No. 1600 C.D. 2006
	:	
Tax Claim Bureau of Northampton County	:	Argued: April 10, 2007
	:	
	:	
v.	:	
	:	
John Heilman and Mary Ann Heilman	:	
a/k/a Mary Heilman	:	

O R D E R

NOW, May 31, 2007, the order of the Court of Common Pleas of Northampton County in the above-captioned matter is hereby **REVERSED**.

RENÉE COHN JUBELIRER, Judge

Appendix F

1. I am the AdministratIve Director of the Internet Archive, located at the Presidio of San Francisco, California. I make this declaration of my own personal knowledge.

2. The internet Archive is a web site that provides access to a digital library of Internet sites and other cultural artifacts in digital form. Like a paper library, we provide free access to researchers, historians, scholars, and the general public. The Internet Archive is affiliated with and receives support from various institutions, including the National Science Foundation and the Library of Congress.

3. The Internet Archive has created a service known as the Wayback Machine. The Wayback Machine makes it possible to surf more than 30 billion pages stored in the Internet Archive's web archive. Visitors to the Wayback Machine can type in a URL (i.e., a web site address), select a date range, and then begin surfing on an archived version of the Web. The links on the archived files, when served by the Wayback Machine, point to other archived files (whether HTML pages or images). If a visitor clicks on a link on an archived page, the Wayback Machine will serve the archived file with the closest available date to the originally requested page.

4. The Internet Archive receives data from third parties who compile the data by using software programs known as crawlers that surf the Web and automatically store copies of web site files at certain points in time as they existed at that point in time. This data is donated to the Internet Archive, which preserves and provides access to it.

5. The Internet Archive assigns a URL on its site to the archived files in the format http://web.archive.org/web/[Year in yyyy][Month in mm][Day in dd][Time code in hh:mm:ss]/[Archived URL]. Thus, the Internet Archive URL http://web.archive.org/web/19970126045828/ http://www.archive.org/ would be the URL for the record of the Internet Archive home page file (http://www.archive.org/) archived on January 26, 1997 at 4:58 a.m. and 28 seconds (1997/01/26 at 04:58:28). Typically,

a printout from a Web browser will show the URL in the footer. The date assigned by the Internet Archive applies to the HTML file but not to image files linked therein. Thus images that appear on the printed page may not have been archived on the same date as the HTML file. Likewise, if a Web site is designed with "frames," the date assigned by the Internet Archive applies to the frameset as a whole, and not the individual pages within each frame.

6. Attached hereto as Exhibit A are true and accurate copies of printouts of the Internet Archive's records of the HTML files archived from the URLs and the dates specified in the footer of the printout.

7. I declare under penalty of perjury that the foregoing is true and correct.

DATE: 5|3|04   _Molly Davis_

For those wishing that the Archive would take a position in their specific case, it should be noted this is unlikely: "The Internet Archive strives to be a disinterested third party in all disputes involving its collection items. If you are using Wayback Machine documents to make a case in your legal dispute, the Internet Archive will not take an idealogical or other position in said dispute." In addition, the Archive explains that its affidavit, "only affirms that the printed document is a true and correct copy of our records. It remains your burden to convince the finder of fact what pages were up when" (**http://www.archive.org/legal/faq.php**). Yet, it seems that there is a chance the Internet Archive would alter its standard affidavit "[a]ccording to particular needs, on a case by case basis. However, if we agree to make such changes, you will be required to reimburse the Internet Archive for its related attorney fees as we ask our attorneys to review and negotiate any changes to the standard affidavit. If you wish to inquire further about this possibility, please contact us via email at info@archive.org."

Appendix G

1. I am the Office Manager at the Internet Archive, located at the Presidio of San Francisco, California. I make this declaration of my own personal knowledge.

2. The Internet Archive is a web site that provides access to a digital library of Internet sites and other cultural artifacts in digital form. Like a paper library, we provide free access to researchers, historians, scholars, and the general public. The Internet Archive is affiliated with and receives support from various institutions, including the Library of Congress.

3. The Internet Archive has created a service known as the Wayback Machine. The Wayback Machine makes it possible to surf more than 85 billion pages stored in the Internet Archive's web archive. Visitors to the Wayback Machine can type in a URL (i.e., a web site address), select a date range, and then begin surfing on an archived version of the Web. The links on the archived files, when served by the Wayback Machine, point to other archived files (whether HTML pages or images). If a visitor clicks on a link on an archived page, the Wayback Machine will serve the archived file with the closest available date to the originally requested page.

4. The Internet Archive receives data from third parties who compile the data by using software programs known as crawlers that surf the Web and automatically store copies of web site files at certain points in time as they existed at that point in time. This data is donated to the Internet Archive, which preserves and provides access to it.

5. The Internet Archive assigns a URL on its site to the archived files in the format http://web.archive.org/web/[Year in yyyy][Month in mm][Day in dd][Time code in hh:mm:ss]/[Archived URL]. Thus, the Internet Archive URL http://web.archive.org/web/19970126045828/http://www.archive.org/ would be the URL for the record of the Internet Archive home page HTML file (http://www.archive.org/) archived on January 26, 1997 at 4:58 a.m. and 28 seconds (1997/01/26 at 04:58:28).

Typically, a printout from a Web browser will show the URL in the footer. The date assigned by the Internet Archive applies to the HTML file but not to image files linked therein. Thus images that appear on the printed page may not have been archived on the same date as the HTML file. Likewise, if a Web site is designed with "frames," the date assigned by the Internet Archive applies to the frameset as a whole, and not the individual pages within each frame.

6. Attached hereto as Exhibit A are true and accurate copies of printouts of the Internet Archive's records of the HTML files archived from the URLs and the dates specified in the footer of the printout.

7. I declare under penalty of perjury that the foregoing is true and correct.

DATE: _____   _____

                                                    Lance Grabmiller

For those wishing that the Archive would take a position in their specific case, it should be noted this is unlikely: "The Internet Archive strives to be a disinterested third party in all disputes involving its collection items. If you are using Wayback Machine documents to make a case in your legal dispute, the Internet Archive will not take an idealogical or other position in said dispute." In addition, the Archive explains that its affidavit, "only affirms that the printed document is a true and correct copy of our records. It remains your burden to convince the finder of fact what pages were up when" (**http://www.archive.org/legal/faq.php**).

Yet, it seems that there is a chance the Internet Archive would alter its standard affidavit "[a]ccording to particular needs, on a case by case basis. However, if we agree to make such changes, you will be required to reimburse the Internet Archive for its related attorney fees as we ask our attorneys to review and negotiate any changes to the standard affidavit. If you wish to inquire further about this possibility, please contact us via email at info@archive.org."

Appendix H

IN THE UNITED STATES DISTRICT COURT FOR THE NORTHERN DISTRICT OF ILLINOIS EASTERN DIVISION

TELEWIZJA POLSKA USA, INC. a Delaware Corporation, Plaintiff, vs. ECHOSTAR SATELLITE CORPORATION, a Colorado corporation, Defendant.	))) Case No. 02 C 3293)) Judge Ronald A. Guzman))) Magistrate Judge) Arlander Keys)))

Memorandum Opinion and Order

Currently before the Court are Plaintiff's 17 Motions *in limine* and Defendant's 38 Motions *in limine*. The Court will address each party's Motions in turn.

Discussion

A Motion *in limine* should be granted only if the evidence clearly is not admissible for any purpose. *See Hawthorne Partners V. AT & T Technologies, Inc.*, 831 F.Supp. 1398, 1400 (N.D. Ill. 1993). Generally, motions *in limine* are disfavored. Instead of barring evidence before trial, the preferred practice is to resolve questions of admissibility as they arise. See *Scarboro v. Travelers Ins. Co.*, 91 F.R.D. 21, 22 (E.D. Tenn. 1980). By deferring evidentiary rulings until trial, courts can properly resolve questions of foundation, relevancy, and prejudice. See *Hawthorne Partners*, 831 F.Supp. at 1401.

I. Plaintiff's Motions in Limine

Plaintiff has filed seventeen separate motions *in limine*. A number of those motions attack the propriety of allowing Defendant to proceed with several affirmative defenses, based upon the evidence produced—or not produced—during discovery. Because a motion *in limine* is not the appropriate vehicle for addressing the strength of the evidence or the substance of a complaint, See *Mid-America Tablewares, Inc. v. Mogi Trading Co.*, 100 F.3d 1353, 1362 (7th Cir. 1996), the Court denies these motions in a fairly cursory manner.

In its First Motion *in limine*, Plaintiff argues that Defendant should be prohibited from arguing that it was entitled to sell subscriptions after the parties' contract was terminated. Plaintiff notes that in *Polska USA, Inc. v. Echostar*, No. 02-4332, 2003 WL 21579968, (7th Cir. July 7, 2003), the Seventh Circuit reversed the district court's conclusion that the only permissible interpretation of the parties' contract permitted Defendant to sell subscriptions during the post-termination period. In reversing the dismissal of Plaintiff's breach of contract claim, the Seventh Circuit stated that the more natural reading of the parties' contract prohibited Defendant from selling subscriptions to the Polska programming after it received Plaintiff's notice of termination. Plaintiff asserts that the law of the case doctrine bars Defendant from arguing that its conduct (i.e., selling subscriptions after the termination of the contract) was permissible, because the Seventh Circuit has held otherwise.

Law of the case is a judicially created doctrine that seeks to limit repeated appeals of issues that have already been decided. *Gertz v. Welch*, 680 F.2d 527 (7th Cir. 1982). While a district court is not free to disregard an appellate ruling, the court may rule on issues not directly decided on appeal. *Id.* at 532 (noting that the law of the case doctrine is not an "immutable rule," depriving the court of jurisdiction over an issue, but is rather a prudential limitation.)

In this case, the Seventh Circuit found that Plaintiff's Complaint stated a cognizable breach of contract claim. On September 1, 2004, Judge Guzman issued a Memorandum opinion and order, finding that Defendant was, nevertheless, "free to argue that it had the right to [sell subscriptions during the post-termination period] because the contract did not explicitly forbid its conduct." *Telewizja Polska USA, Inc. v. Echostar Satellite Corp.*, No. 02 C 3293 (N.D. Ill. Sept. 1, 2004). Because Judge Guzman has decided that the Seventh Circuit's ruling does not prevent Defendant from arguing that its conduct is authorized under the parties' contract, the Motion is denied.

Next, Plaintiff seeks to exclude evidence and testimony supporting Defendants's counterclaim for tortious interference with prospective economic advantage, in its Second Motion *in limine*. Plaintiff argues that Defendant should be precluded from presenting such evidence, because Defendant failed to produce any evidence in support of its tortious interference claim. The Court agrees that Defendant should not be permitted to introduce evidence at trial that it refused to produce during discovery. However, the Court finds that Plaintiff's argument here—that the evidence that Defendant has produced is insufficient to support a claim for tortious interference—is better reserved for a summary judgment motion. *KRW Sales Inc. v. Kristel Corp.*, No. 93 C 4377, 1994 WL 75522, at *1 (N.D. Ill. Mar. 8, 1994) (motions *in limine* should be utilized for resolving evidentiary, not substantive, disputes). Plaintiff's Second Motion *in limine* is denied.

Plaintiff seeks to exclude evidence and testimony supporting Defendant's defamation counterclaim, because Defendant has allegedly failed to produce sufficient evidence in support of this claim. Plaintiff is again seeking a substantive ruling on the sufficiency of Defendant's evidence. The Court denies Plaintiff's Third Motion *in limine*.

In Motion *in limine* 4, Plaintiff claims that, because one of Defendant's officers acknowledged that Defendant was withholding revenue payments, Plaintiff's alleged statement that Echostar was "scamming" Polska was not defamatory. Plaintiff is asking the Court to weigh the evidence and determine whether Defendant has enough evidence in support of its defamation counterclaim to warrant a trial. Because Plaintiff is improperly seeking a ruling on the substance of Defendant's defamation claim, Motion *in limine* 4 is denied.

Plaintiff seeks to prevent Defendant from introducing at trial amendments to the deposition testimony of Mr. Michael Schwimmer. Federal Rule 30(e) allows a witness to review his deposition transcript and make "'any changes in form or substance'" to the answers. *Hawthorne Partners v. AT & T Technologies, Inc.*, 831 F.Supp. 1398, 1406 (N.D. Ill. 1993) (quoting *Lugig v. Thomas*, 89 F.R.D. 639, 641 (N.D. Ill. 1981)). The witness must provide a specific reason for each change made; a blanket, conclusory explanation is insufficient. However, "[a] witness can make changes that contradict the original answers, and the reasons given need not be convincing." *Hawthorne*, 831 F.Supp. at 1406. Courts usually allow such amendments, and stress the fact that these changes can be inquired into on cross-examination. *Hawthorne*, 831 F.Supp. at 1407; *Sanford v. CBS, Inc.*, 594 F.Supp. 713, 715 (N.D. Ill. 1984) (noting that courts typically are reluctant to strike these changes.)

In the instant case, Mr. Schwimmer is not seeking to directly contradict his deposition testimony, but rather to "explain" or put into context answers given during his deposition. See, e.g., *Thorn v. Sundstrand Aerospace Corp.*, 207 F.3d 383, 389 (7th Cir. 2000) (noting that, while it seems dubious to permit a deponent to change his testimony from what he said to what he meant to say via subsequent affidavit, Rule 30(e) clearly permits the practice). While Mr. Schwimmer has offered the identical explanation for each requested change, it is not for the Court "to examine the sufficiency, reasonableness or legitimacy of the reasons for the change"— that is reserved for the trier of fact. *Lugtig*, 89 F.R.D. at 641. Plaintiff is free to explore the distinctions between Mr. Schwimmer's deposition testimony and amended testimony at trial. Motion *in limine* 5 is denied.

In Motion *in limine* 6, Plaintiff seeks to prevent Defendant from introducing evidence and testimony relating to Defendant's lost profits and lost business. Plaintiff asserts that the evidence is inadmissible, because Defendant failed to produce relevant tax returns, evidence of lost subscription sales, and other responsive evidence. Defendant counters that it has produced all relevant, non-privileged evidence, and notes that Plaintiff's reliance upon Illinois state caselaw is misplaced.

Defendant's failure to produce its tax returns and other requested evidence prevents Defendant from introducing such evidence at trial. However, there is no rule stating that a tax return is the exclusive method for proving damages or lost business. The issue of whether Defendant will be unable to establish damages absent this evidence should be addressed in a summary judgment motion.

The cases relied upon by Plaintiff are readily distinguishable, as they involved an Illinois procedural rule not applicable in the instant case, *see Hawkins v. Wiggins*, 415 N.E.2d 1179 (Ill. App. 1980); *Smith v. P.A.C.E.*, 753 N.E.2d 353 (Ill. App. 2001) (both applying Illinois Supreme Court Rule 237(b)), or a court-imposed sanction for failing to comply with a court's discovery order, pursuant to Federal Rule 37, *see Govas v. Chalmers*, 965 F.2d 298 (7th Cir. 1992), which cannot be invoked in the instant case, because there has been no court order compelling discovery. See *FineLine Distributors, Inc. v. Rymer Meats, Inc.*, No. 93 C 5685, 1994 WL 376283, at *4 (N.D. Ill. July 15, 1994) ("the cases interpreting Rule 37(b) clearly establish that the Court should only issue sanctions pursuant to Rule 37(b) for a violation of a court order regarding discovery.")

The Court will grant Plaintiff's Motion, to the extent that Plaintiff seeks to preclude Defendant from introducing evidence that it refused to produce during discovery. But absent evidence that Defendant's failure to produce the documents was in violation of a court order, or was otherwise wilful, the Court denies Plaintiff's Motion.

In its Seventh Motion *in limine*, Plaintiff seeks to preclude Defendant from introducing any evidence in support of its affirmative defenses of waiver, estoppel, ratification, assumption of the risk, failure to mitigate, and unclean hands. Once again, Plaintiff bases its Motion, largely, upon its claim that Defendant's evidence fails to raise a genuine issue of material fact with regard to these claims. Because substantive rulings should be reserved for substantive motions, Plaintiff's Seventh Motion *in limine* is denied.

Similarly, Plaintiff's Eighth Motion *in limine*, seeking to bar Defendant's affirmative defenses of estoppel, unclean hands, and laches, is an attack on the substance of Defendant's affirmative defenses, and is, therefore, denied.

Plaintiff's Ninth, Twelfth, and Thirteenth Motions *in limine* seek to preclude any evidence in support of Defendant's Thirteenth and Fifteenth Affirmative Defenses, and its Illinois Uniform Deceptive Trade Practices Act Counterclaim, respectively. These Motions are denied as moot, however, as Judge Guzman has already granted Plaintiff's Motion to Strike these same affirmative defenses and counterclaim. See *Telewizja Polska USA, Inc. v. Echostar Satellite Corp.*, No. 02 C 3293 (Sept. 1, 2004).

In its Tenth Motion *in limine*, Plaintiff moves for an Order finding that Defendant is a public figure for purposes of its counterclaims. The United States Supreme Court recognizes two classes of public figures: 1) those who are public figures for all purposes; and 2) those who are public figures for a particular public controversy. *Gertz v. Robert Welch, Inc.*, 418 U.S. 323, 342 (1974).

To determine whether an entity is a limited purpose public figure, courts look to "the nature and extent of an individual's participation in the particular controversy giving rise to the defamation." *Id.* at 352. The Court disagrees that Defendant's mere status as a satellite provider renders it a public figure. Nevertheless, Plaintiff has demonstrated that Defendant has sufficiently interjected its position on the controversy into the public realm so as to warrant labeling it a public figure for purposes of this defamation action.

After Plaintiff's programming was pulled from the air, Defendant repeatedly ran a message promoting its version of the events giving rise to the cancellation on the station formerly broadcasting Plaintiff's shows. Defendant had the opportunity to counter Plaintiff's alleged attacks on its reputation, as well as to shape public opinion on the issue by directly addressing the nonparty individuals most interested in the controversy. Under these circumstances, this Court is of the opinion that Defendant is a limited purpose public figure. Therefore, Plaintiff's Tenth Motion *in limine* is granted, in part.

Plaintiff's Eleventh Motion *in limine* seeks to prevent Defendant from introducing any evidence in support of its fourteenth affirmative defense of mistake. Once again, Plaintiff's attack on the substance of Defendant's affirmative defense and the sufficiency of Defendant's evidence is better left to a summary judgment motion. Notably, Judge Guzman denied Plaintiff's Motion to Strike Defendant's Fourteenth Affirmative Defense in his September 1, 2004 Memorandum Opinion and Order. *Telewizja Polska USA, Inc. v. Echostar Satellite Corp.*, No. 02 C 3293, at *10 (N.D. Ill. Sept. 1, 2004).

In its Fourteenth Motion *in limine*, Plaintiff moves to preclude Defendant from introducing any exhibits that it has produced as translations performed by a company identified as Transtelecom. The exhibits purport to transcribe e-mails from unidentified individuals to Plaintiff's officers, in both the original Polish text and English translations, provided by Transtelecom. Plaintiff attacks the admissibility of the exhibits on numerous fronts. The most persuasive attack goes to the accuracy of the translations; the translations are obviously inaccurate on their face.

The exhibits consist of e-mail communications between two alleged consumers and Plaintiff's President, Mr. B.M. Spanski. Both consumers express their frustration, in Polish, with the termination of the Polonia program. Mr. Spanski responded in kind, offering both individuals the *identical* response. Despite the fact that Mr. Spanski gave the same response—verbatim—to both individuals, Transtelecomm has translated the responses quite differently.

Specifically, Transtelecomm interprets the first two sentences of Mr. Spanski's response to a Ms. Barbara Malewicz as follows: "Dish Network ordered us to give them full rights to distribute TV Polonia in the United States. We could not agree to those terms, nor will we agree to those terms, I am very sorry it has come to this." Conversely, Transtelecomm interprets the first two sentences of Mr. Spanski's identical response to "CAC2201" as "Dish Network worked hard to reach an agreement with TV Polonia US sales agent to allow to continue delivering television channels into your homes. There are a lot of unhappy people with this situation."

Defendant offers no explanation for the obvious differences between the translations, and the differences are significant. In this case, Defendant has alleged that Plaintiff defamed it, in part, by claiming that Defendant was demanding exclusive rights to distribute TV Polonia. The translation of Mr. Spanski's response to Ms. Malewicz strongly supports Plaintiff's claim, while the translation of Mr. Spanski's response to CAC2201 is far more benign.

However, a party challenging the authenticity or accuracy of a translation bears the burden of presenting a competing translation, permitting the trier of fact to chose which version to credit. *United States v. Briscoe*, 896 F.2d 1476, 1492 (7th Cir. 1990). In this case, Plaintiff has not offered a competing translation of the emails. Defendant has, however, substantially eased Plaintiff's burden in attacking the accuracy of Defendant's translations.

Next, Plaintiff states that the inaccurate translations are evidence of sanctionable conduct on Defendant's part. The Court disagrees that the translations, standing alone, are sufficient evidence of sanctionable conduct. The translations could be the result of honest human error. There is simply not enough evidence before the Court to sanction Defendant at this time.

Finally, "[a] judge is entitled to exclude unreliable evidence." *Dugan v. R.J. Corman R. Co.*, 344 F.3d 662, 669 (7th Cir. 2002). If the litigants were trying this case before this Court, the Court would likely strike both translations as being inherently unreliable. However, this close decision is better left to the trial judge. Motion denied.

Plaintiff's Fifteenth Motion *in limine* seeks to bar Defendant from introducing an exhibit to prove what Polska's Web site looked like on various dates in 2001. The exhibit is potentially damaging, as it purports to show Polska advertising DISH Network as a provider of TV Polonia on Polska's Web site after the expiration of the contract period. Plaintiff contends that the exhibit constitutes double hearsay, and, therefore, Defendant should not be permitted to present the exhibit at trial. The Court disagrees. "To the extent these images and text are being introduced to show the images and text found on the Web sites, they are not statements at all—and thus fall outside the ambit of the hearsay rule." *Perfect 10, Inc. v. Cybernet Ventures, Inc.*, 213 F.Supp.2d 1146, 1155 (C.D. Cal. 2002) (noting that the printouts of the Web site are admissible pursuant to the best evidence rule.) Moreover, the contents of Polska's Web site may be considered an admission of a party opponent, and are not barred by the hearsay rule. *See Van Westrienen v. Americontinental Collection Corp.*, 94 F.Supp.2d 1087, 1109 (D. Or. 2000).

Plaintiff then contends that the exhibit has not been properly authenticated.[1] Attached to the exhibits is an affidavit from Ms. Molly Davis, verifying that the Internet Archive Company retrieved copies of the Web site as it appeared on the dates in question from its electronic archives. Plaintiff labels the Internet Archive an unreliable source and claims that Defendant has not, therefore, met the threshold requirement for authentication.

Federal Rule of Evidence 901 "requires only a prima facie showing of genuineness and leaves it to the jury to decide the true authenticity and probative value of the evidence." *U.S. v. Harvey*, 117 F.3d 1044, 1049 (7th Cir. 1997). Admittedly, the Internet Archive does not fit neatly into any of the non-exhaustive examples listed in Rule 901; the Internet Archive is a relatively new source for archiving Web sites. Nevertheless, Plaintiff has presented no evidence that the Internet Archive is unreliable or biased. And Plaintiff has neither denied that the exhibit represents the contents of its Web site on the dates in question, nor come forward with its own evidence challenging the veracity of the exhibit. Under these circumstances, the Court is of the opinion that Ms. Davis' affidavit is sufficient to satisfy Rule 901's threshold requirement for admissibility. Plaintiff is free to raise its concerns regarding reliability with the jury.

Finally, Plaintiff asserts that Ms. Davis is an undisclosed expert witness and that her affidavit authenticating the exhibits should be barred. The Court rejects Plaintiff's assertion that Ms. Davis is offering an opinion, expert or otherwise, and rejects Plaintiff's argument. Plaintiff's Fifteenth Motion *in limine* is denied.

In its Sixteenth Motion *in limine*, Plaintiff asks that Defendant be prohibited from introducing any evidence that statements—other than those alleged in its Second Amended Counterclaim—are defamatory.

Plaintiff contends that courts in the Northern District employ the precise language requirement in defamation actions. *Vantassell-Matin v. Nelson*, 741 F. Supp. 698, 707-08 (N.D. Ill. 1990). The precise language requirement ensures that the opposing party has notice of the words alleged to be defamatory in forming its responsive pleadings. *Id.*

However, at least one court in this district has questioned the propriety of employing the judicially-created precise language rule, given Rule 8's liberal notice pleading requirement. In *Socorro v. IMI Data Search Inc.*, Judge Kennelly issued a thorough and well-reasoned opinion tracing the roots of the precise language rule to nonbinding precedent from the

---

[1] Coincidentally, Plaintiff claims that it is unable to access any images of its Web site during the time in question.

Eighth Circuit. No. 02 C 8120, 2003 WL 1964269, at *3 (N.D. Ill. April 28, 2003). Judge Kennelly further notes that "an allegation is considered 'specific enough' if it permits the defendant to understand the specific nature of the claim and form a responsive pleading." *Id.* citing *Cozzi v. Pepsi-Cola Gen. Bottlers Inc.*, No. 96 C 7228, 1997 WL 312048, at *5 (N.D. Ill. June 6, 1997) (stating that "courts in this district . . . have held that the defamatory language need not be quoted verbatim").

For example, in *Harding v. Rosewell*, 22 F. Supp.2d 806, 818 (N.D. Ill. 1998), the court found that once a case proceeds beyond the pleading stage, the appropriate inquiry is whether the opposing party had notice of the defamatory remarks. The court noted that "[t]he defendants, through discovery, have been given all the notice required of the alleged defamatory statements." *Id.*

Similarly, in the case at bar, the pleading stage has long since past; discovery is now closed. While Plaintiff asserts (but does not explain) prejudice, the Court is of the opinion that Plaintiff was given sufficient notice of the alleged defamatory remarks through the discovery process. And the "new" remarks that Defendant seeks to rely upon in support of its defamation counterclaim, like the two statements identified in Defendant's Second Amended Counterclaim, all arise from the parties' falling out over their attempts to renew their contract. Under these circumstances, the Court finds that it would be inappropriate to bar evidence of the allegedly defamatory statements not specifically identified in Defendant's Second Amended Counterclaim. Plaintiff's Sixteenth Motion *in limine* is denied.

Plaintiff seeks to bar Defendant from introducing a redacted email to an unknown recipient from Telewizja's President, B.M. Spanski in its Seventeenth Motion *in limine*. Plaintiff claims that the document should not be admitted because it has not been authenticated, among other reasons. Defendant counters that Mr. Spanski authenticated the email by identifying it in his deposition. A review of the relevant deposition testimony belies Defendant's assertion. Mr. Spanski acknowledged that the email contained his email address, and little more. He neither recognized the email, nor remembered sending it. Because the document has not been authenticated, Plaintiff's Seventeenth Motion *in limine* is granted.

II. Defendant's Motions In Limine

Defendant has filed an astounding 38 Motions *in limine*; very few warrant serious discussion. In half of its motions, Defendant is seeking little more than acknowledgment that it has correctly recited the Federal Rules of Evidence. Plaintiff apparently agrees that Defendant has succeeded in this limited regard, stating that it has no objection to Defendant's Motions *in limine* Nos. 1, 2, 6, 8, 10, 14, 15, 16, 17, 20, 21, 23, 24, 25, 26, 27, 29, 33, and 36.

Motion *in limine* No. 34 (which "claims surprise" as to matters, causes of action, theories of recovery, etc. that Plaintiff hasn't specifically identified) seeks to preclude precisely *nothing*, while Motion No. 38 (a catch-all provision referencing all of the "matters listed above") seeks to preclude almost *everything*. Both Motions are denied.

Defendant's Third Motion *in limine* seeks to preclude Plaintiff's counsel and witnesses from referencing any statement of the law, other than that regarding the burden of proof and the basic legal definitions. Plaintiff does not object to the Motion, but asks that it exclude the Seventh Circuit's holding in *Telewizja Polska USA, Inc. v. EchoStar Satellite Corp.*, No. 02-4332, 2003 WL 21579968, at *2-3 (7th Cir. Sept. 10, 2003).

Plaintiff does not suggest how, precisely, it would like to introduce the Seventh Circuit's opinion into evidence. Of course, it would be inappropriate for a witness to testify as to the contents of the Seventh Circuit's decision. The interpretation of the contract is the province of the court, not the jury; accordingly, the jury does not require assistance from the Seventh Circuit in interpreting and evaluating the scope of the parties' agreement. The Motion is granted.

Defendant's Motions *in limine* Nos. 4, 5, and 18 contend that any reference to prior verdicts, lawsuits, or claims against it is impermissible, pursuant to Federal Rule of Evidence 401 (defining relevant evidence), Rule 402 (stating that relevant evidence is generally admissible), and 403 (noting that relevant evidence should not be admitted if it is unduly prejudicial). Similarly, In Motions 28, 30, 31, and 32, Defendant seeks to exclude evidence of collateral bad acts or character evidence, citing Rule 404.

Plaintiff correctly notes however, that where a movant places its character at issue, evidence of reputation or specific instances of conduct may be admitted to prove character. Fed. R. Evid. 405(a) and (b). A movant may put its character at issue by filing a claim for defamation, "where injury to reputation must be proven." *Johnson v. Pistelli*, No. 95 C 6424, 1996 WL 587554, at *3, n. 5 (N.D. Ill. Oct. 8, 1996).

In this case, Defendant has filed a defamation counterclaim. To the extent that Plaintiff demonstrates at trial that evidence of other claims or lawsuits involving Defendant, or of Defendant's collateral bad acts bears upon its character and reputation, that evidence may be admissible. See *Schafer v. Time, Inc.*, 142 F.3d 1361, 1370 (11th Cir. 1998). Because such evidence may be admissible at trial, upon a proper showing by Plaintiff, motions *in limine* Nos. 4, 5, 18, 28, 30, 31, and 32 are denied.

In Motions *in limine* Nos. 7, 11, 12, and 13, Defendant asserts that evidence of its size, power, net worth, assets, or wealth is irrelevant and, even if relevant, would be unduly prejudicial. See Fed. R. Evid. 402 and 403. In its counterclaims, however, Defendant has alleged that Plaintiff defamed it and otherwise caused it damage by claiming that Defendant is a "monopoly" and has otherwise asserted its powerful market position to bully Plaintiff. Evidence of Defendant's market strength and wealth would likely be relevant in defending against such a claim. To the extent that Defendant places its wealth and/or power at issue, it may open the door to evidence on the issue. Therefore, the motions are denied.

Defendant's Ninth Motion *in limine* seeks to prohibit inquiry into its communications with its attorneys. While privileged communications that have not been waived will remain off limits, Defendant's request captures non-privileged communications with counsel, as well as instances where the privilege has been waived. See, e.g., *C&F Packing Co., Inc. v. IBP, Inc.*, No. 93 C 1601, 1997 WL 619848 (N.D. Ill. Sept. 30, 1997). As such, Defendant's Ninth Motion *in limine* is denied.

Defendant also seeks to prevent Plaintiff from commenting on Defendant's failure to produce a witness, if, in fact, Defendant fails to produce a witness at trial. Permitting or prohibiting attorneys from commenting on its opponents failure to call a witness rest soundly within the discretion of the trial judge. *U.S. v. Simpson*, 974 F.2d 845, 848 (7th Cir. 1992). Because a ruling on the issue is best reserved for trial, Defendant's Nineteenth Motion *in limine* is Denied.

Defendant then asks the Court to prevent Plaintiff from introducing new theories of damages, as well as previously undisclosed damage calculations. Plaintiff counters that granting the motion would eliminate the flexibility required to potentially modify its damages calculations to meet the evidence introduced at trial. The Court grants Defendant's Twenty-second Motion *in limine* in part, barring Plaintiff from introducing at trial any evidence concerning a source of damages that it has failed to disclose. However, to the extent that Plaintiff must modify its damages calculations in light of the evidence presented or rulings made at trial, the Motion is denied.

Defendant's Thirty-fifth Motion *in limine* seeks to bar any reference to the substance of statements of potential witnesses until trial. The Court notes, however, that traditionally, attorneys have referenced potential witnesses and testimony during opening argument arid that granting Defendant's Motion would prevent the parties from doing so. Defendant's Thirty-fifth Motion *in limine*, therefore, is denied.

Finally, Defendant's Thirty-seventh Motion *in limine* requests that Plaintiff be prevented from mentioning that it seeks disgorgement damages from Defendant's profits. Defendant argues that disgorgement is not a valid remedy in a breach of contract action, because the terms of the contract governs the parties' relationship. See *Conseco Group Risk Mgmt. Co. v. Ahrens Fin. Sys. Inc.*, No. 00 C 5467, 2001 WL 219627, at *6 (N.D. Ill. Mar. 6, 2001).

Plaintiff does not dispute Defendant's assertion, but notes that it brought the unjust enrichment claim—which would give rise to a disgorgement remedy—in the alternative to the breach of contract claim. As Judge Guzman has not dismissed Plaintiff's unjust enrichment claim, it would be inappropriate at this stage of the proceedings to preclude Plaintiff from mentioning disgorgement damages. Therefore, Defendant's Motion *in limine* 37 is denied.

Conclusion

As set forth above, the Court grants Plaintiff's Seventeenth Motion *in limine*, and grants in part Plaintiff's Sixth and Tenth Motions *in limine*. The Court denies Plaintiff's remaining Motions *in limine*.

With respect to Defendant's Motions, the Court grants Motions *in limine* Nos. 1, 2, 3, 6, 8, 10, 14, 15, 16, 17, 20, 21, 23, 24, 25, 26, 27, 29, 33, and 36, as Plaintiff has not objected to these Motions. The Court denies Defendant's Motions *in limine* Nos. 4, 5, 7, 9, 11, 12, 13, 18, 19, 28, 30, 31, 32, 35, 37 and 38.

DATED: October 14, 2004   ENTERED:

Arlander Keys
_____
ARLANDER KEYS
United States Magistrate Judge

Appendix I

UNITED STATES DISTRICT COURT
EASTERN DISTRICT OF NEW YORK

No 06-CV-1909 (JFB) (ARL)

ROBERT NOVAK D/B/A PETSWAREHOUSE.COM,

Plaintiff,

VERSUS

TUCOWS, INC., OPENSRS AND NITIN NETWORKS, INC.,

Defendants.

MEMORANDUM AND ORDER
March 26, 2007

JOSEPH F. BIANCO, District Judge:

Pro se plaintiff Robert Novak ("Novak") brings the present action against defendants Tucows, Inc. and its subsidiary, OpenSRS[1] (collectively, "Tucows") and Nitin Networks, Inc. ("Nitin") (collectively, "defendants"), alleging that Defendants' transfer of his internet domain name, "petswarehouse.com," constituted trademark infringement and trademark dilution in violation of the Lanham Act, 15 U.S.C. § 1114, 1117, 1125(a) & 1125(c). Plaintiff also brings pendent state claims, including: conversion, negligence, bailee breach of duty, bailee breach of trust, negligent misrepresentation, breach of contract, tortious interference, and intentional infliction of emotional distress.

---

[1] Tucows, Inc. does business under the name OpenSRS; however, there is no legal entity by the name of OpenSRS that is connected with Tucows. (Lazare Decl., ¶ 3; Tucows' Br., at 6 n.6.) Therefore, this Court shall consider Tucows, Inc. and OpenSRS as a single entity.

Presently before the court are Defendants' motions to dismiss the complaint pursuant to Fed. R. Civ. P. 12(b)(3), on the basis of improper venue, or, in the alternative, under Fed. R. Civ. P. 12(b)(6) and 12(b)(1), on the grounds that Plaintiff fails to state a federal claim upon which relief may be granted and, absent any federal question, this Court lacks jurisdiction due to an absence of complete diversity between the parties. Plaintiff cross-moves to strike certain of both Defendants' declarations and exhibits, and Defendant Tucows moves to strike certain of Plaintiff's exhibits.

For the reasons that follow, Plaintiff's motion to strike is granted in part and denied in part. Defendant Tucows' motion to strike is granted, and both Defendants' motions to dismiss are granted on the basis of improper venue.

I. Background

A. The Facts

The following facts are taken from the amended complaint.

In approximately November 1997, Novak registered for and obtained the Internet domain name "petswarehouse.com" through "Bulkregister .com," an internet domain name registration company. (Am. Compl. ¶¶ 36, 38.) He then commenced selling pet supplies and livestock via his Web site. (*Id.* ¶ 124.) According to Novak, his Web site was the fourth most-visited pet-supply-related site in the United States during 1999. (*Id.* ¶ 5.) On July 30, 2001, Novak trademarked the domain name "petswarehouse.com" and was awarded trademark number 2,600,670. (*Id.* ¶ 36.)

On February 11, 2003, in the Circuit Court of Colbert County, Alabama, an individual named John Benn obtained a default judgment against Novak in the amount of $50,000. (*Id.* ¶ 37.) Faced with the prospect of litigation in Alabama, Novak, a New York resident, opted to transfer the domain name "petswarehouse.com" from "Bulkregister.com," which was based in Maryland, to another company, Nitin, which was located in New York. (*Id.* ¶¶ 38–39.) On March 21, 2003, Novak contacted Nitin by telephone in order to initiate the transfer of his domain name. (*Id.* ¶ 39.) A little over one month later, on May 1, 2003, Benn applied for a writ of execution to obtain Novak's domain name "petswarehouse.com" in an effort to enforce the default judgment that he had been awarded against Novak. (*Id.* ¶ 41.) Novak asserts that it was only as a result of the May 1, 2003 writ of execution that he became aware that his domain name was actually being held by Tucows, a Canadian registration company, rather than the New York-based Nitin. (*Id.* ¶ 42.) Novak contacted Nitin on May 2, 2003, and demanded that Nitin transfer registration of "petswarehouse.com" from Tucows back to Nitin. (*Id.*) Novak was told by Nitin that such a transfer was not possible. (*Id.*)

The Alabama trial court's May 1, 2003 writ of execution required Tucows to suspend domain name hosting of "petswarehouse.com" and to turn over the domain name to the Colbert County Sheriff's Department for public auction. (*Id.* ¶ 45; Ex. C.) On May 23, 2003, Tucows transferred control over the domain name to the Alabama court pursuant to the court's order, and access to Novak's servers through the "petswarehouse.com" web address was suspended. (*Id.* ¶ 47, 124; Ex. D.) Internet users accessing "petswarehouse.com" were directed to a Web page providing notice of the Colbert County Sheriff's Sale of the domain name pursuant to the Alabama trial court's writ of execution. (*Id.* ¶ 68; Ex. E.) On July 28, 2003, Benn purchased "petswarehouse.com" in a public auction held by the Colbert County Sheriff, in which Benn was the only bidder. (*Id.* ¶ 54.) On September 16, 2003, Tucows transferred the domain name to Benn pursuant to the Alabama trial court's order. (*Id.* ¶ 55.)

Novak challenged the Alabama trial court's decision, and on April 2, 2004, the Alabama Court of Civil Appeals reversed Benn's default judgment and writ of execution against Novak on the basis that the judgment had been entered without personal jurisdiction over Novak. (*Id.* ¶ 71.) Armed with the state appellate court decision, Novak demanded that Tucows return control of "petswarehouse.com" to him. (*Id.* ¶ 72.) On October 1, 2004, after Benn was denied rehearing by the Alabama Court of Civil Appeals and the Alabama Supreme Court, Tucows returned the domain name to Novak. (*Id.* ¶ 72–73.)

Plaintiff alleges that the transfer of his domain name out of his control between May 1, 2003 and October 1, 2004 destroyed his pet-supply business. Prior to May 23, 2003, Novak had received approximately 12,000 daily visitors to "petswarehouse.com." (*Id.* ¶ 134.) Following transfer of the domain name, visitors to the Web site were directed to the sheriff's notice of sale, and Novak was unable to process any pet-supply orders. (*Id.*) According to Novak, Tucows and Nitin's transfer of the domain name out of his control diluted the "petswarehouse.com" trademark in violation of the Lanham Act, 15 U.S.C. § 1125(c). Novak also asserts that the transfer deceptively and misleadingly represented Tucows and Nitin's association with "petswarehouse.com," and constituted unfair competition and cyberpiracy under 15 U.S.C. §§ 1114, 1117 & 1125(a).

B. Procedural History

On April 25, 2006, Novak, proceeding *pro se*, filed the instant complaint against defendants Tucows, Inc. and OpenSRS. By letter dated May

11, 2006, Defendant Tucows indicated its intention to move for dismissal on the basis of improper venue. Upon learning of Defendants' proposed motion to dismiss, Plaintiff modified his claims, adding Nitin as a Defendant, and filed an amended complaint on May 16, 2006. On July 10, 2006, Defendants Nitin and Tucows moved to dismiss the complaint on the basis of improper venue, or, in the alternative, failure to state a claim and lack of subject-matter jurisdiction. Plaintiff cross-moved to strike the declarations and exhibits submitted by Defendants in support of their motions to dismiss, and Defendants moved to strike certain of Plaintiff's exhibits. Oral argument and an evidentiary hearing were held on December 22, 2006, January 25, 2007 and February 9, 2007.

II. Evidentiary Objections

A. Plaintiff's Motion to Strike

1. General Objections to Admissibility of Foreign Declarations

According to Novak, the declarations of two of Defendant Tucows' employees in Canada are inadmissible under Fed. R. Evid. 902(12). Rule 902(12) permits foreign documents to be submitted into evidence as self-authenticating business records if accompanied by a declaration signed "in a manner that, if falsely made, would subject the maker to criminal penalty under the laws of the country where the declaration is signed." Fed. R. Evid. 902(12). Novak argues that, in order to meet this requirement, a "jurat including penalty of perjury" under Canadian law should have been provided by Defendants with regard to the declarations submitted by Brenda Lazare ("Lazare"), Tucows' Secretary and General Counsel, and Evgeniy Pirogov ("Pirogov"), Team Leader of the OpenSRS Development Team. (Pl.'s Br., 4 at 25–26.) However, where a matter must be supported by a sworn declaration, a declaration written outside of the United States may be supported "with like force and effect" by a statement in writing that "I declare (or certify, verify, or state) under penalty of perjury under the laws of the United States of America, that the foregoing is true and correct. Executed on (date)." 28 U.S.C. § 1746. In this instance, both the Lazare and Pirogov declarations contain the requisite statement, and are therefore admissible. (See Lazare Decl., at 9; Pirogov Decl., at 6.)

2. Objections to the Lazare Declaration

According to plaintiff, the Lazare declaration is also defective in failing to authenticate the attached Exhibits J-L as business records. The contested exhibits include: Exhibit J, excerpts from the registrar's agreement between Tucows and ICANN, the non-profit corporation that administers the Internet domain name and Internet protocol number system; Exhibit K, excerpts from Tucows' registrar license and the registry-registrar agreement between Tucows and Network Solutions, Inc. a/k/a Verisign, Inc. ("Verisign"), a registry that operates and maintains ".com" top-level domain names; and Exhibit L, excerpts from Nitin's reseller application and the reseller agreement between Tucows and Nitin. (Lazare Decl., Ex. J-L.) In the declaration, Lazare, as Secretary and General Counsel of Tucows, clearly sets forth her personal knowledge of the facts stated therein, explaining that she has held her current position overseeing management of the regulatory compliance and disputes department of Tucows since June 2000. (Lazare Decl., ¶ 1–2.) Specifically, Lazare details Tucows' relationship with ICANN, Verisign and Nitin, and clearly sets forth how the related exhibits were created and maintained in the course of "regularly conducted business activity," pursuant to Fed. R. Evid. 803(6). Therefore, the Court finds that Exhibits J-L are properly authenticated by the Lazare declaration and, moreover, are admissible as business records.

Plaintiff further asserts that the Lazare Declaration should be held inadmissible on the basis that it contains legal argument. The Court finds that the first 26 paragraphs of the declaration contain factual descriptions of the domain name registration and transfer processes. (*Id.* ¶¶ 1–26.) However, paragraphs 27-31 of the declaration present legal argument regarding the applicability of the forum selection clause at issue in this case, and as such, those paragraphs shall be disregarded. (*Id.* ¶¶ 27–31.) See, e.g., *Kamen v. Am. Tel. & Tel. Co.*, 791 F.2d 1006, 1011 (2d Cir. 1986) (holding that it was improper for district court to consider "conclusory and hearsay" statements in an attorney affidavit where the statements were not based upon personal knowledge).

3. *Objections to the Pirogov Declaration*
Novak argues that the Pirogov Declaration lacks personal knowledge, expresses "expert opinion" testimony, and includes hearsay. Pirogov, Team Leader of the OpenSRS Development Team since October 2003, asserts in his declaration that his duties include "supervision of the software development that allows Tucows to process transfers, and maintenance of the logs that archive prior transfers." (Pirogov Decl., ¶¶ 1–4.) Based upon Pirogov's position and his statements, the Court finds that he has sufficient personal knowledge to describe Tucows' domain name transfer process, and to authenticate the exhibits demonstrating that process. Furthermore, the Court finds no basis in the declaration for Novak's assertion that it includes "expert opinion" testimony or hearsay.

In addition, Plaintiff objects to the admissibility of Exhibits B-I, authenticated therein, on the basis that they have been newly created for purposes of this litigation, and were not kept in the ordinary course of business. The Court disagrees. First, the Court finds that these exhibits have been authenticated by Pirogov pursuant to Rule 901(b)(9), which permits the admission of "[e]vidence describing a process or system used to produce a result and showing that the process or system produces an accurate result." Fed. R. Evid. 901(b)(9). Furthermore, to the extent that Exhibits B-I are submitted merely as a demonstrative aid, the Court finds that the hearsay rule is not applicable. "[T]here is no requirement that demonstrative evidence be shown to be totally accurate. Rather, alleged inaccuracies go to the weight and not the admissibility of the evidence." 5-900 *Weinstein's Federal Evidence* § 900.07 (2006); see, e.g., *Datskow v. Teledyne Cont'l Motors Aircraft Prod.*, 826 F. Supp. 677, 686 (W.D.N.Y. 1993) (admitting computer-generated animation used to show theory of how accident occurred). Thus, the Court shall consider Exhibits B-I to the extent that they demonstrate the process of transferring domain names, rather than to show the transfer steps specific to "petswarehouse.com."[2]

4. *Objections to the Agarwal Declaration*

Novak argues that the declaration submitted by Nitin Agarwal ("Agarwal"), CEO and founder of Nitin, contains impermissible hearsay and is not based on personal knowledge. The Court finds, based upon Agarwal's position, that he had personal knowledge of the events relating to Nitin's handling of the transfer of Novak's domain name. Moreover, any potential defects in Agarwal's declaration were subsequently cured by his testimony at the evidentiary hearing, in which he set forth a clear basis for his

---

[2] At the evidentiary hearing, Eliot Noss, CEO of Tucows, testified regarding a series of additional exhibits that recreate the steps taken during Novak's transfer of the domain name "petswarehouse.com" based upon information stored in Tucows' databases. This Court ruled that such exhibits were, in fact, admissible for purposes of showing the transfer steps specific to the transaction in question:

> There are a few documents in which the witness testified the computer took data and put it in the form of how it would have appeared on the page at the time to show where the information would have been inputted on the forms as they currently existed at the time of the transaction. I find that that is also admissible. . . . [T]he witness properly laid the foundation for the[m] having retained the data, and for what forms they used at the time, and it was clear to point out that this was not created at the time, but it was recreated to show, based upon what data they stored, where it would have been inputted on their existing forms. So I think it is admissible under the rules of evidence. . . . I think, based upon [Noss'] testimony, they have laid the proper foundation for the admissibility of the documents. So I am admitting Defense Exhibits T1 through 10.

(Transcript of December 22, 2006 Hearing (hereinafter "Dec. 22, 2006 Tr.," at 125–26.)

personal knowledge of Novak's interactions with Nitin in transferring "petswarehouse.com."

Plaintiff also asserts that the Agarwal Declaration contains the false statement that "[a]t the time of the transfer [March 21, 2003], Nitin Networks was not registering any domain names as a registrar, and was exclusively using Defendant Tucows for all of its registrations and transfers."[3] (Agarwal Decl., ¶ 4.) According to Plaintiff, this statement conflicts with evidence that Nitin Networks was, in fact, registering domain names. However, Plaintiff's objection does not go to the admissibility of the Agarwal Declaration, but to its credibility and weight.

B. Defendants' Motion to Strike

Defendants contend that plaintiff's Exhibits B, J, K, O-R, U and V, which are printouts of Internet pages, constitute inadmissible hearsay and do not fall within any acknowledged exception to the hearsay rule.[4] At the evidentiary hearing, Defendants objected to Plaintiff's Exhibit 1, as well as to Plaintiff's Exhibits N-R. (Jan. 25, 2007 Tr. 125-31.) Plaintiff's Exhibit 1 is a printout from "RegisterSite.com," Nitin's Web site, as it purportedly appeared in 2003. (Pl.'s Ex. 1.) According to Plaintiff, he obtained the printout through a Web site called the Internet Archive, which provides access to a digital library of Internet sites. (Novak Decl., ¶ 2.) The Internet Archive operates a service called the "Wayback Machine," which purports to allow a user to obtain an archived Web page as it appeared at a particular moment in time. (*See id.* ¶¶ 3–5.) The other contested exhibits include: Exhibit B, an online summary of plaintiff's past and pending lawsuits, obtained via the Wayback Machine; Exhibit J, printouts of comments on a web message board by Pirogov; Exhibit K, a news article from the Poughkeepsie Journal Web site featuring Agarwal; Exhibit N, Novak's declaration regarding the authenticity of pages printed from the Wayback Machine; Exhibit O, pages printed from the Internet Archive Web site; Exhibit P, pages printed from the Wayback Machine Web site; Exhibits Q, R and U, all of which constitute pages printed from

---

[3] During the evidentiary hearing, plaintiff cross-examined Agarwal regarding paragraph 4 of his declaration, and Agarwal affirmed "I stand by the full sentence of the statement." (Jan. 25, 2007 Tr. 87.)

[4] During the evidentiary hearing, Defendant Tucows also objected to the admission of Plaintiff's Exhibit S, a document titled "OpenSRS Quickstart Instructions," and dated January 2001, on the basis that the exhibit had not been authenticated by Tucows. (Jan. 25, 2007 Tr. 46- 50.) By letter dated January 30, 2007, Tucows withdrew its objection based upon the authenticity of Exhibit S. (Tucows' January 30, 2007 Letter, at 2.) However, Tucows "reserve[d] the right to argue the immateriality of the document, based both on its contents and the relevance of the 2001 document to events that took place in 2003." (*Id.*)

RegisterSite.com via the Wayback Machine; and Exhibit V, a news article from "The Register," a British Web site, regarding Tucows. (Pl.'s Exs. B, J, K, N-R, U & V.) Where postings from Internet Web sites are not statements made by declarants testifying at trial and are offered to prove the truth of the matter asserted, such postings generally constitute hearsay under Fed. R. Evid. 801. *United States v. Jackson*, 208 F.3d 633, 638 (7th Cir. 2000) (declining to admit web postings where defendant was unable to show that the postings were authentic, and holding that even if such documents qualified under a hearsay exception, they are "inadmissible if the source of information or the method or circumstances of preparation indicate a lack of trustworthiness") (quoting *United States v. Croft*, 750 F.2d 1354, 1367 (7th Cir. 1984)); see also *St. Clair v. Johnny's Oyster & Shrimp, Inc.*, 76 F. Supp. 2d 773, 775 (S.D. Tex. 1999) ("[A]ny evidence procured off the Internet is adequate for almost nothing, even under the most liberal interpretation of the hearsay exception rules.").

Furthermore, in this case, such documents have not been properly authenticated pursuant to Fed. R. Evid. 901. While plaintiff's declaration purports to cure his inability to authenticate the documents printed from the Internet, he in fact lacks the personal knowledge required to set forth with any certainty that the documents obtained via third-party Web sites are, in fact, what he proclaims them to be. This problem is even more acute in the case of documents procured through the Wayback Machine. Plaintiff states that the Web pages archived within the Wayback Machine are based upon "data from third parties who compile the data by using software programs known as crawlers," who then "donate" such data to the Internet Archive, which "preserves and provides access to it." (Novak Decl. ¶ 4.) Based upon Novak's assertions, it is clear that the information posted on the Wayback Machine is only as valid as the third-party donating the page decides to make it—the authorized owners and managers of the archived Web sites play no role in ensuring that the material posted in the Wayback Machine accurately represents what was posted on their official Web sites at the relevant time. As Novak proffers neither testimony nor sworn statements attesting to the authenticity of the contested Web page exhibits by any employee of the companies hosting the sites from which plaintiff printed the pages, such exhibits cannot be authenticated as required under the Rules of Evidence. See, e.g., *Costa v. Keppel Singmarine Dockyard PTE, Ltd.*, No. 01-CV- 11015 MMM (Ex), 2003 U.S. Dist. LEXIS 16295, at *29 n.74 (C.D. Cal. Apr. 25, 2003) (declining to consider evidence downloaded from corporation's Web site in the absence of testimony from the corporation authenticating such documents) (citing

Jackson, 208 F.3d at 638, and *St. Clair*, 76 F. Supp. 2d at 775 ("Anyone can put anything on the [I]nternet. No Web site is monitored for accuracy and nothing contained therein is under oath or even subject to independent verification absent underlying documentation.")). Therefore, in the absence of any authentication of Plaintiff's Internet printouts, combined with the lack of any assertion that such printouts fall under a viable exception to the hearsay rule, Defendants' motion to strike Exhibits B, J, K, N-R, U and V is granted.[5]

III. Standard of Review

Defendants challenge venue in this case pursuant to Federal Rule of Civil Procedure 12(b)(3). However, the Court must first address the question of whether a motion to dismiss based upon a forum selection clause is properly brought under Rule 12(b)(3) as a challenge to venue, rather than under Rule 12(b)(6) for failure to state a claim or Rule 12(b)(1) for lack of subject-matter jurisdiction.

In *New Moon Shipping Co., Ltd. v. Man B&W Diesel A.G.*, the Second Circuit acknowledged the absence of consensus among the courts regarding the correct procedural mechanism for dismissal of a suit pursuant to a valid forum selection clause. 121 F.3d 24, 28 (2d Cir. 1997) (comparing *AVC Nederland B.V. v. Atrium Inv. P'ship*, 740 F.2d 148, 152 (2d Cir. 1984)) (applying Fed. R. Civ. P. 12(b)(1) to a motion to dismiss based upon a forum selection clause), with *Paterson, Zochonis (U.K.) Ltd. v. Compania United Arrows, S.A.*, 493 F. Supp. 626, 629 (S.D.N.Y. 1980) (applying Fed. R. Civ. P. 12(b)(3))); see also *Rainforest Café, Inc. v. EklecCo, L.L.C.*, 340 F.3d 544, 546 n.5 (8th Cir. 2003) (recognizing controversy between whether to apply Fed. R. Civ. P. 12(b)(3) or Fed. R. Civ. P. 12(b)(6) to a motion to dismiss based on forum selection clause). In this instance, Defendants have framed the forum selection clause issue as a motion to dismiss pursuant to Rule 12(b)(3), and in the absence of any objection to this framework by plaintiff, the Court shall consider the jurisdictional issue pursuant to this rule. See, e.g., *Person v. Google, Inc.*, 456 F. Supp. 2d 488, 492-93 (S.D.N.Y. 2006) ("Here, the issue will be considered under Fed. Civ. P. Rule 12(b)(3) because that is how it was framed by the parties.") (citing *J. B. Harris, Inc. v. Razei Bar Indus., Inc.*, 37 F. Supp. 2d 186, 189 (E.D.N.Y. 1998) ("The Court does not decide whether this issue might more properly have been

---

[5] The Court notes that, even if all of Plaintiff's exhibits were admissible, they would not impact the Court's analysis or conclusions on the substantive issues in the instant case.

raised by way of Rule 12(b)(6), as the issue is squarely framed by Defendants under Rule 12(b)(3) and Plaintiff does not argue that this is an improper procedural mechanism.") (internal citation omitted)).

Without resolving the question of whether to treat the motion to dismiss as a 12(b)(1) or 12(b)(3) motion, the Second Circuit held in *New Moon Shipping* that "at the initial stage of litigation, a party seeking to establish jurisdiction need only make a *prima facie* showing by alleging facts which, if true, would support the court's exercise of jurisdiction." 121 F.3d at 29 (citing *Marine Midland Bank, N.A. v. Miller*, 664 F.2d 899, 904 (2d Cir. 1981)); *Gulf Ins. Co. v. Glasbrenner*, 417 F.3d 353, 355 (2d Cir. 2005) ("If the court chooses to rely on pleadings and affidavits, the plaintiff need only make a *prima facie* showing of [venue].") (quoting *CutCo Indus. v. Naughton*, 806 F.2d 361, 364-65 (2d Cir. 1986) and citing *Sunward Elecs. v. McDonald*, 362 F.3d 17, 22 (2d Cir. 2004)). "After limited discovery on the jurisdictional issue, the matter might be appropriate for resolution on motion supported by affidavits, or, if a genuine dispute of material fact exists, the Court may conduct a hearing limited to Article III standing." *Alliance for Envtl. Renewal, Inc. v. Pyramid Crossgates Co.*, 436 F.3d 82, 87-88 (2d Cir. 2006) (citations omitted). Disputed facts may be resolved against the non-moving party only after an evidentiary hearing, where the plaintiff must demonstrate venue by a preponderance of the evidence. *New Moon Shipping*, 121 F.3d at 29 ("A disputed fact may be resolved in a manner adverse to the plaintiff only after an evidentiary hearing. . . . [A] party seeking to avoid enforcement of such a contractual clause is also entitled to have the facts viewed in the light most favorable to it, and no disputed fact should be resolved against that party until it has had an opportunity to be heard.") (citations omitted); *Gulf Ins. Co.*, 417 F.3d at 355 ("[I]f the court holds an evidentiary hearing . . . the plaintiff must demonstrate [venue] by a preponderance of the evidence.") (quoting *CutCo Indus.*, 806 F.2d at 364–65) (additional citation omitted); *Murphy v. Schneider Nat'l, Inc.*, 362 F.3d 1133, 1139 (9th Cir. 2004) ("To resolve such motions when genuine factual issues are raised, it may be appropriate for the district court to hold a Rule 12(b)(3) motion in abeyance until the district court holds an evidentiary hearing on the disputed facts. Whether to hold a hearing on disputed facts and the scope and method of the hearing is within the sound discretion of the district court.") (citations omitted).

In this case, the Court conducted an evidentiary hearing to resolve a disputed material fact as to whether venue is proper in this Court: specifically, whether plaintiff consented to an agreement with defendant Tucows that contained a forum selection clause mandating litigation of all related disputes in Ontario, Canada. At the evidentiary hearing, all parties presented evidence bearing on the question of whether Novak agreed to transfer his domain name to Tucows by clicking his assent to a Domain Name Transfer Agreement ("DNTA") on a Web site. The DNTA in question contained the following forum selection clause at paragraph 27:

> GOVERNING LAW. This agreement shall be governed by and interpreted and enforced in accordance with the laws of [sic] Province of Ontario and the federal laws of Canada applicable therein without reference to rules governing choice of laws. *Any action relating to this agreement must be brought in Ontario* and you irrevocably consent to the jurisdiction of such courts.

(Pirogov Decl., Ex. H.) The legal effect of a forum selection clause depends upon "whether its existence was reasonably communicated to the plaintiff." *Effron v. Sun Line Cruises, Inc.*, 67 F.3d 7, 9 (2d Cir. 1995) (citations omitted). "A forum selection clause stated in clear and unambiguous language . . . is considered reasonably communicated to the plaintiff in determining its enforceability." *Vitricon, Inc. v. Midwest Elastomers, Inc.*, 148 F. Supp. 2d 245, 247 (E.D.N.Y. 2001) (citing *Effron*, 67 F.3d at 9). As there is no question that the language of the forum-selection clause at issue is clear and unambiguous, should this Court find that Novak did, in fact, "click-through" the Tucows DNTA, the Court may fairly conclude that the clause was "reasonably communicated" to the plaintiff. *Id.*

IV. The Evidentiary Hearing

The Court conducted an evidentiary hearing, over several days, to determine whether Novak in fact "clicked-through" his assent to Tucows' DNTA. Based upon the testimony and exhibits presented at the hearing, the Court finds that there is overwhelming evidence that the Plaintiff consented to the DNTA with Tucows. Although it is unclear whether Plaintiff actually read the agreement, the evidence unequivocally demonstrates that he was required to "click-through" his assent to Tucows' DNTA in order to complete the successful transfer of "petswarehouse.com."

The Plaintiff argues that he never agreed to the forum-selection clause, and, further, that he never agreed to enter into any agreement whatsoever with Defendant Tucows. According to Novak, when he transferred the domain name "petswarehouse.com" from its original registrar, "Bulkregister.com," he did so solely by phone agreement with Nitin, whose online transfer system was not operational at the time. (Jan. 25, 2007 Tr. 117.) Novak explained that he was not aware that Nitin was actually a reseller, rather than a registrar, of domain names, nor that Tucows was the actual registrar of "petswarehouse.com" until over a month after the transfer, when Benn issued a writ of execution to obtain the domain name from Tucows. (Jan. 25, 2007 10 Tr. 112, 117; Feb. 9, 2007 Tr. 49.) Novak argues that, in fact, his intent in transferring the domain name from "Bulkregister.com" to Nitin was to bring the domain name under the control of a New York-based registrar. (Jan. 25, 2007 Tr. 110-11; Feb. 9, 2007 Tr. 66-67.) According to Novak, had he received a DNTA from Tucows, a Canadian registrar, he "would have declined the transfer, first because [he] would have felt deceived in seeing another company being involved in this transaction, and moreover a company based not only outside New York, but Canada." (Feb. 9, 2007 Tr. 63.)

In response, Defendants argue that Plaintiff could not possibly have executed transfer of his domain name to Tucows solely by oral agreement with Nitin. According to Tucows, "[p]laintiff's assertion that he transferred the petswarehouse.com domain name orally through Nitin Networks is demonstrably and necessarily false, as the domain name registration system does not permit transfers without the safeguard of an electronic confirmation." (Tucows' Br., at 5.) Contrary to Novak's assertion that he never entered into any agreement with Tucows, Noss testified that such agreements are "necessary" to the domain name transfer process, and that "[t]hey are overwhelmingly—in fact, in our case, almost without exception, they are click-through agreements, ones that are subscribed to on a Web page." (Dec. 22, 2007 Tr. 14.) Tucows asserts that, after Plaintiff communicated with Nitin by phone, he received notification by e-mail from Tucows that he would have to execute further electronic authorization of the transfer. (Tucows' Br., at 5.) According to Tucows, in the confirmation e-mail, plaintiff was instructed to click on a link directing him to Tucows' Web site, where he was required to submit a "Transfer Confirmation Form," affirming that he had "both read and understood the Domain Transfer and Registration Contract," and that he "fully accepts the terms of the Domain Name Transfer and Registration Contract."[6] (Tucows' Br., at 4.) A hyperlink to the DNTA was provided on the Transfer Confirmation Form. (Tucows' Br., at 4.) However, Novak categorically asserts that he "never received the e-mail. If I would have, I would have immediately canceled and gone to another registrar in New York." (Feb. 9, 2007 Tr. 66.)

---

[6] In addition, Tucows argues that it was clear from the electronic confirmation form that Plaintiff would be entering into a contract with Tucows (rather than with Nitin) by language on the form stating that "[t]he domain listed above will be transferred to Registersite.com (An authorized reseller of Tucows)." (Tucows' Br., at 4.)

During the evidentiary hearing, Noss, Tucows' CEO, testified, based upon a review of Tucows' records, that the plaintiff had, in fact, engaged in each of the above steps:

> I can say with certainty that, first, the request for transfer was received by Tucows, that we sent a confirmatory e-mail to bob@petswarehouse.com. We have the IP address, in other words, the specific address of the computer that was connected to the internet that received that e-mail. I can say with certainty that that e-mail, coming from IP address, had a link in it which was clicked on. And that email contained a unique password generated solely for the purpose of confirming this transfer. That password was then entered into the Web page that resulted from clicking on the link. And I can also say with certainty that on the resulting pages, that the box that says, in effect, I agree with the terms and conditions, was ticked.

(Dec. 22, 2006 Tr. 21-22.) Noss' testimony is fully corroborated by exhibits introduced at the hearing, which are printouts from Tucows' computer database that reflect data generated contemporaneously with Novak's domain name transfer. On March 31, 2003, at 12:28 p.m. and 43 seconds Eastern Standard Time, Tucows received a transfer request. (Dec. 22, 2006 Tr. 30; Defs.' Ex. T2.) Three seconds later, Tucows sent a confirmation e-mail to "bob@petswarehouse.com," Novak's e-mail address.[7] (Dec. 22, 2006 Tr. 30; Defs.' Ex. T2.) On the same day, at 5:07 p.m. and 26 seconds, a hyperlink within the e-mail was clicked by the recipient. (Dec. 22, 2006 Tr. at 58-59; Defs.' Ex. T6.) Less than one minute later, at 5:08 p.m. and 15 seconds, the e-mail recipient typed the required domain name and transfer key into the Tucows Web site. (Dec. 22, 2006 Tr. at 59; Defs.' Ex. T6.) Finally, at 5:14 pm and 51 seconds, the contract on the Web site was assented to and the request was submitted. (Dec. 22, 2006 Tr. at 59; Defs.' Ex. T6.) Noss explained that, if Novak had not entered the proper information during each of these steps, or if he had simply ignored the confirmation e-mail from Tucows, the transfer would have failed. (Dec. 22, 2006 Tr. at 60.)

In response, Novak counters that he never engaged in the required steps, and that it was actually Agarwal, CEO of Nitin, who "went directly into the Tucows database, changed the contact info to himself, received the confirmation e-mails, and clicked them off to force the transfer to go through. Alternatively, he modified the database to indicate that that had

---

[7]Novak concedes that he is the sole user of the e-mail address "bob@petswarehouse.com," and that the address is not case sensitive." (Feb. 9, 2007 Tr. 27, 28.)

occurred." (Feb. 9, 2007 Tr. 66.) However, the Court finds Novak's theory that Agarwal manually input false data in order to effect the domain name transfer to be incredible. Based upon the overwhelming evidence that Novak did, in fact, assent to the DNTA, and that a transfer of his domain name to Tucows would not have been possible without such assent, the Court finds, despite Novak's blanket denials and conspiracy theories, that he did enter into such an agreement with Tucows and therefore is subject to the forum-selection clause contained therein, unless there is some ground for the clause to be found invalid. It is the latter issue to which the Court now turns.

V. Validity of Forum Selection Clause

A. Standard

Under the standard set forth by the Supreme Court in *The Bremen v. Zapata Off- Shore Company*, forum selection clauses are *prima-facie* valid and should control questions of venue absent a "strong showing" that enforcement would be "unreasonable and unjust, or that the clause was invalid for such reasons as fraud or overreaching." 407 U.S. 1, 15, 16 (1972). A forum selection clause can bind the parties even where the agreement in question is a form consumer contract that is not subject to negotiation. *Carnival Cruise Lines, Inc. v. Shute*, 499 U.S. 585, 589-95 (1991). Such clauses will be enforced only if found to be exclusive or mandatory. *John Boutari and Son, Wines and Spirits, S.A., v. Attiki Imp. and Distrib., Inc.*, 22 F.3d 51, 52- 53 (2d Cir. 1994). It is clear that the choice of forum is mandatory in this instance, as specific language regarding venue has been included in the clause, specifying that "any action relating to this agreement must be brought in Ontario." See, e.g., *John Boutari and Son, Wines and Spirits, S.A.*, 22 F.3d at 53; *Docksider, Ltd. v. Sea Tech., Ltd.*, 875 F.2d 762, 763-64 (9th Cir. 1989); *Cent. Nat'l- Gottesman, Inc. v. M.V. "Gertrude Oldendorff,"* 204 F. Supp. 2d 675, 678 (S.D.N.Y. 2002) ("For a forum selection clause to be deemed mandatory, jurisdiction and venue must be specified with mandatory or exclusive language.") (citation omitted).

As the forum selection clause at issue is mandatory, it is enforceable, provided that enforcement would not be unreasonable. A clause is unreasonable: (1) if their incorporation into the agreement was the result of fraud or overreaching; (2) if the complaining party will be deprived of his day in court due to the grave inconvenience or unfairness of the selected forum; (3) if the fundamental unfairness of the chosen law may deprive the plaintiff of a remedy; or (4) if the clauses contravene a strong public policy of the forum state. *Roby v. Corp. of Lloyd's*, 996 F.2d 1353, 1363 (2d Cir. 1993) (citing *The Bremen*, 407 U.S. at 10, 15, 18, and *Carnival Cruise*

Lines, Inc., 499 U.S. at 595-96); *S.K.I. Beer Corp. v. Baltika Brewery*, 443 F. Supp. 2d 313, 316 (E.D.N.Y. 2006) (same) (citations omitted). In his moving papers, plaintiff alleges neither that he will be deprived of his day in court due to the inconvenience of litigating this dispute in Ontario,[8] nor that Canadian law is fundamentally unfair and would deprive him of a remedy.[9]

---

[8]In his supplemental reply brief, dated February 21, 2007, Novak asserts for the first time that he is not able to litigate this dispute in Canada for health reasons. In support of this claim, Novak submits a letter from his treating neurologist, Dr. Candice Perkins, M.D., stating that Novak sustained a carotid occlusion and stroke in August 2000 and continues to suffer from a persistent blockage of blood flow to his brain. (Pl.'s Supp. Br., Ex. A.) According to Dr. Perkins, "as a result prolonged travel out of the country (without close contact of [Novak's] medical team) is ill advised." (*Id.*) In fact, while Novak may very well suffer from illnesses that restrict his ability to travel, such impairments did not prevent him from driving cross-country over a two-week span from January 1 to 14, 2007. (Dec. 22, 2006 Tr. 127.) Novak has given no indication that engaging in litigation in Toronto would be more taxing on his health than his recent travel across the United States; therefore, the Court rejects his argument that "[b]ased on [Dr. Perkins'] opinion and my families [sic] concerns I would have to abandon the thought of any cause of action in Canada against Tucows." (Pl.'s Supp. Br., at 2.) Even if Novak were unable to personally attend proceedings in Canada, such deprivation does not necessarily constitute a denial of his day in court. This Circuit has held that "[t]he right to a day in court means not the actual presentation of the case, but the right to be duly cited to appear and to be afforded an opportunity to be heard." *Effron*, 67 F.3d at 11 (quoting *Olsen v. Muskegon Piston Ring Co.*, 117 F.2d 163, 165 (6th Cir. 1941)). "A plaintiff may have his 'day in court' without ever setting foot in a courtroom." *Id.* (citation omitted). While Novak may prefer to bring his case against Tucows in a familiar forum, he consented to bring any such claims in Ontario; in the absence of any showing that plaintiff's health concerns will actually deprive him of his day in court, this Court declines to find that plaintiff should be permitted to evade his contractual obligations.

[9]In his supplemental brief, Novak also raises for the first time the argument that he could be deprived of a remedy under Canadian law because he "doubt[s] very much that court would have jurisdiction over Nitin but more importantly Canada would have no jurisdiction over John Benn as a witness residing in Alabama" and "there is an issue of the statute of limitation in recommencing this action in Canada." (Pl.'s Supp. Br., at 2, 3.)

First, a "statute of limitations bar is not a basis for invalidating [a foreign] forum selection clause." *Asoma Corp. v. M/V. Southgate*, 98-CV- 7407 (CSH), 1999 U.S. Dist. LEXIS 18974, at *9- *12 (S.D.N.Y. Dec. 7, 1999) (collecting cases); see also *Street, Sound Around Elec., Inc. v. M/V Royal Container*, 30 F. Supp. 2d 661, 663 (S.D.N.Y. 1999) ("By bringing suit here and not in Germany, plaintiffs have effectively chosen to ignore the forum selection clause that they previously agreed to; [P]laintiffs will not be heard now to complain of any potential timeliness problems that this choice may have created.") (citations omitted); see also *New Moon Shipping*, 121 F.3d at 33 ("[C]onsideration of a statute of limitations would create a large loophole for the party seeking to avoid enforcement of the forum selection clause. That party could simply postpone its cause of action until the statute of limitations has run in the chosen forum and then file its action in a more convenient forum.").

Second, while it is unclear whether Agarwal and Benn could be compelled to appear before a court in Ontario, the Court is not persuaded that this factor suggests the "fundamental unfairness" of litigating the instant dispute in Canada. At least in the context of transfers of lawsuits pursuant to 28 U.S.C. § 1404(a), courts have held that the availability of witnesses does not "tip the balance" with regard to the choice of a forum, particularly where the testimony of such witnesses may be obtained by videotape or deposition. *Dealtime.com Ltd. v. McNulty*, 123 F. Supp. 2d 750, 757 (S.D.N.Y. 2000); (citing Fed. R. Evid. 804(a)(5) and *Citigroup Inc. v. City Holding Co.*, 97 F. Supp. 2d 549, 561-62 (S.D.N.Y. 2000) ("[T]he unavailability of process over third-party witnesses does not compel transfer when the practical alternative of offering videotaped or deposition testimony of a given witness exists.") (citations omitted). There is no reason to believe that such alternatives to live testimony are not available to Novak in this case.

Plaintiff's contends: (1) that the "petswarehouse.com" domain name was fraudulently transferred from Nitin to Tucows without his permission, and that holding him to the DNTA would therefore be unconscionable under New York state law because he did not consent to the contract terms, and (2) that the forum selection clause contravenes the public policy of New York state, which protects resident consumers against deceptive business acts and practices under New York General Business Law § 349.

B. Fraud

Plaintiff alleges, first, that Nitin misled him by falsely representing that Novak would only be interacting with a New York company when he transferred his domain name to Nitin. Plaintiff claims that Nitin concealed the fact that he was merely a reseller of domain names, and that Tucows, a Canadian company, would be the actual registrar. In other words, according to plaintiff, he was lured into transacting with Nitin on the basis of false information and misrepresentation. Plaintiff also alleges that his domain name was fraudulently transferred without his permission from Nitin, with whom he contracted by phone, to Tucows, with whom he did not contract at all. However, even if plaintiff were able to establish valid fraud claims based on these assertions, which he likely cannot, given his "click-through" assent to the Tucows DNTA, such allegations are insufficient to void a forum selection clause on the basis of fraud.

Actions capable of overcoming the presumption of validity of a forum selection clause "must be *directly related to that clause*, not the contract more generally." *Person*, 456 F. Supp. 2d at 494 (citations omitted). The Supreme Court has held that, where a party attempting to defeat a forum-selection clause alleges fraud, courts must look to whether the inclusion of the clause itself was fraudulent:

> In *The Bremen* we noted that forumselection clauses "should be given full effect" when "a freely negotiated private international agreement [is] unaffected by fraud. . . ." This qualification does not mean that any time a dispute arising out of a transaction is based upon an allegation of fraud, as in this case, the clause is unenforceable. Rather, it means that an arbitration or forum-selection clause in a contract is not enforceable if *the inclusion of that clause in the contract* was the product of fraud or coercion.

Scherk v. Alberto-Culver Co., 417 U.S. 506, 519 n.14 (1974) (internal citation omitted) (emphasis in original). In this case, Novak fails to allege any fraud specifically relating to the forum-selection clause in question. Further, there is no indication that the clause was added to the DNTA in bad faith, or by coercion. Plaintiff therefore has not established grounds for rejecting the clause on the basis of fraud.

C. Unconscionability

Plaintiff also argues that the DNTA is unconscionable under New York law because he was never provided with an opportunity to view the contract or to consent to its terms. According to Plaintiff, he was denied any "meaningful choice" with regard to the selection of Tucows as a registrar, thus demonstrating the contract's unconscionability. (Pl.'s Br., at 40.) However, Plaintiff does not actually identify any particular terms of the contract that are substantively unconscionable; instead, he merely reiterates his assertion that he was never given an opportunity to read the contract, a factor that speaks to the agreement's *procedural* unconscionability.

"Procedural unconscionability involves 'the lack of meaningful choice,' which considers all the circumstances surrounding the contract, including whether each party had a reasonable opportunity to understand the terms of the contract, whether deceptive tactics were employed, the use of fine print, and disparities in education, experience and bargaining power." *Gill v. World Inspection Network Int'l, Inc.*, No. 06-CV-3187 (JFB) (CLO), 2006 U.S. Dist. LEXIS 52426, at *19 (E.D.N.Y. Jul. 31, 2006) (citing *Nelson v. McGoldrick*, 896 P.2d 1258, 1262 (Wash. 1995), and *Gillman v. Chase Manhattan Bank, N.A.*, 534 N.E.2d 824, 828 (N.Y. 1988)). While Plaintiff maintains that he neither read nor assented to any agreement with Tucows, this Court has found that Plaintiff did, in fact, "click-through" his assent to the DNTA. As a result, even if Plaintiff failed to read the terms of the contract, he is nevertheless bound by the forum-selection clause. "[I]t is a fundamental principle of contract law that a person who signs a contract is presumed to know its terms and consents to be bound by them." *Paper Express, Ltd. v. Pfankuch Maschinen GMBH*, 972 F.2d 753, 757 (7th Cir. 1992) (enforcing forum-selection clause where plaintiff had not read the clause prior to signing the contract) (citing 3 Arthur L. Corbin, *Corbin on Contracts* 607 (1989), and 13 Samuel Williston, *Williston on Contracts* 1577 (1988)); see also *Ainsley Skin Care of N.Y., Inc. v. Elizabeth Grady Face First, Inc.*, No. 97-CV-6716 (LAP) (AJP), 1997 U.S. Dist. LEXIS 19102, at *11 (S.D.N.Y. Dec. 2, 1997) ("[A] businessman acting in a commercial context, is held to have understood the consequences of his having signed [contracts], which designate [a particular forum] as the appropriate forum for any action arising thereunder. If [the complaining party] did not read them or hire counsel to do so, he is the victim of his own lack of diligence, not [the opposing party's] misconduct.") (quoting

Elite Parfums, Ltd. v. Rivera, 872 F. Supp. 1269, 1273 (S.D.N.Y. 1995) (internal citation and additional citations omitted)); *Weingrad v. Telepathy, Inc.*, No. 05-CV-2024 (MBM), 2005 U.S. Dist. LEXIS 26952, at *11 (S.D.N.Y. Nov. 7, 2005) ("He is bound by the terms of the forum selection clause even if he did not take the time to read it because 'a signatory to a contract is presumed to have read, understood and agreed to be bound by all terms, including the forum selection clauses, in the documents he or she signed.'") (quoting *Sun Forest Corp. v. Shvili*, 152 F. Supp. 2d 367, 382 (S.D.N.Y. 2001) (internal citation omitted)).

In addition, although the DNTA is a standard form contract offered to all of Tucows' domain name transfer customers, the forum-selection clause may not be defeated for procedural unconscionability on this basis. The Supreme Court has recognized that where a company conducts business in several states, as in the case of Tucows, a nonnegotiated forum-selection clause may be enforced even where it was not the subject of bargaining.[10] *Carnival Cruise Lines, Inc.*, 499 U.S. at 593- 595; *Rosenfeld v. Port Auth. of N.Y. and N.J.*, 108 F. Supp. 2d 156, 164 (E.D.N.Y. 2000) (noting that an agreement "cannot be considered procedurally unconscionable, or a contract of adhesion, simply because it is a form contract").

Finally, the Court cannot find that Novak was so vulnerable or that there was such unequal bargaining power that the contract was procedurally unconscionable, given (1) plaintiff's sophistication in attempting to choose a registrar that would allow him to respond more easily to pending litigation (Am. Compl. ¶ 39), (2) his extensive internet and business experience as owner of an extremely popular web company (Am. Compl. ¶ 134), and (3) plaintiff's broad computer expertise, acquired over the past thirty years (Novak Decl. ¶ 8).

Therefore, this Court cannot find that the forum selection clause at issue should not be enforced on the basis that Tucows' DNTA was either substantively or procedurally unconscionable.

---

[10]Novak contends that Tucows should be subject to jurisdiction before this Court because in an unrelated case, *Bennett v. America Online, Inc.*, No. 06-CV-13221, 2007 WL 241318 (E.D. Mich. Jan. 23, 2007), "Tucows had acquiesed to the jurisdiction of the United States Courts not with standing their forum selection clause." (Pl.'s Supp. Br., at 2.) In *Bennett*, which involved a copyright dispute against Defendants America Online, Inc. ("AOL") and Tucows, the Eastern District of Michigan considered whether to transfer the Plaintiff's case to Virginia pursuant to 28 U.S.C. § 1404(a), based upon AOL's forum-selection clause. *Bennett*, 2007 WL 241318, at *1. While not subject to any agreement with the Plaintiff in that case, Tucows nevertheless consented to personal jurisdiction in Virginia. *Id.* at *6. However, *Bennett* has absolutely no bearing on the instant case, in which the Plaintiff directly entered into a DNTA with Tucows, the Plaintiff is clearly subject to the forum-selection clause contained within the agreement, and neither defendant has consented to jurisdiction before this Court.

D. Public Policy

In *The Bremen*, the Supreme Court stated that forum selection clauses should not be enforced if "enforcement would contravene a strong public policy of the forum in which suit is brought." 407 U.S. at 18 (citing *Boyd v. Grand Trunk W.R. Co.*, 338 U.S. 263 (1949)). Plaintiff alleges that enforcement of the forum selection clause in Tucows' DNTA counters New York state's public policy as expressed in New York General Business Law § 349. Section 349 allows the state attorney general to bring civil actions on behalf of the people of New York state in order to enjoin unlawful deceptive acts or practices. N.Y. Gen. Bus. Law § 349. In addition, subsection (h) of the statute provides for an individual cause of action on the basis of such acts or practices. N.Y. Gen. Bus. Law § 349(h). Plaintiff curiously relies upon this Court's decision in *Gill v. World Inspection Network Int'l, Inc.*, which directly counters his position, in support of the proposition that litigating his case in a foreign forum would contravene Section 349. In *Gill*, the Plaintiff argued that enforcement of an arbitral forum selection clause against franchisees contravened sections of the New York General Business Law that protect franchisees from fraudulent and unlawful practices by franchisors. 2006 U.S. Dist. LEXIS 52426, at *34-36. This Court held that "New York public policy does not operate to undermine the presumptive validity of the arbitral forum selection clause under the preemptive effect of the [Federal Arbitration Act]." *Id.* at *35. Likewise, there is nothing in Section 349 that undermines the presumptive validity of forum selection clauses as articulated by the Supreme Court and by this Circuit in *The Bremen, Shute,* and *Roby. See Person*, 456 F. Supp. 2d at 497 ("It is clear, from Second Circuit precedent, however, that far from being against public policy in this Court's jurisdiction, forum selection clauses are considered 'presumptively valid.'") (citing *Roby*, 996 F.3d at 1363). In fact, New York courts have consistently upheld forum selection clauses in which New York residents would be forced to litigate in another state or country on the basis that such clauses prevent confusion and costly litigation regarding where suits relating to the contract should be brought and defended, and reduce costs to the consumer by limiting the number of fora in which a case may be brought. See, e.g., *Effron*, 67 F.3d at 10 (finding it reasonable for cruise line to select a single venue for passenger suits) (quoting *Shute*, 499 U.S. at 593-94); *Hellex Car Rental Sys., Inc. v. Dollar Sys., Inc.*, No. 04-CV-5580, 2005 U.S. Dist. LEXIS 33858, at *16 (E.D.N.Y. Nov. 9, 2005) ("It is entirely reasonable for [defendant] to require that its franchisees agree to litigate disputes arising from the franchise relationship in Oklahoma, where its corporate headquarters are housed, rather than be required to defend suits in every state where its franchises may be located.") (citing *Carnival Cruise Lines, Inc.*, 499 U.S. at 593). As Plaintiff is unable to show that enforcement of the forum selection clause in question would contravene New York public policy, the Court rejects his contention.

E. Applicability of Forum-Selection Clause to Nitin

Novak also contends that only his claims against Tucows are subject to dismissal pursuant to the forum-selection clause, and thus the case would be severed upon granting a motion to dismiss on this basis. However, this Court has discretion to dismiss the entire lawsuit for improper venue. While it serves only as persuasive authority, this Court finds it notable that the "Third, Seventh and Ninth Circuits have determined that, in certain circumstances, a non-signatory to a contract may be bound by a forum-selection clause found therein." *Hay Acquisition Co., I, Inc. v. Schneider*, No. 04-CV-1236, 2005 U.S. Dist. LEXIS 24490, at *25 (E.D. Pa. Apr. 29, 2005) (collecting cases). Further, at least two courts within this Circuit have held that "[i]t is well established that a 'range of transaction participants, parties and non-parties, should benefit from and be subject to forum selection clauses.'" *Weingrad*, 2005 U.S. Dist. LEXIS 26952, at *15-16 (quoting *Int'l Private Satellite Partners, L.P. v. Lucky Cat Ltd.*, 975 F. Supp. 483, 485-86 (W.D.N.Y. 1997) (internal citation omitted)). A non-party to an agreement may be bound by a forum selection clause where the party is "'closely related' to the dispute such that it becomes 'forseeable' that it will be bound." *Hugel v. Corp. of Lloyd's*, 999 F.2d 206, 209 (7th Cir. 1993) (citing *Manetti-Farrow, Inc. v. Gucci Am., Inc.*, 858 F.2d 509, 514 n.5 (9th Cir. 1988), and *Coastal Steel Corp. v. Tilghman Wheelabrator, Ltd.*, 709 F.2d 190, 203 (3d Cir. 1983)); see also *Weingrad*, 2005 U.S. Dist. LEXIS 26952, at *15-16 ("A non-party is 'closely related' to a dispute if its interests are 'completely derivative' of and 'directly related to, if not predicated upon' the signatory party's interests or conduct.") (quoting *Lipcon v. Underwriters at Lloyd's*, 148 F.3d 1285, 1299 (11th Cir. 1998) (internal citation omitted)). In this instance, plaintiff's claims against Nitin are nearly identical to those against Tucows. Furthermore, all of plaintiff's claims arise out of Novak's single transfer of his domain name, which was effected through both defendants in tandem. It was certainly foreseeable that any claims Novak might raise against Nitin in relation to the transfer could be subject to the terms contained in his agreement with Tucows.[11] Novak's attempt to evade the effect of the

---

[11] Moreover, as a third-party beneficiary of the DNTA, Nitin is, "by definition," "closely related" to the dispute at issue and "forseeably" bound by the forum-selection clause. *Hugel*, 999 F.2d at 209-10 n.7 ("While it may be true that third-party beneficiaries of a contract would, by definition, satisfy the 'closely related' and 'foreseeability' requirements, see e.g., *Coastal Steel*, 709 F.2d at 203

forum-selection clause merely by joining Nitin, a non-signatory to the DNTA, therefore fails. See, e.g., *Hodgson v. Gilmartin*, No. 06- CV-1944, 2006 U.S. Dist. LEXIS 73063, at *45 n.14 (E.D. Pa. Sept. 18, 2006) ("Plaintiff should . . . be prevented from avoiding the impact of a valid forum selection clause by suing [parties] who were not signatories to the Customer Agreement."); *Am. Patriot Ins. Agency, Inc. v. Mutual Risk Mgt., Ltd.*, 248 F. Supp. 2d 779, 785 (N.D.Ill. 2003) ("[W]e also reject Plaintiffs' argument that enforcement of the forum selection clause is precluded by the fact that certain Defendants are not parties to the Agreement. Plaintiffs cannot escape their contractual obligations simply by joining parties who did not sign the contract and then claiming that the forum selection clause does not apply.") (citations omitted), *rev'd on other grounds*, 364 F.3d 884, 889 (7th Cir. 2004).

In summary, the Court finds that plaintiff has not demonstrated that enforcement of the forum-selection clause in this case would be unjust or unreasonable. Therefore, the Court finds that plaintiff has failed to demonstrate venue by a preponderance of the evidence, and grants defendants' motion to dismiss for improper venue.[12]

VI. Lanham Act Claims and Pendent State Claims

Defendants also contend that plaintiff's Lanham Act claims of trademark infringement, trademark dilution and cybersquatting are fatally defective since it cannot be shown that Nitin or Tucows used Novak's alleged trademark, "petswarehouse," "in commerce." According to defendants, because use of "petswarehouse" "in commerce" is a required element of any potential claim that Novak could assert under the Lanham Act, such claims must be dismissed pursuant to Fed. R. Civ. P. 12(b)(6). (Nitin's Br., at 1-4 (citing *Savin Corp. v. Savin Group*, 391 F.3d 439 (2d Cir. 2004) (requiring "commercial use of the mark in commerce" to establish a trademark dilution claim)); Tucows' Br., at 11-15 (citing *Bosley Medical Institute v. Kremer*, 403 F.3d 672, 678-79 (9th Cir. 2005) (use of domain name incorporating plaintiff's mark in Web site critical of plaintiff does not constitute use in commerce), *Lockheed Martin Corp. v. Network Solutions, Inc.*, 194 F.3d 980, 984-85 (9th Cir. 1999) (registrar not liable for con-

---

(refusing to absolve a third-party beneficiary from the strictures of a forum selection clause which was foreseeable); *Clinton v. Janger*, 583 F. Supp. 284, 290 (N.D. Ill. 1984), a third-party beneficiary status is not required."); see also Defs.' Ex. T1, at ¶ 1 ("'Services' refers to the domain name registration provided by us as offered through . . . the Registration Service Provider [Reseller]"); Defs' Ex. T1, at ¶ 3 ("As consideration for the Services, you agree to pay the RSP the applicable service(s) fees.").

[12] Even if the burden to prove venue rested with defendants, rather than plaintiff, that burden would be easily met given the record in this case.

tributory infringement by issuing registration of potentially infringing domain names to third parties), and 15 U.S.C. § 1125(d) (requiring "bad faith intent to profit" from a mark to establish civil liability for cybersquatting under the Lanham Act).) Having concluded that venue is improper before this Court, the Court need not address Defendants' motion to dismiss the Lanham Act claims or pendent state claims for failure to state a cause of action.

VII. Conclusion

For the foregoing reasons, it is hereby ordered that Plaintiff's motion to strike is GRANTED in part and DENIED in part. Defendant Tucows' motion to strike is GRANTED.

It is further ordered that both defendants' motions to dismiss on the basis of improper venue are GRANTED in their entirety.

SO ORDERED.

_____

JOSEPH F. BIANCO
United States District Judge

Dated: March 26, 2007
Central Islip, NY

* * *

Plaintiff appears *pro se*. Defendant Tucows is represented by Glenn Matthew Mitchell, Esq., Schwimmer Mitchell Law Firm, 40 Radio Circle, Suite 7, Mount Kisco, New York, 10549. Defendant Nitin is represented by Gary Adelman, Esq., Adelman & Lavania, LLC, 90 John Street, Suite 304, New York, New York 10038.

Appendix J

THE PHILADELPHIA BAR ASSOCIATION
PROFESSIONAL GUIDANCE COMMITTEE
Opinion 2009-02 (March 2009)

The inquirer deposed an 18-year-old woman (the "witness"). The witness is not a party to the litigation, nor is she represented. Her testimony is helpful to the party adverse to the inquirer's client.

During the course of the deposition, the witness revealed that she has "Facebook" and "Myspace" accounts. Having such accounts permits a user like the witness to create personal "pages" on which he or she posts information on any topic, sometimes including highly personal information. Access to the pages of the user is limited to persons who obtain the user's permission, which permission is obtained after the user is approached online by the person seeking access. The user can grant access to his or her page with almost no information about the person seeking access, or can ask for detailed information about the person seeking access before deciding whether to allow access.

The inquirer believes that the pages maintained by the witness may contain information relevant to the matter in which the witness was deposed, and that could be used to impeach the witness's testimony should she testify at trial. The inquirer did not ask the witness to reveal the contents of her pages, either by permitting access to them on line or otherwise. He has, however, either himself or through agents, visited Facebook and Myspace and attempted to access both accounts. When that was done, it was found that access to the pages can be obtained only by the witness's permission, as discussed in detail above.

The inquirer states that based on what he saw in trying to access the pages, he has determined that the witness tends to allow access to anyone who asks (although it is not clear how he could know that), and states that he does not know if the witness would allow access to him if he asked her directly to do so.

The inquirer proposes to ask a third person, someone whose name the witness will not recognize, to go to the Facebook and Myspace Web sites, contact the witness and seek to "friend" her, to obtain access to the information on the pages. The third person would state only truthful information, for example, his or her true name, but would not reveal that he or she is affiliated with the lawyer or the true purpose for which he or she is seeking access, namely, to provide the information posted on the pages to a lawyer for possible use antagonistic to the witness. If the witness allows access, the third person would then provide the information posted on the pages to the inquirer who would evaluate it for possible use in the litigation.

The inquirer asks the Committee's view as to whether the proposed course of conduct is permissible under the Rules of Professional Conduct, and whether he may use the information obtained from the pages if access is allowed.

Several Pennsylvania Rules of Professional Conduct (the "Rules") are implicated in this inquiry.

Rule 5.3. **Responsibilities Regarding Nonlawyer Assistants** provides in part that,

With respect to a non-lawyer employed or retained by or associated with a lawyer: . . .

(c) a lawyer shall be responsible for conduct of such a person that would be a violation of the Rules of Professional Conduct if engaged in by a lawyer if:
(1) the lawyer orders or, with the knowledge of the specific conduct, ratifies the conduct involved; . . .

Since the proposed course of conduct involves a third person, the first issue that must be addressed is the degree to which the lawyer is responsible under the Rules for the conduct of that third person. The fact that the actual interaction with the witness would be undertaken by a third party who, the committee assumes, is not a lawyer does not insulate the inquirer from ethical responsibility for the conduct.

The Committee cannot say that the lawyer is literally "ordering" the conduct that would be done by the third person. That might depend on whether the inquirer's relationship with the third person is such that he might require such conduct. But the inquirer plainly is procuring the conduct, and, if it were undertaken, would be ratifying it with full knowledge of its propriety or lack thereof, as evidenced by the fact that he wisely is seeking guidance from this Committee. Therefore, he is responsible for the conduct under the Rules even if he is not himself engaging in the actual conduct that may violate a rule. (Of course, if the third party is also a lawyer in the inquirer's firm, then that lawyer's conduct would itself be subject to the Rules, and the inquirer would also be responsible for the third party's conduct under Rule 5.1, dealing with Responsibilities of Partners, Managers and Supervisory Lawyers.)

Rule 8.4. **Misconduct** provides in part that,

It is professional misconduct for a lawyer to:

(a) violate or attempt to violate the Rules of Professional Conduct, knowingly assist or induce another to do so, or do so through the acts of another; . . .

(c) engage in conduct involving dishonesty, fraud, deceit or misrepresentation; . . .

Turning to the ethical substance of the inquiry, the Committee believes that the proposed course of conduct contemplated by the inquirer would violate Rule 8.4(c) because the planned communication by the third party with the witness is deceptive. It omits a highly material fact, namely, that the third party who asks to be allowed access to the witness's pages is doing so only because he or she is intent on obtaining information and sharing it with a lawyer for use in a lawsuit to impeach the testimony of the witness. The omission would purposefully conceal that fact from the witness for the purpose of inducing the witness to allow access, when she may not do so if she knew the third person was associated with the inquirer and the true purpose of the access was to obtain information for the purpose of impeaching her testimony.

The fact that the inquirer asserts he does not know if the witness would permit access to him if he simply asked in forthright fashion does not remove the deception. The inquirer could test that by simply asking the witness forthrightly for access. That would not be deceptive and would of course be permissible. Plainly, the reason for not doing so is that the inquirer is not sure that she will allow access and wants to adopt an approach that will deal with her possible refusal by deceiving her from the outset. In short, in the Committee's view, the possibility that the deception might not be necessary to obtain access does not excuse it.

The possibility or even the certainty that the witness would permit access to her pages to a person not associated with the inquirer who provided no more identifying information than would be provided by the third person associated with the lawyer does not change the Committee's conclusion. Even if, by allowing virtually all would-be "friends" onto her FaceBook and MySpace pages, the witness is exposing herself to risks like that in this case, excusing the deceit on that basis would be improper. Deception is deception, regardless of the victim's wariness in her interactions on the Internet and susceptibility to being deceived. The fact that access to the pages may readily be obtained by others who either are or are not deceiving the witness, and that the witness is perhaps insufficiently wary of deceit by unknown Internet users, does not mean that deception at the direction of the inquirer is ethical.

The inquirer has suggested that his proposed conduct is similar to the common—and ethical—practice of videotaping the public conduct of a plaintiff in a personal injury case to show that he or she is capable of performing physical acts he claims his injury prevents. The Committee disagrees. In the video situation, the videographer simply follows the subject and films him as he presents himself to the public. The videographer does not have to ask to enter a private area to make the video. If he did, then similar issues would be confronted, as for example, if the videographer took a hidden camera and gained access to the inside of a house to make a video by presenting himself as a utility worker.

Rule 4.1. **Truthfulness in Statements to Others** provides in part that,

> In the course of representing a client a lawyer shall not knowingly:
>
> (a) make a false statement of material fact or law to a third person; . . .

The Committee believes that in addition to violating Rule 8.4c, the proposed conduct constitutes the making of a false statement of material fact to the witness and therefore violates Rule 4.1 as well.

Furthermore, since the violative conduct would be done through the acts of another third party, this would also be a violation of Rule 8.4a.[1]

The Committee is aware that there is controversy regarding the ethical propriety of a lawyer engaging in certain kinds of investigative conduct that might be thought to be deceitful. For example, the New York Lawyers' Association Committee on Professional Ethics, in its Formal

---

[1] The Committee also considered the possibility that the proposed conduct would violate Rule 4.3, **Dealing with Unrepresented person,** which provides in part that

(a) In dealing on behalf of a client with a person who is not represented by counsel, a lawyer shall not state or imply that the lawyer is disinterested . . .

(c) When the lawyer knows or reasonably should know that the unrepresented person misunderstands the lawyer's role in the matter the lawyer should make reasonable efforts to correct the misunderstanding.

Since the witness here is unrepresented this rule addresses the interactions between her and the inquirer. However, the Committee does not believe that this rule is implicated by this proposed course of conduct. Rule 4.3 was intended to deal with situations where the unrepresented person with whom a lawyer is dealing knows he or she is dealing with a lawyer, but is under a misapprehension as to the lawyer's role or lack of disinterestedness. In such settings, the rule obligates the lawyer to ensure that unrepresented parties are not misled on those matters. One might argue that the proposed course here would violate this rule because it is designed to induce the unrepresented person to think that the third person with whom she was dealing is not a lawyer at all (or lawyer's representative), let alone the lawyer's role or his lack of disinterestedness. However, the Committee believes that the predominating issue here is the deception discussed above, and that that issue is properly addressed under Rule 8.4.

Opinion No. 737 (May, 2007), approved the use of deception, but limited such use to investigation of civil right or intellectual property right violations where the lawyer believes a violation is taking place or is imminent, other means are not available to obtain evidence and rights of third parties are not violated.

Elsewhere, some states have seemingly endorsed the absolute reach of Rule 8.4. In *People v. Pautler*, 47 P. 3d 1175 (Colo. 2002), for example, the Colorado Supreme Court held that no deception whatsoever is allowed, saying,

> Even noble motive does not warrant departure from the rules of Professional Conduct. . . . We reaffirm that members of our profession must adhere to the highest moral and ethical standards. Those standards apply regardless of motive. Purposeful deception by an attorney licensed in our state is intolerable, even when undertaken as a part of attempting to secure the surrender of a murder suspect. . . . Until a sufficiently compelling scenario presents itself and convinces us our interpretation of Colo. RPC 8.4(c) is too rigid, we stand resolute against any suggestion that licensed attorneys in our state may deceive or lie or misrepresent, regardless of their reasons for doing so.

The opinion can be found at **http://www.cobar.org/opinions/opinion .cfm?opinionid=627&courtid=2**

The Oregon Supreme Court in *In Re Gatti*, 8 P3d 966 (Ore 2000), ruled that no deception at all is permissible, by a private or a government lawyer, even rejecting proposed carve-outs for government or civil rights investigations, stating,

> The Bar contends that whether there is or ought to be a prosecutorial or some other exception to the disciplinary rules is not an issue in this case. Technically, the Bar is correct. However, the issue lies at the heart of this case, and to ignore it here would be to leave unresolved a matter that is vexing to the Bar, government lawyers, and lawyers in the private practice of law. A clear answer from this court regarding exceptions to the disciplinary rules is in order.
>
> As members of the Bar ourselves—some of whom have prior experience as government lawyers and some of whom have prior experience in private practice—this court is aware that there are circumstances in which misrepresentations, often in the form of false statements of fact by those who investigate violations of the law, are useful means for uncovering unlawful and unfair practices, and that lawyers in both the public and private sectors have relied on such tactics. However, . . . [f]aithful adherence to the wording of [the analog of Pennsylvania's Rule 8.4], and this court's case law does not permit recognition of an exception for any lawyer to engage in dishonesty, fraud, deceit, misrepresentation, or false statements. In our view, this court should not create an exception to the rules by judicial decree.

The opinion can be found at **http://www.publications.ojd.state.or.us/ S45801.htm**

Following the *Gatti* ruling, Oregon's Rule 8.4 was changed. It now provides:

(a) It is professional misconduct for a lawyer to: . . . (3) engage in conduct involving dishonesty, fraud, deceit or misrepresentation that reflects adversely on the lawyer's fitness to practice law.

(b) Notwithstanding paragraphs (a)(1), (3) and (4) and Rule 3.3(a)(1), it shall not be professional misconduct for a lawyer to advise clients or others about or to supervise lawful covert activity in the investigation of violations of civil or criminal law or constitutional rights, provided the lawyer's conduct is otherwise in compliance with these Rules of Professional Conduct. "Covert activity," as used in this rule, means an effort to obtain information on unlawful activity through the use of misrepresentations or other subterfuge. "Covert activity" may be commenced by a lawyer or involve a lawyer as an advisor or supervisor only when the lawyer in good faith believes there is a reasonable possibility that unlawful activity has taken place, is taking place or will take place in the foreseeable future.

Iowa has retained the old Rule 8.4, but adopted a comment interpreting the Rule to permit the kind of exception allowed by Oregon.

The Committee also refers the reader to two law review articles collecting other authorities on the issue. See *Deception in Undercover Investigations: Conduct Based v. Status Based Ethical Analysis*, 32 Seattle Univ. L. Rev.123 (2008), and *Ethical Responsibilities of Lawyers for Deception by Undercover Investigators and Discrimination Testers: An Analysis of the Provisions Prohibiting Misrepresentation under Model Rules of Professional Conduct*, 8 Georgetown Journal of Legal Ethics 791 (Summer 1995).

Finally, the inquirer also requested the Committee's opinion as to whether or not, if he obtained the information in the manner described, he could use it in the litigation. The Committee believes that issue is beyond the scope of its charge. If the inquirer disregards the views of the Committee and obtains the information, or if he obtains it in any other fashion, the question of whether or not the evidence would be usable either by him or by subsequent counsel in the case is a matter of substantive and evidentiary law to be addressed by the court.

CAVEAT: The foregoing opinion is advisory only and is based upon the facts set forth above. The opinion is not binding upon the Disciplinary Board of the Supreme Court of Pennsylvania or any other Court. It carries only such weight as an appropriate reviewing authority may choose to give it.

Appendix K

MERLIN INFORMATION SERVICES SERVICE AGREEMENT

IMPORTANT CHECKLIST

The items listed below must be submitted along with Exhibit A. Omitting any of these documents may significantly delay or prevent approval of your application. The approval process takes approximately 24-48 hours.

- ❏ Copy of your Business Letterhead
- ❏ Copy of your Business Card
- ❏ Copy of your city, county, or other municipal Business License (if you are required to have one)
- ❏ Copy of your Professional License (if you are required to have one)
- ❏ Copy of your Wallet ID (if you are required to have one)
- ❏ Copy of original Corporation or other entity Filing (if applicable)
- ❏ Copy of original Fictitious Business Name or Assumed Name Filing (if applicable)
- ❏ Copy of your Sales Tax Permit (if you are required to have one)
- ❏ Copy of your Drivers' License
- ❏ Copy of a recent telephone bill. (Please be sure your current telephone number and address is printed on the bill.)
- ❏ Copy of a blank contract/agreement between your business and your client that clearly outlines the services you perform.

Please remember to . . .

- ❏ Supply your Federal Tax ID/SSN.
- ❏ Checkmark all boxes that apply to you under Gramm Leach Bliley and/or IRSG Acceptable Uses.
- ❏ Complete all required fields on the application.

MERLIN INFORMATION SERVICES SERVICE AGREEMENT

PLEASE PRINT

PART 1

BUSINESS INFORMATION	ACCOUNT CONTACT INFORMATION
Name	Name
Physical Address	Title
City State Zip	Address (if different)
❑ Commercial ❑ Residential	City (if different) State Zip
Mailing Address	Telephone (if different) Ext
City State Zip	Fax
Telephone	E-mail
Company Web Address	Social Security Number
Federal Tax ID	

Describe your type of business: _____

Please provide the following user information:

User Name: _____ Unique User I.D. _____ User E-mail: _____

User Name: _____ Unique User I.D. _____ User E-mail: _____

User Name: _____ Unique User I.D. _____ User E-mail: _____

User Name: _____ Unique User I.D. _____ User E-mail: _____

User Name: _____ Unique User I.D. _____ User E-mail: _____

Please attach a separate page for additional users.

The information submitted in this Agreement will be used to determine eligibility for accessing information provided by Merlin Information Services (Merlin). The Customer hereby authorizes Merlin to independently verify the information provided herein.

PART 2
TERMS AND CONDITIONS

This Agreement is entered into between Merlin Data Publishing Corporation, doing business as Merlin Information Services (Merlin), a corporation with an address of 215 South Complex Drive, Kalispell, MT 59901, and the entity set forth in Part 1 of this agreement (Customer). The parties agree as follows:

1. **SERVICE**. Merlin provides nationwide public record information and related services (Services) using its proprietary databases and information obtained from third parties (Third Parties). Customer hereby sub-

scribes to the use of Merlin's public record database for use solely as a factor in making its business decisions. Customer agrees not to use such information for any purpose for which a credit report may be obtained, such as credit eligibility, or for any other improper purpose. Customer further agrees to pay to Merlin the applicable published rates and charges, as may be revised from time to time, and to abide by the terms and conditions set forth herein. If Customer applies for access to nonpublic information, the attached Exhibit A must be signed. All searches into Merlin's databases must be entered manually.

Merlin reserves the right to periodically verify that Customer's request(s) for nonpublic information is in accordance with this Agreement and applicable law. Customer agrees to cooperate with Merlin in obtaining such verification. Failure of Customer to cooperate with Merlin may result in termination of this Agreement or restriction of access.

2. **PERFORMANCE**. Merlin will use reasonable efforts to provide the Merlin Services requested by Customer and to compile information gathered from selected public records and other sources used in the provision of the Merlin Services; provided, however, that Customer accepts all information "**AS IS**." Customer acknowledges and agrees that Merlin obtains its data from third-party sources, whose data may or may not be completely thorough and accurate, and that Customer shall not rely on Merlin for the accuracy or completeness of information supplied in using Merlin Services. Merlin shall not be responsible for any consequential or other damages arising out of the use of the Services. Merlin does not warrant that the Services will be uninterrupted or error free.

3. **PRICING**. For each response to a request for information, Customer agrees to pay to Merlin the applicable charge then prevailing for the information requested. Merlin reserves the right to change prices, add or delete services, and change the characteristics of any service at any time and without notice. Customer shall pay to Merlin according to prices as updated from time-to-time through online announcements, customer bulletins, and/or published price schedules. Merlin is not responsible for ensuring delivery to Customer of such updates, changes, additions or deletions to any of its prices, which may occur, from time-to-time, and it is Customer's responsibility to check Merlin's Web site (**www.merlindata.com**) and/or publications for such notifications. All current and future Merlin pricing documents are deemed incorporated herein by reference.

4. **INTELLECTUAL PROPERTY**. Customer agrees not to reproduce, retransmit, republish, or otherwise transfer for any commercial or other purpose any information that Customer receives from Merlin or Merlin's Services except in the ordinary and customary course of Customer's bona fide business. Under no circumstances is Customer to resell Merlin's data or Services through a Web site or otherwise without express written approval from Merlin. Customer acknowledges that Merlin (and/or Merlin's third party data providers) shall retain all right, title, and interest in and to the data and information provided by the Merlin Services under applicable contractual, copyright, and related laws, and Customer shall use such materials consistent with Merlin's interests and notify Merlin of any threatened or actual infringement of Merlin's rights. Customer further acknowledges and agrees that it shall acquire no right, title, or interest under applicable copyright or other laws in the databases, services and materials provided or accessed under this agreement.

5. **PAYMENT**. Customer shall pay Merlin for all charges incurred for the use of the Merlin Services on a Prepayment Basis or Monthly Billing Basis. Customer shall be responsible for payment for all Services obtained using Customer's User ID(s), whether or not said User ID is used by Customer or a third party, whether with or without Customer's consent. Merlin reserves the right to terminate this Agreement and the right of Customer to use any information provided hereunder without prior notice to Customer upon any nonpayment of fees by the due date.

   A. **PREPAYMENT BASIS**. A minimum deposit of $250 is required to open an account. Customer's account will be debited after each use of the Service. Customer agrees to prepay for the Service by cash, check, or credit card. Merlin will not debit the Customer's credit card unless authorized by Customer and will only debit the credit card for the amount authorized. **There is no refund for unused credits**.

   B. **MONTHLY BILLING BASIS**. Alternatively, customers with established credit with Merlin and who spend a minimum of $200 per month may qualify for a monthly statement of their account. The minimum invoice amount is $200, even when the Customer's actual monthly search fees fall below $200. If customer does not have established credit with Merlin, an approved credit application is required for this payment option.

6. **MONTHLY SERVICE FEE**. A $20.00 Service Fee will be assessed each month. This fee will be waived for any month in which the Customer's purchases exceed $35.00.

7. **PAYMENT OF MONTHLY SERVICE FEE**. Payment of the monthly Service Fee will be processed on the first day of the following month by an automatic charge to Customer's credit card on file designated for this purpose. If for any reason the Customer's credit card transaction fails, the $20.00 Service Fee will be deducted from Customer's outstanding web balance. If Customer's web balance is less than $20.00, the remaining balance will be applied to the Service Fee and the Customer's account will be disabled.

8. **ACCOUNTS DISABLED FOR INACTIVITY**. Merlin will disable Customer's account if Customer fails to use Merlin's services for a period of 180 consecutive days. If a Customer's account is disabled for inactivity and not reactivated within 60 days of being disabled, Merlin will close the Customer's account. Any remaining Customer web balance is nonrefundable.

9. **DISABLED ACCOUNTS & REACTIVATION FEE**. If Merlin disables a Customer's account, Customer is exempt from the monthly Service Fee until Customer's account is reactivated. Reactivation of a disabled account is subject to Merlin's approval. There is a $20.00 Reactivation Fee to reactivate a disabled account.

10. **TERM OF AGREEMENT**. This Agreement is for services rendered and shall be in full force and effect during such periods of time in which Merlin is providing Services for Customer.

11. **GOVERNING LAW**. The interpretation and enforcement of this Agreement, and all issues relating thereto, including the Services contemplated hereby, shall be governed by and construed in accordance with the laws of the State of Montana, without effect to conflict of law principles. Customer consents to venue and jurisdiction in the courts of Flathead County, Montana.

12. **ASSIGNMENT**. The rights granted to Customer pursuant to this Agreement to use the Merlin Services may not be assigned by Customer, in whole or in part, without the prior written consent of Merlin.

13. **WARRANTIES/LIMITATION OF LIABILITY**. Neither Merlin nor any third party data provider (for purposes of indemnification, warranties, and limitations of liability only, as set forth in this Section and Section 11, Merlin and its data providers are hereby collectively referred to as "Merlin") shall be liable to Customer (or any person claiming through Customer) for any loss or injury arising out of or caused in whole or in part by Merlin's acts, omissions or otherwise, except as expressly set forth in this Section. Merlin makes no warranty or representation of any kind; and any warranty, express or implied, is excluded and disclaimed, including the implied warranties of merchantability and of fitness for a particular purpose.

Without limiting the forgoing, and as part of the consideration for this Agreement, Customer expressly waives any claim against Merlin (including any third party data provider) for any damage or loss caused in whole or in part by Merlin's acts or omissions in procuring, compiling, interpreting, communicating or delivering the Services or the data associated therewith.

It is agreed that Merlin's liability (including the liability of any third party data provider) and Customer's sole remedy, whether in contract, under any warranty, in tort (including negligence), in strict liability or otherwise, shall not exceed the return of the charges paid by Customer, and under no circumstances shall Merlin (or any third party data provider) be liable for any special, incidental, punitive or consequential damages, including, but not limited to, personal injury, property damage, damage to or loss of equipment, lost profits or revenue, costs of obtaining replacement services and other additional expenses, even if Merlin has been advised of the possibility of such damages. The price stated for the Services is a consideration in limiting Merlin's liability and Customer's remedy.

Each Party hereto shall indemnify, defend, and hold harmless the other Party, its directors, officers, employees and agents with respect to any claim, demand, cause of action, debt or liability, including reasonable attorneys' fees, to the extent that it is based upon a claim that, if true, would constitute a breach of any of the indemnifying Party's representations, warranties, or agreements hereunder. In claiming any indemnification hereunder, the Party claiming indemnification (the "Claimant") shall provide the other Party with written notice of any claim which the Claimant believes falls within the scope of this section within ten (10) days after it becomes known to such party, provided, however, that the failure to give such notice shall not relieve the indemnifying party of its obligations to indemnify. The Claimant may, at its own expense, assist in the defense if it so chooses, provided that the other party shall control such defense and all negotiations relative to the settlement of any such claim and further provided that any settlement intended to bind the Claimant shall not be final without the Claimant's written consent.

14. **SURVIVAL OF AGREEMENT**. Provisions hereof related to release of claims, indemnification, use of information and data, payment for Merlin Services and disclaimer of warranties shall survive any termination of this Agreement.

15. **ATTORNEY FEES**. The prevailing party in any action, claim, or lawsuit brought pursuant to this Agreement or to interpret or enforce it is

entitled to payment of all attorney fees and costs expended by such prevailing party in association with such action, claim, or lawsuit.

16. **CUSTOMER CHANGE**. Customer shall notify Merlin immediately of any changes to the information it provided in connection with Merlin's Service Agreement, including all Exhibits and/or Addendums. Merlin reserves the right to terminate Customer's access to the Service or terminate this Agreement without further notice upon receipt of any notice of change which, in its sole discretion, would prevent or hinder Customer in complying with its obligations under this Agreement. Merlin reserves the right to require proof or additional information concerning any such change.

17. **RELATIONSHIP OF PARTIES**. Customer shall at no time represent that it is an authorized agent or representative of Merlin.

18. **CHANGE IN AGREEMENT**. By receipt of the Merlin Services, Customer agrees to, and shall comply with, such revised and/or additional terms, as Merlin shall make from time-to-time. Merlin shall use reasonable efforts to provide notice by online click wrap amendments, facsimile, mail, or other method.

19. **ORGANIZATION, GOOD STANDING AND AUTHORITY OF CUSTOMER**. The Customer represents and warrants the following:

⇨ The Customer is a [Type of Entity, as set forth on Service Agreement], duly organized, existing and in good standing under the laws of the State of _____. The Customer has the requisite power and authority to enter into, and to satisfy all of its obligations under, this Agreement and any related agreements. This Agreement and the transactions contemplated hereby have been duly authorized and approved by the appropriate officers and/or other personnel of Customer, and no further action or proceeding on the part of Customer is necessary or appropriate with respect to the execution by the Customer of this Agreement or any related agreements, or the consummation by the Customer of the transactions contemplated hereby or thereby.

PART 3
AUTHORIZATION AND ACCEPTANCE OF TERMS

I HEREBY CERTIFY that I am authorized to execute this Merlin Service Agreement on behalf of the Customer listed above and that the statements I have provided in this Service Agreement are true and correct. Further, I hereby certify that Customer agrees to the terms and conditions set forth in this Service Agreement.

CUSTOMER
Signature _____
Print Name _____
Title _____
Dated _____

MERLIN
Signature _____
Print Name _____
Title _____
Dated _____

**Please fax completed Agreement to
Merlin Information Services at 406-755-8568 or 406-755-8579**

**Exhibit A
Certification of Uses for Access to NonPublic Information**

The following must accompany this application.
- A copy of your letterhead
- Your business card
- A copy of your current Business License (if you are required to have one)
- A copy of your Professional License (if you are a licensed professional)
- A copy of your wallet ID (if you are required to have one)
- Proof of corporate filing (if applicable)
- Proof of a Fictitious Business Name or Assumed Business Name filing (if applicable)
- A copy of your Sales Tax Permit (if you are required to have one)
- A copy of your drivers license
- A copy of your recent phone bill. Please be sure your current phone number and address is printed on the bill.
- A copy of a blank contract/agreement between your business and your client that clearly outlines the services you perform.

(Check all uses that apply)
Gramm Leach Bliley (GLB) Acceptable Uses
❑ Witness & Victim Locating in a Documented Criminal or Civil Action
❑ Locating Fraud Victims in an Active Criminal or Civil Investigation
❑ Fraud Prevention

❑ Insurance Claims Investigations
❑ Required institutional risk control and/or resolving consumer disputes or inquiries. (Please describe the activities that you feel fall under this category.): _____

_____

_____

IRSG Acceptable Uses
❑ Child Support Enforcement
❑ Collections
❑ Finding Owners of Unclaimed Goods
❑ Legal Process Service
❑ Locate Alumni, Class Reunions
❑ Locate Beneficiaries and Heirs
❑ Locate Former Patients (Medical Industry Only)
❑ Locate Missing Persons
❑ People Locator Service
❑ Employment Verification
❑ Product Recalls
❑ Locating Former Employees
❑ Locating Existing Customers

While other uses for nonpublic records may be allowable under the GLB and the IRSG, the purposes for which we will allow access to these products are limited to those listed above.

I hereby certify that the above checked uses for Merlin services constitute all the purposes for which we will request nonpublic information from Merlin. In signing this certification, I agree to inform Merlin in writing, *in advance,* should my company require nonpublic information for any reason other than those indicated above.

RESTRICTED USES
The following is a list of unacceptable uses for our nonpublic services, products or information:
1. May NOT be used to locate suspects in a criminal or civil lawsuit to develop a news story.
2. May NOT be used to track down victims of fraud, their family members or friends to develop a news story.
3. May NOT be used to locate lost loves, friends, family members or for personal reasons (e.g., dating, etc.).
4. May NOT be used for purposes that may cause physical or emotional harm to the subject of the report (e.g., stalking, harassing, etc.).

5. May NOT be used to search for individuals involved in an adoption (children, parents, siblings, etc.).
6. May NOT be used to locate personal information on well known/ high profile celebrities, government officials, etc.
7. May NOT be used in connection with credit repair services, to locate previous debtors or to assist in the determination of whether or not to file a personal lawsuit or judgment against the subject of the report.
8. May NOT be used to access individual reference data on one's self or out of personal curiosity.
9. May NOT be used by Professional and Commercial users for purposes that are not within their normal course of business (e.g., A collection agency may NOT use our services/products to locate a witness to a crime).
10. May NOT be used for marketing purposes.

ACCESS SECURITY REQUIREMENTS FOR NONPUBLIC RECORD ACCESS

Merlin recognizes and accepts its obligation to support and implement policies that protect the confidential nature of information provided through our services (which include providing access to information contained in national credit bureau databases) and to ensure respect for consumers' privacy rights. Therefore, Merlin provides access to nonpublic information only to pre-approved companies that have an acceptable use for such access.

Merlin strives to achieve and enforce the highest levels of legal and ethical conduct in the use of nonpublic information. Merlin seeks to tailor its products that include nonpublic information, and to limit access to them, in a fair and balanced manner, one that respects both legitimate needs for information and legitimate privacy concerns. Merlin provides the following notice to you so that you may avoid falling under the restrictions imposed by the Fair Credit Reporting Act (FCRA).

You may only use nonpublic information to locate or to further identify the subject of your search. You may not and should not use nonpublic information, in whole or in part, to determine a consumer's eligibility for credit, for employment, or for insurance, nor may you use nonpublic information for any other purpose for which you might properly obtain a consumer report, except in connection with collection of a debt. If adverse action is to be taken against the subject of your search and the basis for such adverse action is information obtained or derived from nonpublic information, you must verify such information from another source before taking such adverse action.

Merlin requires all third party users to take strict precautions to secure any system or device used to access nonpublic information. To that end, Merlin has established the following requirements:

1. You must appoint and identify a Security Designate who will have responsibility within your company to oversee the stipulations listed herein:

   Name: _____   Title: _____

           (Type or Print)   (Type or Print)

2. You must consider and treat your Merlin account number, User ID and password as "sensitive information." You must protect your account number, User ID and password in a way that assures that only key personnel *employed by your company* have access to and knowledge of this sensitive information. Under no circumstances should you give unauthorized persons information concerning your account number, User ID or password. Do not post this information in any manner within your facility. You must notify Merlin immediately so that new passwords can be issued when any of these circumstances occur:

   a. Any company personnel who has access to Merlin's data is terminated from employment, transferred and/or whose job duties have been reassigned where access to data is no longer required;

   b. You become aware of or suspect questionable activity regarding access to Merlin's data;

   c. You become aware of any potential compromise of your systems that may expose Merlin's data to security vulnerabilities.

3. The system access software you use (whether developed by you or purchased from a third party vendor) must "hide" or "embed" your account number, User ID and password so that only supervisory personnel know your account number, User ID and password. You must assign a unique User ID and password to each end user of your system access software. If such access software is replaced by different access software and therefore no longer in use or, alternatively, the hardware upon which such system access software resides is no longer being used or is being disposed of, your password should be changed immediately.

4. You must not discuss your account number, User ID and password over the telephone with any unknown caller, even if the caller claims to be a Merlin employee.

5. You must restrict the ability to obtain nonpublic information to a few key personnel.

6. Place all terminal devices used to obtain sensitive information in a secure location within your facility. You should secure these devices so that unauthorized persons cannot easily access them.

7. After normal business hours, be sure to turn off and lock all devices or systems used to obtain sensitive information.

8. Secure hard copies and electronic files of sensitive information within your facility so that unauthorized persons cannot easily access them.

9. Shred or destroy all hard copy of sensitive information when no longer needed.

10. Erase and overwrite or scramble electronic files containing sensitive information when no longer needed and when applicable regulation(s) permit destruction.

11. Make all employees aware that your company can access sensitive information only for the **Gramm Leach Bliley (GLB) Acceptable Uses** listed above. You or your employees may not access their own information nor should you or your employees access information about a family member or friend unless it is in connection with an appropriate GLB transaction.

12. Nonpublic information obtained through Merlin Information Services CANNOT be sold to the general public, in whole or in part, under any circumstances.

13. Nonpublic information you obtain through Merlin Information Services must be obtained on the basis of an "Acceptable Use," as defined in the industry principles developed by the Individual Reference Service Group (IRSG) with the assistance of the Federal Trade Commission (**http://www.ftc.gov/bcp/privacy/wkshp97/irsdoc1.htm**) and must be used pursuant to an exception as defined by the Gramm-Leach-Bliley Act and/or a permissible purpose as defined by the federal Fair Credit Reporting Act.

14. Merlin Information Services maintains the right to perform an audit of your account at any time to verify that any database searches containing nonpublic information were in fact run for the use specified when the search was executed. This audit may require documentation for searches going back as far as three years. Failure to comply with or pass this audit may result in an immediate termination of your account.

GENERAL PROVISIONS

1. **RESTRICTED LICENSE**. CUSTOMER CERTIFICATION OF USE FOR NONPUBLIC INFORMATION EXCEPTED FROM RESTRICTION. WHEREAS, the Federal Gramm-Leach-Bliley Act, 15 U.S.C.A. Section

6801 *et seq.* (2000), (GLB Act) was enacted to protect the use and disclosure of nonpublic personal information, including, in certain instances, the use of identifying information only; and WHEREAS, the GLB Act provides limited exceptions under which such information may be used; NOW, THEREFORE, _____ (Customer) hereby certifies to Merlin that Customer has determined that Customer's use of certain identification-only products (Reference Products), including but not limited to, Credit Header Products, is pursuant to an exception under the GLB Act and; these Reference Products constitute individual reference products under the Individual Reference Service Group Principles, dated December 15, 1997 (IRSG Principles). Customer acknowledges that it is in its best interest to implement the IRSG Principles and agrees that in addition to using these Reference Products pursuant to a GLB Act exception, it will use these Reference Products in compliance with IRSG Principles. Customer hereby certifies that its use of the Reference Products shall be for the GLB Act exception(s) designated above.

By signing below, Customer acknowledges that Customer has read and does understand the information set forth above and understands that failure to abide by the principles of the IRSG or attempting to access restricted information for any reason other than as designated by Customer will result in immediate termination of access or to other remedies. Further, Customer acknowledges receipt of "Access Security Requirements" and agrees to abide by the terms and conditions described therein.

Customer understands that Merlin cannot provide legal advice regarding the appropriate uses of nonpublic, personal information and that it is Customer's obligation and responsibility to seek legal counsel in interpreting the applicable laws and IRSG principles. However, regardless of the opinion of Customer's legal counsel, Merlin will allow or restrict access to products based on Merlin's understanding of the applicable laws and IRSG principles. All such decisions are the sole discretion of Merlin and shall be final.

2. **BANK REFERENCE.** Customer hereby authorizes release of bank reference information to Merlin only to verify existence of a valid account in Customer's name. This authorization *excludes* release of account number, account balance and/or account activity.

Bank Name _____

Bank Address _____

Bank Contact Name _____

Bank Phone Number _____

By signing below, you acknowledge that you have read and understood the information set forth above, and that you understand that we will deny service to you if you fail to abide by these rules and principles.

Company Name (Customer)	Tax ID or SSN
Company Physical Address	Typed or Printed Name of Authorized Signer
City, State, ZIP Code	Authorized Signature
Company Phone Number	Date
E-mail Address	

Please fax completed application along with all document copies listed on page 1 to 406-755-8568 or 406-755-8579.

Appendix L

OCTOBER TERM, 1999

Syllabus

RENO, ATTORNEY GENERAL, ET AL. *v.*
CONDON, ATTORNEY GENERAL OF SOUTH CAROLINA, ET AL.

CERTIORARI TO THE UNITED STATES
COURT OF APPEALS FOR THE FOURTH CIRCUIT

No. 98-1464. Argued November 10, 1999—Decided January 12, 2000

State departments of motor vehicles (DMVs) require drivers and automobile owners to provide personal information, which may include a person's name, address, telephone number, vehicle description, Social Security number, medical information, and photograph, as a condition of obtaining a driver's license or registering an automobile. Finding that many States sell this information to individuals and businesses for significant revenues, Congress enacted the Driver's Privacy Protection Act of 1994 (DPPA), which establishes a regulatory scheme that restricts the States' ability to disclose a driver's personal information without the driver's consent. South Carolina law conflicts with the DPPA's provisions. Following the DPPA's enactment, South Carolina and its Attorney General filed this suit, alleging that the DPPA violates the Tenth and Eleventh Amendments to the United States Constitution. Concluding that the DPPA is incompatible with the principles of federalism inherent in the Constitution's division of power between the States and the Federal Government, the District Court granted summary judgment for the State and permanently enjoined the DPPA's enforcement against the State and its officers. The Fourth Circuit affirmed, concluding that the DPPA violates constitutional principles of federalism.

Held: In enacting the DPPA, Congress did not run afoul of the federalism principles enunciated in *New York v. United States*, 505 U.S. 144, and *Printz v. United States*, 521 U.S. 898. The Federal Government correctly asserts that the DPPA is a proper exercise of Congress' authority to regulate interstate commerce under the Commerce Clause, U.S. Const., Art. I, § 8, cl. 3. The motor vehicle information, which the States have historically sold, is used by insurers, manufacturers, direct marketers, and others engaged in interstate commerce to contact drivers with customized solicitations. The information is also used in the stream of interstate commerce by various public and private entities for matters related to interstate motoring. Because drivers' personal, identifying information is, in this context, an article of commerce, its sale or release into the interstate stream of business is sufficient to support congressional regulation. See *United States v. Lopez*, 514 U.S. 549, 558-559. This does not conclusively resolve the DPPA's constitutionality because in *New York* and *Printz* the Court held that federal statutes were invalid, not because Congress lacked legislative authority over the subject matter, but because those statutes violated Tenth Amendment federalism principles. However, the DPPA does not violate those principles. This case is instead governed by *South Carolina v. Baker*, 485 U.S. 505, in which a statute prohibiting States from issuing unregistered bonds was upheld because it regulated state activities, rather than seeking to control or influence the manner in which States regulated private parties, *id.*, at 514-515. Like that statute, the DPPA does not require the States in their sovereign capacity to regulate their own citizens; rather, it regulates the States as the owners of data bases. It does not require the South Carolina Legislature to enact any laws or regulations, as did the statute at issue in *New York*, and it does not require state officials to assist in the enforcement of federal statutes regulating private individuals, as did the law considered in *Printz*. Thus, the DPPA is consistent with the principles set forth in those cases. The Court need not address South Carolina's argument that the DPPA unconstitutionally regulates the States exclusively rather than by means of a generally applicable law. The DPPA is generally applicable because it regulates the universe of entities that participate as suppliers to the market for motor vehicle information—the States as initial suppliers of the information in interstate commerce and private resellers or redisclosers of that information in commerce. Pp. 148-151.

155 F.3d 453, reversed.

REHNQUIST, C. J., delivered the opinion for a unanimous Court.

Solicitor General Waxman argued the cause for petitioners. With him on the briefs were *Acting Assistant Attorney General Ogden, Deputy Solicitor General Kneedler, Paul R. Q. Wolfson, Mark B. Stern,* and *Alisa B. Klein.*

Charlie Condon, pro se, Attorney General of South Carolina, argued the cause for respondents. With him on the briefs were *Treva Ashworth*, Deputy Attorney General, and *Kenneth P. Woodington*, Senior Assistant Attorney General.*

Cite as: 528 U.S. 141 (2000)
OPINION OF THE COURT

CHIEF JUSTICE REHNQUIST delivered the opinion of the Court.

The Driver's Privacy Protection Act of 1994 (DPPA or Act), 18 U.S.C. §§ 2721-2725 (1994 ed. and Supp. IV), regulates the disclosure of personal information contained in the records of state motor vehicle departments (DMVs). We hold that in enacting this statute Congress did not run a foul of the federalism principles enunciated in *New York v. United States*, 505 U.S. 144 (1992), and *Printz v. United States*, 521 U.S. 898 (1997).

The DPPA regulates the disclosure and resale of personal information contained in the records of state DMVs. State DMVs require drivers and automobile owners to provide personal information, which may include a person's name, address, telephone number, vehicle description, Social Security number, medical information, and photograph, as a condition of obtaining a driver's license or registering an automobile. Congress found that many States, in turn, sell this personal information to individuals and businesses. See, e.g., 139 Cong. Rec. 29466, 29468, 29469 (1993); 140 Cong. Rec. 7929 (1994) (remarks of Rep. Goss). These sales generate significant revenues for the States. See *Travis v. Reno*, 163 F.3d 1000, 1002 (CA7 1998) (noting that the Wisconsin Department of Transportation receives approximately $8 million each year from the sale of motor vehicle information).

The DPPA establishes a regulatory scheme that restricts the States' ability to disclose a driver's personal information without the driver's consent. The DPPA generally prohibits any state DMV, or officer, employee, or contractor thereof, from "knowingly disclos[ing] or otherwise mak[ing]

---

*Briefs of *amici curiae* urging reversal were filed for the Electronic Privacy Information Center by *Marc Rotenberg*; for the Feminist Majority Foundation et al. by *Erwin Chemerinsky*; and for the Screen Actors Guild, et al.

Briefs of *amici curiae* urging affirmance were filed for the State of Alabama et al. by *Bill Pryor*, Attorney General of Alabama, *John J. Park, Jr.*, Assistant Attorney General, and *Thomas H. Odom*, and by the Attorneys General for their respective States as follows: *Ken Salazar* of Colorado, *Joseph P. Mazurek* of Montana, *Don Stenberg* of Nebraska, *Philip T. McLaughlin* of New Hampshire, *Michael F. Easley* of North Carolina, *W. A. Drew Edmondson* of Oklahoma, *D. Michael Fisher* of Pennsylvania, *Sheldon Whitehouse* of Rhode Island, *Jan Graham* of Utah, *Mark L. Earley* of Virginia, and *James E. Doyle* of Wisconsin; for the Home School Legal Defense Association by *Michael P. Farris*; for the National Conference of State Legislatures et al. by *Richard Ruda* and *Charles A. Rothfeld*; for the Pacific Legal Foundation by *Anne M. Hayes* and *Deborah J. La Fetra*; for the Washington Legal Foundation by *Daniel J. Popeo* and *R. Shawn Gunnarson*; and for the Reporters Committee for Freedom of the Press et al. by *Gregg P. Leslie*.

available to any person or entity personal information about any individual obtained by the department in connection with a motor vehicle record." 18 U.S.C. § 2721(a). The DPPA defines "personal information" as any information "that identifies an individual, including an individual's photograph, social security number, driver identification number, name, address (but not the 5-digit zip code), telephone number, and medical or disability information," but not including "information on vehicular accidents, driving violations, and driver's status." § 2725(3). A "motor vehicle record" is defined as "any record that pertains to a motor vehicle operator's permit, motor vehicle title, motor vehicle registration, or identification card issued by a department of motor vehicles." § 2725(1).

The DPPA's ban on disclosure of personal information does not apply if drivers have consented to the release of their data. When we granted certiorari in this case, the DPPA provided that a DMV could obtain that consent either on a case-by-case basis or could imply consent if the State provided drivers with an opportunity to block disclosure of their personal information when they received or renewed their licenses and drivers did not avail themselves of that opportunity. §§ 2721(b)(11), (13), and (d). However, Public Law 106-69, 113 Stat. 986, which was signed into law on October 9, 1999, changed this "opt-out" alternative to an "opt-in" requirement. Under the amended DPPA, States may not imply consent from a driver's failure to take advantage of a state-afforded opportunity to block disclosure, but must rather obtain a driver's affirmative consent to disclose the driver's personal information for use in surveys, marketing, solicitations, and other restricted purposes. See Pub. L. 106-69, 113 Stat. 986 §§ 350(c), (d), and (e), App. to Supp. Brief for Petitioners 1(a), 2(a).

The DPPA's prohibition of nonconsensual disclosures is also subject to a number of statutory exceptions. For example, the DPPA *requires* disclosure of personal information "for use in connection with matters of motor vehicle or driver safety and theft, motor vehicle emissions, motor vehicle product alterations, recalls, or advisories, performance monitoring of motor vehicles and dealers by motor vehicle manufacturers, and removal of non-owner records from the original owner records of motor vehicle manufacturers to carry out the purposes of titles I and IV of the Anti Car Theft Act of 1992, the Automobile Information Disclosure Act, the Clean Air Act, and chapters 301, 305, and 321-331 of title 49." 18 U.S.C. § 2721(b) (1994 ed., Supp. III) (citations omitted). The DPPA *permits* DMVs to disclose personal information from motor vehicle records for a number of purposes.[1]

---

[1] Disclosure is permitted for use "by any government agency" or by "any private person or entity acting on behalf of a Federal, State or local agency in carrying out its functions." 18 U.S.C. § 2721(b)(1) (1994 ed. and Supp. III). The Act also allows States to divulge drivers' personal infor-

The DPPA's provisions do not apply solely to States. The Act also regulates the resale and redisclosure of drivers' personal information by private persons who have obtained that information from a state DMV. 18 U.S.C. § 2721(c) (1994 ed. and Supp. III). In general, the Act allows private persons who have obtained drivers' personal information for one of the aforementioned permissible purposes to further disclose that information for any one of those purposes. *Ibid.* If a State has obtained drivers' consent to disclose their personal information to private persons generally and a private person has obtained that information, the private person may redisclose the information for any purpose. *Ibid.* Additionally, a private actor who has obtained drivers' information from DMV records specifically for direct-marketing purposes may resell that information for other direct-marketing uses, but not otherwise. *Ibid.* Any person who rediscloses or resells personal information from DMV records must, for five years, maintain records identifying to whom the records were disclosed and the permitted purpose for the resale or redisclosure. *Ibid.*

The DPPA establishes several penalties to be imposed on States and private actors that fail to comply with its requirements. The Act makes it unlawful for any "person" knowingly to obtain or disclose any record for a use that is not permitted under its provisions, or to make a false representation in order to obtain personal information from a motor vehicle record. §§ 2722(a) and (b). Any person who knowingly violates the DPPA may be subject to a criminal fine, §§ 2723(a), 2725(2). Additionally, any person who knowingly obtains, discloses, or uses information from a state motor vehicle record for a use other than those specifically permitted by the DPPA may be subject to liability in a civil action brought by the driver to whom the information pertains. § 2724. While the DPPA defines "person" to exclude States and state agencies, § 2725(2), a state agency that maintains a "policy or practice of substantial noncompliance" with the Act may be subject to a civil penalty imposed by the United States Attorney General of not more than $5,000 per day of substantial noncompliance. § 2723(b).

---

mation for any state-authorized purpose relating to the operation of a motor vehicle or public safety, § 2721(b)(14); for use in connection with car safety, prevention of car theft, and promotion of driver safety, § 2721(b)(2); for use by a business to verify the accuracy of personal information submitted to that business and to prevent fraud or pursue legal remedies if the information that the individual submitted to the business is revealed to have been inaccurate, § 2721(b)(3); in connection with court, agency, or self-regulatory body proceedings, § 2721(b)(4); for research purposes so long as the information is not further disclosed or used to contact the individuals to whom the data pertain, § 2721(b)(5); for use by insurers in connection with claims investigations, antifraud activities, rating or underwriting, § 2721(b)(6); to notify vehicle owners that their vehicle has been towed or impounded, § 2721(b)(7); for use by licensed private investigative agencies or security services for any purpose permitted by the DPPA, § 2721(b)(8); and in connection with private toll transportation services, § 2721(b)(10).

South Carolina law conflicts with the DPPA's provisions. Under that law, the information contained in the State's DMV records is available to any person or entity that fills out a form listing the requester's name and address and stating that the information will not be used for telephone solicitation. S.C. Code Ann. §§ 56-3-510 to 56-3-540 (Supp.1998). South Carolina's DMV retains a copy of all requests for information from the State's motor vehicle records, and it is required to release copies of all requests relating to a person upon that person's written petition. § 56-3-520. State law authorizes the South Carolina DMV to charge a fee for releasing motor vehicle information, and it requires the DMV to allow drivers to prohibit the use of their motor vehicle information for certain commercial activities. §§ 56-3-530, 56-3-540.

Following the DPPA's enactment, South Carolina and its Attorney General, respondent Condon, filed suit in the United States District Court for the District of South Carolina, alleging that the DPPA violates the Tenth and Eleventh Amendments to the United States Constitution. The District Court concluded that the Act is incompatible with the principles of federalism inherent in the Constitution's division of power between the States and the Federal Government. The court accordingly granted summary judgment for the State and permanently enjoined the Act's enforcement against the State and its officers. See 972 F. Supp. 977, 979 (1997). The Court of Appeals for the Fourth Circuit affirmed, concluding that the Act violates constitutional principles of federalism. See 155 F.3d 453 (1998). We granted certiorari, 526 U.S. 1111 (1999), and now reverse.

We of course begin with the time-honored presumption that the DPPA is a "constitutional exercise of legislative power." *Close v. Glenwood Cemetery*, 107 U.S. 466, 475(1883); see also *INS v. Chadha*, 462 U.S. 919, 944 (1983).

The United States asserts that the DPPA is a proper exercise of Congress' authority to regulate interstate commerce under the Commerce Clause, U.S. Const., Art. I, § 8, cl. 3.[2] The United States bases its Commerce Clause argument on the fact that the personal, identifying information that the DPPA regulates is a "thin[g] in interstate commerce," and that the sale or release of that information in interstate commerce is therefore

---

[2] In the lower courts, the United States also asserted that the DPPA was lawfully enacted pursuant to Congress' power under § 5 of the Fourteenth Amendment. See 155 F.3d 453, 463-465 (1998); 972 F. Supp. 977-979, 986-992 (1997). The District Court and Court of Appeals rejected that argument. See 155 F.3d, at 465; 972 F. Supp., at 992. The United States' petition for certiorari and briefs to this Court do not address the § 5 issue and, at oral argument, the Solicitor General expressly disavowed any reliance on it.

a proper subject of congressional regulation. *United States v. Lopez*, 514 U.S. 549, 558-559 (1995). We agree with the United States' contention. The motor vehicle information which the States have historically sold is used by insurers, manufacturers, direct marketers, and others engaged in interstate commerce to contact drivers with customized solicitations. The information is also used in the stream of interstate commerce by various public and private entities for matters related to interstate motoring. Because drivers' information is, in this context, an article of commerce, its sale or release into the interstate stream of business is sufficient to support congressional regulation. We therefore need not address the Government's alternative argument that the States' individual, intrastate activities in gathering, maintaining, and distributing drivers' personal information have a sufficiently substantial impact on interstate commerce to create a constitutional base for federal legislation.

But the fact that drivers' personal information is, in the context of this case, an article in interstate commerce does not conclusively resolve the constitutionality of the DPPA. In *New York* and *Printz*, we held federal statutes invalid, not because Congress lacked legislative authority over the subject matter, but because those statutes violated the principles of federalism contained in the Tenth Amendment. In *New York*, Congress commandeered the state legislative process by requiring a state legislature to enact a particular kind of law. We said:

> While Congress has substantial powers to govern the Nation directly, including in areas of intimate concern to the States, the Constitution has never been understood to confer upon Congress the ability to require the States to govern according to Congress' instructions. See *Coyle v. Smith*, 221 U.S. 559, 565 (1911). 505 U.S., at 162.

In *Printz*, we invalidated a provision of the Brady Act which commanded "state and local enforcement officers to conduct background checks on prospective handgun purchasers." 521 U.S., at 902. We said:

> We held in *New York* that Congress cannot compel the States to enact or enforce a federal regulatory program. Today we hold that Congress cannot circumvent that prohibition by conscripting the States' officers directly. The Federal Government may neither issue directives requiring the States to address particular problems, nor command the States' officers, or those of their political subdivisions, to administer or enforce a federal regulatory program. *Id.*, at 935.

South Carolina contends that the DPPA violates the Tenth Amendment because it "thrusts upon the States all of the day-to-day responsibility for administering its complex provisions," Brief for Respondents 10, and thereby makes "state officials the unwilling implementors of federal policy," *id.*, at 11.[3] South Carolina emphasizes that the DPPA requires the State's employees to learn and apply the Act's substantive restrictions, which are summarized above, and notes that these activities will consume the employees' time and thus the State's resources. South Carolina further notes that the DPPA's penalty provisions hang over the States as a potential punishment should they fail to comply with the Act.

We agree with South Carolina's assertion that the DPPA's provisions will require time and effort on the part of state employees, but reject the State's argument that the DPPA violates the principles laid down in either *New York* or *Printz*. We think, instead, that this case is governed by our decision in *South Carolina* v. *Baker*, 485 U.S. 505 (1988). In *Baker*, we upheld a statute that prohibited States from issuing unregistered bonds because the law "regulate[d] state activities," rather than "seek[ing] to control or influence the manner in which States regulate private parties." *Id.*, at 514-515. We further noted:

> The [National Governor's Association] nonetheless contends that § 310 has commandeered the state legislative and administrative process because many state legislatures had to amend a substantial number of statutes in order to issue bonds in registered form and because state officials had to devote substantial effort to determine how best to implement a registered bond system. Such 'commandeering' is, however, an inevitable consequence of regulating a state activity. Any federal regulation demands compliance. That a State wishing to engage in certain activity must take administrative and sometimes legislative action to comply with federal standards regulating that activity is a commonplace that presents no constitutional defect. *Ibid.*

Like the statute at issue in *Baker*, the DPPA does not require the States in their sovereign capacity to regulate their own citizens. The DPPA regulates the States as the owners of databases. It does not require the South Carolina Legislature to enact any laws or regulations, and it does not require state officials to assist in the enforcement of federal statutes regulating private individuals. We accordingly conclude that the DPPA is consistent with the constitutional principles enunciated in *New York* and *Printz*.

---

[3] South Carolina has not asserted that it does not participate in the interstate market for personal information. Rather, South Carolina asks that the DPPA be invalidated in its entirety, even as it is applied to the States acting purely as commercial sellers.

As a final matter, we turn to South Carolina's argument that the DPPA is unconstitutional because it regulates the States exclusively. The essence of South Carolina's argument is that Congress may only regulate the States by means of "generally applicable" laws, or laws that apply to individuals, as well as States. But we need not address the question whether general applicability is a constitutional requirement for federal regulation of the States, because the DPPA is generally applicable. The DPPA regulates the universe of entities that participate as suppliers to the market for motor vehicle information—the States as initial suppliers of the information in interstate commerce and private resellers or redisclosers of that information in commerce.

The judgment of the Court of Appeals is therefore

Reversed.

Index

Selected Books from . . .
THE ABA LAW PRACTICE MANAGEMENT SECTION

The Lawyer's Guide to Collaboration Tools and Technologies: Smart Ways to Work Together
By Dennis Kennedy and Tom Mighell

This first-of-its-kind guide for the legal profession shows you how to use standard technology you already have and the latest "Web 2.0" resources and other tech tools, like Google Docs, Microsoft Office and Share-Point, and Adobe Acrobat, to work more effectively on projects with colleagues, clients, co-counsel and even opposing counsel. In *The Lawyer's Guide to Collaboration Tools and Technologies: Smart Ways to Work Together*, well-known legal technology authorities Dennis Kennedy and Tom Mighell provides a wealth of information useful to lawyers who are just beginning to try these tools, as well as tips and techniques for those lawyers with intermediate and advanced collaboration experience.

The Lawyer's Guide to Marketing on the Internet, Third Edition
By Gregory H. Siskind, Deborah McMurray, and Richard P. Klau

In today's competitive environment, it is critical to have a comprehensive online marketing strategy that uses all the tools possible to differentiate your firm and gain new clients. The Lawyer's Guide to Marketing on the Internet, in a completely updated and revised third edition, showcases practical online strategies and the latest innovations so that you can immediately participate in decisions about your firm's Web marketing effort. With advice that can be implemented by established and young practices alike, this comprehensive guide will be a crucial component to streamlining your marketing efforts.

The Lawyer's Guide to Adobe Acrobat, Third Edition
By David L. Masters

This book was written to help lawyers increase productivity, decrease costs, and improve client services by moving from paper-based files to digital records. This updated and revised edition focuses on the ways lawyers can benefit from using the most current software, Adobe® Acrobat 8, to create Portable Document Format (PDF) files.

PDF files are reliable, easy-to-use, electronic files for sharing, reviewing, filing, and archiving documents across diverse applications, business processes, and platforms. The format is so reliable that the federal courts' Case Management/Electronic Case Files (CM/ECF) program and state courts that use Lexis-Nexis File & Serve have settled on PDF as the standard.

You'll learn how to:

- Create PDF files from a number of programs, including Microsoft Office
- Use PDF files the smart way
- Markup text and add comments
- Digitally, and securely, sign documents
- Extract content from PDF files
- Create electronic briefs and forms

The Electronic Evidence and Discovery Handbook: Forms, Checklists, and Guidelines
By Sharon D. Nelson, Bruce A. Olson, and John W. Simek

The use of electronic evidence has increased dramatically over the past few years, but many lawyers still struggle with the complexities of electronic discovery. This substantial book provides lawyers with the templates they need to frame their discovery requests and provides helpful advice on what they can subpoena. In addition to the ready-made forms, the authors also supply explanations to bring you up to speed on the electronic discovery field. The accompanying CD-ROM features over 70 forms, including, Motions for Protective Orders, Preservation and Spoliation Documents, Motions to Compel, Electronic Evidence Protocol Agreements, Requests for Production, Internet Services Agreements, and more. Also included is a full electronic evidence case digest with over 300 cases detailed!

The 2010 Solo and Small Firm Legal Technology Guide
By Sharon D. Nelson, Esq., John W. Simek, and Michael C. Maschke

This annual guide is the only one of its kind written to help solo and small firm lawyers find the best technology for their dollar. You'll find the most current information and recommendations on computers, servers, networking equipment, legal software, printers, security products, smart phones, and anything else a law office might need. It's written in clear, easily understandable language to make implementation easier if you choose to do it yourself, or you can use it in conjunction with your IT consultant. Either way, you'll learn how to make technology work for you.

The Law Firm Associate's Guide to Personal Marketing and Selling Skills
By Catherine Alman MacDonagh and Beth Marie Cuzzone

This is the first volume in ABA's new groundbreaking Law Firm Associates Development Series, created to teach important skills that associates and other lawyers need to succeed at their firms, but that they may have not learned in law school. This volume focuses on personal marketing and sales skills. It covers creating a personal marketing plan, finding people within your target market, preparing for client meetings, "asking" for business, realizing marketing opportunities, keeping your clients, staying in touch with your network inside and outside the firm, and more. An accompanying trainer's manual illustrating how to best structure the sessions and use the book is available to firms to facilitate group training sessions.

Many law firms expect their new associates to hit the ground running when they are hired on. Although firms often take the time to bring these associates up to speed on client matters, they can be reluctant to invest the time needed to train them how to improve personal skills such as marketing. This book will serve as a brief, easy-to-digest primer for associates on how to develop and use marketing and selling techniques.

The Lawyer's Guide to Concordance
By Liz M. Weiman

In this age, when trial outcomes depend on the organization of electronic data discovery, *The Lawyer's Guide to Concordance* reveals how attorneys and staff can make Concordance the most powerful tool in their litigation arsenal. Using this easy-to-read hands-on reference guide, individuals who are new to Concordance can get up-to-speed quickly, by following its step-by-step instructions, exercises, and time-saving shortcuts. For those already working with Concordance, this comprehensive resource provides methods, strategies, and technical information to further their knowledge and success using this robust program.

Inside The Lawyer's Guide to Concordance readers will also find:

- Techniques to effectively search database records, create tags for the results, customize printed reports, redline and redact images, create production sets
- Strategies to create and work with transcript, e-document, and e-mail databases, load files from vendors, manage images, troubleshoot, and more
- Real-world case studies from law firms in the United States and England describing Concordance features that have improved case management

The Lawyer's Guide to CT Summation iBlaze, Second Edition
By Tom O'Connor

CT Summation iBlaze gives you complete control over litigation evidence by bringing all you need—transcripts, documents, issues, and events, to your fingertips in one easy-to-use software program. Working in close collaboration with CT Summation, author and noted technology speaker Tom O'Connor has developed this easy-to-understand guide designed to quickly get you up and running on CT Summation software. Fully up-to-date, covering the latest version of iBlaze, the book features step-by-step instructions on the functions of iBlaze and how to get the most from this powerful, yet easy-to-use program.

The Lawyer's Guide to Microsoft Word 2007
By Ben M. Schorr

Microsoft Word is one of the most used applications in the Microsoft Office suite—there are few applications more fundamental than putting words on paper. Most lawyers use Word and few of them get everything they can from it. Because the documents you create are complex and important—your law practice depends, to some degree, upon the quality of the documents you produce and the efficiency with which you can produce them. Focusing on the tools and features that are essential for lawyers in their everyday practice, *The Lawyer's Guide to Microsoft Word* explains in detail the key components to help make you more effective, more efficient and more successful.

The Lawyer's Guide to Microsoft Excel 2007
By John C. Tredennick

Did you know Excel can help you analyze and present your cases more effectively or help you better understand and manage complex business transactions? Designed as a hands-on manual for beginners as well as longtime spreadsheet users, you'll learn how to build spreadsheets from scratch, use them to analyze issues, and to create graphics presentation. Key lessons include:

- Spreadsheets 101: How to get started for beginners
- Advanced Spreadsheets: How to use formulas to calculate values for settlement offers, and damages, business deals
- Simple Graphics and Charts: How to make sophisticated charts for the court or to impress your clients
- Sorting and filtering data and more

How to Start and Build a Law Practice, Platinum Fifth Edition
By Jay G. Foonberg

This classic ABA bestseller has been used by tens of thousands of lawyers as the comprehensive guide to planning, launching, and growing a successful practice. It's packed with over 600 pages of guidance on identifying the right location, finding clients, setting fees, managing your office, maintaining an ethical and responsible practice, maximizing available resources, upholding your standards, and much more. You'll find the information you need to successfully launch your practice, run it at maximum efficiency, and avoid potential pitfalls along the way. If you're committed to starting—and growing—your own practice, this one book will give you the expert advice you need to make it succeed for years to come.

The Lawyer's Guide to Microsoft Outlook 2007
By Ben M. Schorr

Outlook is the most used application in Microsoft Office, but are you using it to your greatest advantage? *The Lawyer's Guide to Microsoft Outlook 2007* is the only guide written specifically for lawyers to help you be more productive, more efficient and more successful. More than just email, Outlook is also a powerful task, contact, and scheduling manager that will improve your practice. From helping you log and track phone calls, meetings, and correspondence to archiving closed case material in one easy-to-store location, this book unlocks the secrets of "underappreciated" features that you will use every day. Written in plain language by a twenty-year veteran of law office technology and ABA member, you'll find:

- Tips and tricks to effectively transfer information between all components of the software
- The eight new features in Outlook 2007 that lawyers will love
- A tour of major product features and how lawyers can best use them
- Mistakes lawyers should avoid when using Outlook
- What to do when you're away from the office

ABA LawPracticeManagementSection
MARKETING • MANAGEMENT • TECHNOLOGY • FINANCE

30-Day Risk-Free Order Form
Call Today! 1-800-285-2221
Monday–Friday, 7:30 AM – 5:30 PM, Central Time

Qty	Title	LPM Price	Regular Price	Total
_____	The Lawyer's Guide to Collaboration Tools and Technologies: Smart Ways to Work Together (5110589)	$59.95	$ 89.95	$_____
_____	The Lawyer's Guide to Marketing on the Internet, Third Edition (5110585)	74.95	84.95	$_____
_____	The Lawyer's Guide to Adobe Acrobat, Third Edition (5110588)	49.95	79.95	$_____
_____	The Electronic Evidence and Discovery Handbook: Forms, Checklists, and Guidelines (5110569)	99.95	129.95	$_____
_____	The 2010 Solo and Small Firm Legal Technology Guide (5110701)	54.95	89.95	$_____
_____	The Law Firm Associate's Guide to Personal Marketing and Selling Skills (5110582)	39.95	49.95	$_____
_____	Trainer's Manual for the Law Firm Associate's Guide to Personal Marketing and Selling Skills (5110581)	49.95	59.95	$_____
_____	The Lawyer's Guide to Concordance (5110666)	49.95	69.95	$_____
_____	The Lawyer's Guide to CT Summation iBlaze, Second Edition (5110698)	49.95	69.95	$_____
_____	The Lawyer's Guide to Microsoft Word 2007 (5110697)	49.95	69.95	$_____
_____	The Lawyer's Guide to Microsoft Excel 2007 (5110665)	49.95	69.95	$_____
_____	How to Start and Build a Law Practice, Platinum Fifth Edition (5110508)	57.95	69.95	$_____
_____	The Lawyer's Guide to Microsoft Outlook 2007 (5110661)	49.99	69.99	$_____

*Postage and Handling	
$10.00 to $49.99	$5.95
$50.00 to $99.99	$7.95
$100.00 to $199.99	$9.95
$200.00+	$12.95

**Tax
DC residents add 5.75%
IL residents add 10.25%

*Postage and Handling	$_____
**Tax	$_____
TOTAL	$_____

PAYMENT

❑ Check enclosed (to the ABA)

❑ Visa ❑ MasterCard ❑ American Express

_____
Account Number   Exp. Date   Signature

Name _____ Firm _____

Address _____

City _____ State _____ Zip _____

Phone Number _____ E-Mail Address _____

Guarantee

If—for any reason—you are not satisfied with your purchase, you may return it within 30 days of receipt for a complete refund of the price of the book(s). No questions asked!

Mail: ABA Publication Orders, P.O. Box 10892, Chicago, Illinois 60610-0892
♦ Phone: 1-800-285-2221 ♦ FAX: 312-988-5568

E-Mail: abasvcctr@abanet.org ♦ Internet: http://www.lawpractice.org/catalog

Are You in Your Element?

Tap into the Resources of the ABA Law Practice Management Section

ABA Law Practice Management Section Membership Benefits

The ABA Law Practice Management Section (LPM) is a professional membership organization of the American Bar Association that helps lawyers and other legal professionals with the business of practicing law. LPM focuses on providing information and resources in the core areas of marketing, management, technology, and finance through its award-winning magazine, teleconference series, Webzine, educational programs (CLE), Web site, and publishing division. For more than thirty years, LPM has established itself as a leader within the ABA and the profession-at-large by producing the world's largest legal technology conference (ABA TECHSHOW®) each year. In addition, LPM's publishing program is one of the largest in the ABA, with more than eighty-five titles in print.

In addition to significant book discounts, LPM Section membership offers these benefits:

ABA TECHSHOW

Membership includes a $100 discount to ABA TECHSHOW, the world's largest legal technology conference & expo!

Teleconference Series

Convenient, monthly CLE teleconferences on hot topics in marketing, management, technology and finance. Access educational opportunities from the comfort of your office chair – today's practical way to earn CLE credits!

LAW|PRACTICE
THE BUSINESS OF PRACTICING LAW

Law Practice Magazine

Eight issues of our award-winning *Law Practice* magazine, full of insightful articles and practical tips on Marketing/Client Development, Practice Management, Legal Technology, and Finance.

Law Practice TODAY

Law Practice Today

LPM's unique Web-based magazine covers all the hot topics in law practice management today — identify current issues, face today's challenges, find solutions quickly. Visit www.lawpracticetoday.org.

LAW TECHNOLOGY TODAY

Law Technology Today

LPM's newest Webzine focuses on legal technology issues in law practice management — covering a broad spectrum of the technology, tools, strategies and their implementation to help lawyers build a successful practice. Visit www.lawtechnologytoday.org.

LawPractice.news
Monthly news and information from the ABA Law Practice Management Section

LawPractice.news

Brings Section news, educational opportunities, book releases, and special offers to members via e-mail each month.

To learn more about the ABA Law Practice Management Section, visit www.lawpractice.org or call 1-800-285-2221.

MARKETING • MANAGEMENT • TECHNOLOGY • FINANCE

ABA LawPracticeManagementSection

MARKETING • MANAGEMENT • TECHNOLOGY • FINANCE

About the CD

The accompanying CD contains a hyperlinked index of Web sites listed in the book (**Find Info Like a Pro, Volume 1 Index.pdf**), as well as the following checklists: Internet Methodology Checklist (**Internet Methodology Checklist.doc**); Internet Source Credibility Checklist (**Internet Source Credibility Checklist.doc**); Search Strategy Checklist (**Search Strategy Checklist.doc**); and Checklist for Finding and Verifying Experts (**Checklist for Finding and Verifying Experts.doc**).

For additional information about the files on the CD, please open and read the "**readme.doc**" file on the CD.

NOTE: The set of files on the CD may only be used on a single computer or moved to and used on another computer. Under no circumstances may the set of files be used on more than one computer at one time. If you are interested in obtaining a license to use the set of files on a local network, please contact: Director, Copyrights and Contracts, American Bar Association, 321 N. Clark Street, Chicago, IL 60654, (312) 988-6101. **Please read the license and warranty statements on the following page before using this CD.**

**Defending Liberty
Pursuing Justice**

CD-Rom to accompany
Find Info Like a Pro, Volume 1:
Mining the Internet's Publicly Available
Resources for Investigative Research